COGNITIVE THEORY
Volume 3

COGNITIVE THEORY
Volume 3

edited by

N. John Castellan, Jr.

Frank Restle

with contributing editors

Michael H. Birnbaum

Stephen W. Link

George R. Potts

 LAWRENCE ERLBAUM ASSOCIATES, PUBLISHERS

1978   Hillsdale, New Jersey

DISTRIBUTED BY THE HALSTED PRESS DIVISION OF

JOHN WILEY & SONS
New York   Toronto   London   Sydney

Lawrence Erlbaum Associates, Inc., Publishers
62 Maria Drive
Hillsdale, New Jersey 07642

Distributed solely by Halsted Press Division

Library of Congress Cataloging in Publication Data (Revised)

Main entry under title:

Cognitive theory.

　　Includes bibliographies and indexes.
　　1. Cognition.　　2. Speech perception.
3. Judgment.　　4. Memory.　　I. Restle, Frank.
BF311.C553　　　153.4　　　75-14293
ISBN　0-470-71732-7　(v. 1)
　　　　0-470-99025-2　(v. 2)
　　　　0-470-26375-X　(v. 3)

Printed in the United States of America

Contents

Preface

This volume of *Cognitive Theory* is the product of the ninth annual conference of mathematical and cognitive psychologists held at Indiana University in April 1976.

Our effort in this book has been to give authors an opportunity and some stimulus to state their theoretical positions and to put contrasting views together. As a result positions are spelled out in somewhat greater detail than is usual in journal articles, and various writers respond to one another. In some cases this seems to resolve what otherwise were serious theoretical conflicts. In other cases this interaction uncovers a theoretical difference that had escaped attention and that now can be clarified and experimentally resolved.

The "theory" in this book is not the sort of finished dogma that appears in textbooks and can be relied on by workers in other fields as a proper summary and explanation of the field. Instead, we deal with theory in action, near or (sometimes) beyond the frontiers of knowledge, full of energy, activity, and error of one sort or another. The reader of this book must be prepared to handle differences of opinion but is rewarded with some of the newest current thinking, the ideas that will infuse and inform new experimental work for some time. These theories are hardly to be thought of as amorphous and free-floating speculation. The issues and many of the processes and entities mentioned in this book have an experimental reality, and most of the writers present new experimental results to support their positions or at least discuss factual results in detail. There is a residue of "mathematical models" in the thinking of these writers, and they formulate their positions carefully and often in quantitative form, define and estimate parameters, and attempt to test the resulting models. The result of such an investigation is not always an unqualified success in a rapidly growing field, because the theorist is motivated to stretch his or her ideas to the utmost in an effort to encompass as many of the newly discovered phenomena as possible and to fit the details of experimental results. Past experience gives us grounds to hope that when the dust has settled, some of these results will remain as solid parts of the emerging exact science of cognitive psychology. It is up to the reader to decide which contributions survive and which are turned under to fertilize new ideas.

The editors did not merely write letters and push papers but attempted to give the papers a careful and creative editorial scrutiny. This has led to many warm interchanges between authors and editors, and we are convinced that both the lines of arguments in the papers and the clarity and completeness of the presentations have been improved by the process. Helping us in this task were our contributing editors: Michael Birnbaum, who took care of psychophysics; Stephen Link, who took care of reaction time; and George Potts, who handled cognitive structures.

The extended paper by Potts and associates is unusual and deserves some explanation. At the meeting, instead of formal set-piece lectures, the group working on linear order structures decided to have a discussion. As it worked out, the members of the "panel" each gave brief talks about their ideas and work, but they cooperated in using the same introduction, and the talks were often interrupted by comments and discussions. In attempting to prepare their material for publication, the writers felt that they could best write a single chapter in which all of their ideas would be brought together. Because sections of the chapters were in many cases drafted by one member of the group and represented his or her ideas or work, these sections are informally indicated as to "authorship." However, all of the writers took part in the writing and rewriting of the whole manuscript.

An earlier volume of this series was described by a reviewer as containing many good ideas for graduate students and young faculty researchers to follow up. We hope that the present volume serves the same purpose.

Bloomington, Indiana

N. JOHN CASTELLAN, JR.
FRANK RESTLE

COGNITIVE THEORY
Volume 3

Part I

THEORIES OF PSYCHOPHYSICAL JUDGMENT

It seems fitting that the history of experimental psychology begins with Fechner's study of psychophysics, because measurement of subjective values is deemed prerequisite to a quantitative science of psychology. Although Fechner's original aim was to specify the relation between physical and psychological energy, it soon became apparent that the construction of psychological measurements could proceed even in cases where the stimuli had no obvious corresponding physical dimensions. Theories of psychophysics expanded to become theories of cognition and judgment. Thus experiments on problems in stimulus comparison and combination, for example, had implications not only for sensory psychologists who hoped to discover properties of neural transducers but also for a larger audience of experimental psychologists concerned with the understanding of information processing and judgment.

The study of judgment should concern students of all areas of psychology for at least three reasons. First, principles of judgment discovered in psychophysical research have been shown to be applicable in a wide variety of experimental situations in which the subject uses a numerical judgment scale to express a psychological value, attitude, opinion, belief, or feeling. Second, theories of measurement become relevant whenever a continuum or structure of psychological value is postulated, as in the recent developments on linear orderings, described elsewhere in this volume. Third, experimental and analytical techniques developed for the study of psychophysical theories can be applied to the study of algebraic models that arise in other areas of psychology.

This section brings together four authors who, though from diverse research traditions, share a common fundamental approach to the study of psychophysical judgment. Each chapter is concerned with criteria for evaluating theories, for ruling out theories that are wrong, and for retaining theories that deserve better treatment. Each is focused on the study of algebraic models; each introduces constraints, both experimental and theoretical, to help resolve theoretical issues of psychophysics.

In Chapter 1 is a charming dialogue, purportedly of recent discovery, between two Athenian scholars who presage important distinctions in the discussion of psychophysics. The dialogue has been translated and annotated by Marks, who compares it with the modern history of psychophysics, including the "direct" scaling approach. The dialogue makes clear the differences between physical measures of intensity and psychological magnitude, and it presents the concept of additivity as a fundamental device for constructing a scale of subjective value.

Marks reviews his recent work on loudness additivity in multicomponent tones. Two simultaneous tones of two different frequencies, in which the intensities of the tones are independently varied, are played to subjects who judge the loudness of the complex tone. Marks uses the principle of additivity together with factorial designs to derive scales of loudness. To account for the differences between scales derived from additive models of multicomponent tones and subtractive models of difference judgment, Marks proposes a stage theory of loudness in which different transformations of intensity occur depending on the subject's processing task.

Chapter 2, by Birnbaum, attacks a long-standing puzzle of psychophysics: the fact that scales derived from "ratio" techniques, such as magnitude estimation, do not agree with scales derived from "interval" techniques, such as category rating. This contradiction poses serious problems for attempts to measure sensation by operational definition, because two "direct" measures do not agree.

Birnbaum notes that "direct" numerical judgments of stimulus "ratios," for example, can be represented as the composition of three functions: a *psychophysical* function relating subjective magnitude to physical magnitude, a *comparison* function that computes the relationship between two stimuli, and a *judgment* function that relates the numerical judgment to subjective impression. Any theory of psychophysics can be considered as a set of premises about these processes, from which predictions for experimental results can be deduced. Birnbaum points out that a severe difficulty in psychophysics has been that too many theories, sets of premises, can account equally well for the data.

The chapter begins with a discussion of "direct" scaling of single stimuli, reviews problems with that approach, and describes the advantages and limitations of the factorial design approach. Key ideas of scale convergence and scale-free tests of algebraic models are introduced to provide diagnostic experiments among alternative theories of ratio and difference judgment. Scale convergence is the additional premise that subjective scale values are independent of the judgment task; that is, that scales of sensation derived from different models applied to different situations should agree. This requirement can be contrasted with Marks' stage theory, which permits different scales.

A series of experiments using the additional constraints are reviewed, showing that a coherent set of premises can account for the data and provide a simple solution to the long-standing disputes over "ratio" and "difference" judgments.

Instructions to judge "ratios" and "differences" of two stimuli lead to the same ordering of stimulus pairs, consistent with the idea that the same comparison process underlies both tasks. Birnbaum's theory contends that for a variety of continua, such as heaviness and loudness, there is no subjective zero point, and under these conditions a subtractive operation underlies judgments of "differences" and "ratios" of two stimuli. A ratio operation can be used to represent judgments of "ratios of differences," possibly because a difference has a well-defined zero point even when the stimuli are inherently only an interval scale. Of equal or greater importance to Birnbaum's conclusions are the methods of experimental and theoretical analysis used to reach those conclusions.

Chapter 3, by Restle, discusses theories that account for the effect of the background on the judgment of a stimulus. Restle devotes most of his attention to the Baldwin illusion, in which the apparent length of a line segment depends on the size of squares drawn at the ends of the lines. The relativity of judgment has been studied in the adaptation level approach (Helson, 1964; Restle & Greeno, 1970), which assumes that all effects of background stimulation can be summarized by one internal psychological state, the adaptation level. Restle notes that recent data for visual illusions appear to contradict a simple version of adaptation level theory, which assumes that the adaptation-level is a constant-weighted average of the stimuli in the field. The recent data show that the judgment of a stimulus is a nonmonotonic function of the background, apparently in contradiction to the theory.

Restle then discusses a modified form of adaptation level theory in which the weights used in the average depend on the similarity of the test and background stimuli. This additional premise, which allows the parameters of the context theory to depend on stimulus relationships, can account for the nonmonotonic effect of background size. An important point made by Restle is that the very strength of mathematical theories, their supreme testability, can be their downfall. There is a danger that theories could be prematurely ruled out by experiments that test auxiliary assumptions rather than the core of the theory. Chapter 3 illustrates how it may be possible to modify theories to account for what may seem at first to be condemning evidence.

In Chapter 4, Falmagne brings together concepts from the Fechner-Thurstone tradition with concepts of fundamental measurement in order to develop the beginnings of a statistical theory of psychological measurement. Falmagne presents a general theoretical treatment of polynomial measurement models, using examples from additive conjoint measurement, extensive measurement, and bisection measurement to illustrate his ideas. Because the paper is highly technical, it will be helpful to discuss some prerequisite concepts that provide a setting for his work.

One of the difficulties encountered by the conjoint measurement approach, Falmagne (1976) notes, is the question of its applicability to experimental data. *Foundations of Measurement* (Krantz, Luce, Suppes, & Tversky, 1971) attempts to specify a set of primitive ordinal assumptions from which one could deduce general premises of addition or subtraction, for example, considered in the chapters by Marks and Birnbaum. The difficulty is that the ordinal axioms of additive conjoint measurement do not have simple applications to data.

To illustrate this difficulty, it is helpful to consider Falmagne's example of loudness additivity. Suppose that the subject listens to dichotic tones consisting of two levels of intensity, one in each ear. Suppose the tone pairs are constructed from a factorial design in which the tones in the left ear are either a, b, or c, combined with tones in the right ear of x, y, or z. Let h and g represent the psychophysical functions for loudness for the left and right ears, respectively. The theory of additive conjoint measurement specifies the conditions under which it is possible to find a representation, h and g, such that (a, x) is louder than (b, y) if and only if $h(a) + g(x) > h(b) + g(y)$. One requirement of additivity is double cancellation: If (a, y) is louder than (b, z) and if (b, x) is louder than (c, y), then (a, x) should be louder than (c, z).

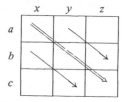

Double cancellation.
Single arrows represent premises;
double arrow represents conclusion.

This property follows from an additive representation, because if $h(a) + g(y) > h(b) + g(z)$ and if $h(b) + g(x) > h(c) + g(y)$, then $h(a) + h(b) + g(y) + g(x) > h(b) + h(c) + g(z) + g(y)$; cancelling $h(b)$ and $g(y)$ from both sides yields $h(a) + g(x) > h(c) + g(z)$, which implies that (a, x) is louder than (c,z).

This implication looks fairly straightforward to test. At first it may seem that all one need do is carry out the experiment and test whether the prediction is confirmed or refuted by the data. But the actual experiment is not that easy. First, what is the operationalization of "louder than"? Three popular definitions are among the posibilities: (1) (a, x) is louder than (b, y) if and only if $CJ(a, x) > CJ(b, y)$, where CJ is the category judgment of the loudness of the pair of tones; (2) magnitude estimation could be used to define the order, replacing category judgment in (1), as in Chapter 1; and (3) subjects could be asked to listen to two pairs and to report which of the pairs was the louder (or even judge the difference between two pairs, as in Chapter 2. A possible definition would be (a, x) is louder than (b, y) if $P(R_{ax;by}) > .5$ where $R_{ax;by}$ is the event that the subject judges the pair (a, x) to be greater than the pair (b, y). These three definitions would hopefully yield the same orderings.

Second, even with a definition, the experimental test remains unclear. Suppose one subject once judges (a, y) louder than (b, z), (b, x) louder than (c, y), and (c, z) louder than (a, x)? It could be attributed to a momentary fluctuation in loudness, to an error of memory, or to statistical fluctuations of proportions used to estimate probabilities. How many violations should it take for the investigator to seriously question the theory?

The statistical issue can be approached by representing the comparison process by an extension of the Thurstone approach. The psychophysical variability is attributed to variability in the psychological magnitudes of the stimuli.

In accord with Thurstone's case V, let $P(R_{12}) = F(\psi_1 - \psi_2)$ where $P(R_{12})$ is the probability that stimulus 1 is judged greater than stimulus 2, ψ_1 and ψ_2 are the subjective values of the stimuli, and F is the cumulative standard normal density function. Now suppose that $P(R_{ay;\ bz}) = .84$. Because .84 corresponds to a standard normal deviate of 1, it follows that $\psi_{ay} - \psi_{bz} = 1$, which implies that $h(a) + g(y) - h(b) - g(z) = 1$. Suppose also that $P(R_{bx;\ cy}) = .84$ then $h(b) + g(x) - h(c) - g(y) = 1$. It follows that $H(a) + h(b) + g(x) + g(y) - h(b) - h(c) - g(z) - g(y) = 2$ or $h(a) + g(x) - h(c) - g(z) = 2$, which implies the specific prediction that $P(R_{ax;\ cz}) = .98$, because F (2) = .98. Thus predictions can be checked against the obtained proportions by standard statistical techniques.

Chapter 4 shows how the method of maximum likelihood can be used to estimate parameters under ascending sequences of constraints to provide likelihood ratio tests to fit. Rather than fitting a model $P(R_{ax;\ by}) = F[g(a) + h(x) - g(b) - h(y)]$, Falmagne argues that it may be advantageous to fit the model $P(R_{ax;\ by}) = F(\theta_{ax;\ by})$ for the parameters $\theta_{ax;\ by}$ under constraints that specify the theory. The key idea is to use functional equations to define the polynomial rather than the polynomial itself. By combining the constraints of a theory of choice to those induced by the structure of the theory of combination, it should be possible to learn more about stimulus comparison and combination processes. Falmagne notes, however, that the development of axiomatic probability measurement theories still awaits a procedure that does not require an assumed form for F.

Any complete theory of psychophysics must deal with the issues of stimulus comparison, representation, combination, and contexual effects. The following chapters offer important contributions that advance the development of coherent psychological theory.

REFERENCES

Falmagne, J. C. Random conjoint measurement and loudness summation. *Psychological Review*, 1976, *83*, 65-79.

Helson, H. *Adaptation-level theory*. New York: Harper & Row, 1964.

Krantz, D. H., Luce, R. D., Suppes, P., & Tversky, A. *Foundations of measurement*. New York: Academic Press, 1971.

Restle, F., & Greeno, J. G. *Introduction to mathematical psychology*. Reading, Mass.: Addison-Wesley, 1970.

1

PHONION: Translation and Annotations Concerning Loudness Scales and the Processing of Auditory Intensity

Lawrence E. Marks
John B. Pierce Foundation Laboratory
   and
Yale University

Translator's note: The manuscript to the dialogue that follows recently came into my possession. The reader will doubtless perceive immediately why a brief glance at the text was all that I needed to make apparent to me the significance of the document—and the prescience of the author and his two protagonists: Protologos and Doutatomas.

Although the subtle analyses and extensive theories of sensation that were proposed by eminent thinkers of antiquity, including the detailed discourses of Plato, Aristotle, and Theophrastos, are well-known to historians of science, none, to the best of my knowledge, deals with the problem of quantifying sensory experience. Certainly none that I am familiar with presages, as *Phonion* does, the interrelationship between sensory scaling and the psychophysics of sensory processes. Most remarkable is the way that Protologos and Doutatomas grasp the very issues that we hear disputed by contemporary psychophysicists in the modern Akademei. Presented forthwith is a full translation of the text, to which I have appended occasional editorial notes, and, more importantly, an account of some of the relevant contemporary material, that is, an analysis of the recent data and modern theories that are—like the dialogue *Phonion*—pertinent to the interrelation between psychoacoustics and the quantification of loudness.

It would, of course, be fascinating to learn whether the author of the dialogue ever developed a complete theory of psychophysical scaling. Unfortunately, the dialogue provides few clues to the author's background or identity, except that he or she would appear to have been an Athenian contemporary of Aristotle. Even more unfortunately, the original manuscript has been destroyed, thereby increasing the difficulty in determining authorship. But the translation remains, and, without further introductory discourse, here it is.

PHONION

Protologos: It is clear, is it not my friend, that our sensory perceptions play a primary role in informing us about the world around us, in teaching us of objects and events.

Doutatomas: Indeed, that is clear.

Protologos: Then it would seem appropriate to begin with an understanding of the senses if we are to comprehend the nature of what is in the world and of what it is that we know. In order to commence our quest, let us consider our sense of hearing and the way that the ear and brain determine the loudness of sounds. You will agree, I'm sure, that loudness—the intensity that we hear in sounds—is one of the salient dimensions of sounds, and hence if we can understand loudness we will be well on our way to comprehending how the ear and brain work.

Doutatomas: I agree fully, for one should always start at the beginning. Surely the onset of this study will be simple. You said that loudness is the intensity of a sound. Can you not just measure the force with which a sound strikes the ear—its physical intensity?

[The terms "force" and "physical intensity" are modern translations of antiquated geometrical terms, used in early physical theories of sound.]

Protologos: Nothetuwonuh.

Doutatomas: Excuse me, Protologos, but I couldn't quite hear you.

Protologos: NO, THAT WON'T DO!

Doutatomas: Oh.

Protologos: My point, Doutatomas, is that loudness is what we *hear* of sound's intensity. Loudness is a psychological dimension, closely related to the physical intensity of a sound, but not identical to physical intensity. Please pardon my little trick, but I believe it will serve my pedagogic purpose. As I gathered, my whisper was much softer than my shout.

Doutatomas: Indeed it was.

Protologos: How much softer? Half as loud, a hundredth, a millionth?

Doutatomas: I'm not sure, except that it was many times softer—less than half as loud, perhaps a hundredth, surely not a millionth.

Protologos: What if I were to tell you that the acoustical intensity of my shout was ten million times as great as that of my whisper.

[If by "acoustical intensity" Protologos means "energy flow," then the ratio of shout to whisper corresponds to a difference of 70 decibels—decibels = 10·log (energy ratio)—a reasonable value. We may, then, assume throughout that Protologos refers to energy flow.]

Doutatomas: By Zeus! Is that so? Then loudness is surely not the same thing as sound's physical intensity.

Protologos: If it were, a chorus of one hundred would sound exactly twice as loud as a chorus of fifty, and Stentor's shout would sound fifty times as loud as my own.

[According to Homer (*Iliad*, V, 785), Stentor could shout as loudly as fifty men.]

From the softest sound that can be heard when the ear is most keen to the loudest that the ear normally tolerates is a range of physical intensity of a trillion to one, or twelve increases of Pythagoras.

> [In the Pythagorean geometry, each "increase"—from point to line, line to square, square to cube—was a tenfold gain.]

Our ear and brain doubtless compress that range into a more manageable proportion. Those of us who seek to comprehend psychoacoustics as well as acoustics endeavor to learn the increases of hearing, among other things. Psychoacoustics, though, is concerned with much more than just the relationship between loudness and physical intensity. We also desire to learn of the acute and grave and of the harmonies and concords. But even if we restrict our domain of inquiry to the psychoacoustics of loudness, there are many other factors besides intensity to take account of, like the speed of the atoms that makes acute instead of grave. Have you noticed how the old men have difficulty hearing the small and fast particles that make the acute? To understand loudness fully is to bring all of the relevant variables into our ken.

Doutatomas: No doubt you are correct in so asserting, but now that you have begun to fertilize my mind the imminent question demanding an answer is, How does loudness depend on physical intensity—when, let us say, these other variables, doubtless important as you say, are held constant?

Protologos: When I whispered, then shouted into your ear, you judged the loudnesses to be in what ratio? About one hundred to one? But the ratio of physical intensities was, as I said, more like ten million to one. Stentor may shout as fifty men, but the shout sounds only three. The chorus of one hundred sounds but twice the loudness of the chorus of ten, and the chorus of ten but twice as loud as a single man.

> [Strikingly similar is Fechner's (1860) remark that "In derselben Beziehung war mir interessant, von einem Musiker (dem Violinvirtuosen v. Wasilewski) die Angabe zu hören, man habe bei den Rheinischen Sängerfersten die Erfahrung gemacht, dass ein Chor von 400 Männerstimmen keinen bedeutend stärkeren Eindruck mache als von 200 [p. 182."][1]

Thus is follows that there is a general rule: With every Pythagorean increase [tenfold gain] in intensity, loudness only doubles.

> [Mathematically, Protologos' rule implies that loudness increases in proportion to acoustical energy raised to the .3 power.]

Doutatomas: Please, a little more slowly, Protologos. I don't have enough fingers.

Translator's note: The contemporary literature on loudness scaling is relevant here. First, it should be noted that Protologos employs a form of the method of ratio estimation in attempting to assess loudness. In ratio estimation a pair of stimuli is presented to a subject, who then tries to estimate numerically the subjective ratio of one member of the pair to the other. It is likely, however, that Protologos employed ratio estimation in this dialogue merely as a convenient

---

[1] "In the same connection, it was interesting to hear the statement from a musician (the virtuoso violinist von Wasilewski), who had the experience at the Rhine choral festival, that a men's choir of 400 voices made no significantly stronger impression than 200."

pedagogical substitute for the method of magnitude estimation; in the latter method, one stimulus at a time is presented to a subject, who then tries to estimate numerically the subjective magnitude of each single stimulus.

Beginning with the seminal papers of S. S. Stevens (1955, 1956), a large body of experimental evidence has been collected with the methods of magnitude estimation and magnitude production (the inverse of estimation, where a subject is given numbers and attempts to set stimulus levels so the sensation magnitudes match the numbers). This evidence suggests that numerically estimated loudness (L) varies approximately with the .3 power of acoustical energy flow (E)

$$L = kE^{.3} \tag{1}$$

L in Eq. (1) corresponds to the sone scale (Stevens, 1955) when the auditory stimulus is a 1000-Hz tone that is heard binaurally, when the proportionality constant k equals 1, and when E has the value of 1 at an acoustical energy corresponding to a sound pressure level (SPL) of 40 decibels. Thus a binaurally heard, 1000-Hz tone has a loudness L of one sone at 40 dB SPL.

The psychophysical relationship given by Eq. (1) holds when the sound stimulus has a frequency greater than about 300 Hz (low frequencies yield larger exponents: Hellman & Zwislocki, 1968; Stevens, 1966) and is heard in the quiet (masking sounds increase the size of the exponent: Hellman & Zwislocki, 1964; Stevens & Guirao, 1967). Although the method of magnitude production yields exponents that are systematically larger than those of magnitude estimation (Stevens & Greenbaum, 1966), and individual differences in exponent can be as great as a two-to-one ratio (J. C. Stevens & Guirao, 1964), nevertheless average values of the exponent are reasonably stable. Values suggested by various investigators go from .27 (Hellman & Zwislocki, 1964) through .30 (Marks, 1974a) to .33 (Stevens, 1972).

Protologos: So you see, Doutatomas, that you are just like everyone else; nay, moreso: For you are quite average.

Doutatomas: The measurement of loudness as a psychological quantity is intriguing, Protologos, and I have no doubt that the computations from these numerical judgments are valuable, but tell me, how do we know that we can rely on such direct quantitative assessments of sensation magnitude? To be sure, your shout is much louder than your whisper, and a hundred times as loud does not seem an unreasonable value, but I do not believe I could honestly say that it is not four or even five hundred times as loud, or thirty or forty.

   [Mathematically, this would put the possible range of exponents of the loudness function as high as .38 or as low as .18.]

Protologos: You are quite correct.

Doutatomas: But something else disturbs me even more. When I listen to you speak— when you don't shout—your voice sounds about three times as loud as that of Telemachos's wife, Xanades, singing across the street.

Protologos: Yes, that seems about right.

Doutatomas: So if the loudness of Xanades's singing is numerically at unity, that of your voice would be three. Antrobus's son Cleon, yelling to his friend, is almost twice as loud as you, to my hearing and judgment a loudness five times that of Xanades, hence a value of five. From these numbers it follows that the difference in loudness between Xanades's song and your speech equals the difference in loudness between your speech and Cleon's shout. But when I listen to these differences directly, and compare them one to the other, the two differences do not sound equal at all. Your voice is not nearly so different from Cleon's wail as it is from Xanades's song.

Protologos: Your observation is most astute. A chorus of one hundred sounds as much louder than a chorus of fifty as a chorus of fifty sounds louder than a chorus of twenty-three. What you have called loudness difference is surely at variance with the calculations of difference in loudness. These two loudness judgments do not seem to measure the same quantity. If I may be allowed, perhaps we could call loudness difference, "different loudness." At one time I attributed this very disagreement to the faculty of judgment, which may trick us by applying quantitative notions of one sort here, of another sort there. But now I know this not to be the case; instead it is one of Orpheus's mysteries. . . .

Translator's note: At this point, the manuscript became illegible, and a short section of about three to four sentences could not be deciphered. The dialogue immediately preceding this point touches closely on a controversial, contemporary issue, which may opportunely be reviewed here.

It has been known for a long time that numerical judgments that are obtained with rating scales—where subjects attempt to partition the psychological domain into subjectively equal steps—often bear a nonlinear relation to numerical judgments that are obtained with magnitude estimations—where subjects attempt to assign numbers in direct proportion to subjective values (Stevens & Galanter, 1957). Ward (1972) suggested that rating scales may vary as the square root of magnitude-estimation scales.

The most potent data that deal with differences or intervals of loudness comprise not ratings of stimuli presented singly but judgments of differences or intervals between the loudnesses of pairs of stimuli. In 1954, Garner published a study in which he generated a scale of loudness by dovetailing results he obtained with two procedures, fractionation and equisection. The fractionations were used in order to equate sensory ratios—the subjects were asked to adjust each variable stimulus to sound half as loud as each standard—but without necessarily accepting at face value the putative subjective size of the ratio (i.e., "half as loud"); the equisections were used in order to equate sensory intervals—the subjects were asked to adjust three or five variable stimuli, between two fixed standards, to mark off four or six successive, equal intervals of loudness. A single, unique scale was devised to conform to both sets of equalities. This scale was called the lambda scale, and it is rather different from prototypical magnitude estimation-magnitude production scales, such as Stevens's sone scale. It is in fact the equisections—the loudness intervals—that are responsible in the main for the form of the lambda scale. If a power function is assumed, the equisections suffice to generate the lambda scale (see Marks, 1968). Loudness in lambda units increases approximately as the .13 power of acoustical energy, whereas loudness in sones increases as approximately the .3 power. Hence lambda is roughly proportional to the square root of sones.

Subsequent studies by Beck and Shaw (1967), Parker and Schneider (1974), and Schneider, Parker, and Stein (1974) investigated intervals and differences in loudness, which their subjects attempted to assess directly with numerical estimates. Results of these experiments clearly demonstrated that loudness differences are judged to be equal when the members of pairs of sounds are separated by equal numbers of lambda units but not when they are separated by equal numbers of sones (see, for example, Beck & Shaw, 1967, figs. 1 and 2). The internal structure of the data obtained in these experiments suffices to constrain the possible underlying loudness scales. Taken as a whole, these studies, together with others, can be interpreted to say that the judgment of difference or dissimilarity in loudness (L_d) between two sounds is a direct function of the algebraic difference between the acoustical energy of each sound raised to a power of about .15:

$$L_d = g\,(E_j{}^{.15} - E_k{}^{.15}) \tag{2}$$

where g is a continuous monotone increasing function (see Marks, 1974a). As Protologos remarked, loudness difference appears to be different from loudness.

Doutatomas: Would it not be much simpler to treat loudness and loudness difference as the same, even though it means relinquishing our quantitative estimates? For sure it is that these are sorely uncertain.

Protologos: Your suggestion is well made, and once upon a time I took it seriously into thought. But tell me, have you not ever watched the stream as it wends its way downhill and through the olive grove at Akademe?

Doutatomas: Indeed, many times.

Protologos: How many streams are there?

Doutatomas: Why, just one, Protologos.

Protologos: Just one—one and the same stream?

Doutatomas: The same, of course.

Protologos: As it cascades down the slope, weaving and dancing between the rocks?

Doutatomas: Yes.

Protologos: Then later, softly lingering, as it passes amongst the trees?

Doutatomas: Yes.

Protologos: One and the same?

Doutatomas: Yes.

Protologos: But does it look the same, this very same stream at once rapidly and more slowly flowing?

Doutatomas: Why, no, Protologos, it looks quite different at different points.

Protologos: But still the same.

Doutatomas: The same, but different—in appearance. It changes as it flows, certainly, but still it is the same stream.

Protologos: Gurgling here, placid there, yet the same stream?

Doutatomas: So I said.

Protologos: So one thing can appear to be different at different points, yet still be the same.

Doutatomas: So it would seem, Protologos.

Protologos: Like a boy respectful and solicitous to his parents, yet mischievous with his friends.

Doutatomas: I would say so.

Protologos: Or like a man happy both when with his wife and when at the theater, but not laughing with one, only the other.

Doutatomas: I suppose. But I pray to Apollo, get to the point. The Dark One [Heraklitos.] already taught us that a person cannot step twice in the same stream.

Protologos: The sounds that we hear, our hearing of them, is like the stream that irrigates the grove at Akademe. Sound is a stream, as Demokritos taught, a stream whose atoms, emitted from objects, pass through the air to our ears. As the passages in the ear and brain dilate or contract, more or fewer atoms flow through to the seat of judgment. How fast they flow through at any point depends on how dilated or constricted is the passage. So they pass through, now fast, now slow, but always it is the same stream.

Doutatomas: One should always take care, Protologos.

Protologos: In what way?

Doutatomas: Lest one not step gingerly enough into a stream, and discover too late how deep it is.

Protologos: Listen, Doutatomas, while I blow this whistle.

Doutatomas: Most pleasing, like the nightingale's lonely moan.

Protologos: Listen again, while I blow two at once.

Doutatomas: I heard but one.

Protologos: The whistles are identical and their sounds blend in near perfect concord. I assure you that there were two.

Doutatomas: But the two together seemed hardly louder than one.

Protologos: Now listen again.

Doutatomas: Shriller, it seems, like the squeal of a carriage, but about as loud as the single one you sounded before.

Protologos: A different one, but only one. Now listen closely.

Doutatomas: Ah, the nightingale's song and carriage's squeal sounded together. Each is distinct and clearly heard.

Protologos: And the loudness, how loud is it? Listen again.

Doutatomas: Much louder, Protologos. Louder, at least, than any of those you sounded before. Neither is the nightingale affected by the carriage squeal, nor carriage squeal by nightingale, so the total is notably greater than either one alone.

Protologos: How much louder? Again.

Doutatomas: Why, about twice as loud.

Protologos: So, two identical sounds are heard as only a little louder than one, whereas two different, but equal sounds are heard as twice as loud.

Doutatomas: So it seems.

Protologos: And, were my mouth large enough, I could show you that two different sounds are heard as loud as ten identical ones. Thus do dissimilar sounds add their loudness—the carriage squeal, the nightingale's plaintive call, even the "brekekekek koax" of the frogs. The atoms from the carriage squeal are elongated and thin, with sharp edges, while those of the nightingale's song are rounder and smoother, and those of Aristophanes's chorus [are] larger and roughly edged. Like-shaped streams add together in one way, whilst dissimilar-shaped streams add in another.

Doutatomas: If it is as you say, then different-shaped atoms must flow through different passages, and thus they must be separated out, one streamlet from another.

Protologos: That certainly makes sense.

Doutatomas: But if this be so, then the streamlets must come together again some point farther on.

Protologos: You understand well.

Doutatomas: They must come together again at another point, as when freshets engendered by heavy rains slide down a hill into the stream in the valley.

Protologos: So what you are saying is that similar sounds come together early in the stream, dissimilar sounds later. And when we judge sounds, compare one to the other, even ones that are heard at different times, must not the sounds, or some resemblance of them, come together again?

Doutatomas: At the seat of judgment.

Protologos: At what Aristotle calls the common sense. So it is that the stream of sound enters the ear as a unitary whole, then sends out tributaries of different size and shape whose manifold flows wend their way through passages and channels until they reunite in the mind, where they combine in simple proportion.

Translator's note: Truly a remarkable passage, this! Protologos has anticipated some of the recent findings in psychoacoustics on what are known as critical bands, and he has suggested one prototype to a Herakitean model for the processing of auditory information. At this point, now that the dialogue is nearly ended, it is germane to present an exposition of the relationship between stages of processing of auditory intensity and the nature of loudness scales.

LOUDNESS SCALES AND THE PROCESSING
OF AUDITORY INTENSITY

Energy Summation, Loudness Summation, and Critical Bands

The concept of critical bands originated with studies of masking (Fletcher, 1940; Zwicker, 1954), from which it was found that a masked sound's loudness is affected only by the energy of the masker that falls within a limited frequency range around the masked sound. The band of frequencies that is effective in producing masking is called a *critical band*. The size of the critical band varies directly with the center frequency. At center frequencies below 500 Hz, the critical band is about 100 Hz wide; by 10,000 Hz, it has grown to about 3000 Hz (Scharf, 1970).

Soon it became apparent that critical bands are relevant to several other auditory phenomena, including loudness summation. In brief, when sounds with different frequencies are combined, the overall loudness that results depends on the frequency relation of the components, as well as their intensities. When the components fall close together in frequency, the overall loudness is smaller than it is when the components are widely spaced (as Protologos demonstrated with his whistles).

If components fall wholly within a single critical band, the overall loudness depends solely on the total acoustical energy (Scharf, 1970; Zwicker et al., 1957). This has been demonstrated with regular and irregular spacing between components (Zwicker et al., 1957) and with unequally intense and equally intense components (Scharf, 1962). If $E_1, E_2, \ldots, E_n$ represent the energies of different components, and if all components fall within a critical band, then total loudness (L_t) is given by

$$L_t = F(\Sigma E_i) \tag{3}$$

When energy is spread out beyond a critical band, loudness is greater than predicted by Eq. (3). Fletcher and Munson (1933) postulated that when components of a complex sound are widely separated in frequency, the total loudness is equal to the simple sum of the loudnesses of the components: If $L_1, L_2, \ldots, L_n$ are the loudnesses of the components, then Fletcher and Munson's proposal is formalized as

$$L_t = \Sigma L_i \tag{4}$$

At moderate and high sound-pressure levels, Fletcher and Munson found that two equally loud sounds, widely spaced in frequency, when played together, have about the loudness that either component alone would have if it were increased in intensity by about 10 decibels (see Zwislocki et al., 1974, fig. 3). For example, a two-component tone that is formed from a 1000-Hz component at 70 dB SPL and a 3000-Hz component of the same loudness gives an overall loudness equal to that of a 1000-Hz tone at an SPL of 80 dB. Because, according to the Fletcher-Munson hypothesis, the two-component tone is twice as loud as either component and is as loud as an 80-dB tone, it follows that an increase of 10 dB from 70 to 80 dB SPL should constitute a doubling of loudness.

Interestingly, the psychophysical loudness Eq. (1), which is based on numerical judgments (magnitude estimations and magnitude productions), predicts that loudness in sones doubles with every 10-dB increase in stimulation. Hence this equation is wholly consistent with Fletcher and Munson's hypothesis that widely separated tones add their loudnesses linearly.

Experiment I: Addition of Loudness in Two-Component Tones

An experiment was conducted in order to try to provide a more complete account of the way that the overall loudness of a two-component tone depends on the intensity levels of the pure tone constituents (Marks, 1975). The frequencies selected were 2000 and 5000 Hz; their geometric average is 3160 Hz, and at such a frequency the critical bandwidth is about 500 Hz (Scharf, 1970). Thus the frequencies used in this experiment are separated by several critical bandwidths.

In order to test the rule of additivity fully, each component took on each of six intensity levels, including zero, and the two-component sounds were constructed by combining every level of one component with every level of the other. Thus there were 36 different stimuli in all. Each stimulus was presented binaurally in a one-second burst (rise and decay times = 10 milliseconds) to the subject, whose task was to assign a number in proportion to the overall loudness (method of magnitude estimation). All 36 stimuli were presented and judged twice in the course of a given session; 15 men and women served as subjects.

Results are depicted in Fig. 1, which gives the geometric averages of the magnitude estimates of loudness plotted against the SPL of the 5000-Hz component. Each contour in the figure represents a different SPL of the 2000-Hz component. The data points determine a set of curves that are almost parallel to one another; there is, however, some small tendency for the functions to converge at high values (come together toward the upper right-hand portion of the figure). From the hypothesis of linear additivity of loudnesses [Eq. (4)], one would expect a set of parallel curves, *given that the response scale accurately represents loudness*. Does it? The fact that the curves are very nearly parallel suggests that the average magnitude-estimation scale used by the subjects in this experiment may have come close to the mark. As a matter of fact, the magnitude-estimation scale that the subjects used here is not quite typical of that obtained in other investigations of loudness. On the average the magnitude estimations of loudness that are obtained with simpler (i.e., single-component) sounds are usually related to the .3 power of acoustical energy [Eq. (1)]. If we take the comparable condition from Experiment I, that is, the condition where only single components were presented (2000 Hz at variable SPL, 5000 Hz at zero; 5000 Hz at variable SPL, 2000 Hz at zero), we find that the magnitude estimations determine a power function with an exponent a little greater than .2. Had the exponent of these functions been .3, and had the other data in the experiment followed suit, the curves in Fig. 1 would have been virtually perfectly parallel.

This conclusion was borne out by a reanalysis of the data in Fig. 1. An iterative procedure was employed whereby the average magnitude estimates were raised to a power (the value varied from iteration to iteration) until the curves became parallel. Figure 2 shows the result of this rescaling. Not only do the transformed data display parallelism, but the new scale values, both for the

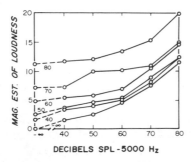

FIG. 1   Magnitude estimates of the loudness of two-component tones, plotted against the SPL of the 5000-Hz component. Each function represents a different SPL of the 2000-Hz component.

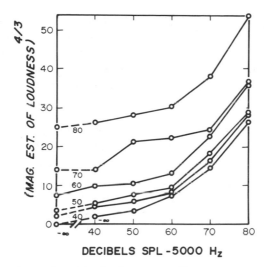

FIG. 2   Magnitude estimates from Fig. 1 raised to the 4/3 power. This is the power transformation that best served to maximize parallelism among the functions.

2000-Hz and for the 5000-Hz components, conform to the .3-power Eq. (1).
That is, after the response scale is transformed through a mildly positively accelerated function, the results are consistent with linear addition of components, and the components are now values defined by the sone scale [Eq. (1)].

A more general rescaling is possible, one that does not require advance knowledge of the mathematical transformation that needs to be imposed on the
responses (that is, where it is not necessary, for instance, to restrict an iterative
search to the class of power transformations). The original data of Fig. 1 were
subjected to conjoint scaling (Guttman-Lingoes), in which the rank-order of the
original data array is preserved and the scale values that satisfy linear addition
between the two components are determined (Luce & Tukey, 1964). Figure 3
shows the outcome, which is quite similar to that of Fig. 2. The underlying
scale values for both components, derived from conjoint scaling, satisfy a power
function with an exponent of .33.

What is the relationship between the present results and those of earlier studies of loudness summation, such as those of Fletcher and Munson (1933), which
employed techniques of loudness matching? In order to answer the question, it
is necessary to examine the present results in terms of loudness equalities; that
is, we must find the different stimulus combinations that produce a given, constant sensation of loudness. This may be done by making horizontal cuts
through the psychophysical functions of Fig. 1 (or those of Fig. 2) and by reading off at each constant level of loudness the various combinations of SPL at
2000 and 5000 Hz that produce it. For example, the same original magnitude

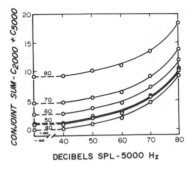

FIG. 3   Rescaling of the data from Fig. 1 on the basis of their rank-order (conjoint scaling).

estimate of "5" in Fig. 1 could be produced by the 2000-Hz tone alone at 60 dB (5000 Hz at zero), by the combination of 5000 Hz at 53 dB and 2000 Hz at 50 dB, by 5000 Hz at 59 dB and 2000 Hz at 40 dB, and by 5000 Hz alone at 61 dB.

The calculated equal-loudness curves are depicted in Fig. 4. Each curve specifies the way that the SPL of the 2000-Hz component must be reduced in order to offset the perceptual effect of increasing the SPL of the 5000-Hz component. If the total sensory effect (loudness) depends on the linear sum of independent contributions from the two components, then

$$L_t = F_1(E_{2000}) + F_2(E_{5000}) \tag{5}$$

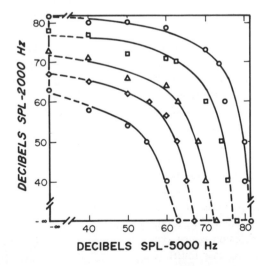

FIG. 4   Equal-loudness curves, constructed from the data in Fig. 1. Each function gives the combinations of SPLs of the 2000- and 5000-Hz components that sound equally loud. The curves represent the equation $(E_{2000})^{.3} + (E_{5000})^{.3}$ = constant.

where F_1 and F_2 are psychophysical transformations of the acoustic input. Given that each curve in Fig. 4 describes a condition of constant loudness, $L_t = c$, it follows that

$$F_1 (E_{2000}) = c - F_2 (E_{5000}) \tag{6}$$

The curves in Fig. 4 describe the equation

$$(E_{2000})^{.3} = c - (E_{5000})^{.3} \tag{7}$$

Hence the psychophysical functions F_1 and F_2 can both be defined by Eq. (1). Note that these equal-loudness curves are consistent with previously reported matches between the loudness of one-component and two-component sounds. Two equally loud components sounded together appear as loud as one component if it were augmented by 10 dB.

A noteworthy feature of the present reanalysis is that it demonstrates how the rule of additivity formalized in Eq. (7) might be derived by means of a loudness-matching procedure. The equal-loudness curves shown in Fig. 4 could have been determined directly by matching the loudness of one multicomponent sound to that of another. That the curves were in fact derived from numerical estimates does not limit their validity, because these invariances (equal-loudness relations) are not themselves dependent on the fidelity of numerical judgments. The only requirement on the magnitude estimates is that they be internally consistent. That is, on the average, subjects must assign the same number to all of the stimuli that produce the same sensation magnitude. Magnitude estimation passes this test of consistency (see Marks, 1974a, 1974b).

What sums in summation?   To conclude at this point that 2000-Hz and 5000-Hz tones combine their *loudnesses* linearly, with no interaction, is to assume the propriety of rescaling the original magnitude estimates. If there were some small deviation from simple linear additivity, given the particular frequencies that were selected, this nonadditivity might be swept up into the rescaling. If so, then loudnesses did not add linearly, and the rescaled values are not loudnesses.

Now, there are two ways to view this objection. One is to demur from accepting the rescaling on the grounds that it may be inappropriate. What this first view entails is the requirement that scaling precede the description of multivariate effects. In order to assess loudness summation, it is necessary first to develop a valid procedure for scaling loudness.

Note that this conclusion is not avoided by devising or selecting a numerical scaling procedure that gives parallel (e.g., linearly additive) functions without rescaling. Both magnitude-estimation scales and rating scales are subject to many systematic effects—of stimulus range, stimulus spacing, number of available rating categories, etc. To discover a procedure that yields linear additivity without rescaling, for instance, is no guarantee that the procedure adequately measures sensation magnitude. The procedure might be "biased" so as to offset the non-linear interaction between components.

Another way to view the objection is to accept the results of rescaling (or the original scaling, if so warranted) as providing a measure of the sensory effects that underlie the rule of combination but to leave in abeyance the question of what it is that the underlying scales represent. What this second view entails is the assertion that the interaction between components, if any, is the outcome of a nonlinear input-output function that operates after the components' effects have combined. Under this view it is accurate to conclude from Experiment I that there is a linear summation $(\Sigma E_i^{.3})$; however, the transformed variables $(E_{2000}^{.3}$ and $E_{5000}^{.3})$ may not represent loudnesses (they might represent some intermediate stage between the acoustic input and loudness). Experiment II helps throw some light on the interpretation of Experiment I.

Experiment II: Loudness Scales and Analytic Addition

One interesting property of the perception of two-component sound stimuli like those used in the previous experiment is their analyzability. Although the complex sounds have an overall loudness, the original components can be heard in the combination, and they are heard distinctly, each with its own constituent loudness. (One piece of evidence to buttress the claim that it is loudnesses that add linearly is the fact that a given component's loudness seems hardly if at all affected by the presence or level of the other component.) The auditory system is analytic to the extent that people are able to parcel out perceptually the constituents of multicomponent sounds. Ohm's acoustical law, which states that the auditory system performs something akin to Fourier analysis on impinging acoustical waves, is one aspect of analyticity. Analyticity is a broader phenomenon. For instance, one may analyze out the tone and noise components of a tone plus noise without being able to analyze the infinitude of frequencies that constitute the noise itself. More importantly, the notion of analyticity may be a property of other sense modalities—such as taste with its four primary qualities—where Fourier analysis of quality does not apply.

The property of analyticity in hearing—more specifically, the property of analytic addition—can be gainfully employed in order to devise a scale of loudness. The only assumption that needs to be made is that the loudnesses of the constituents of a multicomponent sound constitute the overall loudness. This does *not* mean that components have to add their loudnesses linearly without any interaction between them. Even if components do interact and perhaps partially mask one another, they nonetheless can add analytically; all that is meant by analytic addition is that the loudnesses of the components *as they are heard in the multicomponent sound* add up to equal the overall loudness

of the multicomponent sound. The simplest example is a sound of two components that are heard as equally loud in the combination. If the loudness of each
component is defined as unity, the overall loudness equals two. Note that this
relationship says nothing about the stimuli that produce the components, indeed, says nothing about possible interaction between components. All that
needs be said is that as the auditory system yields them, the constituents make
up the whole arithmetically.

Given analytic addition it is simple in principle to generate a psychophysical
scale. The first operation is to set two components to be perceptually equal in a
combination. Next, match a new stimulus, which is the stimulus to be scaled, to
one component of the combination, and define the psychological magnitude of
the matching stimulus as 1. Finally, match the new stimulus again, this time to
the overall magnitude of the two-component stimulus, and define the psychological magnitude of the matching stimulus as 2. This three-step procedure produces a pair of points on a psychological scale; the procedure can be repeated
up and down the scale as desired until a satisfactory function has been generated.

I applied this general procedure to scale the loudness of a 2000-Hz tone (the
matching stimulus). Two different two-component sounds were employed: (1)
combinations of 2000-Hz and 5000-Hz pure tones, set equal in loudness to each
other in the combinations; and (2) combinations of a 2000-Hz tone and a
narrow band of noise centered on 2000 Hz, set equal in loudness to each other.
Condition (1) therefore utilized stimuli like those of Experiment I, so the components were expected to interact minimally with each other. Condition (2)
was selected to maximize mutual masking (nonlinear interaction between components). Nevertheless, because the scaling depends only on the analytic addition of components, that is, on the addition of components as they are perceived
in the combination, the resulting scales derived from the two conditions should
be identical.

Figures 5 and 6 give the results, which are plotted both for individual subjects
(the same ten men and women served in the two conditions) and pooled across
subjects. Although there was considerable variation from subject to subject,
these interindividual differences were not in general maintained across conditions; this suggests that the individual differences are probably largely the result of chance variation.

Most of the scales for individuals, as well as for the average, can be described
well by power functions (straight lines in these log-log coordinates), and the
pooled functions are almost identical for the two conditions. The exponent of
the function relating loudness to acoustical energy is, in Condition (1) .341, in
Condition (2) .346.

From the close agreement between the average scales derived from Experiments I and II, we are in a position to conclude that to a first approximation,

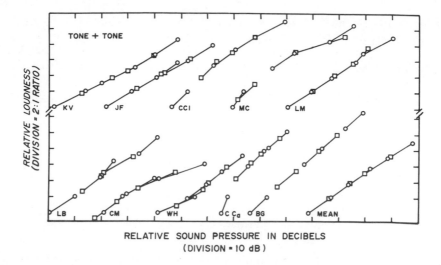

FIG. 5 Psychophysical functions for the loudness of a 2000-Hz tone. Units on the abscissa represent 10-dB changes in SPL; units on the ordinate represent 2:1 ratios of loudness. Shown are individual results for 10 subjects plus results pooled over subjects. The loudness functions are derived through analytic addition in a procedure where the 2000-Hz tone is matched first to the loudness of one constituent of a complex (2000-Hz and 5000-Hz tones equally loud) and then to the overall loudness of the complex. Such pairs of matches were obtained at five places along the loudness dimension.

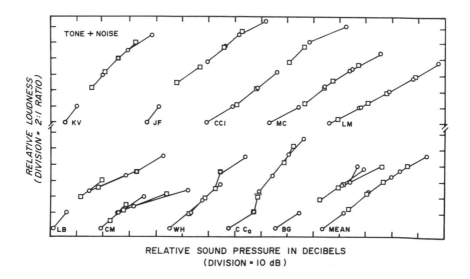

FIG. 6 Same as Fig. 5, except that the equally loud components of the complex were a 2000-Hz tone and a narrow band of noise centered on 2000 Hz.

the rescaled components in Experiment I are loudnesses, and these loudnesses combine linearly. Any nonlinear interaction seems to have been negligible.

Additivity, loudness scales, and auditory processes.   The evidence set forth in the last two sections suggests that the loudness of a sound of constant spectrum grows approximately in proportion to the .3 power of the corresponding acoustical energy and that in complex sounds the loudnesses of components that are widely separated in frequency add up linearly. But it should be kept in mind that there are three distinct points to this conclusion. One is that there exists a psychophysical transfer function from physical intensity to the magnitude of a sensory effect and that this function can be described by a .3-power equation. The second point is that the transfer functions operate on distinct channels, and the sensory effects of different channels (the outputs, after transformation, from widely separated frequency components) add linearly. The third and final point is that these sensory effects are themselves loudnesses.

Experiment I gives both the form of the psychophysical transfer function for loudness and the rule of linear additivity of outputs from widely separated channels. That experiment in itself, however, did not prove that it is loudnesses that add, because the sensory effects could undergo further nonlinear transformations subsequently in the auditory system. That is, after the .3-power transformations are imposed and the transformed sensory values are summed linearly, the summed effect could pass through another nonlinear stage before emerging as a value of loudness. Experiment II, however, does imply that the output of the .3-power function is loudness. Analytic addition is defined on loudness, wherever loudness may emerge in the auditory system.

What is important to bear in mind, however, is the notion that the discovery of a simple rule of concatenation, such as the linear additivity of sensory effects elucidated by Experiment I, does not necessarily specify the nature of the variable that is concatenated. There may be a manifold of stages in the processing of stimulation, with different rules, or perhaps the same rule, of concatenation applying at each stage. (For another viewpoint on this issue, see Anderson, 1970, 1974.) But each stage might involve a different input-output function. As discussed previously, there is a great deal of evidence showing that acoustical energy is integrated within critical bands in the auditory system [see Eq. (3)]. What, we may ask, would be the result of repeating the paradigm of Experiment I on multicomponent sounds whose constituents fell wholly within a single critical band?

Summation within a critical band.   From the extensive data that exist on energy summation within critical bands, it is possible to predict the outcome of an experiment in which subjects are asked to judge the loudness of sounds comprising two components that lie close together in frequency. The predicted outcome is shown in the left-hand section of Fig. 7, which, in analogy with Fig. 1, plots the psychological response as a function of the SPL of one of the components; the level of the second component is the parameter. The particular input-output function that governs the shape of these curves is the .3-power function

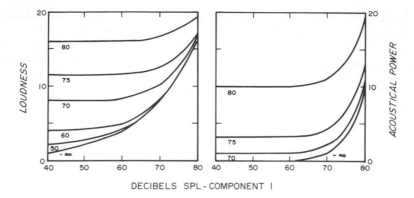

FIG. 7   *Left*: The loudness of two-component sounds, plotted against the SPL of one component. Each function represent a different SPL of the other component. The two components are assumed to fall within a single critical band. *Right*: Loudnesses from left-hand section rescaled so as to make the functions parallel. The rescaled values are now directly proportional to acoustical power (energy flow).

of Eq. (1); however, the general features of this figure would be the same given any negatively accelerated loudness function.

Perhaps the most salient characteristic of the set of curves is their distinct nonparallelism. The curves tend to converge at high levels, an outcome that would seem at first glance to be clearly inconsistent with additivity of components. And so it is if the components are the loudness scales defined by Eq. (1). It is quite easy, though, to transform the response scale in order to make the curves parallel, without disturbing the rank-order of the loudness relationships. The result of rescaling is shown in the right-hand section of Fig. 7. To rescale the curves to parallism though, is merely to redefine the response scale so as to make it wholly proportional to acoustical power (energy flow), because, as previously noted, total loudness is a function of the energy integrated within the critical band.

That it is possible to transform the response scale in order to make the curves parallel in no way assures that the transformed responses provide a "scale of loudness." What we might say is that the rescaled responses provide a scale of the sensory effect that operates at a particular stage of processing. This does not preclude the existence of other scales of sensory effects, that is, sensory scales that operate at other stages.

Sequential Model for the Processing of Auditory Intensity

The pertinent facts about summation within and between critical bands and about the input-output transformations that precede summation are incorporated into the simple scheme depicted in Fig. 8. From my own point of view, the most important stages are the first two. Within each critical band (first stage), some sensory effect that is directly proportional to acoustical energy is summed linearly. This quantity is then fed to the second stage, where there is a nonlinear transformation (roughly according to a .3-power function) imposed on the output from Stage 1 (the output from each critical band), and these transformed quantities—which Experiment II suggests to be loudnesses—are then summed linearly.

The processes that take place at Stages 1 and 2 appear to be describable as energy summation within critical bands and loudness summation across critical bands. Future investigations are needed to determine how well the sequential processing model outlined in Fig. 8 describes additive mechanisms in other portions of the frequency range of hearing. (An intriguing question concerns the rules of summation when two components are separated by more than a critical band but not enough to permit simple loudness summation with no interaction.) Even with the data at hand, it is possible to observe two clearly distinct forms of

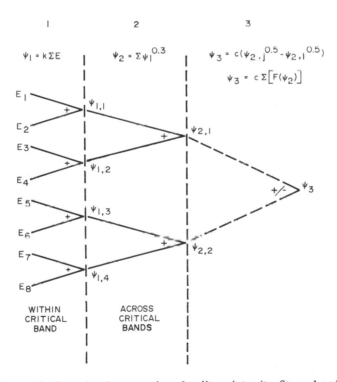

FIG. 8   Sequential scheme for the processing of auditory intensity. Stages 1 and 2 represent the transformations and summations that take place within and between critical bands, respectively. Stage 3 represents the transformations and combinational operations that take place when separate stimuli are related.

input-output relation: a linear relation between the acoustical energy input and the output in the first stage, and a nonlinear relation approximating a .3-power function between the input and output in the second stage. The first two stages of the present model resemble some of the schemes to calculate the loudness of complex sounds (e.g., Zwicker & Scharf, 1970).

Figure 8 displays a third stage (though it may be a parallel set of stages), which seems to be optional. This stage may or may not be called into play; its occurrence often depends on the existence of instructions to the subjects to respond to some relationship between pairs of stimuli. It is tempting to define the division between Stages 2 and 3 as a transaction from "sensation" to "perception." Having said this, I will at least at this time resist the temptation.

Stage 3 is applicable to judgments of loudness differences, which, it may be recalled, yield scale values that are markedly at variance with those defined by Eq. (1). Loudness differences seem to be a function of the algebraic difference between sound intensities raised to approximately the .15 power rather than the .3 power. This would entail a nonlinear effect operating between Stages 2 and 3, where the loudness values undergo a square-root transformation (see Marks, 1974a). Sometimes this transformation can even arise when subjects are asked to judge loudness ratios. Schneider, Parker, Farrell, and Kanow (1976) reported that pairs of sounds that were judged to have the same loudness difference were also judged to have the same loudness ratio (see Chapter 2; and see Birnbaum & Veit, 1974). Garner (1954) reported a related finding: Of 18 subjects asked to match loudness ratios, 13 appeared to match loudness differences. The other 5 seemed to match loudness ratios. Thus there are individual differences among subjects, which might be modified through practice. In terms of the present model, instruction to judge ratios leads in some individuals to a square-root transformation plus linear subtraction at Stage 3.

Similar results are obtained when subjects judge the dissimilarity of auditory stimuli (Parker & Schneider, 1974). Pairs of sounds that are said to have the same loudness difference are also said to be equally dissimilar. I have previously suggested (Marks, 1974a) that sensory magnitudes undergo a square-root transformation when they are to be related to one another on a scale of similarity. In terms of the present scheme, the proposal can be extended to suggest that the optional Stage 3 is brought into action in the generation of multidimensional similarity.

Also indicated in Fig. 8 is a process of psychological addition. This refers to a task where subjects are presented two or more sounds in succession and asked to respond to the "total loudness." This is quite a different situation from that of multicomponent sounds, where, as more and more components are added, the sensory effect itself increases. With sequential presentation of "components," the overall sensory effect does not continue to grow—you don't deafen someone by repeatedly playing an 80 dB tone. The "addition" here has less of a sensory basis. Two questions to be asked of such a psychological addition are: (1) Is the process linearly additive? and (2) Is there a nonlinear transformation imposed on the sensory effects fed from Stage 2 to Stage 3?

Dawson (1971) reported a study in which subjects judged the total loudness of sequentially presented 1000-Hz tones. His results are consistent with: (1) linear summation of sensory effects; and (2) scale values proportional to the .3 power of acoustical energy. Hence Dawson's data imply additivity with no nonlinearity at Stage 3 (see also Zwislocki et al., 1974).

Experiment III: Judgments of "Total Loudness" of Sequentially Presented Tones

Sometimes, though, there may be an additional nonlinear transform imposed in the sequence of processing. The same 15 subjects who served in Experiment I also served in an experiment in which they were asked to judge by magnitude estimation the total loudness of pairs of sounds. Each pair comprised a 2000-Hz and a 5000-Hz tone; the combinations of SPLs were exactly those used in Experiment I. In the present Experiment III, however, the tones were presented sequentially rather than simultaneously. Each tone lasted one second, and one second separated members of each pair (counterbalanced for order). Geometric means of the magnitude estimates are plotted in Fig. 9. These results are analogous to those plotted in Fig. 1, except that the present experiment involved successive rather than simultaneous presentation of components.

In several respects the data shown in Fig. 9 differ notably from those of Fig. 1. For instance, the data in Fig. 9 are "noisier," which is consistent with the subjects' complaints that the judgmental task seemed peculiar and difficult. Also, a

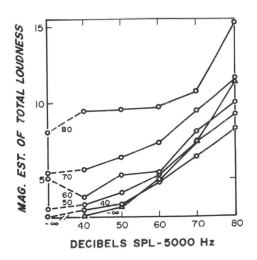

FIG. 9 Magnitude estimates of the "total loudness" of sequentially presented stimuli, one a 2000-Hz tone, the other a 5000-Hz tone. Levels are as in Fig. 1.

strange result was obtained with a subset of the stimuli, namely those where the 5000-Hz tone was presented singly (2000 Hz at zero). The data for this subset have been plotted as triangles in Fig. 9 in order to distinguish them from the remainder of the points. This particular function crosses several of the others, an outcome that precludes the possibility of fitting the entire set of data with a general equation incorporating linear additivity. What may have happened was that this subset of stimuli was judged on a numerical scale different from that used on all of the other stimuli (in fact, comparison to Fig. 1 suggests that the 5000-Hz stimuli, but only that subset, were judged on the same numerical scale used in Experiment 1!). If this subset of the data is ignored, though, the remaining data appear to be reasonably consistent with an additive scheme.

In order to look at this additive scheme in greater detail, the aberrant subset of data was eliminated, and the remainder was subjected to a rescaling that maximized parallelism (additivity) while at the same time maintaining as best possible the rank-order of the values. Figure 10 shows the result. The rescaled values are proportional to the .22 power of acoustical energy; this relationship is virtually identical to the one that Curtis and Mullin (1975) derived from judgments of the average loudness of sequentially presented 1000-Hz tones. It is not consistent, however, with the psychophysical function derived from Experiment I, which employed simultaneous stimulation. Results of that experiment, as well as loudness matches like those obtained by Fletcher and Munson (1933), showed that the loudness gain produced by adding a second, equally loud component is the same as that produced by augmenting the SPL of a single component by 10 dB. In the case of sequential stimulation, the analogous gain in the judgment of "total loudness" is 14 dB. When equal-loudness curves are constructed from the results of Experiment III, they define a set of functions (Fig. 11) that are not consistent with the analogous equal-loudness curves derived from Experiment I (Fig. 4). The process of psychological addition appears sometimes to involve an additional nonlinear transformation on the loudness values.

Just how many different transformations there may be at Stage 3 of the sequential model cannot be said. It is conceivable that the psychological operation that is induced by asking subjects to judge differences (or, sometimes, ratios)

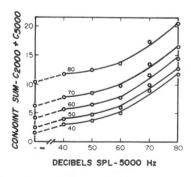

FIG. 10 Rescaling of the data from Fig. 9 on the basis of their rank-order.

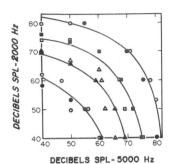

FIG. 11 Equal-"total loudness" curves, constructed from the data in Fig. 9. The curves represent the equation $(E_{2000})^{.2} + (E_{5000})^{.2}$ = constant.

leads to one transformation (a square-root function, bringing the overall exponent down from .3 to .15), whereas asking subjects to judge totals or averages leads to another transformation (a two-thirds power function, bringing the overall exponent down from .3 to .2; or a linear function, leaving the overall exponent unchanged). On the other hand, perhaps there is only one sort of non-linear transformation imposed at Stage 3; the differences in results observed thus far with different tasks may reflect nothing more than variability around an average. It is possible to test directly the question of whether different transformations arise from instructions to add and to subtract: One could, for instance, ask subjects to judge the difference between total loudnesses.

Stages 1 and 2 are auditory stages only, that is, specific to one modality; in fact, the channels described here are presumably specific to the particular domain of auditory intensity. The scope of Stage 3, which is called into action when different stimuli are to be related, presumably is much broader. It is probably not only multidimensional, operating to generate differences or dissimilarities of loudness, pitch, and other auditory dimensions, but also multimodal, operating to generate these differences on all modalities. This would make Stage 3 suprasensory, placing it in what Aristotle called the "common sense" and making it in part responsible for some aspects of the unity of the senses (Marks, in press).

This brings us almost to the end. Before ending, however, let me present the last bit of the dialogue between Protologos and Doutatomas:

Protologos: And that is why these are as they are—our hearing acts in stages, one stage after another.

Doutatomas: That is indeed an interesting theory, Protologos, but tell me—I could say "In all honesty," but I know that is unnecessary—tell me, do you expect others to be convinced of your way of thinking?

Protologos: Certainly, Doutatomas, though perhaps not right away. But in a couple of thousand years. . . .

Doutatomas: That is a long time to wait. Too long for me. I'm off home now to a jug of wine. Care to come along, Protologos?

Protologos: Thank you, no. I'm much too busy just now. I need to give some more thought to another problem that has plagued my mind. Tell me, Doutatomas, have you ever wondered why it is that apples always fall down?

ACKNOWLEDGMENT

Research was supported in part by General Research Support Grant No. RR05692 from the National Institutes of Health. Preparation of the paper was supported in part by Grant No. BNS76-09950 from the National Science Foundation.

REFERENCES

Anderson, N. H. Functional measurement and psychophysical judgment. *Psychological Review*, 1970, *77*, 153-170.

Anderson, N. H. Algebraic models in perception. In E. C. Carterette & M. P. Friedman (Eds.), *Handbook of perception* (Vol. II). *Psychophysical judgment and measurement*. New York: Academic Press, 1974.

Beck, J., & Shaw, W. A. Ratio-estimations of loudness-intervals. *American Journal of Psychology*, 1967, *80*, 59-65.

Birnbaum, M. H., & Veit, C. T. Scale convergence as a criterion for rescaling: Information integration with difference, ratio, and averaging tasks. *Perception and Psychophysics*, 1974, *15*, 7-15.

Curtis, D. W., & Mullin, L. C. Judgments of average magnitude: Analysis in terms of the functional measurement and two-stage models. *Perception and Psychophysics*, 1975, *18*, 299-308.

Dawson, W. E. Magnitude estimation of apparent sums and differences. *Perception and Psychophysics*, 1971, *9*, 368-374.

Fechner, G. T. *Elemente der Psychophysik*. Leipzig: Breitkopf und Härtel, 1860.

Fletcher, H. Auditory patterns. *Review of Modern Physics*, 1940, *12*, 47-65.

Fletcher, H., & Munson, W. A. Loudness, its definition, measurement and calculation. *Journal of the Acoustical Society of America*, 1933, *5*, 82-108.

Garner, W. R. A technique and a scale for loudness measurement. *Journal of the Acoustical Society of America*, 1954, *26*, 73-88.

Hellman, R. P., & Zwislocki, J. J. Loudness function of a 1000-cps tone in the presence of a masking noise. *Journal of the Acoustical Society of America*, 1964, *36*, 1618-1627.

Hellman, R. P., & Zwislocki, J. J. Loudness determination at low sound frequencies. *Journal of the Acoustical Society of America*, 1968, *43*, 60-64.

Luce, R. D., & Tukey, J. W. Simultaneous conjoint measurement: A new type of fundamental measurement. *Journal of Mathematical Psychology*, 1964, *1*, 1-27.

Marks, L. E. Stimulus-range, number of categories, and form of the category-scale. *American Journal of Psychology*, 1968, *81*, 467-479.

Marks, L. E. On scales of sensation: Prolegomena to any future psychophysics that will be able to come forth as science. *Perception and Psychophysics*, 1974, *16*, 338-376. (a)

Marks, L. E. *Sensory processes: The new psychophysics*. New York: Academic Press, 1974. (b)

Marks, L. E. *Mental measurement and the psychophysics of sensory processes*. Lecture presented at The New York Academy of Sciences, December 1975.

Marks, L. E. *The unity of the senses*. New York: Academic Press, in press.

Parker, S., & Schneider, B. Non-metric scaling of loudness and pitch using similarity and difference estimates. *Perception and Psychophysics*, 1974, *15*. 238-242.

Scharf, B. Loudness summation and spectrum shape. *Journal of the Acoustical Society of America*, 1962, *34*, 228-233.

Scharf, B. Critical bands. In J. V. Tobias (Ed.), *Foundations of modern auditory theory* (Vol. I). New York: Academic Press, 1970.

Schneider, B., Parker, S., Farrell, G., & Kanow, G. The perceptual basis of loudness ratio judgments. *Perception and Psychophysics*, 1976, *19*, 309-320.

Schneider, B., Parker, S., & Stein, D. The measurement of loudness using direct comparisons of sensory intervals. *Journal of Mathematical Psychology*, 1974, *11*, 259-273.

Stevens, J. C., & Guirao, M. Individual loudness functions. *Journal of the Acoustical Society of America*, 1964, *36*, 2210-2213.

Stevens, S. S. The measurement of loudness. *Journal of the Acoustical Society of America*, 1955, *27*, 815-829.

Stevens, S. S. The direct estimation of sensory magnitudes—loudness. *American Journal of Psychology*, 1956, *69*, 1-25.

Stevens, S. S. Power-group transformations under glare, masking, and recruitment. *Journal of the Acoustical Society of America*, 1966, *39*, 725-735.

Stevens, S. S. Perceived level of noise by Mark VII and dB(*E*). *Journal of the Acoustical Society of America*, 1972, *51*, 575-601.

Stevens, S. S., & Galanter, E. Ratio scales and category scales for a dozen perceptual continua. *Journal of Experimental Psychology*, 1957, *54*, 377-411.

Stevens, S. S., & Greenbaum, H. B. Regression effect in psychophysical judgment. *Perception and Psychophysics*, 1966, *1*, 439-446.

Stevens, S. S., & Guirao, M. Loudness functions under inhibition. *Perception and Psychophysics*, 1967, *2*, 459-465.

Ward, L. M. Category judgments of loudness in the absence of an experimenter-induced identification function: Sequential effects and power function fit. *Journal of Experimental Psychology*, 1972, *94*, 179-184.

Zwicker, E. Die Verdeckung von Schmalbandgeräuschen durch Sinustöne. *Acustica*, 1954, *4*, 415-420.

Zwicker, E., Flottorp, G., & Stevens, S. S. Critical band width in loudness summation. *Journal of the Acoustical Society of America*, 1957, *29*, 548-557.

Zwicker, E., & Scharf, B. A model of loudness summation. *Psychological Review*, 1970, *72*, 3-26.

Zwislocki, J. J., Ketkar, I., Cannon, M. W., & Nodar, R. H. Loudness enhancement and summation in pairs of short sound bursts. *Perception and Psychophysics*, 1974, *16*, 91-95.

2

Differences and Ratios in Psychological Measurement

Michael H. Birnbaum
University of Illinois at Urbana-Champaign

The purpose of this chapter is to present new approaches to an old problem in psychophysics: the apparent contradiction between so-called "ratio" and "interval" techniques for scaling. The quote marks are used to remind the reader that the numbers obtained when subjects are instructed to judge "ratios" or "differences" need not obey the mathematical properties of the ratio or subtractive models.

The chapter begins with a brief discussion of "direct" scaling, the so-called new psychophysics that was to replace the scaling methods of Fechner and Thurstone. One major problem with this approach is that the empirical contradiction in scales cannot, in principle, be resolved within the unifactor framework typically used in "direct" scaling, which does not allow tests of the theories of measurement.

Newer approaches of psychological measurement that use factorial stimulus designs and algebraic models to assess the data are discussed. It is shown that the additional criterion of scale convergence, the premise that stimulus scales are independent of instructions, can add the extra constraint needed to resolve certain indeterminacies in the measurement approach.

Results of recent research using factorial designs with "ratio" and "difference" tasks illustrate the evidence that for a variety of perceptual continua, instructions to judge "ratios" or "intervals" lead to the same ordering of stimulus pairs, consistent with the interpretation that there is but one comparison operation—which could be either a ratio or difference—for both tasks.

A framework is presented in which ratio and subtractive theories make different ordinal predictions for more complex judgment tasks in which subjects make quantitative comparisons of stimulus pairs. Two experiments are then reviewed in which "ratios" and "differences" of stimulus intervals satisfy predictions of both ratio and subtractive models, yielding a ratio scale of intervals. This scale of intervals is then used to resolve the ratio versus subtractive interpretations for simple "ratios" and "differences" of two stimuli. Data from the two experiments support the contention that the basic operation by which subjects compare two stimuli is best represented by subtraction.

"DIRECT" SCALING

One proposal to obtain a scale of psychological magnitude was to ask subjects to report numbers that "directly" represent the strengths of sensations. The term "direct" was used to emphasize the distinction between this technique and the Fechner-Thurstone approach of "indirectly" inferring psychological differences from measures of discriminability (Stevens, 1957).

An outline of "direct" scaling is shown in Fig. 1. In the outline, Φ_i is the physical measurement of stimulus level i, s_i is the corresponding sensation, and R_i is the overt numerical response. The function relating sensations to physical values is termed the *psychophysical function*, $s_i = H(\Phi_i)$. The function relating responses to subjective values is called the *judgment function*, $R_i = J(s_i)$. A plot of responses against the physical values represents the composition $R_i = J[H(\Phi_i)]$.

Examples of "Direct" Scaling

The bottom of Fig. 2 shows seven squares containing dot patterns that were used as stimuli in an experiment to illustrate typical results obtained with "direct" scaling methods. Subjectively, how "dark" are the dot patterns? Two "direct" methods have been used in attempts to answer this question. The first is to ask subjects to produce numbers that represent subjective intervals using the method of *category rating*. A second procedure is to ask subjects to report numbers that are "directly proportional to their sensations," a technique called *magnitude estimation*. The numbers obtained by these two "direct" methods constitute two operational definitions of "sensation."

FIG. 1   Outline of "direct" scaling. Physical values of the stimuli (Φ_i) are related to psychological scale values (s_i) by the psychophysical function, $s_i = H(\Phi_i)$. Overt responses, R_i, are related to subjective values by the judgment function, $R_i = J(s_i)$, assumed to be strictly monotonic. Since the data observed in a typical unifactor "direct" scaling study are the confounded composition, $R_i = J(H(\Phi_i))$, it is not possible to separate theories of subjective value, comparison processes, or judgmental processes in this framework.

Outline of Direct Scaling

$$\text{Physical Value} \xrightarrow{H} \text{Scale Value} \xrightarrow{J} \text{Overt Response}$$

$$\phi_i \longrightarrow s_i \longrightarrow R_i$$

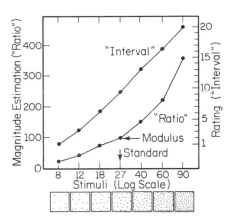

FIG. 2 "Direct" scalings using magnitude estimations and category ratings yield different "scales" of sensation. Upper curve shows mean ratings (1-20) of darkness of dot patterns as a function of the number of dots, spaced logarithimically on the abscissa. Lower curve shows mean magnitude estimations, when the 27-dot pattern (standard "divisor") was designated "100" (modulus).

One group of subjects was instructed to make magnitude estimations of "ratios." They were asked to call the fourth pattern (the standard) "100" and to assign numbers to the other patterns so that the ratio of the two numerical responses would equal the ratio of the subjective darknesses of the two stimuli. They were instructed, if it seemed half as dark, to say "50," if it seemed twice as dark, to say "200," etc.

A second group was asked to make ratings that would represent "intervals." They were told to call the lightest pattern "1," the darkest "20," and to judge each square so that the differences in response would be proportional to subjective intervals of darkness.

Assuming that the subjects follow these instructions, we theorize that the magnitude estimation of "ratio" should be given by the equation:

$$ME_i = 100 \left(\frac{s_i}{s_4} \right) \tag{1}$$

where s_4 is the subjective darkness of stimulus 4 (the standard), s_i is the sensation for stimulus i, and ME_i is the overt magnitude estimation.

Similarly, the category judgments should be given by the equation:

$$CJ_i = 19 \left(\frac{s_i - s_1}{s_7 - s_1} \right) + 1, \tag{2}$$

where CJ_i is the category judgment, and s_1 and s_7 are the two extreme stimuli to be judged "1" and "20," respectively.

Equations (1) and (2) represent theories of the judgment function, J, although they involve deeper assumptions about comparison processes which are discussed later. Equation (1) asserts that magnitude estimation responses are directly proportional to subjective values; Eq. (2) asserts that category ratings are linearly related to subjective values. If the subjective values (s_i in both equations) are the same, solving Eq. (1) for s_i and substituting in Eq. (2) shows that category ratings should be linearly related to magnitude estimations:

$$CJ_i = \frac{19}{s_7 - s_1} \left[\frac{s_4}{100}(ME_i) - s_1 \right] + 1 \tag{3}$$

Equation (3) expresses the idea of the convergence of two operational definitions of sensation. If two procedures for defining the same construct were to agree, there would be no evidence for concern. However, when two procedures do *not* agree, an explanation is required.

An Empirical Contradiction

Figure 2 plots both magnitude estimations ("ratios") and category ratings ("Intervals") as a function of the number of dots in the squares, spaced in equal log steps on the abscissa. It should be apparent that the two procedures yield scales that are not linearly related. These results are typical of the results obtained in a large number of experiments for a variety of psychophysical and social judgment dimensions (Stevens & Galanter, 1957; Stevens, 1966). Instead of a linear function, magnitude estimations are often approximately exponentially related to category ratings.

This violation of converging operations, though it caused some consternation, had good effects for the study of psychological scaling. It caused psychologists to argue about methods, theories, and data, and it caused them to doubt the meaningfulness of the entire enterprise of psychological scaling based on operational definitions (Treisman, 1964; Savage, 1966). Theories were proposed to account for the glaring discrepancy between the two methods. Unfortunately, the theories were untestable in the traditional framework of "direct" scaling.

Theories of the Discrepancy

Three general theories were proposed to account for the finding that the "interval" scaling techniques gave results that were nonlinearly related to the "ratio" techniques: (1) the judgment function, J, depends on the response procedure and is nonlinear for at least one of the methods; (2) there is some bias in the comparison process, C, so that subjects cannot compute both ratios and differences properly; and (3) the subjective values of the stimuli, s, change value, depending on the task.

The first theory is that at least one of the procedures contains a nonlinear judgment bias. Thus this theory rejects the assumptions [of Eqs. (1) and (2)] that J is a linear function in the case of ratings and J is a similarity transformation in the case of magnitude estimation. Just because the subjects have been *instructed* to report a number that is directly proportional to their sensation does not mean that they can use numbers in this way. Attneave (1962) proposed that subjective magnitude of numerals could be a nonlinear power function of objective numerical magnitude, suggesting that the subject selects a magnitude estimation number whose subjective value is equal to the subjective value of the stimulus. Rule, Curtis, and their associates have pursued Attneave's suggestion that the inverse of J is the psychophysical function for numerals (see Rule & Curtis, 1973). Treisman (1964) and Ekman and Sjoberg (1965) have discussed the possibility of a logarithmic psychophysical function for numerals, which would produce an exponential function for J. Poulton (1968) attributed the nonlinearity of J to context effects in the experiments, since the results of "direct" scaling studies using magnitude estimation depended on the stimulus range, frequency distribution, value of the standard, and a variety of other experimental details.

The second type of theory contends that at least one computation is erroneous. Stevens (1971) argued, for example, that subjects can estimate ratios but cannot compute subjective intervals. Rather than argue for a computation error in one of the operations, Torgerson (1961) advanced the conjecture that subjects do not distinguish between "ratios" and "differences," perceiving instead only one quantitative comparison between a pair of stimuli. Subjects (and the experimenters) are willing to call this single relationship either a "ratio" or a "difference."

A third possibility is that the sensation depends on the task. This position contends that we should take the responses in Fig. 2 at face value and conclude that there are at least two kinds of sensations that are nonlinearly related. Marks (1974) has argued that there are two different scales of sensory magnitude, one for "intervals" and one for "ratios," related by the square root function.

Problems with "Direct" Scaling

The major problem with the traditional method of "direct" scaling is that the experimental designs do not provide sufficient ordinal constraints to test the theories of stimulus comparison (Krantz & Tversky, 1971; Birnbaum & Veit, 1974a; Anderson, 1974; Veit, 1974; Shepard, 1976). "Ratios" and "differences" may or may not be consistent with the metric or ordinal predictions of ratio and subtractive models.[1] However, with a unifactor design, it would not be possible to reject a ratio or difference model.

---

[1]Quotation marks are used throughout to indicate "ratio" and "difference" tasks or judgments. Quotation marks are not used for actual (computed) ratios and differences or for models and theoretical statements.

With unifactor designs, used in "direct" scaling research (e.g., Stevens & Galanter, 1957; Torgerson, 1960), "ratios" and "intervals" are necessarily monotonically related. Since the standard (divisor) is fixed, $ME_j = J_R (s_j/c)$, where c is the standard, and J_R is the judgment function for magnitude estimation. For "interval" judgments,

$$CJ_j = J_D \left(\frac{s_j - s_1}{s_7 - s_1} \right),$$

Where s_1 is the smallest stimulus, s_7 is the largest, and J_D is the judgment function for ratings. Hence, since ME_j and CJ_j are both monotonic functions of s_j, ME_j is monotonically related to CJ_j whether the subject computes a difference or a ratio. Therefore, unifactor designs do not permit ordinal tests of theories, such as Torgerson's (1961), that there is only one comparison operation. However, ratios and differences are *not* monotonically related in general (e.g., 2/1 $>$ 7/5, but 2-1 $<$ 7-5). With factorial designs it becomes possible to test theories of comparison processes.

Poulton (1968) has noted that the results of direct scaling studies depend on contextual details of experimental procedure. If the responses are taken at face value, it means that the scale of sensation depends on the stimulus context. But with the direct scaling approach, there is no way to test the alternative theory that the context affects only the judgment, not the sensation.

Basically, since observed data are of the form $R = J [H (\Phi)]$, it is clear that for any reasonable theory of H, it is possible to find a function J such that the composition matches the data in a unifactor design. There is no way to test whether the computation operation can be represented by a difference or a ratio or whether J is linear. There is no way to test whether context affects H or J. The use of factorial designs in the framework of algebraic measurement theories comes close to solving these problems. Certain difficulties still remain but become resolvable with additional constraints. The following section explains how the additional ordinal constraints produced by factorial designs permit tests of algebraic theories of judgment, which allow for distinction between the stimulus scale, $s = H (\Phi)$, and the response transformation, $R = J (\Psi)$.

PSYCHOLOGICAL MEASUREMENT APPROACH

Figure 3 shows an outline of psychological measurement that facilitates discussion of theories of stimulus comparison. In the outline the comparison operation is represented by the function, $\Psi_{ij} = C (s_i, s_j)$, where Ψ_{ij} is the subjective impression of a difference or ratio, s_i and s_j are the subjective scale values of the stimuli, and C is a model of the comparison (integration) process that describes how two stimuli combine to produce the impression of the pair relationship. The judgment function, $R_{ij} = J (\Psi_{ij})$, represents the transformation from impression, Ψ, to overt numerical response.

FIG. 3 Outline of psychological measurement. Subjective scale values of the stimuli are combined by the comparison function, Ψ_{ij} = C (s_i, s_j), and transformed to an overt response by the strictly monotonic judgment function, $R_{ij} = J$ (Ψ_{ij}). In this framework, using factorial stimulus designs, the assumption of a linear J permits a metric test of C. Alternatively, the assumption of a theory of C permits estimation of J and the scale values, s.

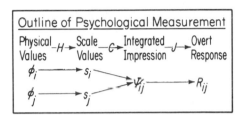

In this framework it is possible in principle to test (i.e., reject) models of the comparison process. Conjoint measurement analysis (Krantz et al., 1971; Krantz & Tversky, 1971) attempts to specify the ordinal relationships that ideal data must satisfy in order to be consistent with particular theories of C. The approach of functional measurement (Anderson, 1970, 1974) has been to attempt to specify theories that reproduce the metric information in the numerical data that are obtained.

Illustrative Factorial Experiments

Figure 4 represents a factorial stimulus design that is used to convey several ideas of psychological measurement. The reader is invited to make two copies of Fig. 4 and to particpate as a psychophysical observer. For one unfamiliar with this area of research, in order to gain a better grasp of the results that follow, it will be helpful to carry out the analyses described below on a set of data. Although these dot experiments are intended for illustrative purposes, they are convenient and reliable demonstrations of results obtained in more formal experimental settings with other psychophysical continua.[2]

Two experiments illustrate important points of the present chapter. For the "ratio" task, judge the ratio of the darkness of each column square to the darkness of every row square. The estimations should be written in the appropriate matrix locations. Judgments should be consistent with the following scheme:

$$12.5 = \text{column is } 1/8 \text{ as dark as row}$$
$$25 = \text{column is } 1/4 \text{ as dark}$$
$$50 = \text{column is } 1/2 \text{ as dark}$$
$$100 = \text{column equals row}$$
$$200 = \text{column is 2 times as dark}$$
$$400 = \text{column is 4 times as dark}$$
$$800 = \text{column is 8 times as dark}$$

[2]In factorial $B \times A$ designs, B refers to rows, indexed by i; A refers to columns, indexed by j. The tasks always specify $A - B$ or A/B, and the data are always plotted against factor A, with a separate curve for each level of B.

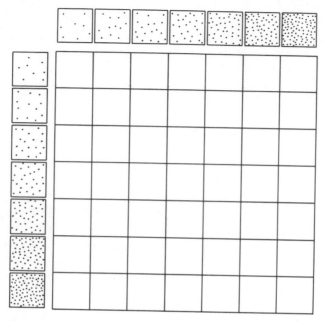

FIG. 4   Representation of factorial experiment. The reader is encouraged to make two copies of this figure and replicate the experiments. For the "ratio" task, judge the ratio of the darkness of the column square to that of the row using a modulus of 100. For the "difference" task, judge the algebraic difference, column minus row, calling the largest difference '100,' a zero difference "0," and using negative numbers when the row stimulus is darker.

Any numbers consistent with this scheme may be used to represent the ratios of subjective, psychological darkness of the dot patterns.

For the "difference" task, the instructions are to judge the difference between the darkness of the column stimulus and the row stimulus. The greatest difference (column-row) is to be called "100." When the column equals the row darkness, the difference would be "0." Negative numbers would be used to express negative differences (i.e., when the row stimulus seems darker than the column stimulus).

The two experiments produce two matrices of numbers that correspond to differential instructions to judge "ratios" and "differences." The following subsections show how the measurement approach permits one to test corresponding ratio and subtractive models and to estimate scale values from the data without using the physical measurements of the stimuli.

Ratio and Subtractive Models

Ratio model.   The *ratio* model can be written:

$$R_{ij} = J_R \left(s_j / s_i \right), \tag{4}$$

where R_{ij} is the numerical estimation of the "ratio" of the jth column stimulus to the ith row stimulus (divisor), having subjective scale values s_j and s_i, respectively, and J_R is the judgmental transformation that relates overt numerical estimations to subjective ratios.

Subtractive model. The *subtractive* model can be written:

$$D_{ij} = J_D (s_j - s_i),$$ (5)

where D_{ij} is the rated difference between the stimulus of column j and the stimulus of row i, s_j and s_i are the scale values, and J_D represents the judgment function that relates overt ratings of differences to subjective intervals.

Metric Implications of the Models

It is useful to initially examine the metric (i.e., numerical) implications of the ratio and subtractive models under the special assumption that the judgment functions, J_R and J_D, are linear. More complex cases that do not restrict the form of the judgmental transformations are discussed later.

Figure 5 shows computed ratios and differences for a 7 X 7 design, as in Fig. 4. The scale values for the seven rows and columns are assumed to be successive integers from 1 to 7 (i.e., let $s_i = i$, and $s_j = j$), and the judgment functions are assumed to be identity functions. Hence $R_{ij} = j/i$, and $D_{ij} = j - i$. Although for simplicity the scale values and judgment functions have been assumed to be known in this example, the measurement approach allows them to be estimated from the data.

Ratio model. The left-hand panel of Fig. 5 plots ratios, R_{ij}, as a function of the column scale value ($s_j = j$), with a separate curve for each row stimulus. The highest curve represents the first row of the matrix, $R_{1j} = j/1$. The lowest curve represents the last row of the matrix, $R_{7j} = j/7$. Each curve is a linear function of the scale value of the column stimulus, with the same (zero) intercept. The slopes are inversely proportional to the scale values of the row stimuli. This sort of diverging fan of straight lines that intersect at a common point is termed a *bilinear fan,* since the interaction in the matrix is located entirely in the bilinear component. Each entry in the matrix could be produced from the equation,

$$R_{ij} = R_{i.} \, R_{.j} / R_{..},$$ (6)

where $R_{i.}$ and $R_{.j}$ are the row and column totals respectively, and $R_{..}$ is the grand total of the matrix. [This equation is analogous to the method for computing predictions under the hypothesis of independence (multiplicative probabilities) for a chi-square table.]

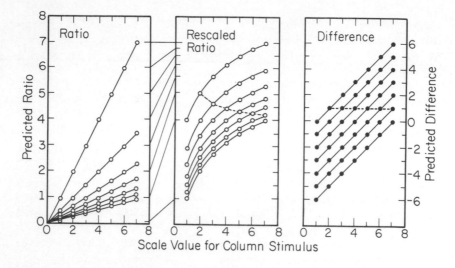

FIG. 5   Predicted ratios and differences assuming two operations on one scale of sensation. The computations have been made using successive integers from 1 to 7 as scale values. *Left:* Plots ratios A/B as a function of the column value (dividend–A) with a separate curve for each row stimulus (divisor–B). *Center:* Shows the ratios rescaled to parallelism by a logarithmic transformation (lines connecting panels). *Right:* Plot differences ($A - B$) as a function of column scale value (minuend), with a separate curve for each row stimulus (subtrahend). Note that ratios and differences are *not* monotonically related. Dashed lines connect differences of 1 and corresponding log ratios.

Equation (6) provides a means for estimating scale values when they are unknown. If there are r rows and k columns, and if $R_{ij} = s_j/s_i$, then

$$R_{\cdot j} = s_j \left(\sum_{i=1}^{r} \frac{1}{s_i} \right)$$

Hence the marginal sum, marginal mean (Anderson, 1970), or $R_{\cdot j}/\sqrt{R_{\cdot\cdot}}$ are all proportional to the scale value, s_j. [The last expression may be recognized as the equation for the first centroid factor of a correlation matrix; it is also presented by Ekman (1958).]

If J_R were a linear function, $R_{ij} = as_j/s_i + c$, the value of the additive constant, c, could be determined from the projection of the point of intersection onto the ordinate. If J_R were of the form, $R_{ij} = a\,(s_j/s_i)^b + c$, the data would still plot as a bilinear fan, since one could define new scale values, $s' = s^b$, against which the curves would be linear. Scales derived from a ratio model are unique to a power transformation, $s' = as^b$, where a and b are arbitrary (Krantz et al., 1971). [The letters a, b, and c are used throughout this chapter for arbitrary constants, with no carryover from equation to equation.]

Some confusion was created by the assertion that marginal means are an "interval scale" of the stimuli in the ratio model. The term "interval scale" has two meanings. Assuming a linear judgment function, the marginal means are linearly related to (and hence an "interval scale" of) the scale values for the ratio model (Anderson, 1970). The concept of "interval scale" has another meaning in terms of ordinal uniqueness. The ratio model does *not* define an interval scale of the stimuli in the ordinal uniqueness sense, since any power transformation of the scale values would yield scales that would reproduce the rank order of the data. That is, substituting $s' = as^b$ for s in Eq. (4), $R_{ij} = J_R (s_j^b/s_i^b) = J_R [(s_j/s_i)^b]$. Since the composition of J_R and a power function is a monotonic function, the rank order of R_{ij} is preserved by any power transformation of the scale values.

In summary, the ratio model predicts a bilinear fan of curves that intersect at a common point. This prediction depends on the judgment function being of the form: $R_{ij} = a (s_j/s_i)^b + c$. When the pattern of bilinearity is observed, it is possible to estimate scale values for the ratio model from marginal sums or means. The scales thus defined are unique to a power transformation.

Subtractive model. The right-hand panel of Fig. 5 shows the computed differences, $D_{ij} = j - i$, plotted in the same fashion as the ratios in the left-hand panel. Again, the curves are linearly related to the column scale value. In the case of the subtractive model, however, the curves are parallel. If $D_{ij} = a (s_j - s_i) + c$, then $D_{ij} - D_{kj} = a (s_k - s_i)$ for all j. Hence the difference between any two rows, say i and k, is independent of the column j.

The parallelism implied by the subtractive model is equivalent to the condition of no row X column interaction in the analysis of variance. Under these conditions, each entry in the matrix can be reproduced by the equation,

$$D_{ij} = \bar{D}_{i.} + \bar{D}_{.j} - \bar{D}_{..}, \tag{7}$$

where $\bar{D}_{i.}$ and $\bar{D}_{.j}$ are the marginal means, and $\bar{D}_{..}$ is the grand mean in the matrix.

Equation (7) provides a means of estimating scale values, since $\bar{D}_{.j} = a [s_j - \Sigma (s_i/r)] + c$. Therefore, when the data fit the model, the curves are parallel and the marginal means are linearly related to the subtractive model scale values.

If J_D were a linear function, $D_{ij} = a (s_j - s_i) + c$, the curves would remain parallel. The scale values for the subtractive model are unique to an interval scale, since any linear transformation of the scale values, $s' = as + b$, would reproduce the rank order of the matrix entries (Krantz et al., 1971).

In summary, the subtractive model predicts no interaction between row and column stimuli, assuming the judgment function is linear. The data should plot as parallel lines. The marginal means can be used to estimate scale values, which are unique to a linear transformation. However, if the judgment function is nonlinear, the model only predicts that it should be possible to rescale the data to parallelism.

Ordinal Indeterminacy

When the overt responses are only considered an ordinal scale (i.e., if J in Fig. 3 is only assumed to be strictly monotonic), it becomes more difficult to test models (Birnbaum, 1974a, 1974b; Birnbaum & Veit, 1974a, 1974b). If the data show ordinal violations of the theory, it is agreed that the model should be rejected. The difficulty occurs when the data are ordinally consistent with the model but metrically (numerically) inconsistent. When is it appropriate to transform data to fit the model and then conclude that the model fits? If the data can be transformed to fit the model, the scale values can be derived from the transformed data, and the inverse transformation could be interpreted as the judgment function (Birnbaum, 1974a, 1974b). However, such transformation may be theoretically inappropriate; the numerical deviations may represent "true" violations of the theory that should not be scaled away. For more extensive discussion of this problem including methods for dealing with it, see Birnbaum (1974a).

The case of ratio and subtractive models is an example of this problem. The ordinal requirements of the subtractive model and the ratio model are equivalent. Hence it is not possible to discriminate these models on the basis of ordinal information in a single experiment without some extra constraint. Data that are numerically consistent with the ratio model can be transformed to fit the subtractive model because $\log(R_{ij}) = \log(s_j/s_i) = \log s_j - \log s_i$. The center panel of Fig. 5 shows the results of a logarithmic transformation of the ratios in the left-hand panel of Fig. 5. Data that are consistent with the subtractive model can be exponentially transformed to fit the ratio model. For a single set of data, $s = \exp(s^*)$, where s is the scale value based on the ratio representation, and s^* is the scale for the subtractive representation.

If we assume that J is linear, then ratio and subtractive models can be distinguished on the basis of the metric properties of the raw (untransformed) data. However, if we do not assume that the judgment function is more than monotonic, we are forced to select a representation on the basis of some arbitrary criterion such as the task given the subjects or convenience. However, additional criteria can be specified to help resolve some of the indeterminancy.

SCALE CONVERGENCE CRITERION

By postulating that scales should be independent of the task, additional constraints are provided that limit the number of permissible transformations of the data. According to the stimulus scale convergence criterion, transformations of the data are deemed *appropriate* if they simultaneously fit models to data and lead to scales that agree. In this framework the scale attains greater status in that it becomes an intervening construct that can be used to account parsimoniously for an otherwise complicated set of relationships (Garner, Hake, & Eriksen,

1956; Krantz, 1972; Krantz et al., 1971; Anderson, 1972; Cliff, 1973; Birnbaum, 1974a; Birnbaum & Veit, 1974a; Shepard, 1976).

Although a single matrix of ordinally consistent data could be rescaled to fit either a ratio model or a subtractive model, Fig. 5 shows that two matrices with the assumption of scale invariance provide greater constraint: Ratios and differences of the *same* scale values are *not* monotonically related. For example, $7 - 5 > 2 - 1$ but $7/5 < 2/1$. The dashed lines in Fig. 5 connect pairs with equal differences of 1. Note that the ratios 2/1, 3/2, 4/3 are not equal but approach 1 as the constant interval (2-1, 3-2, 4-3) is moved up the scale (dashed curve in middle of Fig. 5). If there are both ratio and subtractive operations, then there will be two *different* rank orderings in the matrices. Since the scale that reproduces the order of the ratios is unique to a power function, and the subtractive scale is unique to a linear function, it follows that the common scale that reproduces the two different orders is unique to a similarity transformation. Thus, if the two orders are consistent with the models and interlocked by a common scale, the scale values constitute a ratio scale (Krantz et al., 1971).

On the other hand, if there is only one operation for both "ratios" and "differences," then both instructions will generate the same ordering of the pairs (Birnbaum & Veit, 1974a). If $R_{ij} = J_R (s_j \circ s_i)$ and $D_{ij} = J_D (s_j \circ s_i)$, where $\circ$ represents the comparison operation, then $s_j \circ s_i = J_D^{-1} (D_{ij})$; hence, $R_{ij} = J_R [J_D^{-1} (D_{ij})]$. Since J_R and J_D are strictly monotonic, it follows that R_{ij} will be monotonically related to D_{ij} if there is only one operation.

In summary, there are two simple possibilities: (1) the two rank orders will be distinct, consistent with the respective models and appropriately interlocked by a common scale; (2) the rank order of the data in both matrices will be the same, consistent with the hypothesis that subjects perceive only a single comparison between a pair of stimuli. It is also possible that the data would be inconsistent with both of these alternatives, calling the models and/or the scale convergence criterion itself into question.

Empirical Evidence: One Operation

Figure 6 plots mean estimations of "ratios" of darkness, mean ratings of "differences," and rescaled values. The stimuli were those of Fig. 4, which were administered to 44 undergraduates at the University of Illinois. Half the subjects performed either task first, with no evidence of task order effects.

The left-hand panel of Fig. 6 shows mean "ratio" estimations plotted against marginal means for the column stimulus. The mean estimations (open circles) come very close to the bilinear pattern (lines) predicted by the ratio model.

The right-hand panel plots the mean "difference" estimations against the column marginal means. The data appear nearly parallel, as predicted by the subtractive model. Considering the fit of the raw numerical data to the models implied by the tasks, it would be tempting to conclude that subjects are actually

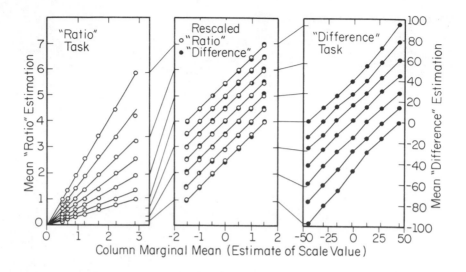

FIG. 6   Mean "ratios" and "differences" of darkness of stimuli in Fig. 4, plotted as in Fig. 5. Although "ratio" task data fit ratio model, and "difference" task data fit subtractive model, both sets of data have equivalent rank orders. Center panel shows data rescaled to parallelism. Transformations are represented by lines connecting panels. Note that the data are *not* like the predictions shown in Fig. 5, since both sets of rescaled values coincide. (From Birnbaum and Stegner, 1976.)

computing ratios for "ratios" and differences for "differences." It is shown later, however, that this interpretation leads to contradiction of the scale convergence criterion.

The center panel shows the results of separate rescalings of both sets of data to parallelism via MONANOVA (Kruskal & Carmone, 1969), a computer program that seeks a monotonic transformation to reduce interactions in analysis of variance. Both the "ratio" task data (open circles) and the "difference" task data (solid points) appear to coincide after transformation. The two tasks seem to generate a single order that can be represented by either a ratio model, or a subtractive model, but not both.

It may seem surprising that subjects given two different tasks provide numbers for the respective matrices that do not obey the ordinal requirements of two operations on one scale. If the subjects had covertly assigned numbers to the stimuli and then calculated ratios and differences on these covert numbers, the results would have been quite different, because the two matrices would have obeyed the predictions of two models on a common scale. Instead, if we accept the premise that the scale values of darkness are independent of the task, it appears that the comparison process is also independent of the task to judge "ratios" or "differences."

More Evidence

The results of this demonstration experiment are typical of results obtained with judgments of the heaviness of lifted weights (Birnbaum & Veit, 1974a), numerical magnitude (Rose & Birnbaum, 1975; Birnbaum, 1974b), shades of gray (Veit, 1974), likeableness of adjectives (Hagerty & Birnbaum, 1976), and loudness (Birnbaum & Elmasian, 1977).

Birnbaum and Elmasian (1977) presented pairs of 1000-Hz tones varying in sound pressure level and asked subjects to compare the loudness of the two tones. The pairs were constructed from a 5 X 9, B X A, factorial design in which the first tone (B) varied from 42- to 90-dB SPL in 12-dB steps; the second tone (A) covered the same range in 6-dB steps. Each subject served in four daily sessions, two for "ratios" and two for "differences," completing 10 replications of the design per session. Separate analyses, performed on the data for each subject-day, led to the conclusion that estimates of "ratios" and ratings of "differences" are each roughly numerically consistent with their respective models. The mean "ratio" estimations, shown in Fig. 7, plotted as in Fig. 6, are nearly bilinear. The mean "difference" ratings (9-point scale), shown in Fig. 8, are nearly parallel. However, the two orders for each subject are approximately the same for both tasks and can therefore be represented by a single comparison operation.

The data for both tasks were transformed to parallelism. Figure 9(A) shows the predicted results for the transformed scores, based on the theory that the subjects can compute both ratios and differences of loudness. In both panels, solid points connected by straight lines represent rescaled "differences," open

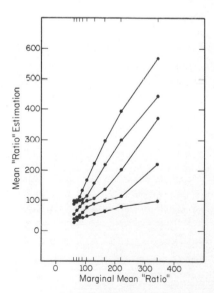

FIG. 7 Mean estimation of "ratio" of loudness, plotted as in left panel of Fig. 6. Modulus was 100. (From Birnbaum and Elmasian, 1977.)

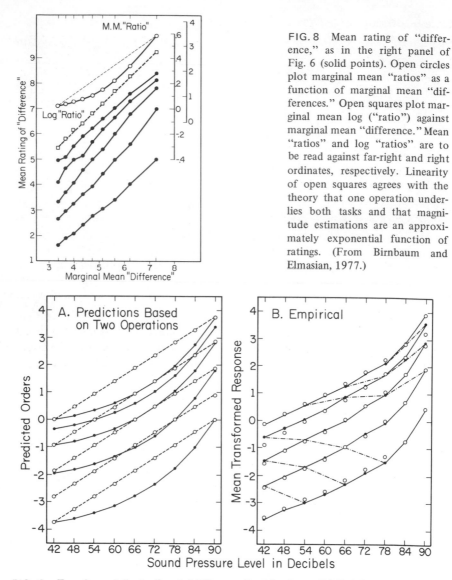

FIG. 8 Mean rating of "difference," as in the right panel of Fig. 6 (solid points). Open circles plot marginal mean "ratios" as a function of marginal mean "differences." Open squares plot marginal mean log ("ratio") against marginal mean "difference." Mean "ratios" and log "ratios" are to be read against far-right and right ordinates, respectively. Linearity of open squares agrees with the theory that one operation underlies both tasks and that magnitude estimations are an approximately exponential function of ratings. (From Birnbaum and Elmasian, 1977.)

FIG. 9 Transformed "ratios" and "differences" of loudness. (A) Left-hand panel shows predicted transformed ratios (open circles) and differences (solid points) assuming power functions for loudness. Hypothetical values were computed by taking ratios and differences of power functions of physical sound pressure and then transforming to parallelism on a common scale. (B) Right-hand panel plots actual mean transformed values as a function of the sound pressure level of tone A with a separate curve for each level of tone B, which varied from 42 dB to 90 dB in 12-dB steps. Solid points connected by solid lines represent transformed "differences"; open circles are transformed "ratios." Broken lines connect pairs of equal physical ratios; lowest broken line is for −36 dB, next is for −24, etc. (From Birnbaum and Elmasian, 1977.)

circles represent rescaled "ratios." Although the particular hypothetical predictions shown in Fig. 9(A) were computed using scale values for both tasks that were power functions of physical intensity, the general relationship between the solid and dashed curves would remain the same for other scale values (transformation of the abscissa). Figure 9(A) shows the relationship between transformed ratios and differences, showing again how different the results should be if subjects actually used two operations.

Figure 9(B) shows the actual mean transformed scores, plotted as a function of sound pressure level for the second stimulus (A) with a separate curve for each level of the first stimulus (B). The mean transformed scores are representative of the single subject data presented by Birnbaum and Elmasian (1977). Each set of rescaled data is nearly parallel, and the two sets are nearly identical. The similarity of the orders can be seen by the coincidence of circles (representing rescaled "ratios") and lines (connecting rescaled "differences"). These results are consistent with the hypothesis that there is but one loudness comparison for "ratios" and "differences."

The broken curves in Fig. 9(B) connect pairs with equal physical ratios. Assuming a ratio model, the power function ($s = a\Phi^b$) implies that equal physical ratios should receive equal "ratio" judgments, since $R_{ij} = J_R (s_j/s_i) = J_R (\Phi_j^b / \Phi_i^b) = J_R [(\Phi_j/\Phi_i)^b]$. Instead, the broken curves of Fig. 9(B) show that equal physical ratios receive more extreme judgments at the upper end of the scale. Scale values for the ratio model are inconsistent with a power function for loudness as a function of physical intensity.

Theories We Can Reject

The finding that instructions to judge "differences" and "ratios" lead to the same ordering of stimulus pairs allows us to reject the theory that subjects use two operations on a common scale. That is, for the continua and conditions studied in our experiments, we reject the theory that can be explicated in the following four premises:

P_1 (independence):   The scale value of a stimulus is independent of the stimulus with which it is compared.

P_2 (scale convergence): $s^* = s$; the scale value of a stimulus is independent of instructions to judge "ratios" or "differences."

P_3 (ratio model): $R_{ij} = J_R (s_j/s_i)$

P_4 (subtractive model): $D_{ij} = j_D (s_j^* - s_i^*)$

The first premise explicitly assumes that the scale value of row or column stimulus is independent of the stimulus with which it is paired. The scale values are assumed to be independent of the task in premise P_2. In premises P_3 and P_4, which state the models, J_R and J_D are any monotonic functions.

The finding that both models fit the data seems inconsistent with previous hypotheses that the reason that "ratio" and "interval" techniques yield different scales is due to a computation error. For example, Stevens (1971) contended that "the human being, despite his great versatility, has a limited ability to effect linear partitions on prothetic continua." The contention that subjects make a miscalculation in computing differences leads to violations of the subtractive model. The present data show that whatever subjects are doing for "intervals," they order the pairs in the same way for "ratios." There seems no evidence to support the contention of two operations with a distortion or bias in one computation, since both sets of data satisfy the ordinal requirements of the subtractive (or ratio) model of comparison.

The data do not support the theory that there are two operations with two scales of sensation, one for "ratios" and another for "intervals," both of which are power functions of physical intensity (Marks, 1974; Stevens, 1971). If $s = \Phi^b$ and $s^* = \Phi^c$, then $s^* = s^{c/b}$. Therefore, the two scales would be related by a power function. This theory turns out to be equivalent in its ordinal predictions to the theory that there are two operations on one scale. In fact, premise P_2 could be replaced by $s^* = as^\beta + \gamma$, and the theory would still predict different orders for the two tasks.

The data do not require more complicated theories, for example, that there is one operation with two scales of sensation or that neither model could provide a representation of either set of data.

Theories We Can Entertain

It would be possible to retain the previous premises P_1, P_3, and P_4 on the basis of the present data if the scale convergence premise (P_2) were replaced with the premise, $s = \exp(s^*)$. However, to retain the scale convergence criterion requires that the other premises be modified, because the entire theory ($P_1 - P_4$) cannot account for the data. There are two simple theories that retain scale convergence and "save the phenomena" (reproduce the data of these experiments).

1. *Ratio theory:*
   P_1: (independence)
   P_2: (scale convergence): $s^* = s$
   P_3: (ratio model): $R_{ij} = J_R (s_j/s_i)$
   P_5: (ratio model): $D_{ij} = J_D (s_j^*/s_i^*)$

This theory asserts that subjects compare stimuli by computing ratios, irrespective of the instructed task. The data for the darkness of the dot patterns (Fig. 6) imply that J_R is at least of the form $R_{ij} = a\,(s_j/s_i)^b + c$, since the data are very nearly bilinear. The judgment function for ratings of "differences," J_D, would have to be approximately logarithmic to account for the near-parallelism of the "difference" ratings.

According to the ratio theory, scale values estimated from the column marginal means, $\bar{R}_{.j}$, are 50, 67, 92, 122, 167, 223, and 287 for the seven levels of darkness. These scale values can be well approximated as a power function of the number of dots, $s = \Phi^{.72}$. Since scale values defined by the ratio model are unique only to a power scale, the exponent would have little meaning unless it were assumed that J_R were linear.

2. *Subtractive theory:* This theory asserts that the basic comparison is a difference, irrespective of task.

P_1 : (independence)
P_2 : (scale convergence): $s^* = s$
P_6 : (subtractive): $R_{ij} = J_R\,(s_j - s_i)$
P_4 : (subtractive): $D_{ij} = J_D\,(s_j^* - s_i^*)$

According to subtraction theory, the data for the darkness example imply that J_R must be nearly exponential, since the "ratio" estimations (left panel of Fig. 6) are nearly bilinear. If $R_{ij} = \exp(s_j - s_i)$, it follows that a subtractive operation would lead to data satisfying the predictions of the ratio model, because $\exp(s_j - s_i) = \exp(s_j)/\exp(s_i)$.

The scale values for the subtractive model, estimated after transforming the data for both tasks to parallelism, are: -1.48, -1.00, $-.50$, $-.02$, $.50$, 1.02, and 1.50. These scale values are very nearly equally spaced, as are the logarithms of the number of dots, indicating that the scale values could be well approximated by a logarithmic psychophysical function of the number of dots, $s = \log \Phi$.

Summary and conclusions.   The data are compatible with the theory that the same comparison operation applies for both tasks, since the two orderings are equivalent. If the operation is represented by a ratio model, then the scale values for darkness can be fit as a power function of number of dots. Furthermore, the ratio interpretation implies that the judgmental transformation for magnitude estimation must be at least a power function and perhaps even linear. To explain the near-parallelism for the difference task would require that the J_D function be approximately logarithmic. If the operation is represented by a subtractive model, however, then the judgmental transformation for "ratios," J_R, would be exponential, and J_D would be approximately linear. The psychophysical function would be well approximated by a logarithmic function. Hence the conclusions for the stimulus and response scales derived from the data depend on the model or theory that is assumed.

The simplest interpretation appears to be that there is only one comparison operation, only one psychophysical scale, and two different judgmental transformations depending on whether the response is a category rating or magnitude estimation. This interpretation is consistent with Torgerson's (1961) theory and is consistent with the data of numerous experiments using factorial designs in which subtractive and ratio models can be evaluated in tandem. If the operation is a ratio, the J_R transformation for magnitude estimation would receive support from the fact that the data are numerically consistent with the model, but the J_D transformation for ratings would be near-logarithmic. On the other hand, if the operation is subtraction, J_D would be nearly linear and J_R exponential.

The inferred psychophysical scales, s, psychophysical function, H, and judgmental transformations, J, all depend on the assumed representation. Does it make sense to ask which operation is "really" correct? Torgerson (1961) noted that this question can not be resolved in the two-stimulus case. The next section discusses a nonmetric four-stimulus approach in which this question becomes meaningful in the sense that experiments could refute one theory or the other.

Scale and Theory Dependence

A simplistic view of functional measurement maintains that the metric fit of a model simultaneously "validates" the model and the response scale. Had the data for only one task (*either* the "difference" or "ratio") been obtained, it might have been tempting to conclude that the fit of the model "validates" both model and scale. However, the scale convergence criterion combined with the data for the two tasks implies, in spite of the metric fit of both models to the raw data, that at least one of the models and one of the scales must be rejected. The present findings show that extreme caution must be used in interpreting the metric fit of a model as evidence for "validity."

Birnbaum and Veit (1974b) introduced the term *scale-dependent* to refer to research in which the determination of the "appropriate" model depends on the arbitrary choice of the "valid" dependent variable, and the "validity" of the response procedure circularly depends on the arbitrary choice of model. For example, if the validity of ratings were assumed for "difference" judgments, the subtractive model would be chosen; the ratio model and magnitude estimation would be rejected. On the other hand, if the validity of magnitude estimations were assumed, then the ratio model would be preferred, and it would be concluded that ratings and the subtractive model are not valid. Thus the choice of model depends on the choice of dependent variable and vice versa.

In scale-dependent tests of the size-weight illusion, Anderson (1972) fit an additive model to rating data; however, J. C. Stevens and Rubin (1970) and Sjoberg (1969) fit ratio models using magnitude estimations. Sarris and Heineken (1976) replicated these results for the size-weight illusion in a single experiment in which only the change of dependent variable sufficed to change the data from parallel to bilinear. Weiss (1972) found that ratings of average darkness of a pair of gray chips were almost consistent with a constant-weight averaging model (additive), whereas magnitude estimations were nearly consistent with a geometric averaging model (multiplicative). Birnbaum and Veit (1974b) have noted that if the response procedure only affects the judgment function, J, and if magnitude estimations are exponentially related to ratings, it follows that if ratings fit an additive (or subtractive) model, magnitude estimations would be expected to fit a multiplicative (or ratio) model.

These scale-dependent experiments, when analyzed in conjunction with the scale-convergence criterion, appear consistent with the proposition that the operations are unaffected by the response procedure, but the judgmental transformation depends on whether category ratings or magnitude estimations are used as the dependent variable. These experiments also illustrate that tests of internal consistency and certain types of "cross-task validation" (e.g., Anderson, 1972), in which the *same* model is applied for both tasks, are not diagnostic tests of the "validity" of the models, scales, or response procedures, since choice of a different dependent variable can alter the apparent form of both models while still retaining cross-task scale convergence.

SCALE-FREE TESTS

The scale-free approach requires only the ordinal information in the data, plus some theoretical assumptions, to test models with far greater constraint than has been achieved in the past. The scale-free approach was developed by Birnbaum (1974a, experiment IV) to test the additive and constant-weight averaging models of impression formation. Birnbaum and Veit (1974b) have applied it to the size-weight illusion, and Veit (1974) has employed a novel application of the technique to the ratio-difference problem. The following subsections expand on the work of Veit (1974, in press) and describe a recent experiment by Hagerty and Birnbaum (1976) that illustrates the scale-free approach for the ratio-difference problem.

Quantitative Relations for Pairs

Suppose for the moment that the "true" operation is subtraction. This could be so for two distinct reasons: (1) it may be that for some reason subjects have only one operation for comparing two stimuli--perhaps, metaphorically, they do not have the neural circuitry to do anything else; and (2) on the other hand, it may be that the operation employed depends on the internal stimulus representation. Perhaps the sensation values should be represented by points on a line with arbitrary origin (i.e., places, not lengths). In such a representation, distances or differences are sensible, but ratios are not. Thus, when asked to judge "ratios," the subject may actually judge differences (Birnbaum & Veit, 1974a).

If the second interpretation were correct, then intervals (differences) would have a well-defined zero point even if the stimulus values did not. Hence subjects might be able to judge both ratios and differences of *pair intervals*, even if they could not judge both ratios and differences of stimulus magnitudes (Veit, 1974). On the other hand, if the interpretation that there is only one operation for such judgments were the case, then only one operation would be observed for comparisons of pairs.

In order to achieve tests of these possibilities, it is necessary to employ tasks in which the subject receives four stimuli on each trial and is asked to compare two pair relations. The four tasks discussed below are "ratio of ratios," "ratio of differences," "difference of ratios," and "difference of differences." The next subsection outlines four models corresponding to these four tasks.

Four Models of Comparison of Pairs

Ratio of ratios model.   This model can be written:

$$RR_{ijkl} = J_{RR} \left[(s_j/s_i) / (s_l/s_k) \right], \tag{8}$$

where RR_{ijkl} is the "ratio of ratios" estimation of the ratio of stimulus levels j to i, relative to the ratio of stimulus levels l to k; J_{RR} is the monotonic judgmental transformation from impressions to overt responses; s_j, s_i, s_l, and s_k are the scale values of the four stimuli, factors A, B, C, and D, respectively, in a four-way factorial design.

Predictions for the ratio of ratios model are shown in Fig. 10, where the calculations are based on scale values of successive integers from 1 to 7. The experimental design portrayed in the upper left of Fig. 10 is a 7 X 7 X 3 design in which the numerator pair is composed of a 7 X 7, A X B, factorial design, and there are three levels of the divisor ratio, C/D, as shown in the figure.

The model predicts a trilinear interaction, in which the bilinear A X B interaction is multiplied by the effect of the divisor ratio. Hence, each A X B interaction should be similar, with greater divergence for smaller divisor ratios. It should be noted that since $J_{RR}^{-1} (RR_{ijkl}) = (s_j/s_i) / (s_l/s_k)$, log $[J_{RR}^{-1} (RR_{ijkl})] = $ log $s_j - $ log $s_i - $ log $s_l + $ log s_k; hence this model is ordinally additive in form.

Ratio of differences model.   This model can be written:

$$RD_{ijkl} = J_{RD} \left[(s_j - s_i) / (s_l - s_k) \right], \tag{9}$$

where RD_{ijkl} is the judged "ratio of differences" of the difference between stimuli s_j and s_i relative to the difference between s_l and s_k; J_{RD} is the judgmental transformation.

Metric predictions for this model are shown in the lower left panel of Fig. 10. Since the numerator contains a subtractive model, the curves for the levels of

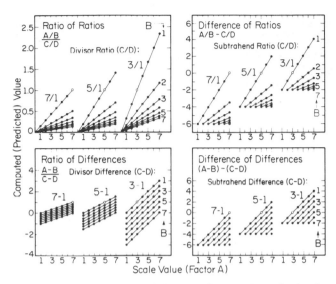

FIG. 10   Predictions for four polynomial theories of comparison of pairs. Successive integers from 1 to 7 are used as scale values for factors A and B. Separate fans of curves are shown for the three divisor or subtrahend pairs (open circles). The two "difference" tasks show predictions only for upper triangular design, in which A-B differences are positive.

$A \times B$ factors $(s_j - s_i)$ are parallel, indicating no interaction between A and B. However, the reciprocal of the divisor difference multiplies this numerator difference. Hence the smaller the divisor difference, the larger the vertical spreads and slopes of the curves. Therefore, the model predicts a bilinear interaction between the numerator and divisor difference. This model is a type of distributive model (Krantz & Tversky, 1971), in which the two dividend factors ($A \times B$) are jointly independent of the divisor (i.e., the ordering in the $A \times B$ matrix for each level of CD is the same), but the other pairs of factors are not (i.e., the ordering of the $A \times$ Divisor matrix depends on the level of B). Hence this model can be distinguished from the others on the basis of ordinal properties of the data. For more detailed discussion of diagnostic analyses for the ratio of differences model, see Veit (1974). Conjoint measurement analyses of general classes of polynomials are discussed by Krantz et al. (1971) and Krantz and Tversky (1971).

Difference of ratios model.   This model can be written:

$$DR_{ijkl} = J_{DR} \left[(s_j/s_i) - (s_l/s_k) \right],   \tag{10}$$

where DR_{ijkl} is the rating of the "difference between two ratios," and J_{DR} is the judgmental transformation for this task.

Predictions for this model are shown in the upper right panel of Fig. 10 for the positive triangle of the 7×7 design (where $s_j - s_i \geqslant 0$), with a separate plot for each subtrahend ratio (s_l/s_k). The predicted pattern is a bilinear $A \times B$ fan for each subtrahend. The bilinear fans for different subtrahends should be congruent, differing only by an additive constant. Thus there is a bilinear interaction between factors A and B, but factors A and B should not interact with the subtrahend pair (CD). This model is a dual-distributive polynomial that can be distinguished from the others on the basis of ordinal information in the data (Krantz & Tversky, 1971).

Difference of differences.   This model can be written:

$$DD_{ijkl} = J_{DD} \; [(s_j - s_i) - (s_l - s_k)] \, , \tag{11}$$

where DD_{ijkl} is the rating of the "difference between two differences," and J_{DD} is the judgmental transformation.

The lower right panel of Fig. 10 shows predictions for the positive upper triangle of the 7 X 7 design (where $s_j - s_i \geqslant 0$). The predicted pattern is one of three-way additivity. Each set of curves is parallel, differing only in an additive constant for each subtrahend pair. Note that although this model is also formally additive and therefore equivalent in an ordinal sense to the ratio of ratios model, scale convergence provides an additional constraint that implies different orderings when the data for the two tasks are compared.

Possible Outcomes

The constraints of the four-stimulus models are such that data can be diagnosed as additive, distributive, or dual-distributive [Eqs. (8) and (11), (9), or (10), respectively] on the basis of the ordinal properties of the data. Scale convergence among the four sets of data (and with the scales from the two-stimulus experiments) provides additional constraints on possible solutions so that different potential outcomes can be distinguished on the basis of the data. Five of these possible outcomes deserve closer attention.

One operation.   One simple possibility is that there is but one operation by which either a pair of stimuli are compared or a pair of stimulus pairs are compared. If this were the case, then the data for all of the four-stimulus tasks could be rescaled to fit either the ratio of ratios model or the difference of differences model. If all of the four-stimulus tasks resulted in the same ordering, the single comparison operation would remain indeterminate.

Subtraction theory.   A second possibility is that the basic operation by which two stimuli are compared is subtraction (Birnbaum & Veit, 1974a; Veit, 1974). This could occur if the subjective stimulus representation is an interval scale, like points along a line with undefined origin. The apparent fit of the ratio model for the "ratio" task would be accounted for by postulating that the judgmental transformation for magnitude estimation of "ratios" is exponential. This theory suggests that subjects could judge ratios of intervals, since differences have a well-defined zero point even when the stimuli do not. Data for the other four-stimulus tasks might be expected to be consistent with the difference of differences model. The "ratio of ratios" tasks would be expected to require a logarithmic transformation to be fit to the difference of differences model, since the dependent variable, magnitude estimation, is presumed to be an exponential function of subjective value. The scales derived from these models would then agree with the subtractive theory of the pair tasks.

Ratio theory.   The basic operation could be a ratio, upon which either differences or ratios could be judged. If this theory were the case, than all of the data could be fit to the ratio and ratio of ratios models, except for the "difference of ratios" task; this task should fit the difference of ratios model, defining scales that agree with the ratio interpretation of the other tasks.

Comparison of pairs validity.   It may be that the data for all of the four-stimulus tasks fit their respective models with a single underlying scale as in Fig. 10. If this outcome were obtained, the common scale could be used to decide between the ratio and subtractive theories for the two-stimulus tasks.

Two worlds.   Perhaps there are two subjective "worlds," one for each operation, with an exponential relationship between the scales. Perhaps the "ratio," "ratio of ratios," and "difference of ratios" data would fit their respective models with one scale. But suppose the "difference," "difference of differences," and "ratio of differences" tasks could be fit to their respective models with another scale that differed from the first. This "impossible figure" outcome, which would look consistent within each realm but inconsistent between realms, could come about if the subject assigned numbers to each *pair* and computed on the numbers to compare pairs.

Evidence for Subtraction Theory

Shades of gray.   Veit (1974, Experiment I) found that ratings of "differences" and estimations of "ratios" of darkness of gray papers were monotonically related, consistent with the theory that one operation applies to both tasks. In a second experiment, she found that magnitude estimations of "differences" generate the same ordering of pairs as magnitude estimations of "ratios" and category ratings of "intervals." However, magnitude estimations of "differences" showed a divergent interaction that required rescaling (interpreted as J^{-1}) to render the curves parallel. This finding is consistent with the interpretation that the comparison operation and scales are independent of the response procedure but that the choice of response procedure affects the judgmental transformation. Beck and Shaw (1967) reached similar conclusions for magnitude estimations of loudness intervals.

In her third experiment, Veit (1974) introduced the ratio of differences model as a test of the subtractive representation. Figure 11 plots the magnitude estimations of "ratios of differences" as in the lower left of Fig. 10, except that larger divisor differences are on the right. The data clearly show the pattern predicted by the ratio of differences model. Consistent with the model, Fig. 12 shows that the small $A \times B$ interactions seen in Fig. 11 can be removed by separate transformation of the data for each divisor difference. It was also possible to fit the ratio model to the numerator/demoninator $[(A - B) / (C - D)]$ comparisons. However, as predicted by the ratio of differences model, it was not possible to eliminate interactions between A or B and the divisor difference. Tests of joint independence (see Krantz et al., 1971) for individual subjects were consistent with the interpretation of the ratio of differences model and inconsistent with the other simple models.

The scale values for the seven levels of reflectance derived from the ratio of differences model were used to evaluate alternative theories for the two-stimulus judgments. These scale values were consistent with the subtractive representation of the simple "difference" and "ratio" tasks. The ratio theory implies scale values that contradict the ratio of differences model. Veit (1974, in press) noted that this finding makes the ratio interpretation implausible. In order to represent

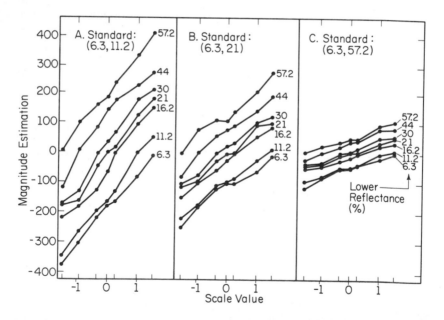

FIG. 11   Mean estimations of "ratios of differences." Each panel shows results for a different divisor difference (C-D), labeled "standard" in the figure. Curve parameters are reflectance values for subtrahend (factor B); abscissa spacing represents estimated scale values for minuend stimulus (factor A). (From Veit, 1974.)

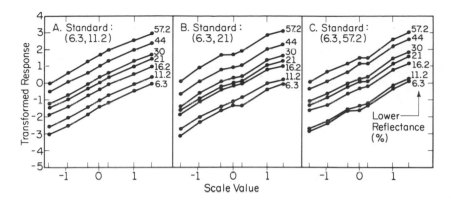

FIG. 12   Transformed mean response as a function of Factor A scale value (minuend) with a separate curve for each level of factor B (subtrahend). A separate rescaling was performed for each divisor (standard) difference. (From Veit, 1974.)

the numerator "difference" with a ratio model and preserve scale convergence, exponential transformation of Eq. (9) represents "ratios of differences" by the model,

$$RD_{ijkl} = \delta_{ij} J_{RD} \{ \exp [(s_j - s_i)/(s_l - s_k)] \} \tag{12}$$

$$= \delta_{ij} J_{RD} \{ [\exp(s_j - s_i)]^{1/(s_l - s_k)} \}$$

hence

$$RD_{ijkl} = \delta_{ij} J_{RD} \{ (s_j^*/s_i^*)^{1/(s_l - s_k)} \} \tag{13}$$

where $s^* = \exp(s)$, and δ_{ij} is the sign of $s_j - s_i$. The ratio interpretation requires two different models for "differences," s_j^*/s_i^* and $s_l - s_k$ (for numerator and denominator "differences," respectively), with two different scales, s^* and s. Furthermore, an instructed "ratio" would be represented by two different models: a ratio model for "ratios" of two stimuli and an exponential-power function for "ratios of differences."

Because of these complexities, Veit (1974) rejected the ratio theory as a viable alternative. Scale values derived from the subtractive representation of magnitude estimations of "ratios," ratings of "differences," magnitude estimations of "differences" and "ratios of differences" were all in close agreement, consistent with the simpler interpretation of the subtractive theory (Veit, 1974; in press).

The possibility remains, however, that the difference of ratios model would fit data obtained in a "difference of ratios" task, yielding scales that would agree with the ratio interpretation of the "ratio" and difference," two-stimulus tasks. This "two worlds" potentiality and others were checked by employing all of the four-stimulus tasks in an experiment by Hagerty and Birnbaum (1976.)

Likeableness of adjectives. Hagerty and Birnbaum (1976) studied judgments of the likeableness of hypothetical persons described by adjectives. For example, how much more would you like someone who is *sincere* than someone who is *mean?* Six tasks were employed, including both of the two-stimulus tasks and all of the four-stimulus tasks. The same subjects performed several tasks the first day for practice, then returned for two more days to complete all of the tasks. Adjectives were chosen on the basis of normative ratings to represent seven levels of likeableness, for example: *cruel, irritating, clumsy, hesitant, thrifty, capable,* and *sincere.*

Data for the "ratio" and "difference" tasks are shown in Fig. 13. The factorial stimulus design was a 4 X 7, *B* X *A*, using different adjectives for the two factors. In the left panel of Fig. 13, the "ratio" estimations (with a modulus of 100) show the approximate bilinear form of diverging curves when plotted against the marginal means. The right panel of Fig. 13 shows that the "difference" ratings (on a 9-point scale) are approximately parallel. Both tasks yield data that can be rescaled to approximate parallelism as shown in the center panel of Fig. 13. The rescaled "ratios" (circles) and "differences" (points) are nearly identical, consistent with previous results and the interpretation that one comparison operation underlies both tasks.

The assumption of the ratio model and the linearity of magnitude estimations would imply that the marginal means (abscissa spacing of Fig. 13) represent a scale of likeableness of the adjectives. The interval between the lowest and middle adjectives *hesitant-cruel* is less than the interval between the two highest adjectives *sincere-capable.* The subtractive representation (abscissa spacing in center panel) leads to the opposite conclusion: The *hesitant-cruel* interval is the larger.

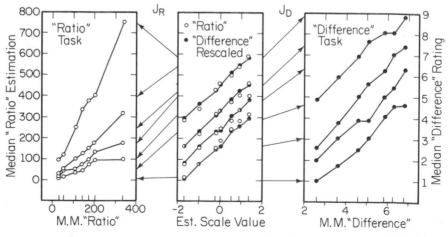

FIG. 13   "Ratios" and "differences" in likeableness of adjectives, plotted as in Fig. 6. *Left:* Shows median "ratios." *Center:* Shows that rank orders for both tasks are nearly identical and that rescaled data are roughly parallel. Assuming a subtractive model for both tasks, the transformations to overt responses (arrows) represent judgmental functions. *Right:* Shows median "differences." (From Hagerty and Birnbaum, 1976.)

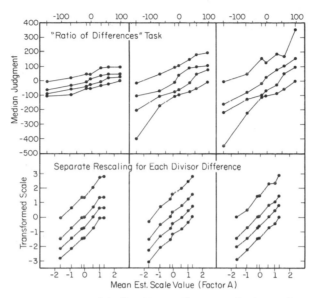

FIG. 14 "Ratios of differences" in likeableness. Upper panels plot median estimates as in Fig. 11. Lower panels plot rescaled values as in Fig. 12. Data are compatible with a ratio of differences model. (From Hagerty and Birnbaum, 1976.)

For the four-stimulus tasks, the 4 X 7 design was combined with three divisor or subtrahend pairs (*truthful-phony, truthful-listless,* and *practical-listless*).

Figure 14 presents the results for the "ratio of differences" task plotted as in Figs. 10 and 11. Data for the largest divisor difference (truthful-phony) are on the left. The curves in Fig. 14 show the form predicted by the ratio of differences model (lower-left of Fig. 10): The smaller the divisor difference, the larger the slopes of the curves and vertical spreads between the curves. The lower panels plot transformed medians, showing that for each divisor, the data can be separately rescaled to parallelism. Other ordinal tests also indicated that the data could be represented by Eq. (9), and that monotonic transformation could not fit the data to any of the other models.

In sum, the "ratios of differences" in likeableness are consistent with the ratio of differences model, in agreement with the findings of Veit (1974).

Results for the "ratio of ratios" task are shown in Fig. 15, plotted as in Fig. 10. The median estimations, plotted in the upper panel as a function of marginal means, show the approximate trilinear divergent interactions anticipated by the ratio of ratios model. The lower panels show the rescaled medians (following monotonic transformation to fit the difference of differences model). Parallelism, linearity, and congruence of the three sets of curves would be evidence that a difference of differences (or ratio of ratios) model is ordinally compatible with the data. In spite of some deviations, the data appear in approximate agreement with the model.

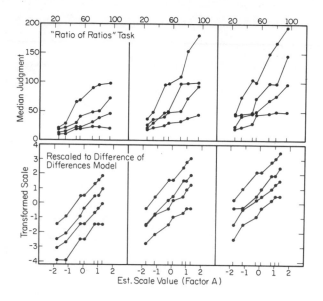

FIG. 15   Results of "ratios of ratios" task for likeableness judgments, plotted as in Fig. 10. Lower panels plot rescaled medians, fit to the difference of differences model. Scale values for difference of differences model agree with scale values for ratio of differences model fit in Fig. 14. (From Hagerty and Birnbaum, 1976.)

Figure 16 shows median ratings of "difference of differences" in likeableness for that portion of the 4 X 7 design in which the column adjective was rated on the average more likeable than the row adjective. Data have been rescaled to fit the difference of differences model; rescaled medians are plotted against estimated scale values in the lower panels. The near-linearity, -parallelism, and -congruence of the sets of curves is consistent with the predictions (Fig. 10) of the difference of differences model.

Median ratings of "difference of ratios" are shown in Fig. 17, plotted as in Fig. 16. The data do not conform to the predictions of the difference of ratios model (see Fig. 10), which predicts diverging fans for each set of curves, nor could the data be transformed to fit the difference of ratios model. Instead, the data are very similar to the data for "difference of differences" (Fig. 16) and can be rescaled to fit the same model, yielding transformed values (lower panel of Fig. 17) that are nearly congruent with transformed values in Fig. 16. It thus appears that the complicated "two worlds" outcome did not materialize, since the "difference of ratios" task can be represented by a difference of differences model.

The scale convergence criterion can be used to select a set of representations for all of the tasks that give a unified picture of these data. Figure 18 provides a summary of tests of scale convergence for the simplest interpretation of the data.

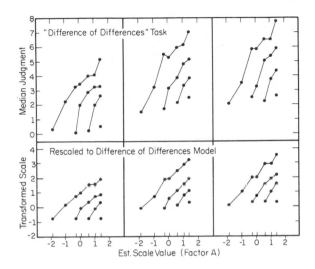

FIG. 16   Results of "difference of differences" task for likeableness judgments. Median ratings are plotted (only for positive differences) as a function of scale values for difference of differences model. Lower panel shows rescaled values, plotted in same fashion. (From Hagerty and Birnbaum, 1976.)

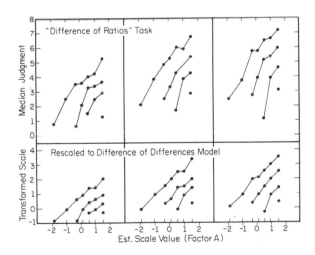

FIG. 17   Results of "difference of ratios" task. Data and rescaled values are plotted as in Fig. 16. Results are compatible with difference of differences model, not difference of ratios model. (From Hagerty and Birnbaum, 1976.)

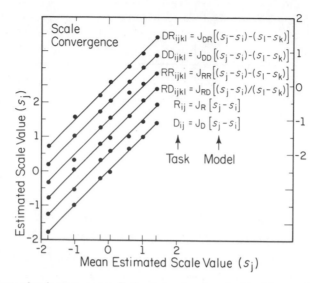

FIG. 18 Tests of scale convergence. Estimated scale values for likeableness of seven column adjectives as a function of mean estimated scale value. Each curve represents scale values derived from a set of data (task) using model shown to the right. Each curve has been displaced .5 units on the ordinate. Linear agreement of the scales is consistent with the theory that the models from which the scales are derived can be interlocked with the same scale values. (From Hagerty and Birnbaum, 1976.)

The most attractive description of all of the data is that the subtractive model applies to "ratios" and "differences" and that the difference of differences model represents not only "differences of differences" but also "ratios of ratios" and "differences of ratios." There is only one ratio operation in all of the models, for "ratios of differences," where the ratio of differences model is applicable. Figure 18 shows the scale values for the seven column adjectives estimated from these models, plotted as a function of the average of the scale value estimates. Each set of scale values has been shifted .5 units on the ordinate; identity lines have been drawn in to aid the examination of linearity.

The two lowest curves show that when the subtractive model is used to derive scales from simple "ratios" and "differences," the scale values are in close agreement with scales derived from the other tasks. The top two curves show that "differences of ratios" and "differences of differences" yield scales that are nearly linearly related to the others when fit to the difference of differences model. The third curve from the top shows that "ratio of ratios" judgments, even though they require drastic (approximate logarithmic) transformation, yield scales in approximate agreement with the others when the data are fit to the difference of differences model. If the subjects were truly computing ratios of ratios using common scale values, the plotted scale values (for the difference of difference model) would have been a logarithmic function of the other scale values. The "ratio of differences" task is the one that really specifies the system. Scale values derived from this model agree with the subtractive theory of all of the other tasks. To replace the subtractive operations in the models with ratios while retaining scale convergence would require that the ratio of differences model be replaced with the complex model of Eq. (13), in which there are two different scales and two different comparison processes for "differences," and in which "ratio" is modeled by a power equal to the reciprocal of a difference. Therefore, the subtractive theory (the set of models shown in Fig. 18) appears to give the simplest and most coherent account of all of the data in terms of a unified scale of likeableness for the adjectives.

TENTATIVE THEORETICAL CONCLUSIONS

The data reviewed here form a simple, consistent picture that justifies discussion of a rather different set of theoretical propositions from those of certain currently popular views. It would be helpful to see replications of the four-stimulus experiments such as those of Veit (1974, in press) and Hagerty and Birnbaum (1976) using other stimuli. If the results of these experiments hold up in further research, they go a long way toward explaining the long-standing controversy of "ratio" versus "interval" scales, clarifying the issues of stimulus comparison, stimulus representation, and judgment.

Comparison Processes

Torgerson's (1961) theory that subjects perceive only a single perceptual comparison between two stimuli was based in part on the approximately logarithmic relationship between category ratings and magnitude estimations (Torgerson 1960). It was also based on Garner's (1954) finding that subjects tended to make the same settings when instructed to adjust a tone to either "bisect" a loudness interval or to establish equal "ratios." Stronger evidence for the idea that there is only one operation is provided by results of factorial experiments in which different theories make different ordinal predictions for the data. In factorial experiments with loudness, darkness, likeableness, and heaviness judgments, it appears that judgments of "differences" and "ratios" of two stimuli are monotonically related, consistent with Torgerson's hypothesis that the comparison process is independent of the task (Birnbaum & Veit, 1974a; Birnbaum & Elmasian, 1977; Hagerty & Birnbaum, 1976; Rose & Birnbaum, 1975; Veit, 1974; see also Schneider et al., 1976).

Torgerson (1961) contended that if the subject appreciates only a single relationship between a pair of stimuli, it would not be possible to test empirically between distance and ratio interpretations of this relation. Some have concluded that it would never be meaningful to ask which representation was the "correct" one, since for a single two-factor design, ratio and subtractive models cannot be differentiated on the basis of ordinal tests. However, the scale-free tests possible with four-stimulus tasks, together with the criterion of scale convergence, provide the leverage to differentiate alternative theories of stimulus comparison. Instructions to judge "ratios" and "differences" *do* lead to two distinct judgment orders when the objects of judgment are stimulus differences. Scales values defined by the subtractive model for both two-stimulus tasks agree with those derived from the ratio of differences model applied to judgments of "ratios of differences" and they agree with scales derived from a difference of differences model applied to the other four-stimulus tasks. Since the results of the four-stimulus experiments interlock with the two-stimulus results, it appears that the process by which two stimuli are compared can best be represented by the subtractive model.

In summary, the following premises are consistent with the data:

P_1 (independence):   The scale value of a stimulus is independent of the stimuli with which it is compared.

P_2 (scale convergence):   The scale value of a stimulus is independent of tasks to judge "ratios," "differences," "ratios of ratios," "ratios of differences," "differences of ratios," or "differences of differences."

P_3 (magnitude estimation): $ME_j = J_M (s_j)$
P_4 (category judgments): $CJ_j = J_C (s_j)$
P_5: $R_{ij} = J_R (s_j - s_i)$
P_6: $D_{ij} = J_D (s_j - s_i)$
P_7: $DR_{ijkl} = J_{DR} [(s_j - s_i) - (s_l - s_k)]$
P_8: $DD_{ijkl} = J_{DD} [(s_j - s_i) - (s_l - s_k)]$
P_9: $RR_{ijkl} = J_{RR} [(s_j - s_i) - (s_l - s_k)]$
P_{10}: $RD_{ijkl} = J_{RD} [(s_j - s_i)/(s_l - s_k)]$

The first premise extends the independence assumption to the four-stimulus tasks. Premise P_2 extends the criterion of scale convergence to include all of the comparison tasks considered here; thus the values of s are assumed to be the same for all of the models. Premises P_3 and P_4 assert that magnitude estimations and category ratings of single stimuli are monotonic functions of subjective value. Premises P_5 and P_6 represent judgments of both "ratios" and "differences" of two stimuli with the subtractive model. Premises P_7, P_8, and P_9 represent the processes underlying three tasks, "differences of ratios," "differences of differences," and "ratios of ratios" with the difference of differences model. Premise 10 represents "ratios of differences" with a ratio of differences model. The judgment functions, J_D, J_R, J_{DR}, J_{DD}, etc., are assumed to be strictly monotonic.

One could ask the question, "Can a ratio theory be saved by replacing the operation of subtraction with division throughout?" The answer is that an exponential transformation of all of the models would yield a set of equations that would reproduce all of the data equally well. However, the "ratios of differences" task would be represented by the complex model of Eq. (13). This modified ratio theory seems too complicated to be seriously considered. Equation (13) not only violates the scale convergence criterion within itself, requiring two different scales, s and s^*, it suggests that two different models apply for "differences" within the same task. This theory represents "ratios" with either a ratio model (for "ratios") or an exponential-power model (for "ratios of differences"). Modified ratio theory also implies that the judgment functions for magnitude estimation are sometimes power functions (for "ratio" judgments) and sometimes logarithmic, since approximate parallelism in the left and right panels of Fig. 11 requires that J_{RD} be logarithmic for "ratios of differences." This theory seems as complicated as Tycho Brahe's geocentric theory of the solar system, which could give as good an account of the heavenly phenomena as Kepler's heliocentric theory if the laws of physics governing celestial events are allowed to be different from the laws describing earthly events. The argument that the earth revolves around the sun is based on simplicity, an assumed coherence between celestial mechanics and mechanics in the physics lab. In the same sense that Brahe's geocentric theory remains consistent with the data, so too does the complicated ratio theory.

It is helpful to show how another line of reasoning also leads to the subtractive theory. "Ratios" and "differences" of two stimuli can be expressed as $R_{ij} = J_R (\Psi_{ij})$ and $D_{ij} = J_D (\Psi_{ij})$, where the comparisons, Ψ_{ij}, are the same, but the monotonic judgment functions, J_R and J_D, are different. Ordinal analysis of the judgments indicates that the Ψ_{ij} form a group; consequently, one can write $\Psi_{ij} = s_j \circ s_i$, where $\circ$ is an unspecified operation. On the basis of two-stimulus judgments alone, Torgerson (1961) was correct in his assertion that the decision to represent $\circ$ with division or subtraction is "only a decision, not a discovery." However, results of four-stimulus experiments provide an empirical basis for testing between theories of the comparison operation. "Ratios of differences" and "differences of differences" demonstrate the appropriate ordinal requirements of ratio and difference operations on a common scale:

$$RD_{ijkl} = J_{RD} \left[\Psi_{ij} / \Psi_{kl} \right] \tag{14}$$

$$DD_{ijkl} = J_{DD} \left[\Psi_{ij} - \Psi_{kl} \right] \tag{15}$$

where the Ψ_{ij} values are the same in both equations and the judgment functions, J_{RD} and J_{DD}, are only assumed to be strictly monotonic. Without assuming anything about the comparison process, $\circ$, it is possible to use Eqs. (14) and (15) to derive values of Ψ_{ij}. These values will be unique to a ratio scale because they must reproduce both differences and ratios; hence the derived values cannot be subjected to nonlinear transformation. The Ψ_{ij} values thus derived are monotonically related to R_{ij} and D_{ij}, indicating that the same comparison operation, ⊖, can be used to represent both two- and four-stimulus judgments. The nature of this operation can be "discovered" by noting that the Ψ_{ij} values derived from Eqs. (14) and (15) are parallel (not bilinear) when plotted against the column values with a separate curve for each row. The parallelism implies that the operation by which two stimuli are combined is subtraction, $\Psi_{ij} = s_j - s_i$. It is conceivable that this plot could have been bilinear, which would have been consistent with ratio theory and inconsistent with subtractive theory. Thus the choice of the subtractive model is based on an empirical test and is not an a priori "decision."

Stimulus Representation

Since "ratios of differences" can be represented by a ratio of differences model, the failure of the ratio model for simple "ratio" judgments cannot be explained by asserting that subjects do not possess the "mental capacity" for two operations. Instead, the stimulus representation may be inherently no more than an interval scale, like points along a line in a subjective space (Veit, 1974). In this case, intervals are meaningful but ratios are not. For example, what is the ratio of the "easterliness" of New York to that of Denver? Without a well-defined zero point, the question does not make sense except in terms of distances. The following question does make sense: "What is the ratio of the distance from New York to Denver, relative to the distance from New York to San Francisco?" It may be that the subject thinks of degrees of darkness or likeableness in the same way that one thinks of locations on a map.[3] When instructed to judge "ratios," the subject cannot make sense of the task and reverts to computing differences. Only when there is a well-defined zero point, as in the case of "ratios of differences," does the subject actually compute ratios.

For certain continua, magnitude estimations and category ratings of single stimuli seem to agree. These continua were named "metathetic" to contrast them with the "prothetic" continua for which the two scales were nonlinearly related (Stevens & Galanter, 1957). A more fundamental distinction would be between continua for which "ratios" and "differences" generate only one or two distinct orderings, suggesting one or two comparison operations. Since stimulus intervals obey this criterion having two orders, one might expect that visual length, which can be thought of as a distance between points, might also allow two operations. Parker, Schneider, & Kanow (1975) represented "ratios" and

---

[3]In a recent experiment, done in collaboration with Barbara Mellers, subjects were indeed asked to make judgments of "ratios" and "differences" of easterliness and westerliness of U.S. cities. The results were consistent with the interpretation that the subtractive operation underlies all four tasks, with estimations of "ratios" exponentially related to subjective intervals.

"differences" of length with two operations, so length may indeed have a well-defined zero point. However, for loudness, likeableness, heaviness, and darkness, it appears that the stimulus representation may be inherently no more than an interval scale.

If subjects compute differences instead of ratios, why do the raw data for "ratios" fit a ratio model? The answer to this question requires a theory of the judgmental transformation.

Judgmental Processes

Premises P_1 through P_{10} account for the ordinal properties of the data. To account for the actual numerical judgments requires additional premises about the nature of the judgmental (J) functions. Although P_1 through P_{10} can be used to estimate these functions from the data, it seems useful to discuss potential explanations of judgment from which the J functions could be predicted.

Category ratings. Parducci's range-frequency theory has been successful in describing ratings of stimuli presented in varying stimulus distributions. (Parducci, 1974; Parducci & Perrett, 1971; Birnbaum 1974b). The theory assumes that ratings reflect a compromise between two tendencies: (1) judges tend to make differences in response proportional to differences in stimulus rank; and (2) judges tend to make differences in response proportional to differences in scale value.

The range-frequency model can be written (Birnbaum, 1974b):

$$CJ_{jk} = (C_m - C_o) [aG_k (s_j) + b(s_j - s_o)/(s_m - s_o)] + C_o, \qquad (16)$$

where CJ_{jk} is the category judgment of stimulus j in context k, on a scale from C_o to C_m; s_m and s_o are scale values of the maximum and minimum stimuli; $G_k^o (s_j)$ is the cumulative density of stimuli having scale values less than or equal to s_j in context k; and a and b are the weights of the frequency and range principles, respectively.

Range-frequency theory predicts that if the stimuli are spaced evenly on the subjective scale and presented with equal frequency, the response will be a linear function of subjective value. The judgmental transformations for the two- and four-stimulus ratings, J_D, J_{DR}, and J_{DD}, are all nearly linear, as evidenced by the near-parallelism in Figs. 6, 8, 13, 16, and 17. The J functions for category ratings have been found to be nearly linear in other studies involving subtractive models (Birnbaum, 1974a; Birnbaum & Veit, 1974a, 1974b).

Although the J functions estimated here are nearly linear, it seems reasonable to suppose that the stimulus distribution for stimulus pairs also affects the J function. Birnbaum, Parducci, and Gifford (1971, Experiment V) found evidence that the form of J in an information integration task can be manipulated in accord with range-frequency theory applied to the distribution of integrated impressions (Ψ). It is tempting to theorize that Eq. (16) would apply to ratings of "differences" with the substitution of $|\Psi|$ for s. Thus ratings of "differences" may be approximated by the equation:

$$D_{ij} = \delta_{ij} (D_m - D_o) [aG (|\Psi_{ij}|) + b \, |\Psi_{ij}| \, / \, \Psi_m] + D_o, \qquad (17)$$

where D_{ij} is the rating of the subjective difference, $\Psi_{ij} = s_j - s_i$; D_m is the maximal response; D_o is the response for "no difference", $\delta_{ij} = -1$ if $\Psi_{ij} < 0$; $\delta_{ij} = 0$ if $\Psi_{ij} = 0$; $\delta_{ij} = 1$ if $\Psi_{ij} > 0$; Ψ_m is the maximum absolute difference in the experiment; and $G(|\Psi_{ij}|)$ is the cumulative density for the absolute difference.

Research is needed to establish the locus of contextual effects in information integration and to test the applicability of Eq. (17) in stimulus comparison experiments.

Magnitude estimation. To account for the approximate bilinearity of "ratio" judgments (Figs. 6, 7, and 13), the trilinearity of "ratios of ratios" judgments (Fig. 15), and the nonlinear relationship between ratings and magnitude estimations (Fig. 2), it is necessary to postulate that the judgmental transformations for magnitude estimation, J_M, J_R, and J_{RR}, are nearly exponential. An exponential transformation for J_R would cause a subtractive operation to lead to bilinear data, since if $R_{ij} = J_R (s_j - s_i) = \exp (s_j - s_i)$, then $R_{ij} = \exp (s_j)/\exp (s_i) = s_j^*/s_i^*$, where $s^* = \exp (s)$.

Birnbaum and Veit (1974a) have proposed an interpretation of J_R that can account for an exponential transformation for magnitude estimation. The idea is shown in Fig. 19, which plots magnitude estimation responses against subjective

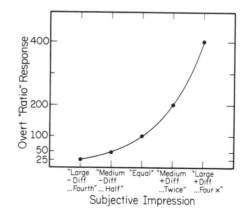

FIG. 19   Theory of the judgment function for magnitude estimations of "ratios." Abscissa represents the subjective continuum of comparisons (Ψ), evenly spaced with category labels of "ratios." It is assumed that reversing the stimulus order corresponds to equal *distances* from "equal" and that the distance from "equal" to "twice" is the same as the distance from "twice" to "four times." This process of response generation induces an exponential transformation. (After Birnbaum and Veit, 1974a).

differences varying from "large minus difference" through "zero difference" to "large positive difference." Suppose a subject is presented with a trial on which a "large difference" is presented. The subject selects a large magnitude estimation response, say "400." If the same pair of stimuli are presented in reverse order, the subjective difference would be the same but reversed in sign. However, the instructions require that the subject respond with the reciprocal "ratio," "25." If reversal in order corresponds to equal psychological distances and if the subject responds with reciprocal "ratios," then J_R will be positively accelerating as in Fig. 19. If, in addition, the subjective distance between "equal" and "twice" equals the subjective distance from "twice" to "four times," then the judgment transformation for magnitude estimation will be exactly exponential. Thus this theory of response generation explains how a ratio model could fit the data even though the comparison process is subtraction.

It is interesting to note that the largest mean "ratio" of loudness (Fig. 7), 5.69, is very nearly equal to the largest mean "ratio" of darkness (left of Fig. 6), 5.84. Teghtsoonian (1971) has discussed a theory of magnitude estimation in which the average log response range ($\log R_{max} - \log R_{min}$) is a constant. In spite of the judge's apparent freedom to choose any response range, Teghtsoonian notes that the average log response range is usually near 1.53. The log response ranges for darkness and loudness (Figs. 6 and 7) are about 1.65 and 1.43, respectively. Birnbaum and Elmasian (1977) found that subjects differed widely in the value assigned to the largest ratio. It may be useful to represent magnitude estimation in terms of an exponential transformation of Eq. (17), allowing the largest response, D_m, to depend on the subject. It may also be possible to manipulate the value of D_m through instructions, possibly in the examples given to illustrate the scale.

The judgmental transformations for magnitude estimations of "ratios of differences" have been estimated to be positively accelerated (Veit, 1974, Experiment II; Beck & Shaw, 1967) when the standard difference is intermediate in value. The curves in the upper-right panel of Fig. 14 show that on either side of zero, the J_{RD} function accelerates. This acceleration is consistent with a positively accelerated judgmental transformation for magnitude estimation. Yet, when the standard difference is the largest difference (Figs. 6 and 11 (C) and upper-left panel of Fig. 14), the J_{RD} function is nearly linear. Perhaps the J_{RD} function has a different form (a smaller slope) for response values less than 100 from the form it has for response values above 100.

A precise theory of magnitude estimation should predict how the subject selects his largest "ratio" response and how such factors as stimulus range, instructions, and modulus affect J. It may prove profitable to solve for J_R by rescaling "ratio" judgments to parallelism, under different conditions of context. For example, this procedure would allow a separation of the effects of stimulus spacing, on J and on s. To date, contextual effects are better understood for ratings than for magnitude estimations.

Summary

The data obtained from sets of factorial experiments suggest that the basic operation by which two stimuli are compared is subtraction. This conclusion depends on the premise that scales are independent of the judgmental task. The metric properties of the data satisfy the theory that magnitude estimations of "ratios" are an exponential function—and category ratings of "differences" are a linear function—of subjective differences. Consistent with the notion that the subjective stimulus representation is inherently an interval scale, "ratios of differences" can be represented by a ratio of differences model even though simple "ratios" are represented by subtraction.

ACKNOWLEDGMENT

This work was facilitated by support from the Research Board of the University of Illinois at Urbana-Champaign. Thanks are due to Robert Elmasian, Michael Hagerty, Barbara Mellers, Barbara Rose, Steven Stegner, and Clairice Veit, who have been collaborators in this research program and who have given helpful criticisms on earlier drafts.

REFERENCES

Anderson, N. H. Functional measurement and psychophysical judgment. *Psychological Review,* 1970, *77,* 153-170.

Anderson, N. H. Cross-task validation of functional measurement. *Perception and Psychophysics,* 1972, *12,* 389-395.

Anderson, N. H. Algebraic models in perception. In E. C. Carterette & M. P. Freidman (Eds.), *Handbook of perception* (Vol. II). New York: Academic Press, 1974.

Attneave, F. Perception and related areas. In S. Koch (Ed.), *Psychology: A study of a science* (Vol. 4) New York: McGraw-Hill, 1962.

Beck, J., & Shaw, W. A. Ratio estimations of loudness intervals. *American Journal of Psychology,* 1967, *80,* 59-65.

Birnbaum, M. H. The nonadditivity of personality impressions. *Journal of Experimental Psychology Monograph,* 1974, *102,* 543-561. (a)

Birnbaum, M. H. Using contextual effects to derive psychophysical scales. *Perception and Psychophysics,* 1974, *15,* 89-96. (b)

Birnbaum, M. H., & Elmasian, R. Loudness "ratios" and "differences" involve the same psychophysical operation. *Perception & Psychophysics,* 1977, *22,* 383-391.

Birnbaum, M. H., Parducci, A., & Gifford, R. K. Contextual effects in information integration. *Journal of Experimental Psychology,* 1971, *88,* 158-170.

Birnbaum, M. H., & Stegner, S. Ratios and differences of darkness. Unpublished experiment, University of Illinois, Urbana-Champaign, 1976.

Birnbaum, M. H., & Veit, C. T. Scale convergence as a criterion for rescaling: Information integration with difference, ratio, and averaging tasks. *Perception and Psychophysics,* 1974, *15,* 7-15. (a)

Birnbaum, M. H., & Veit, C. T. Scale-free tests of an additive model for the size-weight illu - sion. *Perception and Psychophysics,* 1974, *16,* 276-282. (b)

Cliff, N. Scaling. *Annual Review of Psychology,* 1973, *24,* 473-506.

Ekman, G. Two generalized ratio scaling methods. *The Journal of Psychology,* 1958, *45,* 287-295.

Ekman, G., & Sjoberg, L. Scaling. *Annual Review of Psychology,* 1965, *16,* 451-474.

Garner, W. R. A technique and a scale for loudness measurement. *Journal of the Acoustical Society of America,* 1954, *26,* 73-88.

Garner, W. R., Hake, H. W., & Eriksen, C. W. Operationism and the concept of perception. *Psychological Review,* 1956, *63,* 149-159.

Hagerty, M. & Birnbaum, M. H. Nonmetric tests of ratio vs. subtractive theories of stimulus comparison. Unpublished experiment, University of Illinois, Urbana-Champaign, 1976.

Krantz, D. H. Magnitude estimation and cross-modality matching. *Journal of Mathematical Psychology,* 1972, *9,* 168-199.

Krantz, D. H., Luce, R. D., Suppes, P., & Tversky, A. *Foundations of measurement.* New York: Academic Press, 1971.

Krantz, D. H., & Tversky, A. Conjoint measurement analysis of composition rules in psychology. *Psychological Review,* 1971, *78,* 151-169.

Kruskal, J. B. & Carmone, F. J. MONANOVA: A FORTRAN-IV program for monotone analysis of variance. *Behavioral Science,* 1969, *14,* 165-166.

Marks, L. E. On scales of sensation: Prolegomena to any future psychophysics that will be able to come forth as a science. *Perception and Psychophysics,* 1974, *16,* 358-376.

Parducci, A. Contextual effects: A range-frequency analysis. In E. C. Carterette & M. P. Friedman (Eds.), *Handbook of Perception* (Vol. 2). New York: Academic Press, 1974.

Parducci, A., & Perrett, L. Category rating scales: Effects of relative spacing and frequency of stimulus values. *Journal of Experimental Psychology Monograph,* 1971, *89,* 427-452.

Parker, S , Schneider, B., & Kanow, G. Ratio scale measurement of the perceived lengths of lines. *Journal of Experimental Psychology: Human Perception and Performance,* 1975, *104,* 195-204.

Poulton, E. C. The new psychophysics: Six models for magnitude estimation. *Psychological Bulletin,* 1968, *69,* 1-19.

Rose, B. J., & Birnbaum, M. H. Judgments of differences and ratios of numerals. *Perception and Psychophysics,* 1975, *18,* 194-200.

Rule, S. J., & Curtis, D. W. Conjoint scaling of subjective number and weight. *Journal of Experimental Psychology,* 1973, *97,* 305-309.

Sarris, V., & Heineken, E. An experimental test of two mathematical models applied to the size-weight illusion. *Journal of Experimental Psychology: Perception and Performance,* 1976, *2,* 295-298.

Savage, C. W. Introspectionist and behaviorist interpretations of ratio scales of perceptual magnitudes. *Psychological Monographs,* 1966, *80,* 1-32.

Schneider, B., Parker, S., Kanow, G., & Farrell, G. The perceptual basis of loudness ratio judgments. *Perception and Psychophysics,* 1976, *19,* 309-320.

Shepard, R. N. On the status of "direct" psychological measurement. In Savage (Ed.), *Minnesota Studies in the Philosophy of Science* (Vol. IX). Minneapolis: University of Minnesota Press, 1976.

Sjoberg, L. Sensation scales in the size-weight illusion. *Scandinavian Journal of Psychology,* 1969, *10,* 109-112.

Stevens, J. C., & Rubin, L. L. Psychophysical scales of apparent heaviness and the size-weight illusion. *Perception and Psychophysics,* 1970, *8,* 225-230.

Stevens S. S. On the psychophysical law. *Psychological Review*, 1957, *64*, 153-181.

Stevens, S. S. A metric for the social consensus. *Science*, 1966, *151*, 530-541.

Stevens, S. S. Issues in psychophysical measurement. *Psychological Review*, 1971, *78*, 426-450.

Stevens, S S., & Galanter, E. H. Ratio scales and category scales for a dozen perceptual continua. *Journal of Experimental Psychology*, 1957, *54*, 377-411.

Teghtsoonian, R. On the exponents in Steven's law and the constant in Ekman's law. *Psychological Review*. 1971, *78*, 71-80.

Torgerson, W. S. Quantitative judgment scales. In H. Gulliksen & S. Messick (Eds.), *Psychological scaling: Theory and applications*. New York: Wiley, 1960.

Torgerson, W. S. Distances and ratios in psychological scaling. *Acta Psychologica*, 1961, *19*, 201-205.

Treisman, M. Sensory scaling and the psychophysical law. *Quarterly Journal of Experimental Psychology*, 1964, *16*, 11-22.

Veit, C. T. *Ratio and subtractive processes in psychophysical judgment*. Unpublished doctoral dissertation, University of California, Los Angeles, 1974.

Veit, C. T. Ratio and subtractive processes in psychophysical judgment. *Journal of Experimental Psychology: General*, in press.

Weiss, D. J. Averaging: An empirical validity criterion for magnitude estimation. *Perception and Psychophysics*, 1972, *12*, 385-388.

3

Assimilation Predicted by Adaptation-Level Theory With Variable Weights

Frank Restle

Indiana University

This chapter deals with the Adaptation-Level Theory and a factual confrontation with which it has been faced. The Adaptation-Level (AL) model has been used mainly in the analysis of size-contrast illusions, in which the apparent size of a test line gets smaller as it is put in larger and larger contexts. This sort of illusion seems to be an obvious application of a principle of perceptual relativity, the basic concept of AL theory.

Four examples of size-contrast illusions are shown in Fig. 1. In all cases, subjects judge the innermost extent; the middle line in the boxes and wings figures, the inner circle in the Delboeuf concentric-circles illusion, and the central segment in Oyama's divided-line figure. In each case, the main illusion-induc-

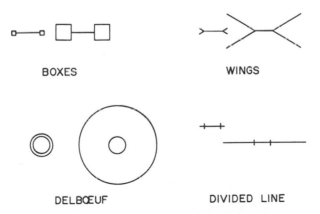

BOXES

WINGS

DELBŒUF

DIVIDED LINE

FIG. 1   Four examples of what are commonly thought of as size-contrast illusions.

ing variable is the size of the surrounding figure—the dimensions of the boxes, the lengths of the wings, the radius of the outer circle, or the length of the extensions of the lines. According to a size-contrast hypothesis, as the outer figure is made larger, the central test line or area should appear progressively smaller.

In the AL model, the judgment (J) of the test line (X) depends on the ratio of X to the adaptation level A.

$$J(X) = X/A, \tag{1}$$

where X is the length of the test line and A is the adaptation level for length at the location of the test figure. Now suppose that the field contains the test line of length X, an illusion-producing figure of length B, and some collection of constant or randomly variable stimuli of mean magnitude K. The adaptation level is a weighted geometric mean of the various factors, which would be

$$A = (X^s B^b K^k)^{\frac{1}{s+b+k}}. \tag{2}$$

If Eqs. (1) and (2) are combined and logarithms taken,

$$\log[J(X)] = [1 - \frac{s}{s+b+k}](\log X) - \frac{b}{s+b+k}(\log B) - \frac{k}{s+b+k}(\log K) \tag{3}$$

$$= \frac{b+k}{s+b+k}(\log X) - \frac{b}{s+b+k}(\log B) - \frac{k}{s+b+k}(\log K).$$

Equation (3) shows that $J(X)$ is a decreasing function of B, the magnitude of the background stimulus. In this sense the model is entirely one of contrast with no qualifications attached.

Restle and Merryman (1968) tested this formulation by having subjects rate the length of a test line X surrounded by square boxes of height B, varying X and B in a factorial design. The judged lengths $J(X)$ decreased as B increased, in apparently close agreement with the model. However, this study did not explore the limiting case of very small boxes. Clavadestscher and Anderson (1977) had their subjects judge test lines as a function of boxes but used a more extreme range of box sizes. They found that when the boxes were very small, $J(X)$ increased with the size of the box. As B was increased from zero, $J(X)$ first rose to a maximum and then fell, finally being slightly lower than the value of $J(X)$ for a line with no boxes.

Oyama (1960), in his review of Japanese studies of illusions, reported an experiment by Ogasawara (1952) on the Delboeuf concentric-circle illusion, in which subjects judged the magnitude of the inner circle as a function of the diameter of the outer one. Ogasawara found that as the larger circle was made larger, the judged size of the inner one increased rapidly up to a maximum in which the gap between the inner and outer circles was approximately one-fourth the diameter of the inner circle. Further increase of the size of the outer circle then produced a decrease in the judged size of the inner circle. Obonai (1954) also shows graphs that have the same general inverted-U shape as those discussed here.

These results seem to dispose of AL theory, because the data do not display a simple contrast effect. In fact, the data are in conflict with a contrast illusion in two respects. First, the test line with boxes appears longer than the line without boxes, so the absolute level of the illusion is in the direction of assimilation rather than contrast. Second, the judgment of the test line increases with increasing box size for small boxes, a trend opposite in direction to that expected of a contrast theory. One would be tempted to conclude that the data refute AL theory.

THEORY

The foregoing conclusion rests on the following chain of argument: (1) Adaptation-Level Theory is a "contrast theory"; (2) all contrast theories predict simple contrast effects; and (3) the experimental results are not contrast effects. The weak link in the argument is (2): All contrast theories predict simple contrast effects. This very simple conclusion makes incomplete use of the potential resources, conceptual and mathematical, available within AL theory.

The adaptation level is a weighted geometric average of factors in the field, in which the weights can be influenced experimentally. A nearby stimulus has more influence on the test line than more distant figures (Restle & Merryman, 1969). One can instruct a subject to ignore part of a field, reducing its weight, and to use another part of the field as the frame of reference, thereby increasing its weight (Restle, 1971). Extents collinear with a test line are more influential than perpendicular extents (Gillam, 1973). Most relevant to the present question, Sarris (1976) has summarized many studies showing that in anchoring studies, where one stimulus affects the judgment of another, the relative influence is greatest when the two stimuli are of approximately the same magnitude. See also Birnbaum, Parducci, and Gifford (1971).

These results should cause us to realize that the weights in an AL equation are not immutable, universal constants. In fact, these weights can be thought of as measurements of the dependent variables of an experiment that summarize the subjects' ways of responding to a set of stimuli. It is clear that the weights may vary from one experiment to another, from one subject to another; and they might vary within one experiment if some relevant aspect of the stimulus situation varies.

The way Eq. (2) is usually interpreted, the numbers b and k are parameters to be estimated (Restle & Greeno, 1970). A simple way to estimate b is to measure the slope of the line relating $\log J(X)$ to $\log B$. This estimation is accurate and valid only if $\log J(X)$ is a linear function of $\log B$. For this slope to be constant and a valid estimator of b, it is necessary that b be independent of the value of B.

In this particular situation, however, the hypothesis that b is constant is quite unreasonable, particularly when the physical size of the box B is relatively very small. Consider what happens to Eq. (3) when B approaches zero. If the weight b is a positive constant, then as B approaches zero, the term $-b \log B$ will approach infinity, because $\log B$ will head for negative infinity without bound. Because $\log J (X)$ contains this explosive quantity as an additive part, this means that $\log J (X)$ will also explode, as will $J (X)$ itself. However, if the box is made smaller and smaller, we approach a display with no box visible. Such a display would be handled by Eqs. (2) and (3) with no reference to B at all, an expression that can be obtained simply by letting b approach zero. This means that instead of b being a constant, b should vary with B:

$$b = f(B). \tag{4}$$

There are two bounding conditions on the function f; namely, when the box is of zero magnitude, it should have a weight of zero, that is,

$$f(0) = 0 \tag{5}$$

and because b is the weight in an adaptation-level function, it should be nonnegative.

The usual prediction of simple contrast (Restle & Merryman, 1968) rests on the assumption of constant b. By letting b depend on B, the magnitude of the box, we open new theoretical possibilities. Two central questions are these:

1. Can AL theory predict other than simple contrast, merely by variation of weight b?
2. Can AL theory fit the observed inverted-U function relating $J (X)$ to box-size B, as observed by Clavadetscher and Anderson (1977)?

Question (1) is answered by substituting $f(B)$ for b in Eq. (3) and differentiating with respect to B. For this analysis we reduce the algebraic complexity by disregarding self-adaptation, letting $s = 0$, because self-adaptation has no bearing on the question at hand. Then, using natural logarithms,

$$\ln J (X) = \ln X - \frac{f(B)}{f(B) + k} (\ln B) - \frac{k}{f(B) + k} (\ln K),$$

Using the notation that $f' = df/dB$,

$$\frac{d}{dB} \ln J(X) = -\frac{kf'(B)(\ln B)}{[f(B) + k]^2} - \frac{f(B)}{[f(B) + k] B} + \frac{kf'(B)(\ln K)}{[f(B) + k]^2}$$

which is positive if

$$kf'(B)(\ln K) > kf'(B)(\ln B) \quad [f^2(B) + kf(B)]/B. \tag{6}$$

All individual terms in this inequality are presumably positive. If the box B is small, because $f(B)$ is nonnegative and $f(0) = 0$, then if f is differentiable and monotonic near 0, its derivative must be somewhere positive. Assuming that f' is positive, then if K is large enough relative to B, the inequality can be satisfied. If so, then the derivative of $J(X)$ with respect to B is positive, which means that $J(X)$ can increase as B increases, an apparent "assimilation" effect. This answers question (1) in the affirmative—AL theory can indeed predict an "assimilation" illusion.

Because the foregoing mathematical derivation depends on assumptions that may seem too convenient to be believed, it may be helpful to give a purely intuitive or phenomenological description of how the result comes about. With no boxes, the short test line is centered in an empty piece of paper or on a dark CRT screen, that is, within a wide open space. The constant K depends in part on the size of the total field that the subject is viewing, which is surely much larger than X. Thus, in the control condition with no boxes, in a sense we may say that $J(X)$ is small, although of course it is recognized that such a statement is exact only when it is made relative to other judgments. When small boxes are introduced at the ends of the test line, they have only a small weight. However, because the boxes themselves are small, much smaller than the background constant field K, they contribute to lowering the adaptation level. This is true because the AL is a weighted average of all factors in the field, and the average of large K and small B will be smaller than K itself. But this lowering of AL, with the test line X held constant, must mean that $J(X)$ increases and the test line is judged to be larger. Now as the boxes are made larger, their larger values of B would tend to increase AL, except that at the same time they also gain increased weight. Increasing the weight of this still-small box may have a net effect in either direction, either raising or lowering AL, and thereby causing the judgment $J(X)$ either to fall or rise. The conditions under which an increase of box size will increase $J(X)$ are shown in Eq. (6); mainly it requires that K be larger than B by a sufficient margin and that the weight of the background, k, be of a large size relative to the weight of the box, $f(B)$.

When the test line is without boxes, then assuming no self-adaptation, its AL is equal to K. When boxes are present, AL is an average of K and B. Now if we set box-size B equal to K, then the weighted average of K and B is equal to K. This means that $J(X)$ is the same when $B = 0$ and when $B = K$. If the experimenter increases box sizes enough, boxes that cause $J(X)$ to decrease should eventually be found. If the function is in fact an inverted-U, the experimenter will eventually find a box size that makes $J(X)$ equal to its "control" value, without any box. This box size then is an estimate of the magnitude K of the constant background. As a general test of the theory, we should expect that this estimated value of K is reasonable, some sensible value for the weighted average of all constant values in the field.

APPLICATION TO DATA

Question (2) raised in the previous section, is whether AL theory can fit the inverted-U function observed by Clavadetscher and Anderson (1977). The process of fitting data requires a specific model and cannot be carried forward merely by using general properties of $f(B)$. We have decided on the hypothsis that $f(0) = 0$ and that $f(B)$ is nonnegative. In a more psychological vein, it seems reasonable that $f(B)$ is greatest when B is approximately the size of the test line X, because a box the same size as X is most useful as a frame of reference and most relevant to the judgment required of the subject. A variety of functions have this property. One, the simplest suggested by Sarris' thinking, is that

$$b = \beta \frac{B}{X} \quad \text{or} \quad \beta \frac{X}{B} \quad \text{whichever is smaller,}$$

where β is the maximum weight of the box, and B/X or X/B are the "similarities." Using this function we found that the model yields an inverted-U function but that the maximum of this function lies approximately at $B = X$, whereas in the data the maximum $J(X)$ is found when $B = 1$ cm and when line length $X = 4$ cm. To fit the Clavadetscher-Anderson data, we therefore chose a function in which the weight of the box approaches its maximum more rapidly as box size increases, namely,

$$b = \beta \left[1 - (1 - \frac{B}{X})^n \right] \quad \text{if} \quad B < X, \tag{7}$$

and

$$b = \beta \left[1 - (1 - \frac{X}{B})^n \right] \quad \text{if} \quad X < B. \tag{8}$$

Equations (7) and (8) are well behaved. Informal estimation suggested that $n = 5$ is a good approximation, and the function assuming $n = 5$ is plotted in Fig. 2. The other parameter to be fit was K, the mean value of the overall field, which we estimated at the large value of 12.4 cm. This is an extrapolation of where the inverted-U function would cross the control value where $B = 0$. The results of the fit are shown in Fig. 3, which reveals that although the fit is perhaps not perfect, the theoretical function faithfully preserves the shape of the empirical function.

The large value of K, 12.4 cm, seems to require some justification. In a subsidiary experiment (their Experiment 4), Clavadetscher and Anderson varied the size of the card on which stimuli were presented, using cards of length 28.0, 36.0, and 56.0 cm, test lines of 2.0 and 4.0 cm, and two sizes each of left box and right box (1 and 6 cm). Let C be the card size, and plot judgments as a function of ln C. If this is a straight line function, then its slope is an estimate of $-c$, the weight of the card size. The values so obtained from the Clavadetscher-

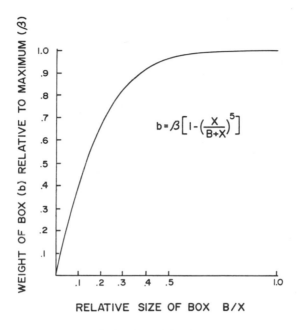

$$b = \beta \left[1 - \left(\frac{X}{B+X} \right)^5 \right]$$

FIG. 2   Hypothetical function relating the weight of an illusion-inducing box to the size of that box relative to the test line. This function is used in calculations in the text.

Anderson data were .014 and .037, which are quite small relative to the maximum box weight of .091. Evidently, the large value of K does not depend very much on the size of the card in the Clavadetscher-Anderson experiments, and we therefore have no serious knowledge of what the components of K may be. One possibility, of course, is that the dimensions of the room itself enter into this K, but without experiments varying room size, this is a mere conjecture.

To pursue this point farther, Susan Dumais and I have performed several experiments using CRT displays viewed through a hood. The viewing distance was fixed at 500 mm, and the maximum display field was a square 125 mm on a side. Lines plotted on the CRT had a width of approximately .25 mm. Nothing but the plotted lines was visible to the subject, who saw the figures in a black expanse, although the subject may have had fairly accurate information as to the true distance and size of the figures from seeing the apparatus before looking into the hood. However, there is no question that extra-experimental visual stimulation was reduced to a minimum in these experiments. The point of limiting the display was to see whether this would increase the importance of general frameworks, corresponding to card size in the Clavedetscher-Anderson experiment. If Dumais were to find that her framework was much more important than did Clavadetscher and Anderson, the result would support the position that room cues were important in the Clavadetscher-Anderson situation and therefore overrode the card size.

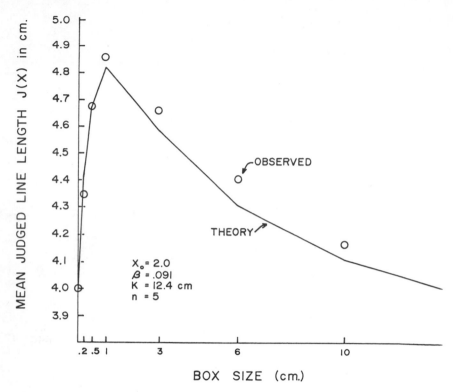

FIG 3 Relation of judged line length to size of boxes at the ends of the line. The line connects points calculated from the model given in the text. (Data from Clavadetscher and Anderson, 1977.)

Dumais' first experiment used test lines of length X = 8, 11, and 15 mm, square boxes of height 0, 2.5, 5.0, 10.0, and 20.0 mm, and a square frame around the figure made up of dotted lines (.5 mm apart). The frames were of sizes 0 (no frame), 60, or 120 mm on a side. This yielded a 3 X 5 X 3 factorial set of 45 displays, which were shown five times in random permutation to 20 subjects. A six-point category rating scale was used.

The results are summarized in Fig. 4. The theoretical lines are from the AL model, expanded to include field size C by the formula

$$J(X) = X/(B^b C^c K^k)^{\frac{1}{b + c + k}}.$$

Because the field size C is larger than X, we assume there is a maximum field effect ϕ and then apply the same formula used for box size, namely, that

$$c = \phi [1 - (1 - X/C)^n].$$

In this case, of course, X must be less than the field size, because the test line is centered within the field.

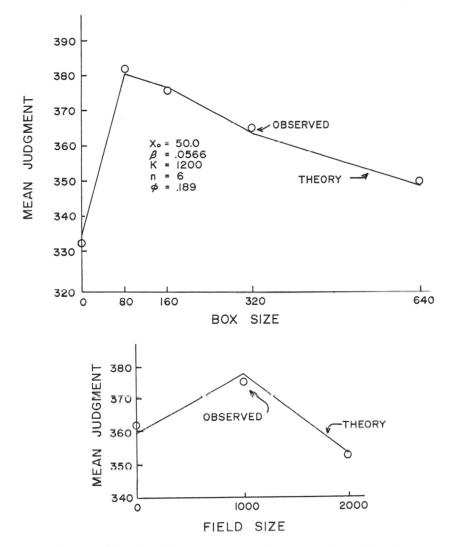

FIG. 4 Mean judged length of line as a function of box size and size of the field drawn around the line-box combination. The total height of field is shown, not the distance used in calculations. Raw responses were six-choice category responses, calibrated into mm by interpolation. Lines connect points calculated from the model. This is the first experiment by Dumais.

The fit of the model to data is, as can be seen, excellent. In the Dumais data, the maximum box weight β was extimated at .057, less than the .091 found with the Clavadetscher-Anderson experiment. However, the total fields were quite different, the brightness contrasts were in opposite directions, and instructions may have been somewhat more analytic in the Dumais experiment. Dumais found a very high maximum weight for the field, $\phi = .189$. Using the same formulation, the Clavadetscher-Anderson data yield two discrepant estimates of ϕ: .153 when the test line is 2 cm but only .033 when the test line is 4 cm. However, recall that Clavadetscher and Anderson's subjects were viewing the display in a lighted room in which many additional stimulus cues were available, whereas Dumais' subjects presumably saw only what was displayed.

Figure 4 confirms the hypothesis that K, the average magnitude of unknown constant stimuli, is large. In the Dumais experiment, K is estimated at 37.2 mm, much larger than the test shafts of 8 to 15 mm and boxes of 2.5 to 20 mm.

An important question is the exact location of the maximum value of the function relating $J(X)$ to B, that is, the box size that maximizes the apparent line length. Dumais repeated the foregoing experiment using much more closely packed values of B in order to get a more precise estimate of the maximum. In this experiment she used line lengths of $X = 7.85, 9.42$, and 11.00 mm, box sizes of 0, .94, 1.88, 2.82, 3.77, 14.13, 28.26, and 37.68 mm, and field sizes of 0, 93, and 124 mm. The intention was to place box sizes close together in the region of the expected maximum and also to find a box larger than K. The above dimensions produce a 3 X 8 X 3, X by B by F, factorial design of 72 displays, each of which was shown three times to 21 subjects, with the procedure the same as in Dumais' other experiment.

The results of this experiment and the calculations fitting it are shown in Fig. 5. Notice that the model fits $J(X)$ as a function of box size and of field size almost perfectly despite the very great range and close packing of values of boxes. Also, the parameter estimates are close to those obtained in the earlier experiment; the values of β, maximum box weight, were .056 and are now .060. The maximum field weight has increased from .180 to .370. The size of K, the residual factor, increased from 1200 to 1400.

In summary, these experiments and analyses have shown that AL theory can fit the inverted-U shaped function found by Clavadetscher and Anderson (1977). It appeared at first that such U-shaped functions would have to be explained as the competition or interaction of two processes, some assimilation process to produce the upward part of the curve, and then a contrast or AL process to produce the downward curve. We have merely taken the AL theory and included explicitly the hypothesis that the weight of each visual object in the field depends in part on the size of that object relative to the test line. That is, we have included the "relevance" hypothesis in our calculations rather than merely setting it aside as a description of the calculations. The reason is that in order to measure the weight of part of the field, one must vary the magnitude of that part and

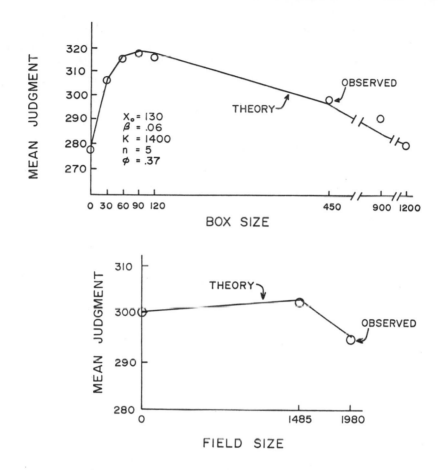

FIG. 5 Mean judged length of line as a function of box size and size of the field. This is the second experiment by Dumais.

observe the effects on response, but the very process of changing the magnitude of B can also change its weight. This means that theoretical procedures become somewhat more complicated and that the predictions become less obvious.

DISCUSSION

This analysis suggests that one can be too hasty in speaking of the "direction" of an illusion. In deciding whether an illusion-inducing context increases or decreases the apparent length of a test line, one is comparing two displays, one with and the other without the context element. In the experiments analyzed in the previous section, it appears that the control line appears in isolation within a relatively large empty area. The test lines appear with small boxes at their ends. It is true that one can say that the boxes seem to make the line longer, but it would be equally correct to say that the control line appears unusually small, and the line with boxes is less small. In fact, all we have is the relative sizes, and we have no absolute standard with which to compare them.

Considerations of relativity permit a theory to predict apparently contradictory experimental outcomes. The success of AL theory does not by any means eliminate alternative theories of the data discussed here. For example, calculations rather like those here could be based on a purely "assimilation" theory like Pressey's, and, in fact, the essential theoretical assumptions have already been published (Pressey & Murray, 1976). Furthermore, as suggested by Clavadetscher and Anderson, a two-process theory involving both contrast and assimilation could also account for the data. In fact, considering that the figure used in these experiments, a line flanked by boxes, appears similar to the Müller-Lyer figure with wings out and apparently has the same factorial composition (Coren et al., 1976) suggests that it is related to the Müller-Lyer figure. The writer has been unable to reconcile data on the Müller-Lyer illusion with the AL theory as presented here. Thus I do not wish to conclude that the foregoing analyses are sufficient to prove the AL theory. The basic point of this paper is not that AL theory is correct, but more philosophically, that inclusion of so reasonable an hypothesis as that the weight of a box depends on the size of the box allows seemingly contradictory data to be easily explained.

Disproving Theories

It is often remarked that for a theory to have empirical content, it must be capable of disproof. This property of falsifiability is particularly important because of the logical fact that a single clear experimental instance disproving a theory is decisive, whereas a single instance agreeing with a theory has no such force to confirm the theory. The credibility of a given theory is enhanced by experiment only to the degree that competing theories are eliminated, which makes the positive support of a theory the product of disproofs of its competitors.

However, any principle, however correct, can be misapplied. Some experimenters feel that a theory should not only be falsifiable in principle but should be falsifiable by an experiment that can be done here and now and that doesn't require too much thought or work. According to this view, a theory must be a sitting duck, or it is not a scientific theory at all.

A theory is most easily falsified if its user bungles the application. For example, suppose that in developing a theory certain simplifying assumptions have been introduced, and these simplifying assumptions are reasonable within a certain middle range of experimental parameters. The theory can be falsified by an experimenter who uses extreme conditions but fails to modify the simplifying assumptions. Here I should say that the theory is falsified not so much because it is wrong as because the experimenter who set out to test it made an error in application. Another easy way to disprove a theory is to take a theory that mentions only one of two possible influences and to do an experiment that measures both factors. Obviously, because the theory does not mention one of the factors, it will be unable to predict the data. However, a more reasonable interpretation would be that the experimenter should have controlled the second variable or else modified the theory to encompass it before doing the experimental test.

In the example used in the main body of this chapter, it was erroneously assumed that AL theory must predict simple contrast effects, and the experiments showed "assimilation." From this it was initially concluded that AL theory was disproved. However, the full argument was not spelled out, and, in fact, if one used the known fact that weights depend on relevance, and used the full resources of AL theory, then that simplistic prediction no longer follows. The original simple prediction came about by assuming that the weight b is a constant as B varies, but such an assumption can be disproved in a particularly simple way by a thought experiment: One can take the formula for adaptation level A, which contains the term B^b, and go to the limit of $B = 0$ while keeping b constant. The result is an absurd conclusion that A would disappear with sufficiently small boxes at the end of the line.

It is not sufficient to find some data that seem to disagree with a theory—the disproof must be "interesting." By this we mean several things: First the disproof should not depend on a mere simplifying assumption but should disprove some basic characteristic of the theory, and second, the disproof should tell us something new about the phenomenon in question. To be of importance, the disproof of a theory should lead to new factual information about the phenomenon or should at least demand a major theoretical restructuring. Although a theorist may be counted on to defend his or her creation, it is really the responsibility of the experimenter claiming to disprove a theory to show that new evidence is an interesting disproof.

The Purpose of Theory

Perhaps one can get a better perspective on this general question if one steps back from the question of how to disprove a theory and questions the purpose of having a theory in the first place.

To many experimenters a theory is primarily a target. Any experiment that disproves a theory is prima facie important, is likely to be accepted for publication, and is thought to be a scientific contribution. This approach is fostered by acceptance and use of the method of "Strong Inference" (Platt, 1964). In Platt's approach the researcher always conjures up two or more working hypotheses and then performs crucial experiments to decide between them. In practice, the aim is to disprove one of the theories. The researcher then further analyzes the survivor, uses it to generate two or more alternative elaborations, and does another experiment to decide. When successfully applied, this process leads to rapid scientific progress. However, each experimental step requires that one or the other hypothesis be shot down, and an impatient experimenter might be inclined to snap off a quick shot and proceed to the next stage of research.

Although the experimenter may see a theory only as a target, as the device for defining an experimental issue, the student sees another value for theory. Instead of having to learn a mass of facts, the student can merely learn a few theoretical principles and the methods of manipulating them and then deduce the "facts" instead of having to memorize them. Not only the college student in a psychology course sees this advantage: The student training to be a school teacher will want to understand principles of learning but will not want to read and remember the whole experimental literature. The businessman interested in consumer behavior, in management practices, in memory training, etc., will have time only for the general principles, not for the detailed facts. A theory, for these users of psychological science, leads to an enormous economy of the students' valuable study time. Of course, if the theory is not exactly correct, then some of the "facts" deduced may be wrong. However, to the student or user, this may seem a small price to pay for a truly efficient mnemonic system.

If a theory is merely the excuse for an experiment, or a mnemonic system for students, then it is not really terribly important. However, theories are often thought to be apices of scientific thought—why? What is there about a theory that makes it the center of scientific attention?

A theory summarizes our beliefs as to the important variables in given situations and how those variables are arranged. Furthermore, good theories make it possible for us to solve scientific problems. If we find that drivers on a certain highway have a tendency to run off the pavement at a curve, a scientific theory of perception might provide us with a list of variables to consider, and some way of combining those variables, to permit us to analyze the situation and determine if there is an illusion of some kind present. The better the theory, the more likely it is to provide a clear and complete analysis of the driver's situation and a helpful account of how errors might be made. Furthermore, such a theory might even help an engineer to formulate a way of changing the highway to reduce the accidents.

Problem solving does not always involve practical problems outside science. A student of attention in the laboratory must control the stimulus variables given the subject and may need a clear theoretical statement of the effects of visual angle, brightness contrast, etc. A student of color vision needs a solid theory of psychophysics. A student of social attitudes needs a theory of rating scales and response biases. A student of the hypothalamus may need a theory of the ethology of rat food-seeking and eating systems. In each case the theory from one area is used to solve problems of practical importance or of experimental control in neighboring areas. It is this problem-solving capacity that justifies the effort devoted to theory and that turns the scientist's attention again and again to theoretical questions, and it is because of this power that we are so anxious to find true theory and, as a means to that end, to disprove or change wrong theory.

The Theoretical Situation With Respect to Illusions

In the study of optico-geometric illusions, there are many theories, most of them first described in the nineteenth century. All of these theories have been disproved, most of them many times.

Many new theories turn out to be elaborations of old positions or old theories dressed in more fashionable conceptual clothes. Certainly the adaptation-level theory differs little from Wundt's principle of perceptual relativity or the principles of "contrast" introduced into many theories. Pressey's theory of assimilation resembles older "confusion" theories (Erlebacher & Sekuler, 1969) or the ancient confluxion theories (Heymans, 1896; Woodworth, 1938). Lateral inhibition is new, but the theory of illusions based on it (Ganz, 1966) differs little from older field theories. The "constancy rescaling" theory of Gregory (1963) has given hope to some experimenters, although its origins date back at least to Ptolemy. It certainly appears that we need a new theory of illusions, because the old theories have been shot by years of experimental attack.

What shall we do until the Muse descends and gives us the new theory? It does not seem to be enough merely to reformulate old theories and then repeat old experiments to disprove them.

I propose that at least some researchers should devote their efforts to detailed analyses of known phenomena, formulating not just general theoretical principles but detailed quantitative models of the data. Naturally, one wants such models to arise from, or at least to be congruent with, more general theoretical positions. However, I propose that we must go deeper into the exact implications of theories and attempt from these investigations to find out some of the factual regularities that are to be explained. The models should be used in a serious way as problem-solving devices and should be extended to the explanation of new figures and new phenomena, with particular attention to problems slightly outside the usual field of study of illusions. For example, it would be useful to design a program for teaching carpenters or machinists to avoid certain perceptual errors that might spoil their work, or to analyze the visual environments of drivers of automobiles [somewhat as Gibson analyzed the situation of the airplane pilot (Gibson, 1950)]. Illusory effects should be used to explain peculiarities of attention, of response scaling, or of stimulus generalization. By this sort of development of the consequences of visual illusions, we may be able to come to understand their place in general psychology.

But what theories are to be used for these problem-solving adventures? There are, it is true, several mathematical theories available, but are they not already disproved and therefore useless? I believe that such theories, including the AL model, have within them useful ideas and theoretical resources that have never been developed and deployed. The use of variable weights, as employed in this chapter, is an example of a theoretical resource, often mentioned in general discussions of the theory, that had simply not been included in the mathematical formulations. Yet the theory of variable weights is of crucial importance in solving most practical problems. First, we need to know not merely whether there is an illusion but its magnitude, and this depends on the weights. It is possible, in principle, to measure the relevant weights in any situation in which an illusion of contrast might exist, but such measurements may be too expensive to be practical (as, for example, if they were to involve rebuilding a highway bridge at four different degrees of curvature in the same environment) or might be so numerous as to be without general significance (as when one considers all the angles and possible distortions worked with by a carpenter in building a frame house). Therefore, we are sure to need a theory of the weights, some general way of predicting the magnitude of weights or of making a few simple measurements in a convenient situation and then generalizing them to other situations. However, the theory of variability of weights provides the foundations of a more practical theory. For example, if it is true that the weight of a factor increases as that factor gets nearer the size of the test object being judged, then this simplifying principle must aid in predicting the weights, because it enables us to take only a few measurements and to predict others.

That a particular theory, adaptation-level, was attacked and defended is not of great general importance, and we cannot suppose that the particular theoretical developments of this paper will be permanently or generally accepted. However, the process by which a theory is specialized into an exact model, criticized because it fails to agree with detailed experimental data, reinforced by attention to a hitherto-neglected theoretical resource, and then, presumably, subjected to new experimental tests—this process is a possible way of coming to understand even such familiar, classic, and knotty problems as the question of optical illusions.

ACKNOWLEDGMENTS

This research was supported by PHS grant MH-16817 from the U.S. Public Health Service. The cooperation of Susan Dumais and the assistance of Roger Ford are gratefully acknowledged.

I should like to thank John Clavadetscher and Norman H. Anderson for providing advance information about their research in the form of prepublication drafts, letters and conversations.

REFERENCES

Birnbaum, M. H., Parducci, A., & Gifford, R. K. Contextual effects in information integration. *Journal of Experimental Psychology*, 1971, *88*, 158-170.

Clavadetscher, J. E., & Anderson, N. H. Comparative judgment: Tests of two theories using the Baldwin Figure. *Journal of Experimental Psychology: Human Perception and Performance*, 1977, *3*, 119-135.

Coren, S., Girgus, J. S., Erlichman, H., & Hakstian, A. R. An empirical taxonomy of visual illusions. *Perception & Psychophysics*, 1976, *20*, 129-137.

Erlebacher, A., & Sekuler, R. Exploration of the Müller-Lyer illusion: Confusion theory examined. *Journal of Experimental Psychology*, 1969, *80*, 462-467.

Ganz, L. Mechanisms of the figural aftereffects. *Psychological Review*, 1966, *73*, 128-150.

Gibson, J. J. *The perception of the visual world*. Boston: Houghton-Mifflin, 1950.

Gillam, B. The nature of size scaling in the Ponzo and related illusions. *Perception & Psychophysics*, 1973, *14*, 353-357.

Gregory, R. L. Distortions of visual space as inappropriate constancy scaling. *Nature*, 1963, *199*, 678-680.

Heymans, G. Untersuchunger über das "optischen paradoxen." *Zeitschrift für Psychologie*, 1896, *9*, 221-225.

Obonai, T. Induction effects in estimates of extent. *Journal of Experimental Psychology*, 1954, *47*, 57-60.

Ogasawara, J. Displacement-effect of concentric circles. *Japanese Journal of Psychology*, 1952, *22*, 224-234.

Oyama, T. Japanese studies on the so-called geometrical-optical illusions. *Psychologia*, 1960, *3*, 7-20.

Platt, J. R. Strong inference. *Science*, 1964, *146*, 347-353.

Pressey, A. W., & Murray, W. Further developments in the assimilation theory of geometric illusions: The adjacency principle. *Perception & Psychophysics*, 1976, *19*, 536-544.

Restle, F. Instructions and the magnitude of an illusion: Cognitive factors in the frame of reference. *Perception & Psychophysics*, 1971, *9*, 31-32.

Restle, F., & Greeno, J. G. *Introduction to mathematical psychology*. Reading, Mass.: Addison-Wesley, 1970.

Restle, F., & Merryman, C. T. An adaptation-level theory account of a relative-size illusion. *Psychonomic Science*, 1968, *12*, 229-230.

Restle, F., & Merryman, C. Distance and an illusion of length of line. *Journal of Experimental Psychology*, 1969, *81*, 297-302.

Sarris, V. Effects of the stimulus-range and anchor value on psychophysical judgment. In H. G. Geissler and Yu. M. Zabrodin (Eds.), *Advances in psychophysics*. Berlin: VEB Deutscher Verlag der Wissenschaften, 1976.

Woodworth, R. S. *Experimental psychology*. New York: Henry Holt & Co., 1938.

4

Probabilistic Choice Behavior Theory: Axioms as Constraints in Optimization

Jean-Claude Falmagne
New York University

ABSTRACT

In choice behavior theory, models specifying the probability of a response $R_{a_1 a_2 \ldots a_m}$ often take the form

$$\mathbf{P}\left\{R_{a_1 a_2 \ldots a_m}\right\} = F\left\{H[h_1(a_1), h_2(a_2), \ldots, h_m(a_m)]\right\}$$

where $a_1, a_2, \ldots, a_m$ are independent variables, $h_1, h_2, \ldots, h_m$ are real valued functions, H is a real valued function in m variables, and F is a distribution function. Occasionally, F and H are completely specified. [For example, in Thurstone-Case V (1927), we have

$$\mathbf{P}(R_{ab}) = \frac{1}{\sqrt{2\pi}} \int_{-\infty}^{h(a)-h(b)} e^{-(\frac{1}{2})z^2} dz$$

as a special case of the above equation.]. It is remarked that the estimation of the parameters, $h_i(a_i)$, can be profitably made via an equivalent model

$$\mathbf{P}\left\{R_{a_1 a_2 \ldots a_m}\right\} = F(\theta_{a_1 a_2 \ldots a_m})$$

where the θs are solutions of the functional equation

$$\theta_{a_1 a_2 \ldots a_m} = H[h_1(a_1), h_2(a_2), \ldots, h_m(a_m)]$$

(e.g., in Thurstone-Case V: $\theta_{ab} = h(a) - h(b)$; i.e., $\theta_{ac} = \theta_{ab} + \theta_{bc}$). This idea is explored in three different models. One example involving the representation

$$\mathbf{P}\left\{R_{ax;by}\right\} = F[g(b) + h(y) - g(a) - h(x)]$$

is developed in detail. Maximum likelihood estimators are provided, and a likelihood ratio statistic is derived.

In a variety of choice behavior situations, data are collected to estimate the probability of some response $R_{a_1 a_2 \ldots a_m}$, characterized by an m-tuple $(a_1, a_2, \ldots, a_m) \in A_1 \times A_2 \times \ldots \times A_m$ of aspects. For instance, $a_1 \in A_1$ might identify the subject , $a_2 \in A_2$ might be some feature of the experimental situation, and $a_3 \in A_3$ to $a_m \in A_m$ might describe the stimuli. (If one wishes, $a_1, a_2, \ldots, a_m$ may be taken as independent variables.) A typical model constraining these probabilities is symbolized by the equation

$$\mathbf{P}\left\{R_{a_1 a_2 \ldots a_m}\right\} = F\left\{H[h_1(a_1), h_2(a_2), \ldots, h_m(a_m)]\right\} \tag{1}$$

in which h_i, $(1 \leqslant i \leqslant m)$ is a function mapping A_i into the reals, H is a real function in m real arguments (e.g., a polynomial), and F is some (cumulative) distribution function (d.f.). Frequently, F and H are completely specified. For example, F might be the d.f. of a standard normal or logistic random variable (r.v.). A classic example is offered by the so-called Thurstone-Case V (1927), in which the probability that a will be judged "greater than" b is given by

$$\mathbf{P}\{R_{ab}\} = \frac{1}{\sqrt{2\pi}} \int_{-\infty}^{h(a)-h(b)} e^{-(\frac{1}{2})z^2} dz \qquad a, b \in A$$

$$= \Phi\left[h(a) - h(b)\right],$$

specializing Eq. (1) (Φ is the d.f. of a standard, normal r.v.).

A problem is that of estimating the $h_i(a_i)$ in (1), considered as parameters of a statistical model. The main point of this chapter is that, in solving this problem, it may be helpful to analyze the function H from the viewpoint of the solutions θ of the functional equation

$$\theta_{a_1 a_2 \ldots a_m} = H[h_1(a_1), h_2(a_2), \ldots, h_m(a_m)]. \tag{2}$$

In other terms, this involves finding axioms on the parameters $\theta_{a_1 a_2 \ldots a_m}$ ensuring the existence of h_i $(1 \leqslant i \leqslant m)$ and H such that (2) holds. This approach provides a clarifying analysis of the constraints set on the probabilities $\mathbf{P}\{R_{a_1 a_2 \ldots a_m}\}$ by the function H, and also simplifies the practical computation of estimators. To illustrate, consider again Thurstone-Case V. Rather than estimating directly the parameters $h(a)$, $h(b)$, ..., we could estimate some parameters θ_{ab}, satisfying both

$$\mathbf{P}(R_{ab}) = \Phi(\theta_{ab})$$

$$\theta_{ac} = \theta_{ab} + \theta_{bc}.$$

It is not difficult to show that the two approaches yield equivalent results. In particular, in the framework of appropriate side conditions, the last equation implies that θ can be written

$$\theta_{ab} = h\,(a) - h\,(b)$$

for some function h (Aczél, 1966). Thurstone-Case V is not discussed in detail here but turns out to be a subcase of two of the models investigated in this chapter. Let us consider three slightly more complex cases of Eq. (1).

THREE SPECIFIC CASES

Model 1.   Additive conjoint measurement.   On each trial of a psychophysical experiment, a subject is presented binaurally with a pair $(a, x) \in A \times X$ of stimuli, followed with another pair $(b, y) \in A \times X$. For example, a, b are two intensities of a pure tone presented in the left auditory channel, and x, y are two intensities of the tone in the right auditory channel. (Thus A, X are two sets of tone intensities for the left and right auditory channels respectively; we may, of course, set $A = X$.) Each pair evokes a sensation of *loudness*. The subject is asked whether the pair (a, x) seems louder than the pair (b, y). The answer must be "yes" or "no." Let $R_{ax;by}$ be the event of a "no" response for the two pairs (a, x), (b, y). Suppose that the effects of the tone in the two auditory channels are additive, in the sense of the following equation:

$$\mathbf{P}\{R_{ax;by}\} = \mathbf{P}\{\mathbf{T}_a + \mathbf{V}_x \leqslant \mathbf{T}_b + \mathbf{V}_y\}, \tag{3}$$

where $\{\mathbf{T}_a \mid a \in A\}$, $\{\mathbf{V}_x \mid x \in X\}$ are two collections of r.v. representing the loudness values of the tones. In other terms, it is assumed that each of the two values of a binaural stimulus has a random effect, that the effects are additive between the two auditory channels, and that the subject's response depends on the outcome of the comparison between the two corresponding sums. Moreover, assume that all these r.v. are independent and that in each of the two collections the r.v. are related by a shift: $\mathbf{T}_a = g\,(a) + \mathbf{Y}$, for all $a \in A$; $\mathbf{V}_x = h\,(x) + \mathbf{Z}$, for all $x \in X$; where g, h are two functions mapping A, X respectively into the reals and $\mathbf{Y}$, $\mathbf{Z}$ are two error r.v. the distribution of which does not vary with the stimulus. With $\mathbf{Y}'$, $\mathbf{Z}'$ identically distributed as $\mathbf{Y}$, $\mathbf{Z}$ respectively,

$$\mathbf{P}\{R_{ax;by}\} = \mathbf{P}\{g\,(a) + \mathbf{Y} + h\,(x) + \mathbf{Z} \leqslant g\,(b) + \mathbf{Y}' + h\,(y) + \mathbf{Z}'\}$$
$$= F[g(b) + h(y) - g(a) - h(x)] \tag{4}$$

where F is the d.f. of $\mathbf{Z} + \mathbf{Y} - \mathbf{Z}' - \mathbf{Y}'$. Equation (4) is a special case of (1), with

$$H[g(b), h(y), g(a), h(x)] = g(b) + h(y) - g(a) - h(x). \tag{5}$$

This model is a natural probabilistic version of (Fundamental) Additive Conjoint Measurement, in the sense of Krantz, Luce, Suppes, and Tversky (1971). Incidentally, the assumption of additivity of the effects in the two auditory channels, of a binaural stimulus of the kind described previously, is in line with some existing data in auditory perception (e.g., Levelt, Riemersa, & Bunt, 1972; see also Falmagne, 1976), so that above model is plausible.

Model 2. Bisection measurement. A subject is facing a screen. On each trial three stimuli, *a, b, c,* are selected from a set A of monochromatic patches of light that differ only in intensities and are flashed on the screen forming a regular horizontal array. The subject is required to compare the brightness of the middle stimulus *b*, with a hypothetical stimulus $a \Delta c$, the brightness of which is imagined to be halfway between that of *a* and *c*. The subject is required to decide whether the brightness of $a \Delta c$ exceeds that of *b*. The answer must be "yes" or "no". Let R_{abc} be the event of a "no" response, and suppose that the probabilities of such events (for $a, b, c \in A$) are constrained by a model of the form

$$P\{R_{abc}\} = P\{\frac{1}{2} [T_a + T_c] \leqslant T_b\} \tag{6}$$

where $\{T_a | a \in A\}$ is a collection of independent r.v. related by a shift: $T_a = h(a) + Y$, with h, Y as in the preceding example. Equation (6) yields successively

$$P\{R_{abc}\} = P\{\frac{1}{2} [h(a) + Y + h(c) + Y'] \leqslant h(b) + Y''\}$$

$$= P\{\frac{1}{2} [Y + Y'] - Y'' \leqslant h(b) - 1/2 [h(a) + h(c)]\}$$

$$= F\{h(b) - \frac{1}{2} [h(a) + h(c)]\} \tag{7}$$

in which Y', Y'' are identically distributed with Y, and F is the d.f. of $\frac{1}{2} [Y + Y'] - Y''$. Equation (7) is another special case of Eq. (1). As far as I know, no experimental test of the foregoing model has ever been made. Such a model, however, is consistent with existing analysis of the so-called bisection method in psychophysics (Pfanzagl, 1968; Krantz et al., 1971). Our last example is from physics.

Model 3. Extensive measurement. Let A be a set of thin rods, and consider the problem of measuring their length. Suppose that no ruler or similar devices are available, but two empirical procedures can be used. A *comparison procedure,* for two rods, involves placing the rods alongside each other in such a way that they coincide at one end and checking whether one of the rods covers the other. We do not assume that this procedure yields reliable results. For instance, for two rods *a, b,* 20 applications of the comparison procedure might conceivably give the following results:

a covers b	b covers a	neither
13 times	4 times	3 times

A *concatenation procedure* for two rods, a, $b \in A$, involves placing a, b end to end along a straight line, forming a new object that we denote ab. Using the comparison procedure, this new object can be placed along some rod c, and it can be checked, for example, whether ab covers c. When the rods of a sequence a_1, a_2, ..., a_n are successively concatenated in the order a_1 with a_2, $a_1 a_2$ with a_3, etc., up to a_n, the final object is denoted $a_1 a_2 \cdots a_n$.

> **Definition 1.** Let A be a set; then x is a *string* of A if there exists a positive integer n, and a_1, a_2, ..., $a_n \in A$ such that $x = a_1\, a_2 \cdots a_n$. (Thus, if x, y are two strings of A, then xy is also a string of A.) The set of strings of A is denoted A^*.

In the context of this example, A^* is thus the set of all strings (of rods) of A that can be constructed by the concatenation procedure. For simplicity, the elements x, y, z, ... $\in A^*$ are also referred to as rods. For any two rods, x, $y \in A^*$, the comparison procedure can be used to check, for example, whether y covers x. Let $R_{x;y}$ be the event that y does not cover x. Consider the following model. For x, $y \in A^*$

$$P\left\{R_{x;y}\right\} = F[h(x) - h(y)], \tag{8}$$

in which F is some d.f., and h is a function mapping A^* into the reals, and satisfying

$$h\,(a_1 a_2 \cdots a_m) = \sum_{i=1}^{m} h\,(a_i), \tag{9}$$

if $a_i \in A$, $1 \leqslant i \leqslant m$. This model extends the usual algebraic analysis of the extensive measurement of length (Krantz et al., chap. 3, 1971). Notice that it cannot very well be derived from assumptions regarding some r.v.s associated with the rods in A, in the style of the two preceding examples. Indeed, such assumptions would naturally lead to a d.f. F depending on the number of terms in each of the rods x, y in Eq. (8). Implicitly, the notion here is that the errors only result from the comparison procedure. Clearly, this position is not without criticism. Equations (7)-(8) constitute our third example of Eq. 1.

In each of these three examples, the function H is linear. It is obvious, however, that the methods of this chapter can be extended to a more general situation.

OUTLINE OF ESTIMATION TECHNIQUES

Consider the problem of estimating the $h_i\,(a_i)$ in Eq. 1 for fixed, known F and H. Suppose that a maximum likelihood method is used. Let $n_{a_1 a_2 \cdots a_m}$ be the number of occurrences of the event $R_{a_1 a_2 \cdots a_m}$ in the course of $n_{a_1 a_2 \cdots a_m} + \bar{n}_{a_1 a_2 \cdots a_m}$ independent trials. Estimates of the $h_i\,(a_i)$ may be obtained by (unconstrained) maximization of the log likelihood function

$$\sum \left[n_{a_1 a_2 \cdots a_m} \ln F\left\{H[h_1(a_1), h_2(a_2), ..., h_m(a_m)]\right\} \right.$$
$$\left. + \bar{n}_{a_1 a_2 \cdots a_m} \ln \left(1 - F\left\{H[h_1(a_1), h_2(a_2), ..., h_m(a_m)]\right\} \right) \right]$$

as a function of the h_i (a_i), the summation extending over the set of all experimental cases $(a_1, a_2, ..., a_m)$.

Alternatively, we can maximize the log likelihood function

$$\Sigma \left\{ n_{a_1 a_2 ... a_m} \ln F(\theta_{a_1 a_2 ... a_m}) + \bar{n}_{a_1 a_2 ... a_m} \ln [1 - F(\theta_{a_1 a_2 ... a_m})] \right\} ,$$

as a function of the θs, satisfying a system of p constraints

$$C_i = 0, \quad i = 1, 2, ..., P \tag{10}$$

in which each of the C_i is an expression of the θs. For concreteness, take, once more, Thurstone-Case V. There, the second method involves maximizing the log likelihood function

$$\Sigma \left\{ n_{ab} \ln \Phi (\theta_{ab}) + \bar{n}_{ab} \ln [1 - \Phi (\theta_{ab})] \right\}$$

under the constraints

$$\theta_{ab} + \theta_{bc} - \theta_{ac} = 0.$$

Going back to the general case, we note that, in principle, the system (10) is equivalent to Eq. (2) in the following sense: if θ, H, and h_i $(1 \leqslant i \leqslant m)$ are such that (2) holds, then the θs must satisfy the system (10); conversely, if the θs satisfy (10), then H and h_i $(1 \leqslant i \leqslant m)$ exist satisfying (2). In principle, thus, the two methods should yield the same values for the estimates for the parameters h_i (a_i). In practice, the second method may be difficult to apply, i.e., the functional Eq. (2) may be hard to solve. In some cases, however, solving this equation is an easy task. The second method is then of interest for the reasons mentioned previously: The computations may be simplified, and the system (10), if suitably chosen, clarifies the constraints involved in the function H. In addition, if (10) involves more than one equation, a sequence of tests of increasing severity becomes available. For example, estimates of the θs can be obtained under the constraint $C_1 = 0$, and a test can be made. Next, the two constraints $C_1 = 0, C_2 = 0$, can be tested against C_1, etc.

In subsection 1-3 of this chapter, we illustrate this method in the case of Models 1-3, respectively. The derivations in subsection 1 is given in some detail. The reader, familiar with the techniques involved, can certainly follow without difficulty the more sketchy treatment in subsections 2 and 3. The last subsection is devoted to some general remarks regarding the uniqueness of the estimates and likelihood ratio tests.

1.   Additive Conjoint Measurement

Let $n_{ax;by}$ be the number of events $R_{ax;by}$ observed in the course of $N_{ax;by} = n_{ax;by} + \bar{n}_{ax;by}$ independent trials. Maximum likelihood estimates of the parameters g (a), h (x) in (4) would result from maximizing the log likelihood function

$$\ln L [g(a), g(b), ...; h(x), h(y), ...] = \Sigma \left(n_{ax;by} \ln F[g(b) + h(y) - g(a) - h(x)] \right.$$
$$\left. + \bar{n}_{ax;by} \ln \left\{ 1 - F[g(b) + h(y) - g(a) - h(x)] \right\} \right)$$

with the summation extending over the set of all events $R_{ax;by}$ considered in the experiment. In some cases, we can equivalently maximize

$$\ln L \left(\theta_{ax;by}, ..\right) = \Sigma\left\{n_{ax;by} \ln F \left(\theta_{ax;by}\right) + \bar{n}_{ax;by} \left[1 - F \left(\theta_{ax;by}\right)\right]\right\}$$

for the θs satisfying the following two constraints:

(A1) $\theta_{ax;by} + \theta_{cy;az} = \theta_{cx;bz}$

(A2) $\theta_{cx;ay} + \theta_{ay;bz} = \theta_{cx;bz}$.

This observation is supported by the following simple result:

Theorem 1. Let $(a,x; b,y) \to \theta_{ax;by}$ be a mapping of $A \times X \times A \times X$ into the reals, where A, X are nonempty sets. Then, the following three conditions are equivalent:

(i) There exists two functions g, h, real valued, respectively defined on A, X, such that for all a, $b \in A$ and x, $y \in X$, $\theta_{ax;by} = g(b) + h(y) - g(a) - h(x)$;

(ii) Axioms (A1) and (A2) hold;

(iii) The following axiom holds: for all a, b, $c \in A$ and x, y, $z \in X$,

(A3) $\theta_{cz;bz} + \theta_{cz;cy} - \theta_{cz;az} - \theta_{cz;cx} = \theta_{ax;by}$.

Moreover, if conditions (i)-(iii) hold, then the two functions g, h are unique up to the translations $g(a) \to g(a) + C$ and $h(x) \to h(x) + C'$ for arbitrary constants, C, C'.

Proof. Clearly, (i) implies both (ii) and (iii). Fixing $c_0 \in A$ and $z_0 \in X$, and defining $g(a) = \theta_{c_0 z_0 ; az_0}$, $h(x) = \theta_{c_0 z_0 ; c_0 x}$, we see that (iii) implies (i). With g, h defined as above, we have for all a, $b \in A$ and x, $y \in X$:

$$\theta_{ax;by} = \theta_{c_0 z_0 ;by} - \theta_{c_0 z_0 ;ax} \qquad\qquad \text{[by (A2)]}$$

$$= \theta_{c_0 z_0 ;bz_0} + \theta_{c_0 z_0 ;c_0 y} - \theta_{c_0 z_0 ;az_0} - \theta_{c_0 z_0 ;c_0 x} \quad \text{[by (A1)]}$$

$$= g(b) + h(y) - g(a) - h(x).$$

Suppose that g', h' are another pair of functions satisfying (i). Then, for all $a \in A$ and $x \in X$:

$$g(a) = \theta_{c_0 z_0 ; az_0} = g'(a) - g'(c_0)$$

$$h(x) = \theta_{c_0 z_0 ; c_0 x} = h'(x) - h'(z_0),$$

and $-g'(c_0)$, $-h'(z_0)$ are the constants C, C' of the Theorem. Q.E.D.

This theorem seems to suggest that all quadruples $(a, x; b, y)$ in some Cartesian product $A \times X \times A \times X$ must be considered as experimental cases. This is not required, however. The same result also holds under weaker conditions; for example, if the function θ of theorem 1 is only defined on certain proper subsets of $A \times X \times A \times X$. In such a case, the equivalence of (i), (ii), and (iii) may hold together with a less restrictive uniqueness condition. We do not develop specific cases theoretically, but an example of this situation is given at the end of the section. This remark is of interest in connection with the uniqueness of the estimates of the parameters $g(a)$, ..., $h(x)$, ...: the θ may be unique while the g, h are not (but clearly not conversely). According to this theorem, we could also maximize $\ln L$ $[\theta_{ax;by}$, ...] under (A3). The choice between (A1)-(A2) and (A3) is influenced by consideration of experimental convenience. Clearly, other equivalent sets of constraints on the θ would be worked out. Notice the complementary character of (A1) and (A2): (A2) involves a separation of the first from the last pair in the quadruple $(a, x; b, y)$; whereas (A1) involves a separation of the terms within each pair.

Assuming that (A1)-(A2) are adopted, maximum likelihood estimates would follow from the development outlined in the following. We define a function K

$$K(\theta_{ax;by}, ...; a_{abc;xyz}, ...; \beta_{abc;xyz}, ...)$$
$$= \ln L(\theta_{ax;by}, ...) + \Sigma a_{abc;xyz}(\theta_{ax;by} + \theta_{cy;az} - \theta_{cx;bz})$$
$$+ \Sigma \beta_{abc;xyz}(\theta_{cx;ay} + \theta_{ay;bz} - \theta_{cx;bz}),$$

in which the $a_{abc;xyz}$ and $\beta_{abc;xyz}$ are the Lagrange multipliers corresponding to the sets of constraints (A1), (A2) respectively, and the two summations extend over all experimental cases where the constraints apply. Maximum likelihood estimates $\hat{\theta}_{ax;by}$ of the parameters $\theta_{ax;by}$ are obtained by solving the system of equations

$$\begin{cases} \dfrac{\delta K}{\delta \theta_{ax;by}} = 0 \\[2em] \dfrac{\delta K}{\delta a_{abc;xyz}} = 0 \\[2em] \dfrac{\delta K}{\delta \beta_{abc;xyz}} = 0 \end{cases}$$

This system contains exactly as many equations as there are parameters $\theta_{ax;by}$, and Lagrange multipliers $a_{abc;xyz}, \beta_{abc;xyz}$ and is linear in the Lagrange multipliers. Once the $\hat{\theta}_{ax;by}$ values have been found, the functions g and h can then be constructed, using for example the method of the proof of Theorem 1.

The theory can be evaluated by performing likelihood ratio tests. For instance, let $\hat{\hat{\theta}}_{ax;by}$ be the set of unconstrained maximum likelihood estimates. [Thus conditions (A1) and A2) are removed.] Suppose that there are k experimental cases, i.e., that the set $\hat{\hat{\theta}}_{ax;by}$ of estimates contains k elements. Suppose also that, under (A1)-(A2), the number of independent parameters is reduced to r.

Then, under the usual conditions (Wilks, 1962),

$$-2 \ln \frac{L(\hat{\theta}_{ax;by,\cdots})}{L(\hat{\hat{\theta}}_{ax;by,\cdots})}$$

is asymptotically $(N_{ax;by} \to \infty)$ distributed chi-square, with $k - r$ degrees of freedom. Obviously, there are other possibilities. For instance, conditions (A1) and (A2) can be tested separately.

In some cases the foregoing method involves only fairly simple computations. This is especially true if F is the d.f. of a standard logistic r.v., as illustrated by the following example.

Example 1. Let $A = \{a, b, c\}$ and $X = \{x, y, z\}$, and suppose that five experimental conditions have been considered, numbered 1 to 5, as shown in Table 1.

TABLE 1

The Five Experimental Conditions

	a	b	c	Case	Case number
z				(b, z; c, y)	1
y				(a, z; b, y)	2
x				(a, z; c, x)	3
				(b, y; c, x)	4
				(a, y; b, x)	5

With the functions g and h defined as in the foregoing, we simplify the notations as follows:

$$g(c) + h(y) - g(b) - h(z) = \theta_1$$
$$g(b) + h(y) - g(a) - h(z) = \theta_2$$
$$g(c) + h(x) - g(a) - h(z) = \theta_3$$
$$g(c) + h(x) - g(b) - h(y) = \theta_4$$
$$g(b) + h(x) - g(a) - h(y) = \theta_5$$

(Notice that the function θ is only defined on a proper subset of the Cartesian product $A \times X \times A \times X$. Nevertheless, Theorem 1 is still relevant, as we shall see.) Let N be the number of observations in each of the five cases: $n_i + \bar{n}_i = N$, $1 \leqslant i \leqslant 5$. Maximum likelihood estimates of the θ_i, under the conditions (A1)-(A2), are obtained from maximizing

$$\ln L(\theta_1, ..., \theta_5) = \sum_{i=1}^{5} \{n_i \ln F(\theta_i) + \bar{n}_i \ln [1 - F(\theta_i)]\}$$

under the constraints

$$\theta_1 + \theta_5 = \theta_3, \qquad \theta_2 + \theta_4 = \theta_3.$$

Forming the function K,

$$K(\theta_1, ..., \theta_5, a, \beta) = \ln L(\theta_1, ..., \theta_5) + a(\theta_1 + \theta_5 - \theta_3) + \beta(\theta_2 + \theta_4 - \theta_3)$$

and computing the derivatives of K in each of its arguments gives the system:

$$F'(\theta_1) [\frac{n_1}{F(\theta_1)} - \frac{\bar{n}_1}{1 - F(\theta_1)}] + a = 0 \tag{11}$$

$$F'(\theta_2) [\frac{n_2}{F(\theta_2)} - \frac{\bar{n}_2}{1 - F(\theta_2)}] + \beta = 0 \tag{12}$$

$$F'(\theta_3) [\frac{n_3}{F(\theta_3)} - \frac{\bar{n}_3}{1 - F(\theta_3)}] - a - \beta = 0 \tag{13}$$

$$F'(\theta_4) [\frac{n_4}{F(\theta_4)} - \frac{\bar{n}_4}{1 - F(\theta_4)}] + \beta = 0 \tag{14}$$

$$F'(\theta_5) [\frac{n_5}{F(\theta_5)} - \frac{\bar{n}_5}{1 - F(\theta_5)}] + a = 0 \tag{15}$$

$$\theta_1 + \theta_5 = \theta_3 \tag{16}$$

$$\theta_2 + \theta_4 = \theta_3 \tag{17}$$

If F is assumed to be the d.f. of a standard logistic r.v. $\mathcal{E}$ [$F(t) = (1 + \exp t)^{-1} \exp t$, $\mathbf{E}(\mathcal{E}) = 0$, $\mathbf{Var}(\mathcal{E}) = \pi^3/3$], then this system takes on a particularly simple form. Equations (11) and (15) reduce to

$$a = \frac{N \exp \theta_1}{1 + \exp \theta_1} - n_1 = \frac{N \exp \theta_5}{1 + \exp \theta_5} - n_5; \tag{18}$$

Equations (12) and (14) reduce to

$$\beta = \frac{N \exp \theta_2}{1 + \exp \theta_2} - n_2 = \frac{N \exp \theta_4}{1 + \exp \theta_4} - n_4; \tag{19}$$

and (13) reduces to

$$a + \beta = n_3 - \frac{N \exp \theta_3}{1 + \exp \theta_3}, \tag{20}$$

Each one of these five equations is linear in one of the $\exp \theta_i$. The parameters $\theta_1, \ldots, \theta_5$ can thus be computed in terms of a, β. Replacing in (16)-(17) the θ_i by their expressions yields the following system:

$$\frac{n_1 + a}{N - (n_1 + a)} \cdot \frac{n_5 + a}{N - (n_5 + a)} = \frac{n_3 - a - \beta}{N - (n_3 - a - \beta)} \tag{21}$$

$$\frac{n_2 + \beta}{N - (n_2 + \beta)} \cdot \frac{n_4 + \beta}{N - (n_4 + \beta)} = \frac{n_3 - a - \beta}{N - (n_3 - a - \beta)} \tag{22}$$

We search for the solutions (a, β) to this system, which also satisfy

$$\max\{-n_1, -n_5\} < a < \min\{N - n_1, N - n_5 , \tag{23}$$

$$\max\{-n_2, -n_4\} < \beta < \min\{N - n_2, N - n_4 , \tag{24}$$

and

$$n_3 - N < a + \beta < n_3. \tag{25}$$

Any solution (a, β) of (21)-(22) that satisfies (23)-(25) is called *acceptable*. Clearly, the data might be such that $\max\{ n_1, -n_5 = 0 = \min N - n_1, N - n_5$, (say, if $n_1 = 0, n_5 = N$); there are thus no acceptable solutions in this case. Also, if $n_1 = n_4 = n_3 = 0$, then $a, \beta > 0$ by (23)-(24), but $a + \beta < 0$ by (25), a contradiction; thus again there is no acceptable solution. It can be shown, however, that except for these and other similar critical cases, an acceptable solution to (21)-(22) always exists, which is then unique. We shall prove this in a moment. The complete list of critical cases is:

(i) $n_1 = 0, n_5 = N$;   (iv) $n_2 = N, n_4 = 0$;

(ii) $n_1 = N, n_5 = 0$;   (v) $\min\{n_1, n_5\} = \min\{n_2, n_4\} = n_3 = 0$;

(iii) $n_2 = 0, n_4 = N$;   (vi) $\max\{n_1, n_5\} = \max\{n_2, n_4\} = n_3 = N$.

Except for these cases, the maximum likelihood estimates of the θ are defined and unique. The rest of this subsection is devoted to a discussion of a practical computation of the estimates, a likelihood ratio test, and the existence and uniqueness of the solutions to (21)-(22).

As a first step, we simplify the system (21)-(22) by a change of variables:

$$\mu = \frac{n_1 + n_5 + 2a}{2N} \tag{26}$$

$$\nu = \frac{n_2 + n_4 + 2\beta}{2N} \tag{27}$$

$$p = \frac{n_1 - n_5}{2N}, \quad q = \frac{n_2 - n_4}{2N}, \quad r = \frac{n_1 + n_2 + n_4 + n_5 + 2n_3}{2N}.$$

This yields, after rearranging

$$\frac{\mu^2 - p^2}{(\mu - 1)^2 - p^2} = \frac{r - \mu - \nu}{1 - (r - \mu - \nu)} \tag{28}$$

$$\frac{\nu^2 - q^2}{(\nu - 1)^2 - q^2} = \frac{r - \mu - \nu}{1 - (r - \mu - \nu)}. \tag{29}$$

This system must be solved for (μ, ν) satisfying

$$|p| < \mu < 1 - |p| \tag{30}$$
$$|q| < \nu < 1 - |q| \tag{31}$$
$$r - 1 < \mu + \nu < r. \tag{32}$$

I leave it to the reader to check the equivalence of (21)-(25) and (28)-(32). Each of (28)-(29) is linear in one of the unknowns. Solving (28) for ν, we obtain:

$$\nu = r - \mu - \gamma_p(\mu) = \Psi_p(\mu), \tag{33}$$

which is a function of μ, with

$$\gamma_p(\mu) = \frac{\mu^2 - p^2}{\mu^2 + (\mu - 1)^2 - 2p^2}.$$

Similarly, (29) yields

$$\mu = r - \nu - \gamma_q(\nu) = \Psi_q(\nu). \tag{34}$$

Replacing ν in (34) by its value in (33), we get

$$\gamma_p(\mu) - \gamma_q[\Psi_p(\mu)] = 0. \tag{35}$$

Notice that the function γ_p is strictly increasing and continuous on $S_p = \{\mu \mid |p| < \mu < 1 - |p|\}$. Similarly, γ_q is strictly increasing and continuous on S_q. (In fact, we have $\gamma_p(S_p) = \gamma_q(S_q) = (0, 1)$, the open interval.) Thus, Ψ_p is strictly decreasing on S_p, and the left member of (35) is a strictly increasing function on $W_{p,q} = \{\mu \in S_p \mid \Psi_p(\mu) \in S_q\}$. Thus there is at most one solution $\mu \in W_{p,q}$ to Eq. (35). This means that there is at most one acceptable solution to the system (21)-(22).

To prove the existence of an acceptable solution, we first show that $W_{p,q}$ is not empty. By continuity, $\Psi_p(S_p)$ is a real interval. Suppose that $|q| > \Psi_p(\mu)$ for all $\mu \in S_p$; then

$$|q| \geqslant \underset{\mu \in S_p}{\text{Sup}} \ \Psi_p(\mu) = r - |p|$$

that yields

$$|q| + |p| \geqslant r.$$

This is impossible, because it implies

$$\min\{n_1, n_5\} = \min\{n_2, n_4\} = n_3 = 0,$$

the critical case (v). Similarly, suppose that $1 - |q| < \Psi_p(\mu)$ for all $\mu \in S_p$. Then

$$1 - |q| < \underset{\mu \in S_p}{\inf} \ \Psi_p(\mu) = r - 1 + |p| - 1$$

yielding

$$|p| + |q| + r \geqslant 3.$$

This is also impossible, because it leads to the critical case (vi). We conclude that $W_{p,q}$ is not empty.

The function Ψ_p maps S_p onto an open interval, say $\Psi_p(S_p) = (q_0, q_1)$. We consider four cases:

1. $|q| \leqslant q_0 < q_1 \leqslant 1 - |q|$;
2. $q_0 < |q| < 1 - |q| < q_1$;
3. $|q| \leqslant q_0 < 1 - |q| < q_1$;
4. $|q_0| < |q| < q_1 \leqslant 1 - |q|$.

It is easy to show that in each case an acceptable solution to (21)-(22) exists. The following proof is based on the fact that the functions γ_p, $\gamma_q \circ \Psi_p$ are respectively strictly increasing and strictly decreasing, with $0 < \gamma_p < 1$, $0 < \gamma_q \circ \Psi_p < 1$. It is argued that in each of the foregoing cases 1-4, $\gamma_p(\mu) - \gamma_q[\Psi_p(\mu)]$ must change sign when μ varies in $W_{p,q}$. The claim follows from continuity. I'll prove Cases 1 and 4 and leave Cases 2 and 3 to the reader.

Case 1. Take $\mu \in W_{p,q}$ and suppose that $0 < \gamma_p(\mu) \leqslant \gamma_q[\Psi_p(\mu)]$ $= s < 1$. Then $\mu' \in W_{p,q}$ exists, $\mu' > \mu$ such that $\gamma_p(\mu') > s > \gamma_q[\Psi_p(\mu')]$ > 0, by strict monotonicity. If $\gamma_q[\Psi_p(\mu)] < \gamma_p(\mu)$, one takes μ' sufficiently close to $|p|$ to reverse the inequality.

Case 4. By continuity, $W_{p,q}$ is an open interval of the form $(|p|, p_0)$ for some $p_0 < 1 - |p|$. Take $\mu \in W_{p,q}$ and suppose that $\gamma_q [\Psi_p(\mu)] \geqslant \gamma_p(\mu) > 0$. Then $\mu' \in W_{p,q}$ exists, $\mu' < \mu$ such that $\Psi_p(\mu')$ is sufficiently close to $|q|$ to yield $0 < \gamma_q [\Psi_p(\mu')] < \gamma_p(\mu')$. If $0 < \gamma_p [\Psi_p(\mu)] < \gamma_p(\mu)$, then μ' exists, $\mu' < \mu$ sufficiently close to $|p|$ to yield $\gamma_p (\mu') < \gamma_q [\Psi_p (\mu')]$.

The left member of (35) is a polynomial of the sixth degree in μ, having thus one useful solution [i.e., exactly one solution leading to an acceptable solution (a, β) to (21)-(22)]. No explicit formula for the solution is available, but it can be found routinely by numerical methods.

Summary of procedure for the example.   Let $n_1, n_2, ..., n_5$ be the data, satisfying $0 < n_i < N$ for $1 \leqslant i \leqslant 5$.

Step 1. Solve Eq. (35) numerically, yielding an estimate $\hat{\mu}$ of μ.

Step 2. Compute estimates of the remaining parameters successively by

$$\hat{v} = \Psi_p(\hat{\mu}), \text{ [cf. Eq. (33)]} \quad \hat{a} = N\hat{\mu} - \frac{n_1 + n_5}{2}, \quad \hat{\beta} = N\hat{v} - \frac{n_2 + n_4}{2},$$

$$\hat{\theta}_1 = \ln \frac{n_1 + \hat{a}}{N - (n_1 + \hat{a})}, \qquad \hat{\theta}_5 = \ln \frac{n_5 + \hat{a}}{N - (n_5 + \hat{a})},$$

$$\hat{\theta}_2 = \ln \frac{n_2 + \hat{\beta}}{N - (n_2 + \hat{\beta})}, \qquad \hat{\theta}_4 = \ln \frac{n_4 + \hat{\beta}}{N - (n_4 + \hat{\beta})},$$

$$\hat{\theta}_3 = \ln \frac{n_3 - \hat{a} - \hat{\beta}}{N - (n_3 - a - \beta)},$$

[which are derived from (33), (25), (27), and (18)-(20), respectively].

Step 3. An admissible set of estimated values for the functions *g, h* can then be obtained from the equations:

$$\hat{g}(a) = 0, \qquad \hat{g}(b) = 1, \qquad \hat{g}(c) = \hat{\theta}_1 - \hat{\theta}_2 + 2$$
$$\hat{h}(x) = \hat{\theta}_2 + \hat{\theta}_5 - 2, \qquad \hat{h}(y) = \hat{\theta}_2 - 1, \qquad \hat{h}(z) = 0$$

Step 4. Define $\hat{\hat{\theta}}_i = \ln \dfrac{n_i}{N - n_i}$, (i.e., $F(\hat{\hat{\theta}}_i) = \dfrac{n_i}{N}$) for $1 \leqslant i \leqslant n$. The statistic

$$-2 \ln \frac{L(\hat{\theta}_1, ..., \hat{\theta}_5)}{L(\hat{\hat{\theta}}_1, ..., \hat{\hat{\theta}}_5)} \tag{36}$$

is then asymptotically ($N \to \infty$) distributed chi-square, with $5 - 3 = 2$ degrees of freedom.

Preliminary Monte Carlo simulation of the likelihood ratio statistic (36) for various values of N and of the five probabilities $\mathbf{P}\{R_{ax;by}\}$ of the example indicates that the convergence is fairly fast. For not too extreme values of the probabilities ($.05 < P < .95$), the power of the test seems to be virtually identical to that of the asymptotic chi-square when N is of the order of 40.[1]

We have a numerical example. Let $N = 50, n_1 = 10, n_2 = 20, n_3 = 21, n_4 = 30,$ $n_5 = 43$. Using the foregoing procedure, we obtain $\hat{a} = -1.900, \hat{\beta} = -.681, \hat{\theta}_1 = -1.643, \hat{\theta}_2 = -.462, \hat{\theta}_3 = -.114, \hat{\theta}_4 = .348, \hat{\theta}_5 = 1.529$, Eq. (35) being solved numerically (by the "halving method," with a programmable desk calculator). This yields a value of 1.446 for the log likelihood ratio statistic (36). The scale values for the functions g, h are: $\hat{g}(a) = 0, \hat{g}(b) = 1, \hat{g}(c) = .819, \hat{h}(x) = -.933, \hat{h}(y) = -1.462, \hat{h}(z) = 0$. Notice in passing, in connection with the earlier remark, that in this example the function θ (in the terminology of Theorem 1) is only assumed to be defined on a proper subset of the Cartesian product $A \times X \times A \times X$. As a consequence the uniqueness part of Theorem 1 fails. Indeed, the following set of scale values is also acceptable [in the sense that these values satisfy the equation $\hat{\theta}_{dv;ew} = g(e) + h(w) - g(d) - h(v)$]: $g'(a) = -.538,$ $g'(b) = 0, g'(c) = -.643, h'(x) = .991, h'(y) = 0, h'(z) = 1$. But g', h' are not translations of g, h respectively.

Finally, we remark that, in the case where X contains only one element and F is assumed to be the d.f. of a standard normal r.v., the model of this subsection becomes identical to Thurstone-Case V. In this case, Axioms (A1)-(A2) reduce to a single axiom of the form $\theta_{a;b} + \theta_{b;c} = \theta_{a;b}$ [cf. Axiom (A8) in the following].

2.   Bisection Measurement

Let $A, R_{abc}, F,$ and h be as in Model 2; let n_{abc} be the number of events R_{abc} observed in $n_{abc} + \bar{n}_{abc}$ independent trials. Estimates of the $h(a)$ in Eq. (7) result from maximizing

$$\ln L(\theta_{abc}, \ldots) = \Sigma\{n_{abc} \ln F(\theta_{abc}) + \bar{n}_{abc} \ln [1 - F(\theta_{abc})]\}$$

(where the summation extends over the set of all events R_{abc} observed in the course of the experiment), under the constraint

(A4) $\theta_{acd} - \theta_{abc} + \theta_{fkl} - \theta_{fhk} = \theta_{hdl}$

Indeed:

Theorem 2.   Let $(a, b, c) \rightarrow \theta_{abc}$ be a mapping of $A \times A \times A$ into the reals, where A is a nonempty set. Then, the following three conditions are equivalent:

---

[1] I am grateful to Steven Marcovici for helping with the simulation of the process for various sets of probabilities.

(i) There exists a real valued function h on A satisfying

$$\theta_{abc} = h\,(a) - \frac{1}{2}[h\,(b) + h\,(c)]$$

for all $a, b, c \in A$;

(ii) Axiom (A4) holds:

(iii) The following three axioms hold: For all $a, b, c, d, f, k \in A$:

(A5) $\theta_{aaa} = 0$;

(A6) $\theta_{abc} = \theta_{acb}$;

(A7) $\theta_{acd} - \theta_{acb} = \theta_{fkd} - \theta_{fkb}$

Moreover, if conditions (i)-(iii) hold, then the function h is unique up to the translations $h\,(a) \rightarrow h\,(a) + C$ for some arbitrary C.

Proof. It is easy to check that (i) implies (ii) [and in fact also (iii)]. We show that (ii) implies (iii). If we set $a = b = c = d = f = k = l$, Axiom (A4) reduces to (A5). On the other hand, if the set, $b = c = d$ in (A4), we get

$$0 = \theta_{add} - \theta_{add} = \theta_{ddl} - \theta_{fkl} + \theta_{fdk}$$
$$= \theta_{ac'd} - \theta_{adc'}$$

for any $c' \in A$, by Axiom (A4). Thus, in general, $\theta_{abc} = \theta_{acb}$ for any $a, b, c \in A$, establishing (A6). Axiom (A7) follows from (A4) and (A6). Indeed, if we replace a by f and c by k in (A4), we get, using also (A6),

$$\theta_{fkd} - \theta_{fkb} = \theta_{fkb} - \theta_{fkl} + \theta_{bdl}$$
$$= \theta_{acd} - \theta_{acb}$$

by (A4) and (A6), yielding (A7). Next, we prove that (iii) implies (i). Fixing $a_0, b_0, c_0 \in A$, we define two function g, m respectively on $A \times A, A$, by

$$g\,(a, b) = \theta_{abc_0}$$

$$m\,(a) = \theta_{a_0 b_0 c_0} - \theta_{a_0 b_0 a}$$

Using (A7), we obtain

$$\theta_{abc} = \theta_{abc_0} + \theta_{a_0 b_0 c} - \theta_{a_0 b_0 c_0}$$
$$= g\,(a, b) - m\,(c)$$
$$= g\,(a, c) - m\,(b) \qquad\qquad \text{[by (A6)]}$$

Setting $c = c_0$ in the previous equation and noting that $m\ (c_0) = 0$, we get $g\ (a,\ b) = g\ (a,\ c_0) - m\ (b)$. That is, with $h\ (a) = g\ (a,\ c_0)$,

$$\theta_{abc} = h\ (a) - m\ (b) - m\ (c)$$

for all a, b, $c \in A$. Using (A5), we obtained $h\ (a) - 2\ m\ (a) = 0$, or $m\ (a) = \frac{1}{2}\ [h\ (a)]$, as required. Finally, the uniqueness property of h comes from the fact that if v is some other function satisfying $\theta_{abc} = v(a) - \frac{1}{2}[v(b) + v(c)]$, for all a, b, $c \in A$, then, in particular,

$$\theta_{ac_0c_0} = h(a) = v(a) - \frac{1}{2}[v(c_0) + v(c_0)]$$
$$= v(a) - v(c_0)$$

and $-v(c_0)$ is the constant C of the theorem. Q.E.D.

As indicated by this theorem, the maximization of the likelihood function under (A4), on the one hand, and under (A5)-(A7), on the other hand, yield identical restults. This last set of constraints appears, however, more interesting in that it provides a detailed analysis of the functional equation

$$\theta_{abc} = h\ (a) - \frac{1}{2}\ [h\ (b) + h\ (c)],$$

suggesting a variety of research strategies. For example, the experimenter may occasionally be willing to take for granted that (A5) and (A6) hold as a consequence (for instance) of some symmetry inherent in the experimental conditions. In such a case, the experimenter may be contented with a time-saving experiment testing only (A7). Another possibility, as previously noted, involves a nested sequence of tests, such as:

(A5)   [against no constraints]
(A5)-(A6)   [against (A5)]
(A5)-(A7)   [against (A5)-(A6)] .

No example of a practical application is given. We trust that the reader is able, at this point, to develop his or her own example, along the lines of Example 1.

3. Extensive Measurement

Let A, A^*, $R_{x;y}$, F, and h be as in Model 3 (in particular, Definition 1); let $n_{x;y}$ be the number of events $R_{x;y}$ observed in the course of $n_{x;y} + \bar{n}_{x;y}$ independent trials. Estimates of the $h\ (x)$, $h\ (y)$ in Eq. (8) and (9) result from maximizing the log likelihood function

$$\ln L\ (\theta_{x;y},\ ...) = \Sigma\{n_{x;y}\ \ln F\ (\theta_{x;y}) + \bar{n}_{x;y}\ \ln\ [1 - F\ (\theta_{x;y})]\}$$

(the summation extending over all events $R_{x;y}$ observed in the experiment) under the two constraints:

(A8) $\theta_{x;y} + \theta_{y;z} = \theta_{x;z}$;

(A9) $\theta_{xz;yz} = \theta_{zx;zy} = \theta_{x;y}$

The following theorem justifies this claim.

> **Theorem 3.**   Let A be a nonempty set; let A^* be the set of all strings of A; Let $(x;y) \to \theta_{x;y}$ be a mapping of $A^* \times A^*$ into the reals. Then, the following two conditions are equivalent:
>
> (i) There exists a unique function h on A^*, real valued, such that for any $x = a_1 a_2...a_n$, $y = b_1 b_2...b_m \in A^*$
>
> $$\theta_{x;y} = \sum_{i=1}^{n} h(a_i) - \sum_{j=1}^{m} h(b_j); \tag{37}$$
>
> (ii) Axioms (A8) and (A9) hold.
>
> **Proof.**   Clearly, (i) implies (ii). Axiom (A8) is well known (Sincov, 1903a, 1903b; Aczél, 1966) to imply the existence of a function h, satisfying
>
> $$\theta_{x;y} = h(x) - h(y) \tag{38}$$
>
> for all $x, y \in A^*$. This function is defined up to arbitrary translation $h \to h + C$. Thus we can assume without loss of generality that $h(zz) = 2\,h(z)$ for some $z \in A^*$. We have for any $x, y \in A^*$, using (A9) and (38),
>
> $$\theta_{xy;zy} = h(xy) - h(zy) = \theta_{x;z} = h(x) - h(z),$$
>
> and
>
> $$\theta_{zy;zz} = h(zy) - h(zz) = \theta_{y;z} = h(y) - h(z).$$
>
> Summing the foregoing equations and simplifying appropriately yields
>
> $$h(xy) = h(x) + h(y)$$
>
> for all $x, y \in A^*$, which implies (37). The uniqueness of h is clear, because if v is another function satisfying (37), then, for any $x \in A^*$, successively
>
> $$\theta_{xx;x} = h(xx) - h(x) = h(x) = v(xx) - v(x) = v(x) \qquad \text{Q.E.D.}$$

Here also we shall let the reader develop his or her own example.

4.   General Remarks

Some of the results obtained in Example 1 can be extended without difficulty to Models 2 and 3 and, in fact, to a much more general situation. Simplifying our notations somewhat, we consider the problem of finding the maximum
of a log likelihood function

$$\ln L\,(\theta_1, \theta_2, ..., \theta_n) = \sum_{i=1}^{m} \left\{ n_j \ln F\,(\theta_j) + \bar{n}_j \ln\,[1 - F\,(\theta_j)] \right\} \tag{39}$$

$(n_j, \bar{n}_j$ strictly positive integers, $n_j + \bar{n}_j = N$, $j = 1, 2, ..., n)$ for n parameters θ_j,
$j = 1, 2, ..., n$, satisfying a system of constraints

$$C_i\,(\theta_1, \theta_2, ..., \theta_n) \gtreqless 0, \quad i = 1, 2, ..., p \tag{40}$$

Each of the $C_i(i = 1, 2, ..., p)$ is an expression in the θ_j; any of the p formulas
in the system (40) are equalities or (strict or nonstrict) inequalities. Let S be
the set of solutions to the system (40),

$$S = \left\{ \Theta \, \epsilon \, \mathrm{IR}^n \,|\, C_i(\Theta) \gtreqless 0, i = 1, 2, ..., p \right\}.$$

As parameter space, we have an open convex region $\Omega \subset \mathrm{IR}^n$; the model specified by (40) defines a subset $\omega = S \cap \Omega$ of the parameter space.

It will be shown that if S is a convex set, and F is the d.f. of a standard normal or logistic r.v. (or more generally, if both F and $1 - F$ are strictly ln-concave), then any local maximum $\Theta_0 \, \epsilon \, \omega$ of $\ln L$ is in fact the unique maximum of
that function in ω. In the case where (40) is a system of linear equalities (for
example, in Models 1-3), S is a r-dimensional subspace of IR^n (for some $r < n$),
thus a convex set. If the model is correct, that is, if the data has been generated
from some $\Theta_0 \, \epsilon \, \omega$, then, under appropriate regularity conditions (which are
fulfilled in the normal and logistic cases), the statistic

$$-2 \ln \frac{\underset{\Theta \, \epsilon \, \omega}{\mathrm{Sup}} \;\; L\,(\Theta)}{\underset{\Theta \, \epsilon \, \Omega}{\mathrm{Sup}} \;\; L\,(\Theta)}$$

is distributed chi-square, with $n - r$ degrees of freedom (Wilks, 1962). These
results have important practical values, because determination of local maxima
can be made routinely by numerical methods. A tempting question is whether
any useful results can be obtained when: (1) Eq. (40) is not a system of linear
equalities; and (2) S is not a convex set. Undoubtedly, this question raises much
more difficult problems than those discussed in this chapter. I limit myself here

to a few remarks that suggest that the situation would not necessarily be hopeless in those cases.

1. Obviously, S can be convex even though (40) is not a linear system of equalities. For instance, if each of the p expressions in (40) is a linear inequality, then S is the intersection of p half subspaces, i.e., a convex set.
2. In any event, the convexity of S is not a necessary condition for the uniqueness of a global maximum.
3. The main difficulty, however, is the construction of an appropriate statistical test in the nonlinear case.

Generalizations of Wilks' result in the nonlinear case have been worked out, which might potentially be applicable here (Chernoff, 1954; Feder, 1968). Suppose, for example, that S is an $(n - 1)$ dimensional smooth surface in $\mathrm{IR}^n = \Omega$ and that the true value Θ_0 lies in S. Suppose that one tests whether Θ lies on one side or the other of S, using a likelihood ratio method; then (under the regularity conditions needed to ensure the normality of the maximum likelihood estimators) the log likelihood ratio statistic is a random variable with value zero half of the time and distributed chi-square with one degree of freedom half of the time (Chernoff, 1954).

Let us prove that any local maximum $\Theta_0 \in \omega$ is a unique global maximum, in the case where S is a convex set and both F and $1 - F$ are strictly ln-concave (in particular, when F is the d.f. of a standard normal or logistic r.v.). This result, which generalizes a result of Dorfman (1973), is an immediate consequence of the following lemma, which lists a number of well-known (or obvious) properties of (strictly) concave functions (e.g., Royden, 1963; Chocquet, 1966).

> **Lemma.**   (i) Any linear combination with (strictly) positive coefficients, of (strictly) concave real functions is (strictly) concave.
>   Let f be a (strictly) concave real function on IR. For $i = 1, 2, ...,$ n, define f_i on IR^n by $f_i (x_1, x_2, ..., x_i, ..., x_n) = f(x_i)$. Then:
> (ii) f_i is (strictly) concave, for $i = 1, 2, ..., n$;
> (iii) If f has an everywhere defined second derivative f'', the strict concavity of f is equivalent to the condition $f'' < 0$.
>   Let f be a strictly concave real function on IR^n, and W a convex subset of IR^n, then:
> (iv) The restriction $f|_W$ of f to W is strictly concave;
> (v) If $f|_W(x_0) > f|_W(x)$ for some $x_0 \in W$ and all x is in the neighborhood of x_0 in W, then x_0 is the unique maximum of that function in W.

We use (v) and show that $\ln L|_S$ is strictly concave if S is convex and if both $\ln F$ and $\ln (1 - F)$ are strictly concave. In view of (iv), it suffices to show that $\ln L$ is strictly concave. Define for $i = 1, 2, ..., n$, $\zeta_i(\theta_1, \theta_2, ..., \theta_i, ..., \theta_n) = \ln F(\theta_i)$, and $\bar{\zeta}_i(\theta_1, \theta_2, ..., \theta_i, ..., \theta_n) = \ln [1 - F(\theta_i)]$. Thus both $\zeta_i, \bar{\zeta}_i$ are real valued functions on IR^n, which are strictly concave by (ii). Thus,

$$\ln L\,(\Theta) = \sum_{i=1}^{n} \left[n_i \, \zeta_i\,(\Theta) + \overline{n}_i \, \overline{\zeta}_i\,(\Theta) \right]$$

is strictly concave by (i), because by hypothesis n_i, $\overline{n}_i > 0$. Finally, it can be checked by direct computation (Dorfman, 1973) that, in the case of the normal or logistic standard r.v., we have $(\ln F)'' < 0$, $[\ln (1 - F)]'' < 0$.

A word of conclusion. The methods discussed in this chapter are useful when the function F of Eq. (1) is completely specified. In subsection 1, an example was analyzed in which F was assumed to be the d.f. of a standard logistic r.v. The method would remain applicable with different assumptions. A natural question at this point is: How critical are the assumptions on F regarding the decisions on the function H? This raises the question of the robustness of the method. Besides practical applications, there are three possible developments of this work:

1. Investigate other assumptions on H. Work along those lines is in progress (Cohen & Iverson, in preparation).
2. Develop parameter estimation procedures involving different assumptions on F.
3. Investigate robustness with regard to the assumptions on F.

ACKNOWLEDGMENTS

The research reported here was supported by a grant from the National Science Foundation (BMS75–09533). I thank Geoffrey Iverson, John Van Praag, and especially Hans-Henning Schulze for a number of useful discussions on this material. I am also grateful to Michael Birnbaum for his remarks on a previous draft.

REFERENCES

Aczél, J. *Lectures on functional equations and their applications.* New York: Academic Press, 1966.

Chernoff, H. On the distribution of the likelihood ratio. *The Annals of Mathematical Statistics*, 1954, *25*, 573-578.

Chocquet, G. *Topology.* New York: Academic Press, 1966.

Cohen, S., & Iverson, G. *Subjective area of rectangles: Test of various polynomial formulas.* Manuscript in preparation, 1977.

Dorfman, D. D. The likelihood function of additive learning models: Sufficient conditions for strict log-concavity and uniqueness of maximum. *Journal of Mathematical Psychology*, 1973, *10*, 73-85.

Falmagne, J. C. Random conjoint measurement and loudness summation. *Psychological Review*, 1976, *83*, 65-79.

Feder, P. I. On the distribution of the log likelihood ratio test statistic when the true parameter is "near" the boundaries of the hypothesis regions. *The Annals of Mathematical Statistics,* 1968, *39,* 2044-2055.

Krantz, D. H., Luce, R. D., Suppes, P., & Tversky, A. *Foundations of measurement* (Vol. 1). New York: Academic Press, 1971.

Levelt, W. J. M., Riemersa, J. B., & Bunt, A. A. Binaural additivity of loudness. *British Journal of Mathematical Statistical Psychology,* 1972, *25,* 51-68.

Pfanzagl, J. *Theory of measurement.* New York: Wiley, 1968.

Royden, H. L. *Real analysis.* New York: Macmillan, 1963.

Sincov, D. M. Notes sur le calcul fonctionnel (Russ.) *Bull. Soc. Phys. Math.* 1903, *13,* 48-72. (a)

Sincov, D. M. Über eine Funktionalgleichung. *Arch. Math. Phys.,* 1903, *6,* 216-217. (b)

Thurstone, L. L. A law of comparative judgment. *Psychological Review,* 1927, *34,* 273-286.

Wilks, S. S. *Mathematical statistics.* New York: Wiley, 1962.

Part II

NEW VIEWS OF REACTION
TIME AND ACCURACY

Psychologists maintain a continued interest in the relation between speed and accuracy of responding in judgment tasks, but only recently has major success in understanding the underlying processes been achieved. These successes are revealed in new theories and models that provide increasingly accurate accounts of empirical data. A clear implication of these theoretical and empirical developments is that theories of information processing in psychophysical and other judgment tasks must deal with both speed and accuracy.

The chapters in this section provide a comprehensive view of recent developments in the area. In Chapter 5, Link discusses theories that provide various interpretations of effects elicited by the use of experimenter-defined reaction-time deadline procedures. One of these theories, Relative Judgment Theory, proposes that a person changes the total comparative difference necessary to discriminate between stimuli in order to accommodate changes in the deadline time. Link then analyzes three experiments—two in signal detection and one concerning line length discrimination. Each analysis demonstrates that as reaction-time deadlines increase, the subject increases the total comparative difference.

In Chapter 6, Lappin is concerned with the effect of prior knowledge on the speed and accuracy of recognition. In this context, prior knowledge is a broad term that includes any information or expectation that the person has about the stimulus prior to its presentation. In particular, Lappin is concerned with the manner in which varying amounts of prior knowledge lead to increased efficiency in processing and responding. In developing his model, Lappin assumes that choice behavior can be represented by two processes—a perceptual process for recognizing and categorizing stimuli and a decision process for selecting among the response alternatives. He then shows the locus of effect of prior knowledge on the two processes.

In Chapter 7, Pachella, Smith, and Stanovich examine the relationship between the speed and accuracy of human information-processing performance and describe a methodology for the study of information processing based on this bivariate relation. They review the logical and empirical problems faced by current cognitive research that measures only reaction times. With Link and Lappin, they argue that an alternative methodology dealing with speed and accuracy relations is necessary in order to study effectively more general cognitive problems. Their experimental tasks involve instructing subjects to perform at a number of controlled response speeds in order to produce data that permit an analysis of the relations among the errors in performance. The application of recent models of error analysis and the development of new models are discussed along with data from three representative experiments.

Chapter 8, by Townsend and Ashby, represents a strikingly new approach to the investigation of cognitive capacity. They are concerned with general models of "capacity" in feature matching, pattern matching, and comparison tasks. For Townsend and Ashby, capacity is a global construct that can be applied to different levels and types of information processing and has varying interpretations depending on the particular experimental paradigm and task. They adopt a twofold approach to the analysis of capacity. One approach is based on a linear correlation model, and the other is presented in the context of stochastic latency theory. A major portion of their chapter is concerned with the dynamics of capacity as it relates to detection and latency; thus they link their work with the other chapters in this section.

Taken in their entirety, these chapters represent a comprehensive current treatment of the general speed/accuracy issue. A careful reading of them will reward the reader with detailed understanding of one of the major issues in contemporary cognitive psychology.

5

The Relative Judgment Theory Analysis
of Response Time Deadline Experiments

Stephen W. Link
McMaster University, Hamilton, Ontario, Canada

Our knowledge of the solar system would be quite limited if ancient astronomers had measured only the latencies, from dusk to first appearance, of the various planets. Given several centuries of such measures, astronomers could argue convincingly that the accumulated observations produced more confusion than order and that less refined measures of planetary performance might expose otherwise undiscoverable natural laws. A clear candidate for simplified data would be the presence or absence of a planet from the night sky, because this measure avoids the awkward problem of defining latencies for planets that do not appear. Armed with these binary performance measures, astronomers could produce an impressive array of statistics, but the heliocentric theory would most likely exist only in stargazers' eyes. Moreover, the call to reason, proclaiming that it would be better to obtain more than one response measure (e.g., latency and spatial position), might drown beneath a chorus of assertions that, like music from the spheres, drones out the common refrain: We can't understand the performance of one variable, so why measure two?

The meaning of our astronomical canard will not be lost on contemporary students of psychophysics. For more than a century, experimental psychophysics maintained the view that the simultaneous measurement of more than a single response variable produced more confusion than order. Of course there were some exceptions; Henmon's (1906, 1911) studies of speed and accuracy in line length discrimination; Garrett's (1922) well-remembered study of the relation of accuracy to speed; Kellogg's (1931) investigation of the psychometric function; Hollingworth's (1939) study of the speed and accuracy of typing while chewing; and Cartwright and Festinger (1943) and Festinger's (1943) experiments, to name a few. But, by and large, two qualitatively different measures of psychophysical performance have been the focus of psychophysical theories. These are, of course, the measures of response frequency versus measures of response time.

Recent experiments, in which response choice and response time are measured simultaneously, provide the data base for new theories of psychophysical performance. Although previous theories account for changes in a single response measure as experimental conditions vary, an increasing number of newer theories predict relationships between response probability and response time. Examples of such theories are the Fast Guess Theory (Ollman, 1966; Yellott, 1971), the Fixed Sample Size Signal Detection Theory (cf. Green & Luce, 1973), the Neural Timing Theory (Luce & Green, 1972), and Relative Judgment Theory (Link & Heath, 1975; Link, 1975).

A particularly useful experimental method for investigating theoretical predictions relating response probability (RP) and response time (RT) utilizes experimenter-defined RT deadlines (Fitts, 1966). Using this method in a typical two-stimulus-two-response paradigm, the experimenter informs the subject of an RT deadline prior to the presentation of a randomly selected stimulus. The experimental subject must, somehow, attempt to produce an RT less than the deadline. Of course on some trials the observed RT may exceed the RT deadline, but numerous experiments show subjects able to respond mostly within the RT deadline even when the deadline randomly changes from trial to trial (Link, 1971).

A decrease in RT deadline has two effects. Not only does mean RT decline, but the probability of responding correctly also declines. This concomitant change in RT and RP is often imagined as a trade-off of speed and accuracy. Basic to the postulation of a speed-accuracy trade-off is the assumption that the subject may either control RT, thereby changing response accuracy, or control response accuracy to produce a change in RT. That is, the locus of control over performance rests in control of a single response measure variable.

Examples of these two distinct views of the speed-accuracy trade-off are found in the Fast Guess Theory, FGT, (Ollman, 1966; Yellott, 1971) and the Fixed Sample Size Signal Detection Theory investigated by Green and Luce (1973). The FGT assumes that on the average, Ss can beat an RT deadline by increasing the number of guesses as the RT deadline is reduced. By assuming guesses to occur more quickly on the average than discriminative responses, a reduction in mean RT will occur as the number of guesses increases. Thus, for the Fast Guess Theory, the emphasis is on controlling response accuracy through the proportion of guesses. Changes in mean RT are a byproduct of changes in response accuracy.

The Fixed Sample Size model assumes, instead, that for a given RT deadline a certain number of sensory samples are accrued. By summing these samples, a subject may improve accuracy in the same way as an experimenter who increases the sample size. If each sample requires a fixed average sampling time, then the average time to collect a fixed number of samples is constant, regardless of the stimulus presented or the response made. Accuracy, however, depends on the number of samples accrued. Thus, as the number of samples, which is taken as equivalent to time, increases, so does the accuracy. Therefore, accuracy is dependent on the sampling time manageable within a given RT deadline.

In contrast, other theories assume both response frequency and duration to be controlled indirectly. For these theories measurements of RP and RT provide different windows through which the discriminative mechanism can be viewed. In addition, these theories also predict relationships between RP and RT that depend on parameters that are considered to be under subjective control. For example, Relative Judgment Theory specifies how subject-controlled changes in two response thresholds simultaneously affect both response measures. When RT deadlines are applied in two-stimulus-two-response paradigms, Relative Judgment Theory proposes a locus of control for both RT and RP.

The three experiments described in the following sections illustrate how RP and RT vary as RT deadlines change. Two experiments on signal detection are analyzed by using the Relative Judgment Theory prediction relating mean RT to response proportions. The third experiment examines both response measures when line lengths are discriminated and RT deadlines vary randomly from trial to trial. In all experiments subjects increase the total comparative difference required for a decision as the RT deadline increases.

THE THEORY OF RELATIVE JUDGMENT

Briefly described, Relative Judgment Theory (RJT) maintains that stimulus presentations provide the basis for development of an internal psychological referent or "mental" standard. During an experimental trial, a stimulus presented to the subject is compared to an already established mental standard by subtraction. The process of comparison, which occurs during a unit of time Δt, results in a discrepancy that is added to an accumulator of discrepancies. When the accumulated discrepancy first exceeds a preset response threshold, A, response R_A is elicited. If the accumulated discrepancy is first smaller than a second preset response threshold, $-A$, then response R_B occurs; otherwise, another discrepancy is obtained during the next unit of time and is added to the accumulator of discrepancies. The analysis of this process of discrimination generates predictions for both response probability and response time.

We assume here that the presentation of stimuli has provided the subject with a mental standard, or referent, which can be sampled during the decision process. A sampled value of the referent will be a value of a random variable X_r. The properties of the referent are captured by the probability density function (pdf) for X_r, $f_r(x)$, and we assume this distribution to be stationary during the duration of the decision process.

When a stimulus S_i $(i = A, B)$ is presented to the subject, psychological values of the stimulus are available for sampling. We let X_i be a random variable representing these psychological values of stimulus S_i. The pdf $f_i(x)$ represents the distribution of X_i, and assume again that $f_i(x)$ is stationary during the decision process.

Over time units of size Δt, repeatedly sampled values of the stimulus are compared to sampled values of the referent. The discrepancy obtained by subtracting X_r from X_i during the kth time interval of size Δt is $d_{ik} = X_{ik} - X_{rk}$. The expected discrepancy $E(d_{ik})$ is the average discrepancy between the presented stimulus and the subject's mental standard. Because the referent is based on previous exposure to the stimuli and is a composite of both S_A and S_B, we assume that the expected value of the referent is bounded by the expected values of the stimulus representations, in particular, $EX_{Bk} < EX_{rk} < EX_{Ak}$. Furthermore, the assumption of stationarity provides that the average discrepancy is constant over time. Thus for any k, $Ed_{Bk} < 0 < Ed_{Ak}$, and it will be convenient to define these expected values as rates of drift; μ_B and μ_A, respectively.

In Fig. 1 the decision process is represented as an accumulation of discrepancies. Over n units of time, the accumulated discrepancy is

$$D_{i,n} = d_{i1} + d_{i2} + ... + d_{in}.$$

The random variable $D_{i,n}$ performs a random walk, with stationary drift rate μ_i, on a dimension of comparative difference bounded by response threshold values placed at A and $-A$. A presentation of stimulus S_A results in a positive drift, μ_A, to the walk, thereby driving the walk, on the average, toward the R_A response threshold. A presentation of S_B generates negative drift, μ_B. The value $2A$ is the total comparative difference adopted by the subject in order to make a decision.

Also shown in Fig. 1 is the starting position of the decision process at time zero. By varying the starting position, C, toward the response threshold at A, the subject biases responding in favor of response R_A. Any bias toward A leads to a simultaneous bias away from $-A$. The result of such bias is to increase the probability of an R_A response when either S_A or S_B is presented. Moreover, mean RT to S_A is reduced, and mean RT to S_B is increased.

The interaction between response bias and rates of drift can now be examined. The rate of drift is a major determinant of response time; in general, the mean decision time, conditioned on the stimulus presented, equals the average distance traveled by the walk divided by the rate of drift. Let the rate of drift when S_B is presented, μ_B, be equal in magnitude to the rate of drift when S_A is presented, μ_A. The subject, we assume, is required by the experimenter to maintain responses within a fixed deadline time regardless of which stimulus is presented. In this case control over the response times for R_A and R_B responses can be effected by maintaining zero bias and by manipulating the size of A. As the value of A is reduced, mean RT is also reduced, but accuracy declines.

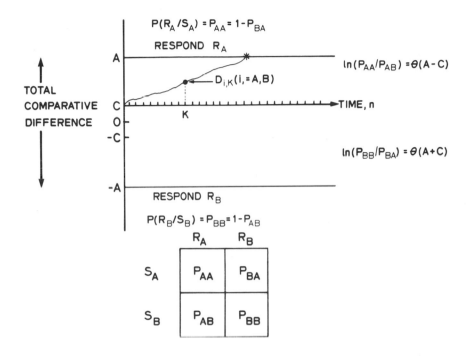

FIG. 1   An illustration of the random walk decision space. The starting position C reflects bias toward one or the other of two response thresholds having values A and $-A$. P_{ij} is the probability of response R_j given stimulus S_i. D_{ik} is the value of the random walk at time unit k, given a presentation of S_i. At the bottom of the figure is a table representing the probabilities P_{ij} of response R_j to stimulus S_i.

Suppose again that the two drift rates are equal in absolute value and that the subject is required to maintain responses within the RT deadline only when stimulus S_A occurs. Of course the instruction at first appears odd, because how is the subject to know that S_A occurred without having first made at least an implicit decision? And, if the decision process requires a minimum time to completion, then the subject should be unable to implement the decision in time to beat very low RT deadlines. If, however, the subject interprets the instruction to imply control of R_A responses, so that regardless of which stimulus is presented an R_A response should occur faster than the deadline, then a bias toward the R_A response threshold will meet the experimenter's requirement. Correct responses to S_A will be made faster than correct responses to S_B.

Although qualitative arguments suggest how subjects may control RT, they do not provide predictions relating RT and RP. Only by demonstrating that RT and RP behave and are related as predicted by theory will we be able to establish the existence of a locus of control over performance. The needed predictions are developed in the next section.

THEORETICAL PREDICTIONS

The theory permits derivations of relations between response probabilities and response times as the total comparative difference, $2A$, changes. In this regard it will be useful to summarize the more general predictions presented in Link and Heath (1975). Let P_{ji} be the probability of responding R_j when stimulus S_i is presented $(j = A, B; i = A, B)$. Then

$$P_{Ai} = \frac{e^{(A + C)\theta_i} - 1}{e^{(A + C)\theta_i} - e^{-(A - C)\theta_i}}.$$
$$= 1 - P_{Bi}, \tag{1}$$

where θ_i is a nonzero value of θ satisfying $E(e^{-\theta d_i}) = 1$, θ_i is of the same sign as μ_i, A is the value of the response threshold for response R_A, and C is the starting position of the random walk, $(-A < C < A)$. Assuming that $\theta_A = -\theta_B = \theta$, we find that

$$\ln\left(\frac{P_{AA}}{P_{AB}}\right) = (A - C)\theta \tag{2}$$

$$\ln\left(\frac{P_{BB}}{P_{BA}}\right) = (A + C)\theta \tag{3}$$

Estimates of $A\theta$ and $C\theta$ are easily obtainable from Eq. (2) and (3) by using empirical estimates of P_{ji}.

The effect of bias on response probability is shown in the following. Note first that when no response bias exists, the parameter C assumes the value zero. The conditional probability of response R_A given stimulus S_A is then

$$P(R_A | S_A, C = 0) = \frac{e^{A\theta} - 1}{e^{A\theta} - e^{-A\theta}} = p$$

and in general we have,

$$P(R_A | S_A, C) = \frac{e^{A\theta} - e^{-C\theta}}{e^{A\theta} - e^{-A\theta}}$$

$$= P(R_A | S_A, C = 0) + \frac{1 - e^{-C\theta}}{e^{A\theta} - e^{-A\theta}}$$

$$= p + b$$

where $b = (1 - e^{-C\theta})/(e^{A\theta} - e^{-A\theta})$. Therefore, for fixed A the effect of response bias is to add or subtract a bias component to the response probability when no bias exists. When the value of C is positive, the bias is added to $P(R_A|S_A, C = 0)$, and when C is negative, the bias component is subtracted. Examining the probability of response R_B to stimulus S_A, we find that

$$P(R_A \mid S_A, C) = P(R_B \mid S_A, C = 0) - b$$
$$= pe^{-A\theta} - b.$$

Similar computations reveal relations among the four possible response probabilities. Table 1 summarizes these relations in a standard two-by-two format. Entries in Table 1 are response probabilities conditioned on the stimulus presented. The convention adopted here specifies the upper left-hand cell to contain a Hit probability P_{AA} and the lower left-hand cell to be a probability of False Alarm P_{AB}. In general, the relation between Hit and False Alarm probabilities can be expressed as $P_{AA} = e^{(A-C)\theta} P_{AB}$.

RESPONSE TIME PREDICTIONS

Although it has been assumed that the values of θ satisfying $E(e^{-\theta d_i}) = 1$ are equal but opposite in sign, it is not necessary to restrict our analysis in other ways. This becomes especially important in the consideration of the response time predictions given in the following, where EDT_{ji} is the expected decision time for R_j given S_i.

$$EDT_{Ai} = \frac{1}{\mu_i \gamma_i} \left[M_i - \left(\frac{e^{\beta\theta_i} + \gamma_i}{e^{\beta\theta_i} - 1} \right) \right] \tag{4a}$$

$$EDT_{Bi} = \frac{1}{\mu_i \gamma_i} \left[M_i + \left(\frac{e^{a\theta_i} + \gamma_i}{e^{-a\theta_i} - 1} \right) \right] \tag{4b}$$

where

$$M_i = \frac{(a\gamma_i + \beta) e^{\beta\theta_i} + (a + \beta\gamma_i) e^{-a\theta_i}}{e^{\beta\theta_i} - e^{-a\theta_i}}$$

$$a = A - C, \qquad \beta = A + C, \qquad \text{and} \qquad \theta_A = -\theta_B$$

TABLE 1
Conditional Response Probabilities for the
Equal θ Case of Relative Judgment Theory

	Response	
Stimulus	R_A	R_B
S_A	$p + b$	$pe^{-A\theta} - b$
S_B	$pe^{-A\theta} + be^{C\theta}$	$p - be^{C\theta}$

Multiplying the numerators and denominators of Eq. (4a, b) by θ_i gives equations similar to those given by Link (1975). From Eq. (1) and (4a, b), we find that the average decision time given a presentation of stimulus S_i is

$$\text{EDT}_i = \frac{1}{\mu_i \theta_i} \left[(P_{Ai} - P_{Bi}) A\theta_i - C\theta_i \right] \tag{5}$$

The value, $[(P_{Ai} - P_{Bi}) A\theta_i - C\theta_i] = Z_i$, is the average distance traveled by the decision process, multiplied by θ_i. Thus Z_i is a scaled measure of the average amount of comparative difference required for the discrimination. In contrast, $2A$ is the total amount of comparative difference. In general, as the total amount of comparative difference increases, so does the value of Z_i. Rewriting Eq. (5) we find that the average decision time is

$$\text{EDT}_i = \frac{Z_i}{\mu_i \theta_i}$$

Therefore, if the values μ_i and θ_i remain constant while the total comparative difference increases, we should find a linear relationship between mean decision time and estimates of Z_i. Furthermore, values of Z_i can be determined entirely from response probability estimates and Eqs. (2) and (3). Thus we have succeeded in establishing a method of testing the predicted relationship between decision time and response probability.

For fixed stimuli we now wish to determine how mean response time will change when A is allowed to vary. Collecting together all components of response time that do not overlap decision time and defining EK to be the expected value of these nondecision components of mean response time, we have for the expected response time to stimulus S_i,

$$ERT_i = EDT_i + EK \tag{6}$$

Thus, as A increases, we find that ERT_i increases linearly as a function of Z_i with slope $(\mu_i \theta_i)^{-1}$ and intercept EK.

Using estimates of the slopes $(\mu_i \theta_i)^{-1}$ obtained from the data for presentations of stimulus S_i, an average relationship between mean RT and Z can be obtained. Letting $q = \mu_A \theta_A / (\mu_A \theta_A + \mu_B \theta_B)$, we have as an estimate of the weighted average performance

$$\overline{RT} = q ERT_A + (1 - q) ERT_B \tag{7}$$

$$= 2 (\mu_A \theta_A + \mu_B \theta_B)^{-1} Z + EK,$$

where $Z = (Z_A + Z_B)/2$. The linear relationships expressed in Eqs. (6) and (7) provide a simple test of RJT predictions relating response time and response probability.

A measure of the difference between average sensory representations of S_A and S_B is obtained by letting $\pi = \theta_B / (\theta_B - \theta_A)$. Then

$$\frac{\mu_A \theta_A \bar{\pi}}{\mu_A \theta_A \pi + \mu_B \theta_B (1 - \pi)} = \frac{\mu_A}{\mu_A - \mu_B} \tag{8}$$

is the proportion of the distance between μ_B and μ_A accounted for by the distance from the mental standard to the average sensory representation of S_A. When values of θ are known to be equal, Eq. (8) provides a useful summary of the relationship between μ_A and μ_B that does not require scaling in terms of standard deviations or higher-order moments of the discrepancy distributions.

Moreover, having at hand estimates of $\mu_i \theta_i$ and $A\theta_i$ permits us to define the total comparative difference, $2A$, in terms of the drift rate, μ_i. The ratio $2A\theta_i / \mu_i \theta_i = 2A/\mu_i$ measures $2A$ in units of the average discrepancy between S_i and the mental standard. When μ_i can be specified in units of the physical stimulus (e.g., degrees visual angle), then $2A$ can also be defined in units of the physical stimulus.

APPLICATION TO RT DEADLINE METHODS

The use of response time deadlines permits an investigation of three phases in a subject's discriminative performance. During the first phase, the subject, in order to meet the demands required by very low deadline times, varies the nondecision component of response time. In the second phase, with the RT deadlines relaxed, both response time and response accuracy may increase as the subject increases the total comparative difference required for a decision. The third phase occurs when the response time deadline is far in excess of the time required for a decision to be reached, but the total comparative difference used by the subject has already been pushed to a maximum. In this last case several possibilities exist; among them, either the decision occurs but the overt report is delayed, or the sequential sampling process is delayed and then the decision occurs.

Let us now engage in a conceptual experiment. The experimenter imposes on the subject a response time deadline that is less than the value of EK, the expected value for nondecision components of latency. How is the subject to meet this performance demand? In the context of RJT, this demand is met by not entering the decision process at all and simply responding as quickly as possible. If no decision is made, then $A = C = 0$, and the value of Z_i also equals zero. We would expect to find from parameter estimates that $Z_i = 0$ and that changes in response probabilities represent chance phenomena.

When RT deadlines exceed the value of EK, the subject may process the presented stimulus by increasing the total comparative difference to $2A$ from zero. As the RT deadline is relaxed further, the total comparative difference may again be increased. In this way, by controlling the total comparative difference required for a discriminative response, the subject simultaneously controls both response probability and response time.

We must also provide for cases in which the subject's decision is made well in advance of the RT deadline but then delayed. If no new decision is effected during this postdecision delay, the observed value of Z_i provides a means of estimating the maximum total comparative difference that can be maintained by the experimental subject.

These relations between mean RT_i and Z_i are shown in Fig. 2. When response times are forced to levels for which accuracy is at chance, mean RT depends on nondecisional factors, and Z_i remains zero. As the subject increases the total comparative difference from zero to a maximal value, mean RT increases linearly with slope $(\mu_i \, \theta_i)^{-1}$, as shown in the midsection of Fig. 2. Finally, when the maximum total comparative difference is reached, Z_i remains constant, and delays in responding permit mean RT_i to increase. The linear relation between mean RT_i and Z_i predicted for the second phase of performance provides data for estimating the minimum decision time, not from the data of simple RT experiments, nor from the method of stages, but from the response times and response probabilities themselves.

A major test of parameter stationarity is also provided by the second performance phase. If the distributions driving the random walk decision process are stationary, then as decision time increases, the parameters μ_i and θ_i should remain constant. Any systematic changes in these parameters should be revealed by data points deviating systematically from the best-fitting straight line.

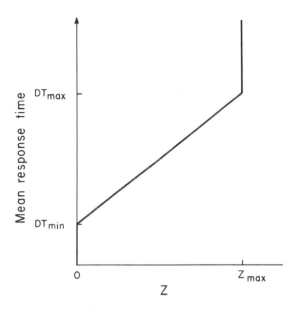

FIG. 2   The relationship between mean RT and Z for three phases of performance in RT deadline experiments.

Having established these preliminary results, we can now examine the effect of instructing subjects to respond within a time deadline only on trials when, say, stimulus S_A is presented. We assume that in order to more carefully control RT when S_A is presented, the subject simply biases the starting position of the decision process toward the R_A response threshold. Predictions for mean RT versus Z remain unaltered, but the amount of bias should be reflected in estimates of θC, which should be positive. Subjects required to employ a deadline on only S_B trials should bias the starting position toward $-A$, resulting in negative estimates of θC.

EXPERIMENTAL TESTS

Green and Luce (1973) reported a series of Yes-No detection experiments designed to examine counting, timing, fast guess, and sequential likelihood ratio models. Their experiments are of particular interest because, at the time, closed form expressions for random walk theories were not readily obtained. Thus, for our purposes, we can consider the experiment to have been performed without prior knowledge of the predictions of RJT. An important feature of these experiments is the response-terminated trial structure. Were the stimuli to be presented for only short durations, and terminated prior to the response, a failure to find linearity in RT_i versus Z_i might be attributable to a lack of stationarity resulting from the termination of the stimulus.

Green and Luce, in the best tradition of scientific inquiry, have very kindly provided me with a detailed subject by condition summary of the five experiments reported in Green and Luce (1973). For two experiments employing RT deadline manipulations, the number of responses and mean response times are reported in the following tables.

Experiment 1

The precise experimental details are discussed by Green and Luce (1973). To summarize, one stimulus was white Gaussian noise with a spectrum level of 40 dB. The remaining stimulus was a 1000-Hz sinusoid 20 dB above the noise power density ($10 \log p/N_0$). Response deadlines of 250, 300, 400, 500, 600, 800, 1000, 1500, and 2000 msec were employed, and three subjects were instructed to use one time deadline on all trials within a 250-trial block. A system of response payoffs provided heavy fines for anticipatory responses and a moderate fine for RTs exceeding the RT deadline.

Results from Experiment 1 are given in Table 2. The average number of responses across the three subjects has been rounded to the nearest integer. It is easily seen that both the relative number of correct responses and the mean response time decrease with reductions in the RT deadline. For the 250-msec deadline, the marginal correct response probability, (594 + 679)/1394, equals .493, and the mean response time is only 153 msec. At the other extreme, we find for the 2000-msec deadline a marginal correct-response probability of .913 and a mean response time of 938 msec. The 785-msec range in mean response time should certainly allow for a strong test of the stationarity assumption.

Least squares estimates of the slope and intercept values obtained from plotting ERT_i against Z_i, assuming $\theta = \theta_A = -\theta_B$, were obtained. For Signal trials the slope and intercept were found to be 266 and 286-msec, and the Noise trials yielded values for the slope and intercept of 295 and 291 msec respectively. With an estimated standard deviation for the intercept of approximately 11 msec, there was no difference between the intercept values of 286 and 291 msec.

Estimated values of $\theta\mu_A$ and $\theta\mu_B$ obtained from the slopes for Signal and Noise trials are $\theta\mu_A = 3.766 \times 10^{-3}$ and $\theta\mu_B = 3.392 \times 10^{-3}$. Using Eq. (8) we find that the mean for the referent, which may be taken to have a value of zero, is placed 47.4% of the distance from μ_B and to μ_A. Estimates of mean RT and values of Z obtained from Eq. (7) yielded the results shown in Fig. 3. The 250- and 300-msec time deadlines were apparently met by subjects performing phase 1 responding. There is no discrimination when the RT deadline is as short as 300 msec. Applying least squares methods to Eq. (7) yielded an estimated intercept of 288 msec and a slope of 279. The linearity in Fig. 3 is readily apparent.

The results from this experiment are compatible with changes in performance due to increases in the value of A as RT deadlines increase. As seen in Table 2, estimates of $A\theta$ are at first zero and then increase as the RT deadline increases.

TABLE 2
Results from Experiment 1
(Green & Luce, 1973)

Deadline	$P(S_A)$	$\overline{N}_{AA}$	$\overline{RT}_{AA}$	$\overline{N}_{BA}$	$\overline{RT}_{BA}$	$\overline{N}_{AB}$	$\overline{RT}_{AB}$	$\overline{N}_{BB}$	$\overline{RT}_{BB}$	$\widehat{A\theta}$	$\widehat{C\theta}$
2000	.468	594	921	59	889	62	1030	679	952	2.35	−.04
1500	.504	479	764	60	772	48	869	483	781	2.19	−.09
1000	.514	468	538	97	647	65	702	470	654	1.78	−.14
800	.517	389	477	120	474	90	479	386	495	1.32	−.08
600	.483	605	434	288	427	204	426	687	455	1.10	−.06
500	.513	364	345	204	345	197	327	343	367	.57	0
400	.533	258	293	172	288	168	277	209	312	.31	.02
300	.492	311	189	228	180	314	184	242	186	.03	0
250	.505	134	151	106	158	135	150	100	155	0	0

Note: $\overline{N}_{ji}$ = the average number of R_j responses to stimulus S_i.
$\overline{RT}_{ji}$ = the average RT (msec) for response R_j given stimulus S_i.

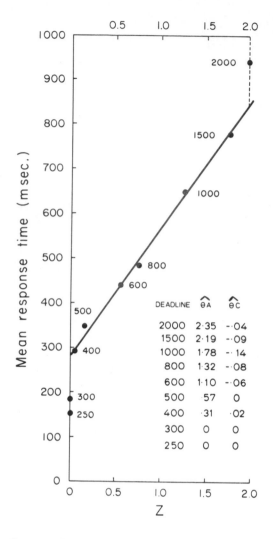

FIG. 3   Data from Green and Luce (1973) analyzed with respect to the Relative Judgment Theory of two choice discrimination. Numbers within the figure indicate the RT deadline for the nearest data point. Estimates of θA and θC are also shown.

In contrast, values of $C\theta$ remain near zero as the RT deadline increases. The very close fit of data points to the linear relation between mean RT and estimates of Z demonstrate the assumption of parameter invariance to be supported. Thus the only parameter that appears to change across RT deadlines is A, indicating that $2A$, the total comparative difference, is increased to permit greater accuracy and longer response times.

Experiment 2

The purpose of the second experiment was to examine changes in performance when the RT deadline is to be used only when S_A is presented. Three subjects who had not participated in Experiment 1 were instructed to beat the RT deadline on Signal trials. The stimuli remained identical to those employed in Experiment 1, and RT deadlines remained the same except for the 250-msec deadline, which was deleted. In all other respects, the experiment was identical to Experiment 1.

The results from Experiment 2 are given in Table 3. To compare these results with those of Experiment 1, the data from the 400-msec to 1500-msec RT deadline conditions were used. From a least squares analysis of Z_i versus ERT_i, estimates of $\theta\mu_A$ and $\theta\mu_B$ were found to be 9.47 × 10^{-3} and 8.34 × 10^{-3}. With respect to these estimates, we find that the average value of the mental referent is placed 46.8% of the distance from μ_B to μ_A. In terms of this estimate, the placement of the referent is remarkably near that found for Experiment 1 (47.4) even though the subjects participating in this experiment did not participate in Experiment 1.

The data from Experiment 2 also demonstrates stationarity of parameters over a wide range of response times. From Eq. (7) the intercept value is 288 msec (quite close to that of Experiment 1), and the slope is 112. Again it appears that the 300-msec RT deadline did not provide sufficient time for discrimination to occur. Also, responses in the 2000-msec condition appear to be delayed.

Estimates of θA and θC, given in Table 3, illustrate how subjects may have interpreted the experimenter's instructions. As the RT deadline increased, the value of θA also increased. We conclude that as in Experiment 1, the subjects in Experiment 2 increased the total comparative difference as the RT deadline increased. Estimates of θC demonstrate a strong bias toward the R_A response threshold, as if subjects were attempting to obtain greater control over the R_A rather than the R_B response.

We expect that with a bias toward the R_A threshold, the mean RT on Signal trials will be less than the mean RT on Noise trials. These differences, computed from the 2000-msec to the 300-msec deadline, are 360, 272, 226, 234, 184, 132, 171, and 51 msec, respectively. Although the differences between mean RTs appear to be in the correct direction, the differences are rather large. In part, the size of these differences results from an unexpected result found in graphs of RT_i versus Z_i ($i = A, B$).

In Experiment 1 these functions had nearly identical intercepts; 286 msec for Signal and 291 msec for Noise trials. In Experiment 2 the corresponding values are 244 and 339 msec, respectively; that is, the intercept values differ by nearly 100 msec. At the present time, it is not known whether this discrepancy can be attributed to a combination of response bias and differential response preparation or whether the result indicates that the conception of stimulus

TABLE 3
Results From Green and Luce (1973) With RT Deadlines
to be Used Only on Signal Trials

Deadline	$P(S_A)$	$\overline{N}_{AA}$	$\overline{RT}_{AA}$	$\overline{N}_{BA}$	$\overline{RT}_{BA}$	$\overline{N}_{AB}$	$\overline{RT}_{AB}$	$\overline{N}_{BB}$	$\overline{RT}_{BB}$	$\widehat{A\theta}$	$\widehat{C\theta}$
2000	.500	705	927	2	1180	4	1154	702	1289	5.52	.35
1500	.498	589	758	2	930	5	1151	592	1030	5.23	.45
1000	.466	605	589	9	664	22	602	683	823	3.82	.37
800	.504	675	538	10	736	34	562	640	786	3.57	.60
600	.500	708	426	27	573	82	410	654	641	2.67	.52
500	.541	658	350	61	421	179	335	431	552	1.63	.49
400	.519	627	325	49	409	199	282	428	605	1.66	.59
300	.492	569	243	136	218	460	205	268	427	.45	.20

Note: $\overline{N}_{ji}$ = the average number of R_j responses to stimulus S_i.

$\overline{RT}_{ji}$ = the average RT (msec) for response R_j given stimulus S_i.

sampling, as presented here, requires modification. In spite of these speculations, an analysis of data averaged across the two stimuli, using $(RT_A + RT_B)/2$ versus $(Z_A + Z_B)/2$ yielded the results shown in Fig. 4. For the average data, the relationship between RT and Z is shown by using results from the 300-msec to 1500-msec RT deadlines, and the clearly linear relationship suggests the conclusion that the μ and θ parameters remain fixed across deadline conditions.

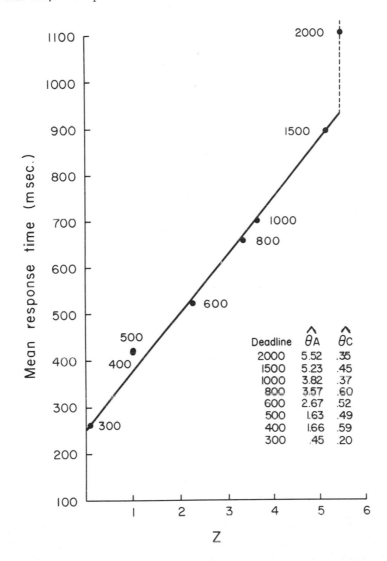

Deadline	$\hat{\theta}_A$	$\hat{\theta}_C$
2000	5.52	.35
1500	5.23	.45
1000	3.82	.37
800	3.57	.60
600	2.67	.52
500	1.63	.49
400	1.66	.59
300	.45	.20

FIG. 4   The relationship between mean RT and Z when subjects are instructed to beat the RT deadline when a signal is present. These results, obtained from different subjects than those in Experiment 1, show $(RT_A + RT_B)/2$ versus $(Z_A + Z_B)/2$ for the 300- to 1500-msec RT deadlines.

Of course the results from this experiment only open up the possibilities for examining how subjects respond to the experimenter's instructions. To demonstrate convincingly that subjects use bias to implement greater control over, say, R_A rather than R_B, a within-subject experiment, in which stimuli, RT deadlines, and the application of the deadlines to either a particular stimulus or response, is a necessity.

Experiment 3

The last experiment to be described is the application of RJT to line length discrimination. During the experiment (cf. Link, 1971), subjects were first presented a fixed standard line length and then, 200 msec following termination of the standard, a variable comparison length appeared. The subjects determined whether the comparison stimulus was either the same as or different from the standard. The experiment also imposed on the subjects RT deadlines that varied from trial to trial.

The most important feature of the experiment rests in the nature of the comparison stimuli. Of these stimuli 50% were of the same length as the standard, but for a particular subject, the remaining comparisons always deviated from the standard in a fixed direction, i.e., either always longer or always shorter depending on the subject. These comparison stimuli deviated from the standard by 1, 2, 3, or 4 mm (at a distance of 1 meter) and were presented at random with probability .125. Thus a subject observed a comparison of the same length as the standard on a randomly selected 50% of the trials and on the remaining trials observed a randomly selected comparison of varying discrepancy from the standard.

In addition to varying the discrepancy between the standard and comparison stimuli, one of three different equiprobable randomly presented RT deadlines was visually presented at the start of each trial. The deadlines, selected on the basis of previous experimentation, were 260 msec, 460 msec, or Accuracy. Subjects were instructed to respond as accurately as possible, given the time deadlines imposed on the task, and were informed at the end of each trial whether the response was correct and whether the RT was within the deadline.

There are two theoretical variables under manipulation: the referent established by the subject, and the total comparative difference, which is, as we have seen, influenced by changes in RT deadlines. Given the small range of stimulus magnitudes, we will assume that the psychological values for individual comparison stimuli preserve the equal spacing of the physical stimuli. Even over a large range of line lengths, estimated magnitudes are approximately a similarity transformation of physical magnitude (Stevens, 1975), and thus a similarity transformation may also provide a useful approximation to our more limited range of stimuli. By adopting the notation that $i = 0, 1, 2, 3, 4$ defines the difference in mm between the experimenter's standard and a comparison stimulus, we have that the psychological value of a stimulus is $X_i = mS_i$.

A reasonable assumption about the subject's referent is that its average value lies somewhere between the average values of X_0 and X_4. The unknown referent we label X_r and observe that there corresponds to the average value of X_r an unknown physical magnitude S_r such that $S_0 < S_r < S_4$. We see that $X_i - X_r = mS_i - mS_r = m (S_i - S_r)$ is thus the average difference between the psychological value of comparison stimulus S_i and the unknown subjective referent.

The decision time when comparison S_i is present depends on both $S_i - S_r$ and the total comparative difference adopted by the subject. When deadline j, $(j = 1, 2, 3)$ is in effect, $2A_j$ denotes the total comparative difference. Bias is probably a minimal factor in our results, because first, a stimulus difference greater than zero either was or was not presented on 50% of the trials; second, subjects were given feedback on each trial; third, accuracy was to be maintained regardless of the type of stimulus presented; and fourth, the RT deadline applied equally to either response. The mean decision time to S_i with the response bias set to zero, and deadline j is,

$$DT_{ij} = \frac{A_j}{m (S_i - S_r)} (2P_{ij} - 1), \qquad i = 0, ..., 4$$

where P_{ij} is the probability of a correct response to stimulus S_i given deadline j.

To examine whether there exists a different intercept value for each deadline condition, we define the expected response time as

$$ERT_{ij} = DT_{ij} + K_j, \tag{9}$$

When estimates of ERT_{ij} are plotted against estimates of $(2P_{ij} - 1)/ (S_i - S_r)$, we should observe a linear function with slope A_j/m and intercept K_j. The slope is a scaled measure of the response threshold, and the value of K_j can be compared across deadlines.

To investigate Eq. (9), the three different deadline conditions were treated separately. For each condition a value of S_r was found that minimized squared deviations of ERT_{ij} from values predicted by Eq. (9) across the five stimuli. The best linear fits, subject to $A \geq 0$, and the resulting independent values of S_r are shown in Fig. 5. For the 260-msec condition, the minimum value for A was 0, and the minimum squared deviations changed little across a wide range of S_r, indicating that responding was at chance. However, it is clear that with mean squared errors of 3.8 and 2.7 msec squared for the 460 msec and Accuracy conditions, respectively, the linearity is quite good.

A major result from this analysis is reflected in values of S_r, which are nearly identical for the 460 msec and Accuracy conditions. The average value of these separate values is $S_0 + .76$, which is the physical stimulus magnitude corresponding to the subjects' internal standard. The very close correspondence for the estimates of S_r indicates that the referent is not affected by changes in RT deadlines. Also, the result is not compatible with the Thurstonian argument that a

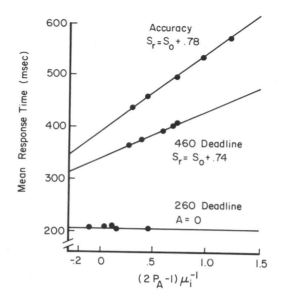

FIG. 5   Estimates of S_r, the physical value corresponding to the average mental standard, obtained from data reported by Link (1971). For each of three RT deadline conditions, the linear relation between mean RT was obtained by setting $\mu_i = S_i - S_r$ and minimizing least squares. Data from each deadline condition were analyzed separately.

standard presented by the experimenter provides the basis for decision through means of a pair comparison. However, a fixed value for S_r is consistent with Fechner's early use of a mental referent in developing the method of right and wrong cases.

Changes in slope are consistent with increases in total comparative difference as the RT deadline increases. For the 260-msec deadline condition, the slope is zero, indicating that the value of A is zero and that response performance is the result of guessing. The 460-msec deadline condition shows variations in mean RT, yielding a slope estimate of 89. The estimated slope increases to 146 in the Accuracy condition. Considered jointly, the estimates of slope again indicate that to meet RT deadline requirements, subjects increase total comparative difference, thereby producing longer RTs and higher correct-response probabilities.

The analysis of intercept values shows changes across the RT deadlines. For the 260-msec, 460-msec, and Accuracy conditions, the intercepts are 205, 339, and 392 msec, respectively. These large differences are a clear indication that although Relative Judgment Theory predicts correctly the relationship between decision time and response probability, there are other effects that cause large changes in the nondecision component of mean RT.

Conclusion

These experiments clearly demonstrate that in controlling speed and accuracy of various psychophysical judgments, subjects control the total comparative difference required for a decision. The effect of imposing a time deadline is to force subjects to reduce the total comparative difference as the RT deadline is reduced. Moreover, the relation between RP and RT permits estimation of a physical magnitude corresponding to the average mental referent adopted by the subject, and permits definition, as Fechner suggested many years ago, of a mental construct in units of the physical stimulus.

The method of analysis used for these experiments pits a particular theory against the relationships between RT and RP observed in three experiments. In this regard an important assumption concerning stationarity of the parameter $\mu_i\theta$ has been tested. When $\mu_i\theta$ is constant, we have assumed that θ is constant, and thus changes in estimates of $A\theta$ and $C\theta$ are due to changes in A and C, respectively. The parameters A and C are clearly under the subject's control and vary as the subject attempts to meet various experimenter-imposed conditions on the judgment task. Thus the purpose of this analysis has not been to suggest the specifics of how the subject chooses his values of A and C but rather to demonstrate that the changes in these two variables account for the changes in performance as RT deadlines are manipulated.

The analysis of the three experiments illustrates that the measurement of two response measures permits a deeper analysis of discriminative mechanisms than that obtained from either measure considered separately. In addition to the theory presented here, other theories of psychophysical performance that relate RP and RT response measures signal a major advance in psychophysical theories; because it is by defining the time course of discrimination that we place mental behavior in the stochastic context where it rightly belongs.

ACKNOWLEDGMENTS

This project was supported by USPHS Grant #MH23878 awarded to Rockefeller University, by National Research Council of Canada Grant A0229, and completed during my tenure at The Rockefeller University and at New York University. My special thanks extend to Professor W. K. Estes and to Professor J. C. Falmagne, who made my visit to New York intellectually rewarding and exciting.

REFERENCES

Cartwright, D., & Festinger, L. A quantitative theory of decision. *Psychological Review*, 1943, *50*, 595-621.

Festinger, L. Studies in decision: 1 Decision-time, relative frequency of judgment and subjective confidence as related to physical stimulus difference. *Psychological Review*, 1943, *50*, 291-306.

Fitts, P. M. Cognitive aspects of information processing: III. Set for speed versus accuracy. *Journal of Experimental Psychology*, 1966, *71*, 849-857.

Garrett, H. E. A study of the relation of accuracy to speed. *Archives of Psychology*, 1922, *56*, 1-104.

Green, D. M., & Luce, R. D. Speed-accuracy tradeoff in auditory detection. In S. Kornblum (Ed.), *Attention and performance* (Vol. IV). New York: Academic Press, 1973.

Henmon, V. A. C. The time of perception as a measure of differences in sensation. *Archives of Philosophy, Psychology, and Scientific Methods*, 1906, *8*, 5-75.

Henmon, V. A. C. The relation of the time of a judgment to its accuracy. *Psychological Review*, 1911, *18*, 186-201.

Hollingworth, H. L. Psycho-dynamics of chewing. *Archives of Psychology*, 1939, *239*, 1-90.

Kellogg, W. N. Time of judgment of psychometric measures. *American Journal of Psychology*, 1931, *43*, 65-86.

Link, S. W. Applying RT deadlines to discrimination reaction time. *Psychonomic Science*, 1971, *25*, 355-358.

Link, S. W. The relative judgment theory of two choice reaction time. *Journal of Mathematical Psychology*, 1975, *12*, 114-136.

Link, S. W., & Heath, R. A. A sequential theory of psychological discrimination. *Psychometrika*, 1975, *40*, 77-105.

Luce, R. D., & Green, D. M. A neural timing theory for response times and the psychophysics of intensity. *Psychological Review*, 1972, *79*, 14-57.

Ollman, R. T. Fast guesses in choice reaction time. *Psychonomic Science*, 1966, *6*, 155-156.

Stevens, S. S. *Psychophysics*. New York: Wiley, 1975.

Yellott, J. I. Correction for fast guessing and the speed-accuracy tradeoff in choice reaction time. *Journal of Mathematical Psychology*, 1971, *8*, 159-199.

6

The Relativity of Choice Behavior and the Effect of Prior Knowledge on the Speed and Accuracy of Recognition

Joseph S. Lappin
Vanderbilt University

1. TWO RELATED PROBLEMS

This paper is concerned with two related problems, one empirical and the other methodological.

The empirical problem concerns the effect of prior knowledge about a stimulus on the speed and accuracy with which it is recognized. "Prior knowledge" is used as a generic term to refer to any information the subject has about the probable parameters or features of the stimulus before it is presented; the present usage is similar to that in Bayesian statistics. Prior knowledge might permit more efficient processing due to the operation of expectancy, preparedness, selective attention, adaptive heuristics, directed memory searches, and the like. In terms of experimental operations, prior knowledge derives from characteristics of the set of alternative stimuli and is manipulated by varying the number, the relative probability, and the similarity of the members of this set. Determining the effects of these manipulations on the subject's perceptual processing of stimuli constitutes a fundamental research problem related to the general issue of how information from past and present experience is combined in the process of pattern recognition. Although research has been directed at various facets of this problem, a general theoretical understanding is lacking.

Determining the role of prior knowledge in recognition is complicated by a basic methodological problem namely, distinguishing the contributions of perceptual and decision processes in the observed performance. The concepts "perception" and "decision" also are used generically to distinguish two logically separate functions involved in responding to stimuli: "Perceptual" processes refer to the general class of processes for obtaining information about stimuli, permitting the discrimination of one stimulus from another; "decision" processes refer to the general class of processes for choosing overt responses, based not only on the current perceptual information but also on the subject's prior expectations for the occurrence of various stimuli and on the anticipated outcomes contingent on the responses to these stimuli. Thus the two component processes are distinguished by different dependencies on the stimulus and task variables. A more precise formal definition of these two processes is given in Sec. 3. Because any observed behavior results from the joint operation of both processes, inferences about the perception of the stimuli rest on assumptions about the subject's decision strategy for choosing responses to the perceived stimulus events.

However, decision processes usually have not been considered important in the performance of reaction-time (RT) tasks. Because the stimuli are typically easy to detect, and because the tasks usually can be performed without error, such concepts as decision criteria often have seemed irrelevant and immeasurable. Indeed, a major motivation for the use of RT as a dependent measure has been the analysis of error-free performance. Nevertheless, the assumption that decision processes can be disregarded in RT tasks may be unwarranted; decision processes may sometimes exert a significant influence on RT.

In theoretical characterizations of choice behavior, the decision process is usually regarded as a fundamental complement to the perceptual process, translating the perceptually processed information about the stimuli into the observed responses. Accordingly, investigations of the perceptual process must rely on an interpretation of the behavioral language that has been used to represent the perceptual events. Unless RT performance is considered fundamentally different from other forms of choice behavior, some understanding of the corresping decision process seems essential to the interpretation of RT data. If, for example, the lengthening of RT by some particular stimulus variable could be attributed to the decision strategy employed by a theoretically ideal observer with perfect perception of the stimuli, then it would be unparsimonious and potentially misleading to infer limitations on perceptual information processing to account for such an effect.

A basic thesis of this chapter is that RT performance is essentially no different from other forms of choice behavior. The same general explanatory processes and the same interpretive rationale should apply whether the dependent measure is the speed or the accuracy of performance. The logic of interpretation should not be determined by the experimenter's choice of a dependent measure.

Consideration of RT as an aspect of choice behavior, involving the same combination of perceptual and decision processes as in other examples of choice behavior, is important particularly in investigating the effect of prior knowledge on recognition: According to well-accepted theories of decision making, it is to be expected that prior knowledge *should* have an effect on the decision process for selecting responses and should therefore also have an effect on observed behavior. This is a familiar idea from Bayesian conceptions of statistical inference and from the application of these concepts in signal detection theory. Application of the Bayesian approach allows us to express the transformation from prior knowledge (prior to the acquisition of present perceptual data) to posterior knowledge by the following familiar but elegant formula:

$$\frac{P(H_i \mid x)}{P(H_j \mid x)} = \frac{P(x \mid H_i)}{P(x \mid H_j)} \cdot \frac{P(H_i)}{P(H_j)} \tag{1}$$

where x is a random variable corresponding to the perceptual data obtained from some stimulus presentation, and H_i and H_j are two hypotheses about the actual stimulus conditions that gave rise to the evidence x. The ratio on the left side of the equation is the *posterior odds* of hypothesis H_i over H_j; the ratio on the far right side is the *prior odds* of H_i over H_j; and the middle term is known as the *likelihood ratio* for H_i over H_j. All of the information about the relative validity of the hypotheses provided by the perceptual event x is specified in the likelihood ratio. Thus the posterior odds in favor of one response over another is determined by both the prior odds and the likelihood ratio; it is to be expected that observed behavior should also reflect this functional relation between prior knowledge and present perception.

Therefore, it is not sufficient to find that prior knowledge affects *behavior*, because this result is anticipated from characteristics of the *decision* process whether or not prior knowledge affects *perception*. Consequently, the methodological problem is to distinguish the contributions of these two functionally distinct processes, both of which may produce a similar effect on observed performance. Parsimony demands that performance limitations should not be attributed to perceptual information processing if the same effects could have been produced solely by the decision process of a theoretically ideal observer.

As we shall see, the operation of the decision process may suffice to account for a significant portion of the experimental data on the effects of prior knowledge on the speed and accuracy of recognition. First, however, it is important to examine the formal structure of the choice experiment in order to identify the isomorphism of data structures based on measures of speed and accuracy.

2.   THE CHOICE EXPERIMENT

The design of the task most frequently employed for the study of perception is very simple: The subject merely categorizes each stimulus presentation as belonging to one or another of a set of mutually exclusive categories. The experimentally relevant behavior typically is restricted to a small set of discrete responses that serve simply as category labels for classifying the stimuli. Such tasks may require detection, discrimination, recognition, or identification—and these are referred to collectively as *choice experiments*. The formal characteristics of the general class of choice experiments have been described in detail by Bush, Galanter, and Luce (1963). The following brief description is focused on only certain pertinent aspects.

The principal defining characteristic of the choice experiment is that the relational structure of the responses is only categorical. That is, the meaning of the responses is based on their correspondence to the categories of the stimulus presentations; the various responses simply designate different categories. Thus the choice experiment imposes strong restrictions on the subject's options and responsibilities for choosing responses and consequently depends on minimal and testable assumptions in interpreting the subject's behavior. In contrast, other psychophysical methods utilize richer semantics available in natural language and request subjects to characterize more abstract relations between stimuli, such as ratios, differences, or ordered similarities. The chapters in Part I of this volume describe rationale for interpreting the perceptual processes underlying such responses and also illustrate the fruitfulness of these psychophysical methods. Whereas there are obvious benefits from investing greater semantic significance in the subjects' responses, these benefits often are gained at the cost of ambiguities in distinguishing the contributions of decision strategies to experimental data. Ironically, models for the decision process have been developed more fully for choice experiments that permit fewer alternative decisions. The particular advantage of the choice experiment derives from simplifying the decision process and distinguishing its role in observed behavior.

The subject's task in a choice experiment is determined by the rules that specify the correct response for each stimulus presentation. It is assumed that the subject has full knowledge of these rules and also, therefore, knowledge of the sets of alternative stimuli and responses. The subject's objective in the task is to maximize the accuracy and/or speed of his or her choices.

The data structure of a choice experiment can be represented by a stimulus-response (S-R) matrix, where the rows correspond to stimuli and the columns to responses, and the data in the cells measure the conditional proximity of the responses to the stimuli. The data are frequently conditional probabilities, $P(r_j \mid s_i)$, but may also be reaction times, $RT(r_j \mid s_i)$, or some other measure of response strength. (Often, the trials are considered as sequentially independent and stationary observations of the same process, but there is no inherent necessity for disregarding sequential dependencies among the trials.) Whatever the specific dependent variable, speed or accuracy, the relationship that is measured is the strength of association, or *proximity*, of a stimulus and response. The proximity of a particular response to a particular stimulus, however, is meaningful only in relation to the proximities of other responses to the same stimulus and the proximities of the same response to other stimuli. Thus the interpretation of data from a choice experiment derives from the full set of proximities as given by the complete *S-R* matrix.

As Shepard (1957) pointed out, the data of an *S-R* matrix can be characterized by two separate sets of parameters—one set for the *S-S* relations between pairs of stimuli and the other set for the *R-R* relations between pairs of responses. In the present context, these two sets of parameters correspond to the structures of relationships resulting from two underlying processes—a perceptual process for discriminating between the stimuli that is characterized by the proximities of pairs of stimuli, and a decision process for choosing among the response alternatives that is characterized by the relative bias or preference for one response over another. (This theoretical representation is discussed in more detail in the next section.) The best-known models are signal detection theory (cf. Green & Swets, 1966) and choice theory (Luce, 1959, 1963), as applied primarily to the analysis of 2 X 2 *S-R* matrices of conditional probabilities. Both models provide a measure of stimulus discriminability as a *distance* between the two stimuli that ostensibly is invariant with changes in the relative bias between the two responses. Such models have been employed less frequently for analyzing larger matrices of conditional probabilities, though several applicable models are available, as exemplified by Luce's (1963) choice theory, Townsend's (1971) "overlap activation model," Nakatani's (1972) "confusion-choice model," and Smith's "informed guessing model" (see Chapter 7 of this text). The same general conception of processes for choosing among the alternative stimuli and alternative responses was basic to previous work with information theory (see Garner, 1962), although analogous parameters for all of the pairwise relations among the stimuli and among the responses were not estimated. Similar decision-theoretic models for choice behavior have been applied only rarely to RT data; the chapters in this symposium are an important exception to this questionable practice.

The common procedure of describing RT performance solely by the RTs of correct responses (i.e., from only the main diagonal of the *S-R* matrix) implicitly assumes that the proximities of the off-diagonal *S-R* pairs are zero. Actually, the proximities of these off-diagonal *S-R* pairs are unknown, because they have not been measured. Furthermore, this analytic procedure disguises the essential isomorphism of data based on speed and accuracy. It should be understood, however, that if some experimental manipulation produces longer RTs at a fixed error rate, then the same manipulation should be expected to produce greater errors at a fixed RT.

Despite the obvious isomorphism of the speed and accuracy of performance, RT data are often considered as somehow fundamentally different from other aspects of choice behavior—as not involving the same processes of discrimination and choice among competing stimulus and response alternatives. Rather, information-processing models for RT experiments typically represent stimulus input as a set of discrete component elements and represent the processing of this input as a sequence of operations that transform its symbolic representation. Presumably, the RT is determined by the number of processing operations required to transform a given individual stimulus into the appropriate individual response. The important assumption that departs from decision-theoretic models of choice behavior is that stimuli and responses may be represented as discrete events defined independently of their context.

The basic issue is not empirical. Rather, it involves competing epistemologies and alternative axiomatic representations of stimulus information and choice behavior. The selection of one of these representations has crucial consequences for the interpretation of human perception and performance. A formalization of the approach adopted in this chapter is given in the following section.

3.   FUNDAMENTAL ASSUMPTION: THE RELATIVITY OF CHOICE BEHAVIOR

The general epistemological assumption underlying the present analysis is that knowledge about any particular object or event can be represented only in relation to other objects and events. The knowledge of component elements arises within the context of some functional organization; the relations define the components. Although this approach has been often overlooked, the relativity of concepts has fundamental applications in logic, mathematics, science, and language (see Bohm, 1969; Cassirer, 1923). Certainly, this approach is not new to the study of perception and performance. For example, the crucial role of the context provided by the sets of alternative stimuli and responses was explicitly emphasized in psychological applications of information theory. As Garner (1974) expresses it, "information theory has provided psychology with the basic concept of information itself, and it has clarified that information is a function not of what the stimulus is, but rather of what it might have been, of its alternatives [p. 194]." An analogous statement might be made for the role of the response alternatives in the choice of a response. The relativity of the choice of a response was clarified especially by the application of statistical decision theory to problems in signal detection and psychophysics. Ironically, what is known currently as the "information-processing" approach usually relies on fundamentally different representations of information and choice, in which the sets of alternatives are no longer basic to the definitions of stimulus, response, and perception.

For the special case of choice experiments, the present assumption is that *the tendency for a specific stimulus to evoke a specific response should be interpreted in relation to the tendency of the same stimulus to evoke other responses and the tendency of other stimuli to evoke the same response.* That is, the observed *S-R* relations are assumed to derive from *S-S* relations and *R-R* relations that are defined on the sets $S \times S$ and $R \times R$ respectively.

More formally, the observed *S-R* proximities may be represented by two logically distinct processes or transformations—a perceptual process that maps the set of stimuli onto a (unobservable) set of perceptual events, and a decision process that maps the perceptual events onto the set of responses. Symbolically, this representation can be expressed as

$$
\begin{aligned}
\Psi : \quad & S \rightarrow X \\
\Delta : \quad & X \rightarrow R \\
\Delta(\Psi) : \quad & S \rightarrow R
\end{aligned}
\tag{2}
$$

where S and R are the sets of stimuli and responses designated by the experimenter, X is a set of perceptual events, Ψ is the perceptual process, and Δ is the decision process for choosing responses to the perceptions. The set of perceptual events, X, is entirely hypothetical; its theoretical role is simply a device for interpreting observed *S-R* relations in terms of perceptual relations among stimuli and decisional relations among responses.

Presumably, the perceptual process Ψ is a stochasitc process that produces a many-to-many mapping from S onto X where each stimulus $s_i \in S$ may give rise on different trials to a variety of different images $x \in X$ with a probability distribution $p_i(x)$, and where an individual perception x may be an image on different trials for several different stimuli. This imperfect correspondence between the elements of S and X typically is assumed to result from the addition of random noise in the physical process of stimulus presentation and in the biological process of sensory encoding. Because the perceptual event produced by any stimulus presentation is certainly the composite of a large number of elementary events occurring in many neurons over a period of time, it is appropriate to regard each composite perceptual observation as a vector composed of many spatially and temporally separate variables, $x = (x_1, x_2, ..., x_T)$, where T is a combined index of the number of neural and temporal units included in the total observation. Thus longer durations of observation and processing are assumed to increase the total amount of perceptual data and thereby increase the discriminability of the stimulus from its alternatives. The similarity or confusability of any pair of stimuli is assumed to correspond to the volume of overlap of the multivariate distributions of perceptual events produced by the two stimuli. The greater the overlap, the greater is the probability of an error in classifying the stimuli after any given duration of processing and the longer is the RT for discriminating between them with any given degree of accuracy.

The similarity or confusability of any pair of stimuli may be represented by the proximity of the pair, and the proximities of all of the pairs characterizes the structure of perceptual relations among the complete set of stimuli. Usually it is sufficient to consider these proximity relations among stimuli as reflexive, symmetric, and monotonic measures of discriminability. That is, if s_i and s_j are any two nonidentical stimuli and if ψ (s_i, s_j) is the measure of proximity, then

$$\psi(s_i, s_i) = \psi(s_j, s_j) \leqslant \psi(s_i, s_j) = \psi(s_j, s_i),$$

It follows that if there are n stimuli, then n $(n-1)/2$ *parameters* are required to represent the multidimensional structure of perceptual relations among the stimuli.

In many cases, a stronger or more detailed representation of the perceptual relations among stimuli is useful and justifiable. For example, by employing the rationale and computational procedures of signal detection theory (Green & Swets, 1966) or choice theory (Luce, 1959, 1963), the measure ψ (s_i, s_j) may be interpreted as the distance between the two centroids of the distributions of perceptual events produced by the stimuli s_i and s_j. Further, such a representation may be regarded as a special case of a general class of models that more completely describe the stochastic distributions of the perceptual events, in terms of variances, correlations, etc., rather than only average proximities. Such a detailed characterization would require a larger number of parameters than can be estimated from a single *S-R* matrix and could be defined only by interdependencies among multiple matrices of response probabilities or RTs.

Just as the perceptual process can be considered as a mapping from S onto X that is characterized by pair-wise relations among the stimuli, correspondingly, the decision process can be considered as a mapping from X onto R that is characterized by pair-wise relations among the responses. The basic assumption is that responses are chosen by partitioning the space of perceptual events into mutually exclusive and exhaustive subsets or regions, with a different response assigned to each region. If R_j designates the region of the perceptual space to which response r_j is assigned, and if p_i (x) is a continuous distribution conditional on stimulus s_i, then presumably the probability that stimulus s_i yields response r_j is given by

$$P(r_j \mid s_i) = \int_{R_j} p_i(x)\, dx \tag{3}$$

Decision strategies are assumed to differ in terms of the location of the criterion boundaries that divide one response region from another. The optimum decision procedure for achieving any one of several objectives (e.g., maximizing the expected value of the responses, minimizing the maximum expected loss) is generally a Bayesian procedure involving comparison of the conditional probabilities

$$\frac{p(s_i)p_i(x)}{\sum_{k=1}^{n} p(s_k)p_k(x)}$$

that the observation x could have been produced by each stimulus s_i (see Anderson, 1958; Green & Swets, 1966). For example, the probability of a correct response is maximized by choosing the response associated with the stimulus for which $p(s_i) \, p_i \, (x)$ is a maximum; the corresponding response region R_i is given by the set of observations x for which $p_i \, (x)/p_k \, (x) \geqslant p \, (s_k)/p \, (s_i)$ for all $k \neq i$. Provided that the likelihood ratios $p_i \, (x)/p_k \, (x)$ are continuous over the perceptual space X, then optimum decision criteria can be defined on the likelihood ratios—pair-wise measures on the space of perceptual events.

The important point is that the decision process can be regarded as a partitioning of the perceptual space that is characterized by relations among pairs of responses. As with the perceptual process, these pair-wise relations between responses, say $\delta \, (r_i, r_j)$, are assumed to be reflexive and symmetric [in the sense that $\delta \, (r_i, r_j)$ is completely determined by $\delta \, (r_j, r_i)$]. Thus, if there are m responses, then $m \, (m - 1)/2$ *parameters* are required to describe the multidimensional structure of relations among the response alternatives.

The characterization of the decision process by relations between pairs of responses rather than by the biases of individual responses constitutes a potentially important issue. A common assumption implicit in the design of many experiments and explicit in some theories (e.g., Luce's choice theory) is that the decision process may be specified by a single bias parameter for each response. In the latter case, the number of parameters is only $m - 1$, in contrast to $m \, (m - 1)/2$ for the relational representation, differing by a factor of $m/2$. Thus characterization by the biases for individual responses implies a restriction on the degrees of freedom of the decision process that may be unrealistically strong for some experiments. If subjects are able to exercise more freedom in choosing responses, then their decision strategies may produce effects that are attributed erroneously to the perceptual process. If the smaller parameter set is sufficient, then fewer restrictions are imposed on the experimental designs and analyses required in order to distinguish between the contributions of the perceptual and decision processes in performance. Furthermore, if the structure of perceptual relations among the stimuli is assumed to be multidimensional, then it seems intuitively implausible to suppose that the organization of this space into response categories is constrained by a smaller number of dimensions. On the other hand, characterizing the decision process by pair-wise relations among the responses is consistent with the Bayesian assumption—adopted, for example, in signal detection theory—that response criteria should be defined on likelihood ratios.

To summarize, the Relativity of Choice Behavior concerns two general ideas: (1) perceptual knowledge is based on relations among stimuli; and (2) responses are choices among the alternatives. Presumably, these choices are governed by the odds and utilities in favor of the various responses. Although these simple ideas are conventional in the well-known applications of statistical decision theory to the study of perception, they are often disregarded in representing human performance as the processing of information in individual stimulus events.

Careful adherence to this relativistic representation of choice behavior turns out to have some surprising (to me, at least) consequences for the design and interpretation of experiments on the effects of prior knowledge. Four implications, discussed in the following sections, concern the following topics: (1) a methodological restriction on the design of choice experiments for distinguishing perceptual and decision processes; (2) the effect of stimulus probability on response criteria; (3) differences in the response criteria for stimuli with the same response; and (4) the effect of set size on the selection of response criteria.

4.   A METHODOLOGICAL THEOREM

The fundamental assumption about the relativity of choice behavior leads to a simple theorem about the requirements for a choice experiment to be able to distinguish the contributions of perceptual and decision processes: *If the dimensionality of the perceptual relations among stimuli is unknown, then the number of responses should[1] either be the same as or one greater than the number of stimuli; otherwise, the perceptual structure cannot be distinguished from the effects of decision strategies.*

The proof of this theorem follows from the requirement that the degrees of freedom in an *S-R* matrix should be greater than or equal to the number of parameters to be estimated. For an $n \times m$ *S-R* matrix, the degrees of freedom are $n(m-1)$—for each of the n stimuli presented by the experimenter, the subject must choose among m response alternatives. As indicated in the previous section, $n(n-1)/2$ is the number of parameters needed to specify the perceptual process, and the number for the decision process is $m(m-1)/2$. Thus the following inequality must be satisfied:

$$n(m-1) \geqslant \frac{n(n-1)}{2} + \frac{m(m-1)}{2} \tag{4}$$

where n and m are positive integers. Now let $m = n + k$. Substituting in Eq. (4) gives

$$n(n+k-1) \geqslant \frac{n(n-1)}{2} + \frac{(n+k)(n+k-1)}{2}$$

Multiplying and rearranging terms yields

$$0 \geqslant k(k-1)$$

---

[1] I use the word "should" rather than "must" because of the demonstrated success of Pachella, Smith, and Stanovich (see Chapter 7 of this text) in using a "nonidentifiable" model with more parameters than degrees of freedom. This fascinating accomplishment, however, requires some dependencies among the parameters and is not representative of the usual requirements for estimating parameters.

which is satisfied if and only if $k = 0$ or $k = 1$. Thus $m = n$ or $m = n + 1$.

A corollary to this theorem is that *the number of perceptual parameters that can be estimated from an S-R matrix is not greater than the number of pairs of responses.*

This restriction is avoidable only by means of assumptions about the perceptual structure of relations among the stimuli that permit a reduction in the number of parameters needed to represent the data. This may be appropriate, for example, when the stimuli are constructed from several mutually independent physical variables, so that the perceptual proximity corresponding to a given difference on a given physical variable can be assumed to be the same for all pairs of stimuli with that difference. However, such a linear representation constitutes a strong assumption about the independence and additivity of dimensions that should be checked against the data.

Ironically, the problem of requiring more parameters than can be identified by the data matrix often arises in the attempt to control the decision process by assigning multiple stimuli to the same response. Examples of this problem are examined in Secs. 6 and 7.

5. STIMULUS PROBABILITY AND RESPONSE CRITERIA

One of the most familiar ideas from the application of Bayesian statistical decision theory to the study of perception is that the criterion for choosing a response should depend in part on the prior probability of success of that response. The well-known formula for posterior odds, as given in Eq. (1), states that the posterior odds in favor of one hypothesis over another depends equally on two distinct quantities: the likelihood ratio, which measures the information provided by a given piece of evidence, and the prior odds before the present evidence was obtained. [The linearity of this formula may be made more obvious by a logarithmic transform of Eq. (1). Accordingly, the relationship can be expressed as "the log posterior odds equals the sum of the log prior odds and the log likelihood ratio."] An optimal decision strategy involves adopting a specific criterion value of the likelihood ratio and then choosing the corresponding response whenever the likelihood ratio is equal or greater than this value—i.e., whenever "the likelihood ratio is within the criterion." In general, then, the higher the prior odds, the lower the likelihood ratio needed to meet the criteron. This principle of choice behavior ranks as perhaps one of the best established principles in the study of human perception and performance. It merits mention here only because its relevance to RT tasks often is disregarded, because performance often is not conceptualized as a form of choice behavior.

Stimulus probability should be expected to influence the response criterion in RT experiments as well as in other choice experiments. More probable stimuli should lead to faster responses, because a reasonable decision strategy should demand less perceptual evidence for responding to these stimuli. This reasoning would apply as long as there is a trade-off between speed and accuracy, as has been amply demonstrated in recent years (e.g., see Pachella, 1974, and the other chapters in Part II of this volume). The general indication from studies of the speed-accuracy trade-off is that perceptual information about the stimulus increases with time from stimulus onset. (Probably, the reliability of the decision process for selecting responses also increases with time, but in any case the net effect is a rapidly developing control of responses by stimuli.) Link (in Chapter 5 of this volume) presents a detailed and plausible theory for interpreting many such findings in terms of a random walk over the space of comparative relations between stimuli. According to such conceptions, slower responses are usually more accurate, because they stand to benefit from a greater accumulation of perceptual information. If less information is required to meet a response criterion that has been lowered as the result of prior knowledge about the stimulus presentation, then that criterial amount of information may be obtained sooner and the response made more rapidly; similarly, less probable stimuli should elicit slower responses. The same effect of prior knowledge of the presentation probability should obtain even in a "simple RT" task requiring a single response, because RT tasks require a decision about when to respond as well as about which response to choose.

The operation of these processes can be illustrated by an experiment[2] that Joe Harm and I conducted on the question of whether prior knowledge could facilitate the speed of recognition in a task wtih only two stimuli and two responses. As a dependent measure of performance we used not only the RTs but also the trade-off relation between RT and discrimination accuracy. Specifically, we examined the discrimination accuracy of responses falling within various bands of RT—a measure that we refer to here as the *conditional accuracy function* (CAF),[3] because it is discrimination accuracy conditionalized on RT. We had found in previous experiments using the CAF (Lappin & Disch, 1972; Harm & Lappin, 1973), that performance was no more efficient when one of the stimuli was made more predictable than when the two stimuli were equiprobable. Although the average RTs were faster when the stimuli were more predictable, as reported by many other experimenters, this apparently resulted from the opportunity

---

[2] We gratefully acknowledge the patient and competent help of Phil Vickery and Whitley Courtnay in the collection and analysis of this data.

[3] In several previous reports, we have referred to this measure as the "latency operating characteristic," to suggest its analogy with the "receiver operating characteristic." However, this previous term has not been generally adopted in the literature and is less descriptive than the present term, which was suggested by Robert Ollman. This measure has also been referred to as the "micro-tradeoff" (e.g., Pachella, 1974), distinguishing it from the "macro-tradeoff" between mean RT and accuracy for a given block of trials. Although the CAF is conceptually similar to the macro- or speed-accuracy trade-off between mean RT and accuracy, the two measures have several different characteristics (see Pachella, 1974; Wood & Jennings, 1976).

for using a lower criterion for the more probable response. When performance was analyzed in terms of the CAF, using a measure of discrimination accuracy
that was ostensibly invariant with the subject's response criterion (d' or the similar measure — ln η from the choice theory), then discrimination accuracy was
unaffected by stimulus probability. Thus prior knowledge about the stimulus
evidently influenced only the decision process but not the perceptual process.

The stimuli in our previous experiments, however, had been highly discriminable spots of light varying only in spatial position. We wondered whether prior
knowledge might facilitate recognition when the stimulus patterns were more
complex and were discriminable only on the basis of more subtle features. The
stimuli in the present experiment were patterns of eight dots randomly distributed in the cells of an (invisible) 8 X 8 matrix. Although this task provided only
an elementary form of prior knowledge, we wondered if such limited information
might be sufficient to improve the speed of the perceptual process.

The stimulus patterns were displayed on a cathode ray tube under control by
a small computer. At the beginning of each experimental session, a new pair of
patterns was generated by a random process, and both patterns were displayed
simultaneously for as long as the subject wished to study and compare them.
During this initial study period, the stimulus assigned to the left response key
appeared on the left of the display scope, and the stimulus assigned to the right
response key appeared on the right. During the experiment proper, each trial
was initiated when the subject depressed both response keys, one with each hand;
½ sec later the stimulus appeared in the center of the display; the subject responded by releasing one of the two keys; the stimulus then disappeared and feedback was provided about both RT (by the position of a spot of light on the display
screen) and accuracy (by a teletype bell for correct responses) of the response;
and the subject could then initiate the next trial as soon as he or she wished.

Two experimental conditions differed in the relative frequencies of the two
stimuli: In the 50/50 condition, the two stimuli occurred equally often, and in
the 75/25 condition, one of the stimuli (assigned to the left response key) occurred on 75% and the other on 25% of the trials.

In order to obtain data reflecting the trade-off between speed and accuracy,
the subjects were asked to try to maintain their RTs in a 100-msec band (175-
275 for three subjects and 200-300 for another) within which they could be
correct on only about 75% of the trials. These bands were determined for each
subject during four practice sessions. Four paid volunteers each served for six
experimental sessions, each consisting of 500 trials preceded by 50 warm-up
trials. Three sessions were devoted to each of the two experimental conditions,
in counterbalanced order.

The effect of prior knowledge on the speed and accuracy of recognition is
indicated by the CAFs for the two conditions, as shown in Fig. 1. Discrimination
accuracy was computed from confusion matrices for just those trials on which
the RT was within a specific 20-msec band. Figure 1 gives the average discrimina-

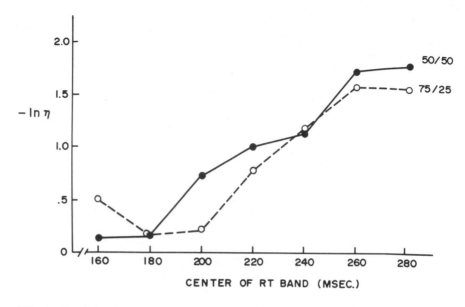

FIG. 1   Conditional accuracy functions for two conditions defined by the relative probabilities of two stimulus alternatives. The measure of discrimination accuracy, $-\ln \eta$, is
taken from Luce's (1963) choice theory and is calculated by

$$-\ln \eta = -\frac{1}{2} \ln\left[\frac{P(r_2 \mid s_1)}{P(r_1 \mid s_1)} \cdot \frac{P(r_1 \mid s_2)}{P(r_2 \mid s_2)}\right]$$

This measure is similar to the measure d' in signal detection theory in ostensibly being invariant with changes in response bias and in its interpretation as a measure of perceptual
distance between the two stimuli. This measure of discrimination was computed from confusion matrices for responses occurring in 20-msec bands of RT, centered at the points
shown on the abscissa.

tion accuracy (as measured by $-\ln \eta$, from the choice theory) at seven values of
RT, in 20-msec bands from 150 to 289 msec. As may be seen, the CAF is no
better for the 75/25 condition than for the 50/50 condition. Therefore, stimulus
probability does not seem to have facilitated the perceptual process for recognizing the stimulus patterns in this task.

That is not to say, of course, that stimulus probability had no effect on performance—the average RT was about 25 msec faster and the overall accuracy
slightly higher in the 75/25 condition. However, these apparent benefits to performance in the 75/25 condition were primarily due to a lower criterion for the
more probable response. Data on the response biases are given in Fig. 2, which
plots a logarithmic measure of bias comparable to the measure of discrimination
used in Fig. 1, again conditionalized on RT. As may be seen, the response criterion
varied systematically with the speed of the response, with the bias for the probable response strongest at the fastest RTs and diminishing steadily as the RTs

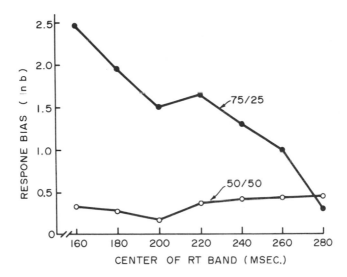

FIG. 2   Response bias conditionalized on RT. The calculation of this measure was similar to that for the discrimination measure shown in Fig. 1. The calculation formula is

$$\ln \beta = \frac{1}{2} \ln\left[\frac{P(r_1 \mid s_1)}{P(r_2 \mid s_1)} \cdot \frac{P(r_1 \mid s_2)}{P(r_2 \mid s_2)}\right]$$

became slower. That is, prior knowledge about the probable stimulus tended to produce fast but indiscriminate responses in anticipation of that stimulus.

The results of this experiment indicate that prior knowledge influenced the decision process as expected from the standpoint of statistical decision theory—by lowering the criterion for the probable response. On the other hand, prior knowledge seems to have provided no benefit to the perceptual process for discriminating between the stimuli.

6.   EQUATING RESPONSES DOES NOT EQUATE CRITERIA

Most investigators who have studied the effect of stimulus probability on performance have been aware of the potentially misleading influence of response criteria. Comparing the RTs to stimuli with different presentation probabilities has usually been regarded as equivocal for tasks with a one:one stimulus-response mapping—because faster responses to the more probable stimuli can be expected to result solely from biases in decision criteria. One strategy for avoiding this problem has been to use a many:one stimulus-response mapping, where several stimuli with different presentation probabilities are assigned to the same response (e.g., LaBerge & Tweedy, 1964). Because the responses have been equated, it is natural to assume that the response criteria for the various stimuli have also been equated. Presumably, response biases should be associated solely with the responses, independently of how the stimuli are assigned to them.

This assumption is mistaken, however. One of the implications of the Relativity of Choice Behavior, as stated in the theorem of Sec. 4, is that perceptual and decision processes typically cannot be distinguished when the number of stimuli is greater than the number of responses. According to this representation of performance, the decision process consists of the mapping from the perceptual structure of relations among stimuli to the behavioral structure of relations among responses. When there are fewer responses than stimuli, the responses may be insufficient to characterize the relational structure of the stimuli; the S-R matrix may have too few degrees of freedom to identify and distinguish the two sets of parameters.

Consider, for example, a 3:2 design, with two stimuli, s_1 and s_2, assigned to one response, r_1, and a single stimulus, s_0, to the other response, r_0. In an attempt to assess the perceptual effects of stimulus probability isolated from the influence of response bias, the two stimuli sharing the same response may have different presentation probabilities. The perceptual relations among these stimuli might be represented spatially, with the discriminability of each pair of stimuli indicated by the spatial separation between them. The corresponding decision rule for translating the perceptual events in this space into the two responses could be described by a partition of this space into two categories separated by some criterion boundary, assigning the events on one side of the boundary to one response and those on the other side to the other response. Accordingly, the perceptual proximities among the three pairs of stimuli are characterized by three parameters and the preference relation among the two responses by a fourth parameter. The S-R matrix, however, has only three degrees of freedom and can be described by many different four-parameter models. The effect of stimulus probability therefore cannot be determined, because the structure of relations among the stimuli is not identifiable. Expressed differently, when the subject erroneously gives response r_1 to stimulus s_0, there is no way to determine whether this error involves the discrimination between s_0 and s_1 or between s_0 and s_2.

This problem of nonidentifiability is illustrated by Fig. 3, which shows a perceptual space of three stimuli divided into two different response regions by the location of two different criterion boundaries. Suppose in this illustration that s_1 has a higher presentation probability than s_2. The subject's task in this situation would be to discriminate s_0 from s_1 and also from s_2. In analyzing the data matrix of S-R proximities—either conditional response probabilities or RTs—the experimenter might attempt to determine the discriminabilities of s_0 from s_1 and from s_2, the relation between s_1 and s_2 being irrelevant to the subject's task and presumably irrelevant to the empirical question about stimulus probability. But consider the behavioral effects of different decision strategies for translating the given perceptual structure into two responses. Figure 3 shows

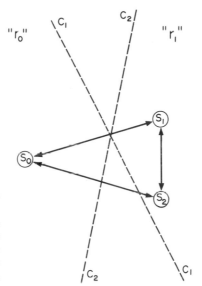

FIG. 3 A hypothetical perceptual space consisting of three stimuli and partitioned into two response regions by means of two different decision criteria. Criterion C_1 would be associated with a discriminant vector that is adapted primarily to discriminating between s_0 and s_1. Criterion C_2, on the other hand, would give greater weight to discriminations between s_0 and s_2 while maintaining the same criterion for responding differentially to s_0 and s_1.

two criteria (C_1 and C_2) that are roughly equivalent with respect to their bias in differentiating s_0 and s_1 but are quite different in their bias in differentiating s_0 and s_2. Thus use of criterion C_1 would yield data indicating an appreciable decrement in the recognizability of s_2, whereas use of criterion C_2 would indicate little or no difference in the recognizability of s_1 and s_2. On the basis of a given data matrix, it is impossible to know whether the poor discrimination of s_2 from s_0 is due to the fact that these two stimuli are indeed confused and located near each other in the perceptual space or whether the subject's decision strategy is just not adapted to differentiating these stimuli. It may be noted that the latter alternative—a misdirected response criterion—is the rational and predictable effect from presenting s_2 infrequently and thereby rendering it less relevant to most of the decisions required by the task.

The moral is that assigning the same response to different stimuli does not guarantee that they will have an equal opportunity for guiding the subject's choice of responses. A biased response criterion can deny equal weighting of equally recognizable stimuli on the subject's behavior.

7.   THE EFFECT OF SET SIZE ON DECISION CRITERIA

The glib suggestion that choice experiments should provide as many responses as stimuli is apt to appear superficial and out of touch with contemporary research on information processing. The fact is that tasks requiring identifying responses to *sets* of stimuli rather than merely to individual stimuli have provided an extraordinarily rich experimental paradigm. And properly so, because the task of classifying a large set of patterns into subsets corresponding to different prototypes or concepts is basic to the very definition of pattern recognition. This general task structure is inherent in the phenomena of perceptual constancy and recognition memory. Thus investigation of how recognition is affected by the composition of the set of stimuli assigned to a given response constitutes a research problem of fundamental importance. For the same reasons, an understanding of the demands on the decision process is crucial to the interpretation of research on this problem. As it turns out, the difficulty of the decision problem depends heavily on the number of stimuli in the set assigned to a given response (the "set size"). Large and systematic effects of set size can be anticipated as inherent aspects of the decision problem, aside from any effects of set size on perceptual information processing.

The design of many:one recognition experiments need not be taken as a violation of the principle that the number of perceptual parameters cannot exceed the number of pairs of responses, because the perceptual relations of interest are between *sets* of stimuli rather than between the individual members within the sets. The question is not the feasibility of these experiments but the attribution of their results to the perceptual and decision processes.

Increased set size typically brings an increased number of relevant attributes required to distinguish between stimuli and, therefore, increased dimensionality of the perceptual space of interstimulus relations. The *identification* of an individual stimulus selected from this space must involve the *discrimination* of more attributes defined on more dimensions. Insofar as random perturbation or "noise" is associated with the acquisition of information about any one attribute or dimension, then there is a greater opportunity for this noise to appear spuriously as true stimulus information as the number of dimensions increases. Identification of any given stimulus becomes less accurate as the number of alternative stimuli is increased, simply because there are more opportunities for confusion with other stimuli.

At first glance such potential confusions would not appear to hamper detection and recognition tasks with just two alternative response categories, but this initial appearance is misleading. What must be remembered is that all such tasks ultimately depend on the discrimination of one stimulus from another. Because the subject does not know at the beginning of any trial which one of the possible stimuli has been presented, he or she cannot be sure which one of the several potentially relevant perceptual dimensions is most appropriate for discriminating between the two response categories on that trial. The perception of information on the relevant dimension is diluted by the perception of noise events on irrelevant dimensions. The resulting decrement in performance derives from a reduction in the stimulus information available to the subject and from the inherent ambiguity about which perceptual information is relevant to the decision process, independently of any possible limitation on the perceptual process as such. A performance decrement associated with increased set size is predictable for an ideal observer with access to unlimited perceptual information. Prior knowledge about the relevant stimulus attributes simply permits the ideal observer to ignore much of the available perceptual information in choosing a response.

A heuristic illustration of how set size affects the decision process may be described as follows. Consider a task in which a positive set of two stimuli, s_1 and s_2, must be discriminated from a single stimulus, s_0. When only one of the stimuli, s_1 or s_2, must be discriminated from s_0, we can imagine the task as involving decisions based on the location of the perceptual events along a discriminant vector extending between the two alternatives, from s_0 to s_1 or from s_0 to s_2. When there are two alternatives, however, the observer is uncertain on any trial about which of these two vectors to employ in the decision process. A reasonable decision strategy, which is described more fully later, is to cross-correlate the perceptual events with a linear combination of the two stimuli, s_1 and s_2. If both of these components are weighted equally, the effect is the formation of a new discriminant vector that lies between the two original vectors. Decisions are now based on the projected positions of perceptual events onto this new vector.

This situation is illustrated in Fig. 4. As may be seen, the projected positions of perceptual events onto this new vector are distributed over a shorter distance than when there were only two stimuli, and the discriminant vector was oriented so as to maximize the distance between the average perceptual events associated with the two stimuli. Elementary trigonometry yields the relationship shown in Fig. 4 for the average vector lengths in the two cases, for positive sets of one and of two stimuli. If the original discriminant vectors are orthogonal—i.e., at right angles in the perceptual space—and if the two alternatives, s_1 and s_2, are equally discriminable from s_0, then the discriminal distance is decreased by a factor of $(1/\sqrt{2})$ when the set size is increased from one to two alternatives.

A more general and precise theory for the effect of set size on recognition can be developed as follows. First, let us represent the perceptual event associated

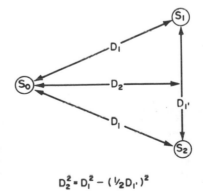

FIG. 4 A hypothetical perceptual space consisting of three stimuli, showing the relations between the lengths of discriminant vectors when there are only two alternative stimuli (D_1) and when both s_1 and s_2 are included in the same set (D_2). Decisions would be based on the projected positions of perceptual events onto one of these vectors.

$$D_2^2 = D_1^2 - (\tfrac{1}{2}D_{1'})^2$$

with the presentation of any stimulus, s_i, as a vector

$$x_i(t) = s_i(t) + n(t),$$ (5)

where the component variables indexed by t correspond to observations at separate points in time, space, frequency, neural elements, etc. Variability is associated with the vector $n(t)$, in which the values for each interval dt are assumed to be distributed with zero mean and unit variance. We will also assume that $n(t)$ is generated by a Poisson process in which the values at separate points in t are stochastically independent, that is

$$E \int_0^T n(t)\,dt = 0$$ (6)

$$E \int_0^T n(t)^2\,dt = T$$ (7)

$$E \int_0^T n(t) \cdot n(t+u)\,dt = 0, \qquad u \neq 0$$ (8)

The vector $s_i(t)$ is assumed to be a constant, the expected value of the perceptual event evoked by the stimulus s_i—i.e.,

$$E \int_0^T x_i(t)\,dt = s_i(t)$$ (9)

The limit of integration, T, can be regarded as the bandwidth of the system.

When the observer is uncertain about which of several alternative stimuli may be presented, a decision procedure for recognizing any one of them—i.e., discriminating it from a null stimulus, s_0—is to base decisions on a cross-correlation of the perceived event with a linear combination of the several alternative stimuli. This procedure is analogous to that in communications engineering for constructing an optimum linear filter for maximizing signal/noise ratios (see Anderson, 1973; Green & Swets, Chap. 6, 1966; Harman, sec. 11, 1963; Nolte & Jaarsma, 1967; Townsend & Ashby, Chapter 8, of this text). Thus the linear filter can be represented by

$$h(t) = \sum_{i=1}^M w_i s_i(t),$$

where the coefficients w_i are the weights for each of the component vectors; $\sum_{i=1}^M w_i^2 = 1$. A reasonable decision procedure is to respond "yes" whevever the cross-correlation

$$Y = \int_0^T h(t) \cdot x(t)\,dt$$ (10)

is within some criterion.[4]

Before considering the special case of M equally likely orthogonal alternatives, it is useful to develop an overall picture of the performance of this system. The expected value of the filter output when the stimulus s_i is presented can be written as

$$E(Y \mid s_i, h) = E \int_0^T h(t) \cdot [s_i(t) + n(t)] \, dt$$

$$= \int_0^T h(t) \cdot s_i(t) \, dt \qquad (11)$$

Suppose that s_0 is a null stimulus, orthogonal to all those represented in the filter—i.e.,

$$\int_0^T h(t) \cdot s_0(t) \, dt = 0,$$

Accordingly, the expected filter output when stimulus s_0 is presented is $E(Y \mid s_0, h) = 0$, and the difference in the expected outputs for the two stimuli is given by

$$d_h(s_i, s_j) = E(Y \mid s_i, h) - E(Y \mid s_0, h)$$

$$= \int_0^T h(t) \cdot s_i(t) \, dt. \qquad (12)$$

---

[4]This decision procedure is not optimal. The optimal procedure is based on the likelihood ratio for each perceived event, $1(x) = 1/M \sum_{i=1}^{M} [P(x|s_i)/P(x|n)]$. When the noise is normally distributed with zero mean and unit variance, the likelihood ratio for the case of M orthogonal signals has the form

$$1(x) = \frac{1}{M} \sum_{i=1}^{M} \exp(xs_i - \frac{1}{2}s_i^2),$$

where the term xs_i denotes the cross-correlation of the vectors $x(t)$ and $s_i(t)$, and s_i^2 denotes the energy of the vector $s_i(t)$. Thus, this optimum, maximum-likelihood procedure involves adding the likelihood ratios associated with each of the cross-correlations rather than adding the cross-correlations themselves. When the signal energy is low (e.g., $d' < 1.5$), the two procedures are essentially the same; but when the signal energy is high, the maximum-likelihood procedure yields much better performance with little decrement from increases in M. Which of the two procedures has greater validity as a perceptual model is unclear, but Anderson (1973) argues for the neurophysiological reasonableness of adding cross-correlations, and Kinchla (1974) describes supporting data on human performance. For present purposes I consider the procedure of adding cross-correlations, in part because it is mathematically much simpler. It may also be noted that these are not the only reasonable alternatives. A third important formulation that is different from both of the preceding ones can be derived from Luce's choice theory (for an equivalent formula, see Luce, 1963, pp. 140, 181-184; Lappin & Uttal, 1976). I am indebted to David M. Green for helping to clarify this problem for me.

Let us now consider the variance of the filter output:

$$\text{var}(Y \mid h) = E \int_0^T \{h(t) \cdot [s_i(t) + n(t)]\}^2 \, dt - \{E \int_0^T h(t) \cdot [s_i(t) + n(t)] \, dt\}^2$$

$$= E \int_0^T [h(t) \cdot n(t)]^2 \, dt$$

$$= \int_0^T h(t)^2 \, dt \tag{13}$$

(The last step is based on the assumption that $n(t)$ has unit variance within each interval dt.) In other words, the variance of the output of the filter depends only on its bandwidth, $\int_0^T h(t) \, dt$, independent of the input. Thus, if we measure detectability by the signal/noise ratio,

$$D_h(s_i, s_0) = d_h(s_i, s_0) / \sqrt{\text{Var}(Y \mid h)}$$

then we find

$$D_h(s_i, s_0) = \frac{\int_0^T h(t) \cdot s_i(t) \, dt}{[\int_0^T h(t)^2 \, dt]^{\frac{1}{2}}} \tag{14}$$

The important point expressed in Eq. (14) is that we have a linear system in which the signal/noise ratio is proportional to the input signal intensity. That is,

$$D_h(k \cdot s_i, s_0) = k D_h(s_i, s_0)$$

and if s_i and s_j are orthogonal stimuli, then

$$D_h[(s_i + s_j), s_0] = D_h(s_i, s_0) + D_h(s_j, s_0).$$

It may also be seen that when the filter is exactly matched to the stimulus presentation, $h(t) = s_1(t)$, the difference in mean output for stimulus s_1 and s_0 is equal to the variance of the filter output

$$d_1(s_1, s_0) = \int_0^T s_1(t)^2 \, dt = \text{var}(Y \mid 1)$$

Thus for this case the signal/noise ratio is equal to the signal intensity

$$D_1 = [\int_0^T s_1(t)^2 \, dt]^{\frac{1}{2}} \tag{15}$$

Now consider the case of M equally likely and orthogonal alternatives. The optimal filter for this case consists of a weighted sum of the several alternatives, and if the alternatives are equally likely and equally detectable, then we may set their weights to the same value, $w_i = (1\sqrt{M})$. Substituting into the appropriate preceding equations, we find

$$E(Y \mid s_i, M) = \int_0^T s_i(t) \left[\sum_{j=1}^{M} \frac{1}{\sqrt{M}} s_j(t) \right] dt$$

$$= \frac{1}{\sqrt{M}} \int_0^T s_i(t)^2 \, dt$$

$$d_m(s_i, s_0) = \frac{1}{\sqrt{M}} d_i$$

$$\mathrm{var}(Y \mid M) = \int_0^T \left[\sum_{j=1}^{M} \frac{1}{\sqrt{M}} s_j(t) \right]^2 dt = \frac{1}{M} \sum_{j=1}^{M} \cdot \int_0^T s_j(t)^2 \, dt$$

$$= \mathrm{var}(Y \mid 1) = d_1$$

$$D_m = \frac{d_m}{\sqrt{\mathrm{var}(Y \mid M)}} = \frac{\frac{1}{\sqrt{M}} d_1}{\sqrt{d_1}}$$

$$= \frac{1}{\sqrt{M}} \sqrt{d_1} \; .$$

Thus we come to the following expression for the effect of set size on recognition accuracy:

$$D_m = \frac{1}{\sqrt{M}} D_1 \tag{16}$$

The relationship expressed in Eq. (16) is essentially the same as that derived from similar models by Tanner (1956) and by Anderson (1973, p. 422). The predictions from this equation are also very similar to those of a formula given by Lappin and Uttal (1976) for the percentages of correct responses in a two-alternative forced-choice detection task, when one of M alternative stimuli is presented in one of two observation intervals. Peterson, Birdsall, and Fox (1954) developed a different formula based on an approximation to the distribution of the likelihood ratio for a signal detection task with additive white Gaussian noise. At lower levels of detectability, their formula also predicts very similar performance decrements with increasing set size, but as Nolte and Jaarsma (1967) demonstrate, their formula predicts too small a performance decrement from increased set size at high levels of detectability.

Finally, we can consider how RT varies with the set size, M. First we need to assume that RT is a linear function of the observation interval, T—i.e., RT = $a + bT$.[5] Additionally, suppose that the perceived stimulus information is homogeneous in time—i.e.,

$$\frac{\int_0^T s_i(t)\,dt}{\int_0^{T'} s_i(t)\,dt} = \frac{T}{T'}$$

Recall also that the noise $n(t)$ is assumed to have a homogeneous and stationary distribution with variance proportional to the observation interval, T. If the filter, $h(t)$, is also defined to give equal weight to observations over the whole interval T, then we have from the preceding equations

$$d_{MT} = \frac{1}{\sqrt{M}} \int_0^T s_i(t)^2\,dt,$$

so that

$$\frac{d_{MT}}{d_{MT'}} = \frac{T}{T'}$$

Similarily, from the assumed characteristics of the noise process, the variance of the filter output, var $(Y \mid h, T)$, is also directly proportional to the observation interval—i.e.,

$$\frac{\text{var}(Y \mid h, T)}{\text{var}(Y \mid h, T')} = \frac{T}{T'} \tag{18}$$

[5]It may be noticed that T has been used to represent both time and any other component variables on which the observations may be defined. For present purposes, it is necessary to assume simply that T is proportional to the total duration of observation. Whatever other components might be included in the total bandwidth, we assume that they are constant. It may also be noted that the limit of integration, T plays the same role as the bandwidth of the filter, $h(t)$. By defining $h(t)$ to have nonzero values only over a specific interval, T, we could accomplish the same results by restrictions on the bandwidth of the filter and allow the integration to extend from 0 to $+\infty$. The present construction, with arbitrary limits on the range of integration over a single dimension, seems less cumbersome than more complete constructions.

Now we find the dependence of the discrimination accuracy, D_{MT}, on the interval T as follows:

$$\frac{D_{MT}}{D_{MT'}} = \frac{d_{MT}/\sqrt{\text{Var}(Y \mid h, T)}}{d_{MT'}/\sqrt{\text{Var}(Y \mid h, T')}} = \frac{T}{T'} \cdot \left(\frac{T'}{T}\right)^{\frac{1}{2}}$$

$$= \left(\frac{T}{T'}\right)^{\frac{1}{2}} \tag{19}$$

In other words, discriminability as measured by the signal/noise ratio, D_{MT}, is proportional to the square root of the observation interval, $\sqrt{T}$. Indeed, the predicted linear relationship between RT and the squared discrimination measure $(d')^2$ has been reported by several investigators (e.g., see Green & Luce, 1973; Lappin & Disch, 1972; Taylor, Lindsay, & Forbes, 1967).

In order to find the relation between set size, M, and RT for a constant level of discrimination accuracy, notice that the discrimination measure D_{MT} is inversely proportional to the square root of the set size. That is,

$$\frac{D_{MT}}{D_{M'T}} = \left(\frac{M'}{M}\right)^{\frac{1}{2}} \tag{20}$$

Accordingly, the decrement in discrimination associated with an increase in set size can be compensated by a corresponding increase in the observation interval. Suppose that the set size is increased from M to kM; then the resulting decrement in discrimination accuracy can be offset by increasing the observation interval from T to kT:

$$D_{(kM)T} = \left(\frac{1}{k}\right)^{\frac{1}{2}} D_{MT}$$

$$D_{M(kT)} = k^{\frac{1}{2}} D_{MT}$$

$$D_{(kM)(kT)} = D_{MT}$$

Recalling that RT is linearly related to T, this completes the demonstration. RT should be a linearly increasing function of M.

Thus this linear system for discriminating between stimuli will produce the same relation between set size and RT that often has been obtained experimentally (e.g., see Sternberg, 1975). In the same way the linear relation between set size and the variance of the RTs (Sternberg, 1969) follows immediately from the assumption that the variability or noise is generated by a Poisson process, where the variance in the waiting time for the nth event is proportional to n. Further, the present system also yields additive effects on RT from variations in stimulus intensity or clarity and from set size, as shown in Eq. 14 and as has been found experimentally (e.g., Sternberg, 1969). The fundamental reason why these relationships occur in the present system is the same as the reason for their occurrence in most theories of memory scanning—namely, both are linear systems.

In contrast to many theories about memory scanning, however, the present analysis does not attribute these additive effects on RT to the serial addition of temporally distinct stages. Rather, these additive effects are attributed to the linearity of a parallel discrimination system. The present demonstration merely illustrates the isomorphism of many serial and parallel systems—a topic that has been studied in greater detail and generality by Townsend (1976).

Moreover, these effects of prior knowledge on the speed and accuracy of recognition are predicted for an *ideal observer* with no limitations on perception, memory, etc. Whether or not set size might affect the *perceptual* process, effects of set size on observed recognition performance may be expected to result from the observer's uncertainty about which stimulus variables to employ in his *decision* process.

Are these effects of prior knowledge about the set of alternatives produced by perceptual or by decision processes? The question is moot. The concept of a "filter" as employed in the preceding development may suggest some type of perceptual or attentional channel that transmits only some limited portion of the available stimulus information. No limitations on the availability of information are necessary, however. Actually, the observed effects of this filter would be the same in many tasks, including those considered in this chapter, whether the filter were located nearer the input or the output of the system. The performance characteristic most closely associated with the distinction between perceptual and decision processes is the response latency for modifying the filter to adapt to newly acquired information and the decay rate for information from the recent past that might be reevaluated in the light of new information about its relevance. An examination of this important problem is beyond the scope of this paper, but it seems apparent that a great deal remains to be learned. Perhaps the most relevant studies have been contributed by Eriksen and his colleagues (e.g., Eriksen & Hoffman, 1972). As far as the present results are concerned, the observer could be assumed to have unlimited access to past information. The so-called filter could be associated entirely with the particular information the observer employs as decision criteria in choosing a response.

The inevitability of the detrimental effects of increased set size, whether their origin is considered as perception or decision, is suggested by an experiment recently conducted with William Uttal (Lappin & Uttal, 1976). A forced-choice detection task was used to investigate the effect of set size on visual form detection. In separate experimental conditions, a target form was presented at one of either two, four, or eight alternative positions in either of two successive patterns of random visual noise. The observer's task was simply to decide whether the form occurred in the first or the second of the two patterns of noise presented on each trial. We reasoned that with a smaller set of potential target positions, the observer might be able to focus his attention more effectively, thereby improving the detectability of the form.

Detection accuracy was found to decrease sharply with increased set size, but the decrease was fully accounted for by the assumption that noise events occurring at each of the possible target positions were independently confusable with the true target. Evidently, the prior knowledge associated with a smaller set of possible positions merely allowed the observer to ignore irrelevant information occurring at impossible target positions. Because the obtained effect of set size on detection accuracy did not depart from the predicted performance of an ideal observer, there was no evidence that prior knowledge permitted the allocation of greater perceptual resources to the potential target positions. Without some clear evidence for variations in the availability of perceptual information, it seems safer to attribute the effect of prior knowledge to the decision process.

The words of Green and Swets (1966) are helpful:

> If a change in the stimulus situation makes the signal harder to detect for the ideal observer, then we shall not be surprised if the same change makes the signal harder to detect for the human observer. The principle is parsimony—it is unnecessary to invent psychological mechanisms to explain a change that may be traced to the stimulus situation itself [p. 152].

8. CONCLUSION

The length and formalisms of this chapter should not disguise the simplicity of the basic ideas. The origin of many of these ideas owes as much, perhaps, to the seminal work of Tanner (e.g., Tanner, 1956; Tanner & Birdsall, 1958) as to any other single source. In particular, the concept of the ideal observer and the analysis of the effects of the observer's uncertainty about stimulus parameters provide the foundation for the theory in Sec. 7. This chapter merely applies these concepts to the interpretation of performance in tasks used for studying human information processing. When stimulus presentations are regarded as information for discriminating among the alternatives, and when responses are regarded as choices based on rational decisions about this information, then certain aspects of human information processing seem less complicated than they first appeared. At any rate, the aim of this chapter is to reveal simplicity in certain aspects of the role of prior knowledge in recognition.

The most important assumption is what is termed the *Relativity of Choice Behavior.* The assumption is: (1) perceptual information about stimuli should be represented in terms of relations between stimuli; and (2) responses should be represented as choices among alternative classifications of any given perceptual information. Presumably, the same representation should apply equally to interpretations of both the speed and accuracy of performance. In both cases, prior knowledge is considered as the coequal of present information in choosing a response. The meaning of this relativistic representation is to be understood by contrast with the representation of human perception and performance as the processing of digital information about individual stimuli and responses. The justification for the relativistic representation derives in part from a more general epistemology.

The second most important assumption is that the source of uncertainty in perception and the source of errors and latency in responses is a stochastic process that is: (1) independent of the stimulus presentation; (2) stochastically independent at separate points in space and time; and (3) homogeneously distributed with the same parameters at separate points in space and time. Parts (2) and (3) of this assumption define a Poisson process. Parts (1) and (2) are the most important; modest violations of part (3) could probably be tolerated with comparatively small impact on overall performance. Although this simple assumption was adopted partly as a matter of convenience for developing the theory in Sec. 7, it turns out to have broad implications not only for the role of prior knowledge in recognition but also for the neurophysiological functioning of the brain as a whole. Insofar as the assumption may be valid, the brain may be said to function as a "parallel coherent detection system" (Trehub, 1971), which is optimal for a large class of detection tasks. This is a linear system in which the output signal/noise ratio remains proportional to the input signal/noise ratio. It may be noted that this assumption about the stochastic processes underlying perception can be empirically tested in a variety of experiments, although an examination of the available evidence is beyond the scope of this chapter. A significant body of evidence can be found to lend at least indirect support for this assumption, but many clear examples of nonlinearity can also be found. The task is to develop an understanding of the conditions under which this assumption can be expected to apply. Questions about the validity of this stochastic assumption are not unrelated to questions about the validity of the Relativity of Choice Behavior.

ACKNOWLEDGMENTS

Preparation of this report was supported by NSF Grant # BMS−75−19103. Some of the experimental work was also supported by NIMH Grant # MH−21105. The present version of this paper has benefited very significantly from the insightful criticisms of James Townsend, the unusually attentive editing of John Castellan and Steve Link, and helpful discussions with Bruce Bloxom and Saul Sternberg. Their contributions are gratefully acknowledged.

REFERENCES

Anderson, J. A. A theory for the recognition of items for short memorized lists. *Psychological Review*, 1973, *80*, 417-438.

Anderson, T. W. *An introduction to multivariate statistical analysis.* New York: Wiley, 1958.

Bohm, D. Some remarks on the notion of order, *and* further remarks on order. In C. H. Waddington (Ed.), *Towards a theoretical biology* (Vol. 2). Chicago: Aldine, 1969.

Bush, R. R., Galanter, E., & Luce, R. D. Characterization and classification of choice experiments. In R. D. Luce, R. R. Bush, & E. Galanter (Eds.), *Handbook of mathematical psychology* (Vol. I). New York: Wiley, 1963.

Cassirer, E. *Substance and function and Einstein's theory of relativity.* Chicago: Open Court, 1923. Also republished by Dover, New York, 1953.

Eriksen, C. W., & Hoffman, J. E. Temporal and spatial characteristics of selective encoding from visual displays. *Perception & Psychophysics*, 1972, *12*, 201-204.

Garner, W. R. *Uncertainty and structure as psychological concepts.* New York: Wiley, 1962.

Garner, W. R. *The processing of information and structure.* Potomac, Md.: Lawrence Erlbaum Associates, 1974.

Green, D. M., & Luce, R. D. Speed-accuracy trade off in auditory detection. In S. Kornblum (Ed.), *Attention and performance IV. New York: Academic Press, 1973.*

Green, D. M., & Swets, J. A. *Signal detection theory and psychophysics.* New York: Wiley, 1966.

Harm, O. J., & Lappin, J. S. Probability, compatibility, speed, and accuracy. *Journal of Experimental Psychology*, 1973, *100*, 416-418.

Harman, W. W. *Principles of the statistical theory of communication.* New York: McGraw-Hill, 1963.

Kinchla, R. A. Detecting target elements in multielement arrays: A confusability model. *Perception and Psychophysics*, 1974, *15*, 149-158.

LaBerge, D., & Tweedy, J. R. Presentation probability and choice time. *Journal of Experimental Psychology*, 1964, *68*, 477-481.

Lappin, J. S., & Disch, K. The latency operating characteristic: I. Effects of stimulus probability on choice reaction time. *Journal of Experimental Psychology*, 1972, *92*, 419-427.

Lappin, J. S., & Uttal, W. R. Does prior knowledge facilitate the detection of visual targets in random noise? *Perception & Psychophysics*, 1976, *20*, 367-374.

Luce, R. D. *Individual choice behavior.* New York: Wiley, 1959.

Luce, R. D. Detection and recognition. In R. D. Luce, R. R. Bush, & E. Galanter (Eds.), *Handbook of mathematical psychology* (Vol. I). New York: Wiley, 1963.

Nakatani, L. H. Confusion-choice model for multidimensional psychophysics. *Journal of Mathematical Psychology*, 1972, *9*, 104-127.

Nolte, L. W., & Jaarsma, D. More on the detection of one of M orthogonal signals. *Journal of the Acoustical Society of America*, 1967, *41*, 497-505.

Pachella, R. G. The interpretation of reaction time in information-processing research. In B. H. Kantowitz (Ed.), *Human information processing: Tutorials in performance and cognition.* Hillsdale, N.J.: Lawrence Erlbaum Associates, 1974.

Peterson, W. W., Birdsall, T. G., & Fox, W. C. The theory of signal detectability. *IRE Transactions on Information Theory*, 1954, *4*, 171-212.

Shepard, R. N. Stimulus and response generalization: A stochastic model relating generalization to distance in psychological space. *Psychometrika*, 1957, *22*, 325-345.

Sternberg, S. The discovery of processing stages: Extensions of Donders' method. *(Attention and Performance II) Acta Psychologica*, 1969, *30*, 276-315.

Sternberg, S. Memory scanning: New findings and current controversies. *Quarterly Journal of Experimental Psychology,* 1975, *27,* 1-32.

Tanner, W. P., Jr. Theory of recognition. *Journal of Acoustical Society of America,* 1956, *28,* 882-888. Also in J. A. Swets (Ed.), *Signal detection and recognition by human observers.* New York: Wiley, 1974.

Tanner, W. P. Jr., & Birdsall, T. G. Definitions of d' and η as psychophysical measures. *Journal of Acoustical Society of America,* 1958, *30,* 922-928. Also in J. A. Swets (Ed.), *Signal detection and recognition by human observers.* New York: Wiley, 1964.

Taylor, M. M., Lindsay, P. H., & Forbes, S. M. Quantification of shared capacity processing in auditory and visual discrimination. *Acta Psychologica,* 1967, *27,* 223-229.

Townsend, J. T. Theoretical analysis of an alphabetic confusion matrix. *Perception & Psychophysics,* 1971, *9,* 40-50.

Townsend, J. T. Serial and within-stage independent parallel model equivalence on the minimum completion time. *Journal of Mathematical Psychology,* 1976, *14,* 219-238.

Trehub, A. The brain as a parallel coherent detector. *Science,* 1971, *174,* 722-723.

Wood, C. C., & Jennings, J. R. Speed-accuracy tradeoff functions in choice reaction time: Experimental designs and computational procedures. *Perception & Psychophysics,* 1976, *19,* 92-101.

7

Qualitative Error Analysis and Speeded Classification

Robert G. Pachella
J. E. Keith Smith
Human Performance Center, University of Michigan
   and
Keith E. Stanovich
Oakland University

INTRODUCTION

A number of writers (Pachella, 1974; Wickelgren, 1977; Ollman, 1977) have recently expressed concern with the growing dependency of cognitive psychology on experimental paradigms that utilize reaction time as their basic dependent variable. This concern has focused on the manner in which the majority of investigators who have used these paradigms have interpreted the obtained reaction times in the theoretical accounts of the phenomena that they have studied. Typically, reaction times have been interpreted in a manner that is simple, straightforward, and intuitively appealing. However, recent empirical findings about the nature of reaction time measures (Pachella, 1974; Ollman, 1977) have indicated that there may be some serious and fundamental problems associated with this naive interpretation; and with such an extensive effort of cognitive psychologists centering around the use of this single variable, it has become crucial that the variable come under close scrutiny. Problems and limitations that are basic to the use of reaction time paradigms in general are likely to have far-reaching effects on our understanding of many substantive issues. Thus the research presented in this Chapter is a product of such a scrutiny, and it is the hope of the investigators that it leads to both a fuller understanding of the limitations of reaction time methodology and points in the direction of some useful alternatives.

The typical intuitive interpretation of reaction time involves a number of assumptions. The most important of these is that reaction time is a direct measure of the duration of mental activity. It is the nature of mental events that they are often not accompanied by any overt behavioral activity. Other dependent variables such as "percent correct" tend not to be properties of mental events but rather consequences of them. Thus the only simple property of mental events that can be studied directly, while the events are taking place, is their duration.

Second, reaction time is taken not only to be a measure of the duration of mental activity, but it is also assumed to be the *minimum* duration for which an accurate performance can be obtained. Under the usual interpretation of reaction time, it is believed that the mental activity taking place is densely packed, that there is no wasted time. Quite obviously subjects could produce times that are longer than this minimum simply by delaying their response (or by delaying any particular mental activity necessary for the completion of the task), but they are instructed not to do this. They are instructed to respond as quickly as possible. Furthermore, in addition to being asked not to waste any time, subjects are also asked not to rush their responses. In other words, they are asked not to make errors. Thus the reaction times interpreted by most theorists represent an optimal or an ideal performance: They are the minimum durations for which maximum accuracy can be maintained.

Finally, there is a methodological assumption that underlies the use of reaction time paradigms. Simply stated, it is the belief that subjects are capable of finding this optimal level of performance and that they can maintain their performance during an experiment at this level when simply instructed to do so. In other words, reaction times are interpreted on the basis of the instruction to the subject to respond as quickly and as accurately as possible, and there is seldom any converging methodological operation to check whether performance actually meets this criterion. Indeed, common practice has been to remove trials from the data on which the subject has made an error, and undoubtedly this practice is motivated by the belief that the resulting data conform to the desired norm. However, such a practice makes additional theoretical assumptions about the nature of the reaction time interval. In particular, it assumes that an error represents a local perturbation of performance, confined solely to the trial on which the error occurred, and that the remaining reaction times are unaffected.

The major consequence of these assumptions is that reaction time is assumed to be a real, *physical* property of mental activity, namely its duration. As a physical variable, time has certain scaling and measurement properties that many other dependent variables available to the psychologist do not have. In particular, it is a ratio measure and differs from other measures, like percent correct or trials to criterion, by permitting the theorist to interpret statistical interactions (or the lack thereof), the particular shapes of functions, or the slopes of regression lines, without having to worry about the scaling of the dependent variable. Thus the range of quantitative and statistical procedures and the modes of theoretical explanation that are available to the experimenter who uses reaction time measures is greatly increased.

There are a number of serious logical and empirical problems with this intuitive interpretation of reaction time. These problems call into question the idea that reaction time can be considered a direct index of the duration of mental activity; and, at the very least, they suggest that only ordinal measurement properties can be assumed for these measures.

In order to understand the problems associated with reaction-time measurement, one must carefully consider another measure of performance, performance accuracy. Subjects invariably make errors in reaction-time tasks. They do so in spite of the fact that they are instructed not to make errors and in spite of the fact that the tasks used in most reaction-time paradigms are trivially simple. For example, it is not unusual to have subjects make from two to six percent errors in a task that simply calls on them to name a single letter when it is presented (e.g., Theios, 1973). Clearly, the circumstances surrounding the measurement of reaction time lead subjects to make errors that they would avoid under other circumstances.

The study of the relation of error rates to reaction-time measures has come to be known as the speed-accuracy trade-off (Fitts, 1966). It is clear intuitively, and has been demonstrated empirically, that for any information-processing task there exists a family of possible performances. Subjects can work very slowly and carefully making no errors at all; they can work at high rates while making numerous errors, or they can work at some point in between these two extremes. Over the past 10 years, many investigators have caused subjects to produce these various performances by differentially emphasizing speed or accuracy and have been able to trace the relationship of these two variables for a particular task in the form of an operating characteristic. An idealization of such a function is illustrated in Fig. 1.

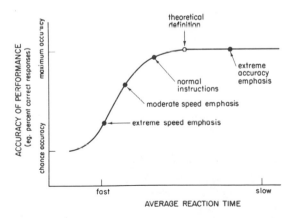

FIG. 1   An idealized speed-accuracy trade-off function.

Although there are at least two distinct ways of obtaining speed-accuracy operating characteristics, all of the functions that have been reported in the literature share the general characteristics depicted in Fig. 1: Performance accuracy, when transformed into a measure of percentage of correct responses, is a monotonically increasing, negatively accelerated function of reaction time. There are several important implications of this function with regard to the interpretation of reaction-time measures.

First, only one point on the function corresponds to the performance necessary for the usual interpretation given to reaction time. This point, indicated with the open circle and labeled "theoretical definition," is the fastest reaction time at which maximum accuracy is maintained. As noted above, the normal instructions to a subject yield a performance somewhat below this value.

Second, if subjects actually produced no errors in an experiment, the theorist would be at a loss to interpret the obtained reaction times, because there are an infinite number of reaction times that can result in zero errors (i.e., all of the points to the right of the open circle). The problem that confronts the subject when performing in a reaction-time experiment is essentially the same as that confronting the theorist: If a subject never made an error, how would he know if he were anywhere close to the optimum operating point? Although the usual interpretation of reaction time assumes that a subject can find this point when instructed to do so, it is clear from empirical evidence that there are situations (tasks) in which he or she cannot (Rabbitt, 1966). Moreover, the subject must find this point and *continue to track it* by making at least an occasional error (Rabbitt & Vyas, 1970). Thus, in order to come close to optimum performance, the subject must perform at a point that is slightly below the optimum value assumed by the usual interpretation of reaction time.

Third, it should not matter that subjects do not perform at the point assumed by most cognitive theorists. Of greater importance is the possibility that differences in the criterion for speed versus accuracy may be correlated with experimental conditions. The danger in this possibility is that in many experiments, although the differences in error rates go unreported (perhaps because of a lack of statistical significance due to their small number), they may be correlated with the experimental conditions. Thus it is possible that subjects may vary from condition to condition to the extent to which they tend to rush their responses.

Finally, the limitations on the interpretability of reaction time due to variability in error rates is accentuated by the general form of the speed-accuracy operating characteristic. Given percent correct as the accuracy measure, the practical significance of the observed negative acceleration lies in the fact that small differences in error rate can be associated with large differences in reaction time. This is particularly true for the range of high overall accuracy (90% to 100%) typically found in reaction-time experiments. This means that what may look like relatively meaningless differences in accuracy may contaminate reaction-time values extensively.

Recently, there have been a number of findings about classical reaction-time phenomena that have illustrated the dangers indicated in the foregoing. For example, Posner, Klein, Summers, and Buggie (1973) found that the decrease in reaction time due to short foreperiods, which has classically been attributed to increased alertness, is at least partially due to a speed-accuracy trade-off: Subjects respond more quickly but at a cost in accuracy. Likewise, Swensson (1972b) was able to show that in serial reaction-time tasks, part of the repetition effect (the decreased reaction time for repeated responses) was attributable to differences in the speed-accuracy criterion. Further, Pachella (1972) argued that the equality of the slopes of memory-scanning functions for "yes" and "no" responses may be an artifact: When the slopes are adjusted to account for error-rate difference, the obtained equality may vanish.

Some recent findings in applied situations also have illustrated dramatic speed-accuracy effects. For example, Jennings, Wood, and Lawrence (1976) investigated the effects of alcohol doses on reaction time. They found that the inconsistency in previous results concerning the effects of alcohol were related to trade-off effects: Whereas alcohol reduced performance efficiency by decreasing the rate of increase of accuracy per unit time, changes in subjects' criterion for speed yielded faster reaction times, particularly at high dose levels.

The previous considerations seem to force the conclusion that the interpretation of reaction-time measures is not nearly as straightforward as has been generally believed. Instead of assuming reaction time to have ratio or interval measurement properties, investigators would undoubtedly be more realistic if they would assume reaction-time data to have only ordinal interpretations. That is, they would be more accurate in the theoretical use of data if they were to assume that the reaction-time measures merely ordered experimental conditions. However, even this level of measurement may be inappropriate in the presence of a strong negative correlation between reaction time and error rate. Fast reaction times and high error rates in one condition and slow reaction times and low error rates in another could result even though the former condition was the more difficult or involved the more complex mental processing. In this situation even the direction of the reaction-time difference could be the result of artifactual differences in criteria for speed versus accuracy.

In many less extreme circumstances, the correlation between reaction time and error is positive: The "more difficult" conditions yield both slower reaction times and higher error rates than the "easier" conditions. Here, the assumption of ordinal measurement is more reasonable. However, interval properties for the data still may not be assumed. If the observed error differences are a result of differential speed-accuracy criteria, then the possibility exists that the magnitude of the observed reaction time difference is artifactually too small. Thus the magnitude of differences, even in the presence of a positive correlation of reaction time and errors, cannot be interpreted directly.

Finally, there is another class of logical problems that further attests to the need for the exploration of the relationship between the speed and the accuracy of performance. These problems concern the extent to which reaction-time paradigms resemble the conditions of "normal" information processing. For the moment assume that there are no methodological problems associated with the collection of reaction-time data and that the errors that occur represent insignificant variability that does not interact with any experimental manipulation of interest. In other words, assume that subjects are perfectly capable of producing responses that correspond to the point of minimum time at which maximum accuracy can be maintained. Then theoretical models based solely on this single class of data would be limited, because they would be based on a single point in what is obviously a continuum of performances. There is no doubt that people can control the speed of their responses to stimuli and that this ability is related to the accuracy of their performance. It is also likely that the speed at which people normally function is *not* that which corresponds to a rate that is consistent with typical reaction-time instructions. For certain kinds of cognitive functioning, the normal speed of operation is probably much slower than this rate; for other human abilities, normal performance may be much faster than this rate. Further, the particular nature of the mental activity underlying performance may change as a function of speed criterion. Thus, without the appropriate data base, there is no way of knowing whether or not the data typically collected can be reasonably generalized to these other classes of performance.

Given these problems with reaction-time paradigms and the limitations of the data derived from them, it should be clear that there is need to examine in detail the nature of the errors that occur when subjects make speeded reactions in cognitive experiments. Furthermore, theories need to be developed that not only account for the occurrence of these errors but also describe both the quantitative and qualitative changes that take place as a result of changes in the operating criterion for speed versus accuracy.

AN ALTERNATIVE RESEARCH STRATEGY

If reaction time, as an index of the duration of mental processes, has only an ordinal relation to the actual durations of those processes. then it is no better as a measure than many other dependent variables that might be chosen in the study of information processing. In particular, it is probably no better as a measure than the error rates obtained in reaction-time experiments. Statistical problems in the use of error rates as a performance measure do become particularly severe when subjects are instructed to perform with high accuracy as has been common. In this region (see Fig. 1), very different speed-accuracy trade-off functions (SATFs) generate very small differences in error rates. Except for this, the error rates could function just as well as an index of mental processing complexity. In order to understand the importance of this assertion, the implicit methodological assumptions underlying the typical reaction-time experiment must again be considered. The typical experiment involves presenting a task to the subject and asking him to produce an errorless performance (as noted previously, a feat that is rarely accomplished). Differences in reaction time are then used to imply differences in the structure of the underlying mental operations. However, given the notion of speed-accuracy operating characteristic developed earlier, the logic of this experiment can be reversed without modifying the interpretation of the resulting performance measure: A subject could be asked to produce responses of some constant (or equally distributed) duration across all conditions of an experiment. Differences in error rate for the various conditions could then be taken as an index of the structure of mental operations. Ideally, this latter experiment would produce error rates that would correlate perfectly with the reaction times obtained in the former experiment. If reaction time has only ordinal properties, the two experiments are completely equivalent with regard to their ability to assess the level of processing difficulty of the experimental conditions.

Under these circumstances, however, the error measures can yield more information about the nature of the underlying mental operations than can the corresponding reaction-time measures. The reaction-time measures, even when produced under errorless performance, produce only an ordering of the level of difficulty of the experimental conditions. They produce no qualitative information about the relationships between various stimuli and responses. The error measures, on the other hand, not only produce the same ordering among the conditions but, in addition, supply a descriptive profile of the specific confusions produced by the subject. That is, from the distribution of the specific incorrect responses made to each stimulus, it is possible to reconstruct relationships between stimuli and responses from which detailed models of mental processing can be deduced. Many of these models (e.g., Luce's Choice Model) have had extensive theoretical and empirical development, and the application of these models to the errors produced in the context of reaction-time experimentation can supply additional qualitative information that cannot be obtained from latency measures by themselves.

The research discussed in the following makes extensive use of the general experimental strategy alluded to earlier. This paradigm has been developed and used extensively by the present investigators for the past 10 years (Pachella & Pew, 1968; Pachella & Fisher, 1972; Stanovich, Pachella, Smith, 1977), and similar methods have independently appeared elsewhere (Schouten & Bekker, 1967; Link, 1971; Yellott, 1971; Reed, 1973). The fundamental object of the paradigm is to have the subject of the experiment systematically vary his or her "operating point" on the speed-accuracy operating characteristic. The accuracy is then measured at each different speed at which the subject works, and, in particular, the manner in which his or her performance changes as a function of speed emphasis is studied in detail. In contrast to the more typical approach, the subject is trained to emit responses within a particular time interval and to sacrifice accuracy in order to achieve this goal. There are several alternative methods used to produce this performance in subjects (see Reed, 1976, or Schouten & Bekker, 1967), but the one developed by the present investigators (Pachella & Pew, 1968) involves specifying a response-time deadline, which the subject attempts to beat. With appropriate feedback and with a minimum of training, subjects acquire the ability to produce responses within the deadlines. Thus the technique allows the subject to effectively manipulate response time.

The basic datum that arises from this paradigm is an operating characteristic such as that pictured in Fig. 1. Substantive questions of interest then involve asking how this bivariate relation changes as a function of various experimental conditions. Potentially recoverable from this operating characteristic approach, either by extrapolation or interpolation (depending on the range of the speed-accuracy manipulation), is the point that corresponds to the definition of reaction time used in much current theory development in cognitive psychology, i.e., the minimum time to produce maximum accuracy. Thus the data of the normal or usual reaction-time paradigm is, under ideal circumstances, a derivative subset of the data acquired under this alternative methodology. It represents just a single point from each operating characteristic for each experimental condition.

Previous research that has utilized the foregoing strategy generally has been focused on the form of the speed-accuracy operating characteristic or derivative measures (e.g., Pachella, 1974; Reed, 1976; or Wood & Jennings, 1976). Further, most of this previous research has been limited to experimental tasks that involve only two alternative responses. The reason for this limitation has been theoretical: Most of the relevant theories about the generation of reaction time make precise predictions only for the case with two alternatives. However, the experimental work discussed here uses multiple stimuli and multiple response tasks. In its fullest development, the speed-accuracy operating characteristic consists of a confusion matrix for each speed-constraint condition. The present research strategy, then, consists of the analysis of each of these confusion matrices according both to known psychometric models (e.g., Luce, 1963) and to models developed in this chapter. The analysis of experimental data consists of the estimation of the parameters for the confusion matrices, the investigation of the changes in these parameters as a function of experimental conditions, and the extrapolation of these changes back into inferences about the structure of the information-processing dynamics of the subjects.

MODELS FOR CONFUSION DATA

The experimental paradigm described in the final section involves an experimental task in which a series of stimuli are presented to a highly practiced subject for verbal identification under a number of experimental conditions. The subjects are practiced at responding under various speed-constraint conditions defined by response-time deadlines. The basic data of the experiment consists of confusion matrices for each experimental and speed-constraint condition. The foci of interest are these distributions of errors as well as a new model that gives a rather precise account of the errors. The new model, which we call the Informed Guessing Model, is intimately related to the Luce (1963) Biased Choice Model and the model that Townsend (1971) has called the "Stimulus Activation" Model, or more simply, the "Overlap" Model. Technically, this new model is not identifiably different from either of the two previous models, which we show are not identifiably different from each other. However, the new model has advantages over each of the others in terms of the interpretations that may be made of subject performance.

The Luce Biased Choice Model

The Biased Choice Model states that the probability, p_{ij}, of Response j when Stimulus i is presented can be represented as proportional to the product of a parameter representing the tendency to use Response j, call it β_j, and a parameter representing the similarity of Stimuli i and j, call it η_{ij}. It is further assumed that similarity, and hence η, is a symmetric concept $(\eta_{ij} = \eta_{ji})$, and without loss of generality that the similarity of a stimulus with itself is equal to 1 $(\eta_{ii} = 1)$. Algebraically,

$$p_{ij} = \frac{\beta_j \eta_{ij}}{\alpha_i} \tag{1}$$

where $\Sigma \beta_j = 1$, and $\alpha_i = \Sigma_j \beta_j \eta_{ij}$.

This model has proved to be extremely robust with regard to analyzing confusion matrices from perceptual identification experiments, but it has the important disadvantage of not yielding an account of itself in terms of a process. That is, it is a purely descriptive model and does not describe a mechanism whereby Stimulus i leads to Response j. By contrast, the Townsend Overlap Model and the Informed Guessing Model each supply an elementary (perhaps the most elementary) processing account.

The Townsend Overlap Model

The overlap model asserts that when Stimulus i is presented, it is processed enough to be identified with probability ξ_i, or at least enough so that the only uncertainty that remains is whether the stimulus is i or j, with probability ξ_{ij}. In the latter case, Response i is made with odds $b_i:b_j$, where b has an interpretation similar to that of β in the foregoing. It is assumed that $\xi_{ij} = \xi_{ji}$, i.e., the probability of the confusion set (i, j) is the same whether the stimulus is i or j. One justification for this assumption is that were it not the case, the mere existence of the confusion set would be informative about which stimulus had, in fact, been presented. In general, the algebraic representation is

$$p_{ij} = \frac{b_j}{b_i + b_j} \xi_{ij}, \qquad j \neq i$$

$$p_{ii} = c_i = 1 - \sum_{j \neq i} p_{ij} \tag{2}$$

where $\xi_{ij} = \xi_{ji}$, $\sum b_i = 1$, and $\xi_i = 1 - \sum_{j \neq i} \xi_{ij}$.

Identifiability of Alternative Models

Two model types are nonidentifiable with respect to a set of data if for each model of one type there exists a model of the other type that yields the same description of the data. In the cases of the Biased Choice Model and the Overlap Model, there exists a one-to-one transformation of each parameter space into the other:

Townsend parameters in Luce terms:

$$b_i = \frac{\beta_i \alpha_i}{\Sigma_j \beta_j \alpha_j}$$

$$\xi_{ij} = \eta_{ij} \left(\frac{\beta_i}{\alpha_j} + \frac{\beta_j}{\alpha_i} \right), \qquad i \neq j$$

$$c_i = \frac{\beta_i}{\alpha_i} \tag{3}$$

Luce parameters in Townsend terms:

$$\beta_i = \frac{\sqrt{b_i c_i}}{\Sigma_j \sqrt{b_j c_j}}$$

$$\eta_{ij} = \left(\frac{\xi_{ij}}{b_i + b_j} \right) \sqrt{\frac{b_i b_j}{c_i c_j}}, \qquad i \neq j$$

$$\alpha_i = \left(\frac{1}{c_i} \right) \frac{\sqrt{b_i c_i}}{\Sigma_j \sqrt{b_j c_j}}. \tag{4}$$

The nonidentifiability demonstrated by Eqs. (2), (3), and (4) holds, however, only where no further constraints are imposed on ξ_i. Equation (3), for a particular set of Luce parameters, may lead to negative values of ξ_i, contrary to the interpretation of ξ_i as a probability. The region of the Luce parameter space corresponding to valid Overlap Model parameters is nevertheless measurable with respect to the total Luce parameter space, so that likelihood ratio tests cannot be applied for testing the Overlap Model relative to the Luce Model. We define two model-types to be quasi-nonidentifiable (QNI) if the image of each is measurable in the parameter space of the other. This anomaly arises when errors are numerous; moreover, it is shown that the Overlap Model imposes restrictions on the data that are intuitively unappealing. The Informed Guessing Model, discussed later, is also QNI with respect to the Luce Model, but in no data so far observed has this problem arisen using the Informed Guessing Model.

Parameter estimation.   These two model types are among many that are not identifiable (QNI) on the basis of identification experiments alone. All share the property that predicts the following characteristic of the data. Let e_{ij} be the predicted number of times that Response j is made to Stimulus i by any one of the models. Then, for data fitting these models,

$$e_{ij}e_{jk}e_{ki} = e_{ji}e_{ik}e_{kj} \qquad \text{for all } i, j, k \tag{5}$$

This property defines a "quasi-symmetric" contingency table, and maximum likelihood procedures exist for finding the best-fitting e_{ij} (Bishop, Fienberg, & Holland, 1975, p. 289). Specifically, it can be shown that the maximum likelihood estimates, $e_{ij} = (n_i \cdot \hat{\beta}_j \hat{n}_{ij})/\hat{\alpha}_i$, satisfy the following equations:

$$\sum_j e_{ij} = \sum_j n_{ij},$$

$$\sum_i e_{ij} = \sum_i n_{ij},$$

$$e_{ij} + e_{ji} = n_{ij} + n_{ji} \qquad i \neq j, \tag{6}$$

$$e_{ii} = n_{ii}.$$

Although solutions for these e_{ij} cannot be found in closed form, estimates with any degree of accuracy can be obtained by the following iterative procedure:

$$e_{ij}^{(0)} = 1 \qquad i \neq j, e_{ii}^{(0)} = n_{ij}$$

$$e_{ij}^{(3r+1)} = e_{ij}^{(3r)} \frac{n_{i\cdot}'}{e_{i\cdot}'^{(3r)}}$$

where

$$n_{i\cdot}' = \sum_{j \neq i} n_{ij} \qquad \text{and} \qquad e_{i\cdot}'^{(r)} = \sum_{j \neq i} e_{ij}^{(r)} \tag{7a}$$

$$e_{ij}^{(3r+2)} = e_{ij}^{(3r+1)} \frac{n_{j\cdot}'}{e_j'^{(3r+1)}} \tag{7b}$$

$$e_{ij}^{(3r+3)} = e_{ij}^{(3r+2)} \frac{n_{ij} + n_{ji}}{e_{ij}^{(3r+2)} + e_{ji}^{(3r+2)}} \tag{7c}$$

where r indexes the iteration cycles $(r = 0, 1, \ldots)$.

That is, a first approximation setting all expected values to one is iteratively modified by proportional adjustment first to row totals, then column totals, then symmetric error cells. It can be shown that all $e_{ij}(r)$ satisfy (5) and that the limiting values of the e_{ij}s are maximum likelihood estimates of cell frequencies. Once the expected frequencies are estimated, maximum likelihood estimates of either type of parameter can be obtained simply by algebraic manipulation; specifically,

$$\hat{\eta}_{ij} = \sqrt{\frac{e_{ij}e_{ji}}{e_{ii}e_{jj}}} \quad \text{and} \quad \frac{\hat{\beta}_j}{\hat{\beta}_i} = \sqrt{\frac{e_{ij}e_{jj}}{e_{ji}e_{ii}}} \tag{8}$$

The Informed Guessing Model

The Informed Guessing Model merely adds a parameter g to the parameters of the overlap model. The process is generalized to allow the possibility, with probability g, that not enough information was extracted from the stimulus to rule out any of the set of stimuli, i.e., g is the probability that *all* stimuli remain in the confusion set. Algebraically,

$$p_{ij} = \frac{b_j}{b_i + b_j} \xi_{ij} + b_j g, \qquad i \neq j,$$

$$p_{ii} = 1 - \sum_{j \neq i} p_{ij} \tag{9}$$

$$g + \xi_i + \sum_{j \neq i} \xi_{ij} = 1.$$

It seems reasonable to consider a model that allows for some proportion of stimulus-independent responding. As seen later, this condition is particularly attractive for the class of experiments in which the confusions are generated by subjects responding under extreme speed requirements in a reaction-time situation. This model also satisfies (6) and thus has the same expected values as the Biased Choice Model or the Overlap Model for any particular set of data. The parameters discussed in the following should be assumed to be based on the expected values derived by the maximum likelihood procedure.

Estimates of the bias parameters, b_j, are the same as in the Overlap Model and are unique. However, g and the ξs are no longer unique. In general, there is an entire range of the values for g and the corresponding ξs, which yield data corresponding exactly to the expected values.

Maximum g. From Eq. (9) it is clear that $b_j g$ could not be larger than the smallest p_{ij}. Consequently,

$$g_{\max} = \min_{i,j} \frac{p_{ij}}{b_j} \tag{10}$$

Minimum g.   Consider the sum of the *i*th column and the *i*th row of the conditional probability matrix, i.e., $p_{i\cdot} + p_{\cdot i}$. Using Eq. (9), this is

$$p_{i\cdot} + p_{\cdot i} = 2p_{ii} + \sum_{j \neq i} \xi_{ij} + g[1 + (R-2)b_i] \qquad (11)$$

where R is the size of the stimulus set. Then,

$$1 + p_{\cdot i} = 2p_{ii} + 1 - \xi_i + (R-2)gb_i$$

and

$$g = \frac{p_{\cdot i} - 2p_{ii} + \xi_i}{(R-2)b_i}$$

and because $\xi_i \geqslant 0$,

$$g \geqslant \frac{p_{\cdot i} - 2p_{ii}}{(R-2)b_i}$$

and because g is to have a probability interpretation,

$$g_{\min} = \max_i \left\{ 0, \frac{p_{\cdot i} - 2p_{ii}}{(R-2)b_i} \right\} \qquad (12)$$

If the Overlap Model is to hold, $g_{\min}$ would have to equal zero, implying that

$$p_{\cdot i} < 2p_{ii} \qquad \text{for all } i ,$$

and summing

$$p_{\cdot \cdot} < 2 \sum p_{ii} ,$$

but because this is an $R \times R$ conditional probability matrix $p_{\cdot \cdot} = R$, so that the average percent correct, $\sum p_{ii}/R = \bar{p}_c$ is constrained, i.e., $\bar{p}_c \geqslant \frac{1}{2}$. That is, the Overlap Model cannot fit whenever the average percent correct is less than 50%. That this is true whatever the number of stimuli or the stimulating conditions is what we found intuitively unappealing about this model.

The Informed Guessing Model has the advantage of being related to a number of theoretical ideas that have been around for some time. It performs the service, in a sense, of illustrating the relationship between these diverse models by way of its mutual relationship with each of them. The relation between the Informed Guessing Model and Luce's Biased Choice Model is clear from the foregoing discussion. The importance of this relation is the fact that the Informed Guessing Model supplies an elementary process account for data that can be fit with the Luce model. However, the Informed Guessing Model is also a special case of a general class of models known as Sophisticated Guessing Models (see Broadbent, 1967), which is discussed in the next subsection.

With regard to reaction-time data, the Informed Guessing Model bears an important similarity to the Fast Guess Model put forward by Yellott (1971), which hypothesizes that subjects in a reaction-time experiment emit two kinds of responses. Either they process the stimulus, in which case their response is a correct identification, or they fail to process the stimulus, in which case they produce a guess response. The Informed Guessing Model includes both of these states and in addition a third intermediate state—one that allows for the partial processing of the stimulus. Of course, the Fast Guess Model specifies the relation of these states to reaction-time measures, and the Informed Guessing Model does not. However, given the definition of these states by the model, that relation becomes an empirical question.

The Sophisticated Guessing Model

The Sophisticated Guessing Model discussed here is based directly on that described by Broadbent. His model allows for the possibility of confusion sets of any size, the only restriction being that the correct response is assumed always to be contained in the confusion set, because he assumes that the stimulu event acts only to delete a subset of responses, perhaps empty, that are inconsistent with the stimulus. The natural parameters of Broadbent's model are the confusion-set probabilities and the relative response biases. The extension made by our model is to assume that the probability of any confusion set is the same no matter which of its response elements is the correct response. As pointed out earlier, this assumption rules out the possibility of the confusion-set identity itself being a useful clue to the correct response within the set. Although this may appear to be a technical assumption, it is necessary not only to reduce the number of parameters but also to give some unambiguous meaning to the concept of a confusion set.

The number of parameters is a serious problem. Even when the additional assumption is made, there remain $2^R - 2$ parameters, $R - 1$ bias parameters and $2^R - R - 1$ confusion-set probabilities, a number that is larger than the number of degrees of freedom in the confusion matrix, $R(R-1)$ if R, the number of stimuli, is greater than 2.

It should now be clear how the Stimulus Overlap Model and the Informed Guessing Model occur as special cases of the Sophisticated Guessing Model. They are obtained by setting the probabilities of appropriate collections of confusion sets equal to zero.

The Sophisticated Guessing Model is a special case of the Luce Biased Choice model in that every assignment of probability values to confusion-set and bias parameters leads to a probability description of a confusion matrix that fits the Luce Model. Indeed, because of the excess of parameters, many such assignments may lead to the *same* confusion matrix. It is not the case, however, that every Luce confusion matrix can be described as a sophisticated guessing matrix. For example, we have proved that if the Sophisticated Guessing Model is to hold, for any particular response, its probability must be higher for the appropriate stimulus than for any other stimulus. These two model types are also QNI. It is important to determine both necessary and sufficient conditions if we are ever to determine which model is more descriptive. If data matrices can be reliably generated that fit the Luce conditions but not the Sophisticated Guessing conditions, the Biased Choice Model will be supported. If not, the Sophisticated Guessing Model would be preferred on theoretical grounds as providing a simpler process description.

In the latter case, the Biased Choice Model would still be useful for statistical reasons. The iterative estimation procedure previously described derives from the fact that the Biased Choice Model is itself a special case of a log-linear model, i.e., a model in which the logarithms of cell frequencies can be written as linear functions of the basic parameters. In recent years methods of analysis for such models have been extensively and systematically developed (Bishop, Fienberg, & Holland, 1975). In particular, valid statistical procedures are available for comparing biases and similarities both within and between experiments and for assigning confidence intervals for the various parameters. This is of course invaluable not only for assessing experimental outcomes but for designing experiments with the precision needed to distinguish models.

When the parametrization of interest is that of Sophisticated Guessing Model, the Biased Choice Model statistics provide maximum likelihood adjustment of cell frequencies, which lead to maximum likelihood estimates of Sophisticated Guessing parameters. Further research is needed, however, to determine how these estimates can be constrained to satisfy interesting side conditions. An example that has been solved is how to test for equality of bias parameters in the Sophisticated Guessing Model—parameters that are not simply related to those of the Choice Model.

EXPERIMENT I

The purpose of this section is to present an experiment that is prototypical of the paradigm that was described in the second section of this chapter. This prototype experiment demonstrates the scope and the precision of the research that can be achieved with this particular experimental technique.

The work leading up to the present experiment was reported by Stanovich, Pachella, and Smith (1977). That experiment, like the present one, involved the verbal identification of single letters presented visually to subjects, who produced responses that were constrained by response-time deadlines. Confusion matrices for each deadline condition were fit with Luce's (1963) Biased Choice Model using maximum likelihood estimation techniques. This pilot work established a number of facts that are confirmed and extended by the present experiment. First, subjects were able to perform the basic task. This was not a trivial finding, because the application of the response-time deadline technique had previously not been attempted with verbal responding. Second, the subjects produced "meaningful" confusion matrices. That is, the confusions were clearly stimulus-dependent and could not be fit with simple independence assumptions. This result was also not trivial, because on the basis of work by Ollman (1966), Yellott (1971), and Swensson (1972a), subjects could have accommodated the speed demands by producing strings of essentially random guessing responses. That possibility seemed particularly relevant, because the earlier work (Swensson, 1972a) had indicated that this strategy might tend to be associated with simple tasks using highly discriminable stimuli. Third, a model of the type characterized by Eq. (5), e.g., Luce's model, provided a good description of the Stanovich et al. data. Thus, on the basis of the identifiability relations described in the previous section, it seemed reasonable that data could be obtained that could be described adequately by the Informed Guessing Model.

The specific purpose of the present experiment, then, was to produce a set of data for which a particular Informed Guessing Model could be developed and tested. To this end, stimuli were designed that were intended to constrain the potential confusion sets available to the subject. These stimuli were based on the font developed by Rumelhart (1971; Rumelhart & Siple, 1974) and are illustrated in Fig. 2. In other words, from inspection it should be clear that certain pair-wise confusions of these letters (e.g., *DB* and *CE)* *should* be more likely, given partial information processing, than other confusions.

Method

Subjects: The subjects were six male, paid volunteers recruited on the University of Michigan campus.

Apparatus: A PDP-1 computer controlled the presentation of stimuli and recorded response latencies by means of voice key. The stimuli were the letters *B, C, D, E* presented on a Hewlett Packard 1311A display device. The letters were of a font used by Rumelhart (1971; Rumelhart & Siple, 1974), in which 14 line segments are used to construct the 26 letters of the alphabet. The letters were approximately .5 cm high, and subjects sat about 65 cm from the display screen. The experimenter sat behind the subject and recorded each response as a *B, C, D,* or *E* on a microswitch keyboard.

Procedure.   Each session consisted of four blocks of 200 trials. The sessions lasted approximately one hour and were run on separate days. The first session

FIG. 2   Experimental stimuli.

was a practice day on which the naming task and the response-time deadline procedure—to be used throughout the study—were introduced to the subject. Before every block the subject was informed of an experimenter-defined response-time deadline that he was to beat on every trial. After each trial the subject was given the feedback "fast" or "slow" in the lower left corner of the display device, depending on whether he had emitted his response prior to or subsequent to the response-time deadline.

On the practice day each of the four blocks was assigned a different deadline ranging from 340 msec to 525 msec. This procedure provided sufficient data on the subjects' speed-accuracy trade-off function that appropriate deadlines for each subject could be chosen for the remainder of the experiment. Subsequent to the practice day, each subject completed sessions on each of six consecutive days under four different speed-accuracy criteria each day. One was an accuracy condition for which there was no deadline on the subject's response. In addition to the accuracy condition, three other deadlines were chosen individually for each subject. These deadlines ranged from 425 msec to 335 msec and were chosen to produce approximately 10%, 15%, and 20% to 30% errors respectively. Each of the six sessions consisted of four blocks of trials, one under each of the four speed-accuracy conditions. Each subject thus produced a total of 4800 responses. The order of the deadline conditions was either descending or ascending in speed stress and was alternated over days. Stimulus sequences were generated by a pseudorandom computer algorithm subject to the constraint that each stimulus appear an equal number of times in each 200-trial block. Subjects were informed of the deadline to be used on each block, and three-minute rest periods were given between blocks.

Results and discussion.   All data were tabulated and analyzed, and all models were fit to individual subjects. However, for expository purposes, because the pattern of results was identical for all subjects, data averaged across subjects, subsequent to model fitting, are presented.

Figure 3 shows the speed-accuracy trade-off function (SATF) for the six subjects. This function plots probability correct as a function of the average reaction time for the four speed-constraint conditions. This function is quite typical of those that have been previously reported (e.g., Pew, 1969), and it shares the basic features of Fig. 1: It is monotonically increasing and negatively accelerated. Under normal reaction time instructions, the subjects averaged 96% correct. With the fastest deadlines, the subjects averaged 73% correct. These accuracy differences were produced over a range of 100 msec of reaction-time difference (446 msec versus 346 msec).

The purpose of the present paradigm is to note not only the percentage of accuracy for each condition but, more importantly, the distribution of errors within each condition. It should be noted that corresponding to each point of Fig. 3 is a confusion matrix. Consequently, the confusion matrix for each subject at each speed-constraint condition was analyzed. This analysis consisted of

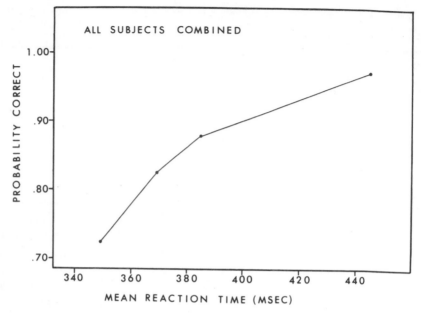

FIG. 3   Speed-accuracy trade-off function for Experiment I.

fitting, by maximum likelihood procedures, the Informed Guessing Model specified by Eq. (6) to each matrix. The chi-square measure for these fits ranged from 1.86 to 19.08 and averaged about two and one-half times the degrees of freedom (the median chi-square was 8.11, and there are 3 d.f. for each fit; 14 were insignificant at the 5% level, 10 were significant at the 5% level), which, with a total frequency of 1200 responses for each matrix, is quite good. Descriptively, in each case the model accounted for better than 95% of the variance, and for five of the six subjects, the model accounted for better than 99% of the variance, for all speed constraints. Thus the model accounts well for the data but not perfectly, i.e., the chi-square values indicate that the small residual variation is systematic.

Because this is an unfamiliar method of analysis, we present an example of the procedure. Table 1(a) contains the data generated by Subject JH using his most stringent deadline, 360 msec, and, in parentheses, the expected values generated by the iterative procedure. Chi-square for this data is 12.39, the fourth worst of the 16 fits used in this analysis. Table 1(b) contains the parameter values of the Biased Choice Model corresponding to this fit, and Table 1(c) contains the Informed Guessing Model parameters. Note that the confusion set DE has probability zero precisely. This is due to g having been set at its maximum value, .28. But the fact that confusion sets BE, CD, and BC have probabilities on the order of .02 is a finding of the study. In fact, for the 96 estimates of these four confusion probabilities in this experiment, the median value is .005. Consequently, these values are not plotted in Figs. 4 and 6.

TABLE 1
Sample Data Analysis

Subject: JH
Deadline: 360 msec

(a) Stimulus

	B	C	*Response* D	E
B	201 (201)	23 (23.94)	59 (54.24)	10 (13.82)
C	37 (36.06)	203 (203)	20 (28.90)	50 (42.04)
D	86 (90.76)	41 (32.10)	162 (162)	9 (13.14)
E	37 (33.18)	59 (66.96)	23 (18.86)	181 (181)

(b) Choice Model parameters

	B	C	η D	E	β
B	1	0.145	0.389	0.112	0.320
C		1	0.168	0.277	0.262
D			1	0.092	0.222
E				1	0.196

(c) Informed Guessing parameters

$g = P\ (BCDE) = 0.283$

P (BC) = 0.022	P (CD) = 0.066	P (DE) = 0	
P (BD) = 0.323	P (CE) = 0.242		
P (BE) = 0.010			
P (B) = 0.361	P (C) = 0.387	P (D) = 0.328	P (E) = 0.465
b_B = 0.365	b_C = 0.257	b_D = 0.222	b_E = 0.156

The ξ-parameter values averaged across subjects are presented in Fig. 4. This set of functions is referred to as an expanded SATF, indicating that it represents the expansion of each point of Fig. 3. This figure shows the probability that the subject found himself in a particular confusion set, given an appropriate stimulus. The confusion sets consisting of single letters indicate correct detections. They would correspond to stimulus-controlled responses in Yellott's (1971) model. The confusion set consisting of all four stimulus letters, *BCDE,* indicates the pure guess responses, discussed earlier as the *g* parameter. In other words, when the subject is in this state his response is completely determined by his response biases. As discussed earlier, this guessing parameter can take on a range of values. In the present instance, the guessing parameter was always set at its maximum. Thus, the function in Fig. 4 shows the maximum guessing rate that is consistent with the data.

Figure 4 shows two of the possible six pair-wise confusion sets, *BD* and *CE.* The reason only these two sets are shown is that the probabilities of each of the other sets was effectively zero. The actual probabilities for each of the other confusion sets averaged less than one percent at all speed-constraint conditions.

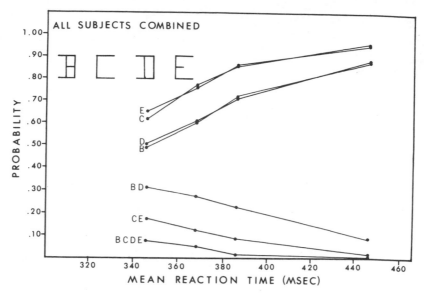

FIG. 4   Expanded speed-accuracy trade-off function. The ordinate corresponds to confusion set probabilities estimated using the Informed Guessing Model.

It is important to note that this does not mean that subjects did not produce confusions of this type. It means that when the data are corrected for guessing, the probability of these confusions resulting from the subject being in the relevant pair-wise confusion set was effectively zero. In other words, the observed pair-wise confusion was the result of the subject being in the pure guessing state.

A concrete example will perhaps clarify this important point. As can be seen from Table 1, subject JH, when working with his fastest deadline, responded "C" 8% of the time when the letter B was presented. Furthermore, he responded "B" 12% of the time when the letter C was presented. Thus he made a BC confusion about 10% of the time when a relevant letter was presented. However, when the subject's confusion matrix was corrected for pure guess responses, these probabilities were reduced to about two percent. In other words, the erroneous "C" responses to the letter B and the erroneous "B" responses to the letter C were not the result of the subject being in the BC confusion set but rather from being in the BCDE confusion set.

Figure 4 shows the systematic changes in the probabilities of each of the confusion sets as a function of the subject's average reaction time. As the subject is allowed more time to respond, the probability of a correct detection increases, and the probability of a confusion set decreases. However, there are a number of more subtle points that demonstrate the precision of the data and the adequacy of the informed guessing model for dealing with it.

The appropriate Informed Guessing Model for these data yields the following account. If a B or a D is presented to the subject, the subject is in the pure guessing state if he has not picked up any relevant features. He may pick up some intermediate information, however, which allows him to discriminate B and D from C and E, because he never confuses B or D with C or E except when guessing. Finally, he can pick up the cue (i.e., the short horizontal line half-way up the letter) that allows him to discriminate B from D or C from E. If the stimulus is B or D, and if the subject is not guessing, he is then in either the DB confusion set, or he knows the identity of the letter. Likewise, if either C or E is presented, and the subject is not guessing, then he is either in the CE confusion set, or he knows the identity of the letter. It follows from this account that the probability of detecting a B should equal the probability of detecting a D, and likewise, the probability of detecting a C should equal the probability of detecting an E. Furthermore, the differences between being in the BD confusion set on the one hand, and being in the CE confusion set on the other hand, should exactly equal the difference between detecting B or D and detecting C or E. In other words, if the subject is not guessing, he has at least enough information to place him in either the BD or the CE confusion set. If in addition he perceives the small horizontal line, then he knows whether or not the stimulus is either B or D, or C or E.

Figure 4 quite precisely demonstrates these features. It should be noted carefully that the regularity of the data in Fig. 4 is not simply a mathematical necessity but rather is a reflection of the underlying processing. The foregoing account represents a true prediction that is empirically demonstrated by the data of Fig. 4. The only mathematical constraint on the probabilities for each speed condition is that the probabilities for confusion sets containing any one letter must sum to 1.0. The regularity of the data in Fig. 4 is due to the fact that observed non-BD or CE confusions can be accounted for by pure guessing behavior and that this simple mechanism continues to work systematically as speed stress varies.

There are two other interesting features of Fig. 4 that should be noted. First, the BD stimulus pair, which is the slightly more complex stimulus type (i.e., it contains one more line than the CE pair), is the more difficult stimulus pair to detect. Second, the short horizontal line that distinguishes either the B from the D, or the C from the E, which is basically the same kind of feature in either case, is more difficult to perceive in the context of the more complex stimulus. In other words, the BD confusion set function and the CE confusion set function can be thought of as tracing out the temporal course of the probability of detecting the small horizontal line (i.e., if this feature is not detected, the subject will be in the intermediate confusion state), and the probability is higher that the subject will be in the BD set than in the CE set.

Thus the Informed Guessing Model analysis is able to give a precise and detailed account of this identification experiment. The experiment and the analysis taken together demonstrate clearly the nature of the process from which errors are generated when a subject is called on to work under speed stress, and the paradigm allows for the detailed analysis of the acquisition of information over time.

EXPERIMENT II

The purpose of Experiment II was to imbed the paradigm developed in Experiment I into a substantive problem in order to test new analytic dimensions for the potential solution for that problem. The substantive problem is that of determining the effects of stimulus probability.

The evaluation of the effects of stimulus probability has been a topic of considerable interest in cognitive psychology for a number of years. Among the important questions that have been considered is the question of whether an effect of this variable can be demonstrated on encoding or perceptual stages of processing. Most recently, the effect of stimulus probability has been at the center of attempts to distinguish between various models of memory scanning and choice reaction time (for various points of view in this controversy, see Pachella & Miller, 1976; Miller & Pachella, 1976; Theios, 1975; Sternberg, 1975; Falmagne, 1965; and Link, 1975).

Stanovich, Pachella, and Smith (1977) varied stimulus probability for subjects working under speed stress and fit the resulting confusion matrices with the Biased Choice Model. The results indicated systematic effects of probability on the bias parameters of that model and also effects on the similarity parameters. However, the experiment utilized only one level of speed stress and did not attempt to trace out the entire trade-off function. Because different numbers of errors were present under the two levels of probability manipulation, the comparison of the similarity parameters was ambiguous. With only one level of speed stress, the same number of errors must be obtained for two conditions in order for a direct comparison to be valid.

Method

Subjects: The subjects were five of the six male, paid volunteers who participated in Experiment I.

Apparatus: The apparatus and stimuli were the same as those in Experiment I.

Procedure.   Subjects participated in six sessions consisting of four blocks of 200 trials. Subsequent to their particpiation in Experiment I, these subjects participated in six sessions of another study using a similar methodology. Thus the six sessions of the present experiment represent Days 14-19 of their experimental participation.

The procedure of this experiment differed from that of Experiment I in only two ways. First, the stimuli did not appear with equal probabilities. The letter B was presented 40% of the time, C and D were present 25% of the time, and E was presented 10% of the time. These stimulus probabilities remained the same throughout the six sessions. Second, subjects worked under only two response deadlines individually chosen to yield approximately 15% and 25% errors, respectively. The deadlines ranged from 400 msec to 315 msec. The manipulation of speed stress was blocked, and the order of conditions (two fast blocks followed by two slow blocks and vice versa) alternated over days.

Results and discussion. The results of Experiment II are summarized in Figs. 5 and 6. Each of these figures compares the results from this experiment to comparable points in Experiment I, in which all stimuli were equally likely. Figure 5 shows the effect of stimulus probability on the bias parameter of the Informed Guessing Model. The amount of bias for each stimulus is shown relative to stimulus D, which was presented with probability .25 in both experiments. The left panel depicts the bias parameters from two speed stress conditions of Experiment I, where the stimulus presentation probabilities were equal. The bias parameters clearly are not affected by speed stress. In addition, it appears that the biases are nearly equal. This is in sharp contrast to the parameter values depicted in the right panel, which come from Experiment II, where probability was manipulated. Although speed stress again has no effect, the equality of biases obviously does not hold for this experiment. The data show the same pattern as those of Stanovich, Pachella, and Smith (1977). Probability systematically affects biases in a manner consistent with presentation probability. Thus subjects are biased away from stimulus E (with presentation probability of .10) and toward stimulus B (with presentation probability of .40).

Figure 5 shows the effect of probability on the confusion-set probabilities. The solid lines in the figure connect the parameter values of two deadline conditions of Experiment I. The dashed lines connect the two deadline conditions of the present experiment, in which stimulus probability was manipulated. All

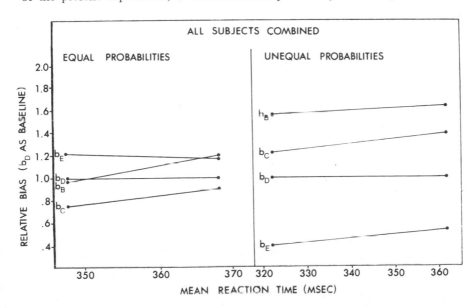

FIG. 5   The effect of stimulus probability on relative response bias.

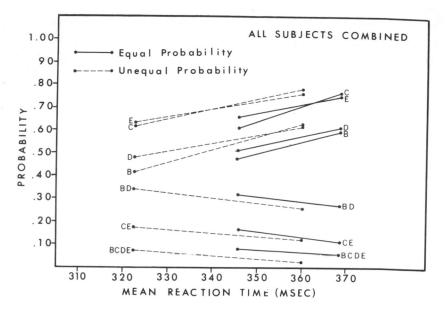

FIG. 6 Expanded speed-accuracy trade-off function from Experiment II. The ordinate corresponds to confusion set probabilities estimated using the Informed Guessing Model.

of the relations between the various parameters that were described in the previous section appear to hold when probability is manipulated. The similarity of the functions from Experiments I and II seems quite impressive and is indicative of a lack of dramatic probability effects on encoding.

These data, however, are problematic for a number of reasons. First, they involve grossly different amounts of practice. The equal probability condition (i.e., the prototype experiment) involved the first 6 days of experience for the subjects. The unequal probability condition was conducted after the subjects had a total of 13 days of practice (i.e., the unequal probability condition was run on Days 14 through 19). The observable differences in Fig. 6 are consistent with these practice effects. That is, the subjects are both faster and more accurate after practice. The second problem with regard to this comparison is the small amount of overlap of reaction time between the two sets of functions. Ideally, all of the points should be directly comparable with regard to the amount of speed stress. Nevertheless, the obtained functions are again suggestive of the potential precision of the present paradigm.

EXPERIMENT III

In addition to reaction-time experiments, much contemporary cognitive psychology, particularly within the field of perception, is based on methodology involving the tachistoscopic presentation of stimulus materials. Furthermore, these two classes of data are often used interchangeably in order to reinforce certain theoretical positions. The purpose of Experiment III was to investigate the relation between the methodology developed in the present project and that using tachistoscopic presentation. Both methodologies are based on the analysis of errors. Both methodologies implicitly involve the notion of limiting the opportunity for the subject to process information. On the one hand, the attempt is to limit processing from the stimulus side, and on the other hand, the attempt is to limit processing from the response side. The models that have been discussed in this chapter have had a wide previous application to the errors obtained under tachistoscopic presentation (see Townsend, 1971), and the basic question of the present experiments is whether or not the pattern of confusions for the two situations are related to one another.

Method

Subjects: The subjects were five male, paid volunteers recruited on the University of Michigan campus. None of the subjects had participated in Experiments I and II.

Apparatus: The apparatus and stimuli were the same as in Experiments I and II.

Procedure.   The experiment consisted of eight sessions. The first session was a practice day on which the naming task and the response-time deadline procedure were introduced to the subject. Before every block the subject was informed of an experimenter-defined response-time deadline that he was to beat on every trial. After each trial the subject was given feedback "fast" or "slow" in the lower left corner of the display device depending on whether he had emitted his response prior or subsequent to the response-time deadline.

On this first practice day, each of the four blocks was assigned a different deadline ranging from 340 msec to 525 msec. This procedure provided the information on the subject's speed-accuracy trade-off that allowed the experimenter to choose a deadline for the remainder of the experiment.

Each subject participated in a second practice day, consisting of four blocks of 200 trials each, in which the tachistoscopic condition was introduced. Subjects were to identify which of the four stimuli had appeared in a tachistoscopic presentation ranging from 2 msec to 12 msec in duration. There was no response deadline on the subject's response, and no feedback was given.

Following the two practice days, subjects participated in six sessions, each consisting of four blocks of 200 trials. On each day, subjects completed two blocks under tachistoscopic conditions and two blocks under the response-deadline procedure. Order of tasks (two tachistoscopic blocks first or two response-deadline blocks first) alternated over days. The response-deadline and stimulus-exposure duration were individually chosen, based on the results of the practice days, for each subject so that approximately 35% errors would result in both conditions. The four letters were presented with equal probability. Three-minute rest periods were given between each block.

Results and discussion.   The Informed Guessing Model was applied to both sets of data. For each condition the comparison of the estimated confusion-set probabilities was averaged across subjects and is presented in Fig. 7. It should be noted that, given the equality of the error rates, this figure captures the change in the pattern of the confusability of the letters.

First, the Informed Guessing Model produced excellent fits to both sets of data. Second, as with the previous experiment, the probability of non-*BD* and *CE* confusion sets was effectively zero for both sets of data. The pattern of fit, as indicated in Fig. 7, was quite different for the two conditions, however. Under speed stress the subject has a much higher probability of emitting a pure guess P *(BCDE)*, or a correct detection P *(B)*, P *(C)*, P *(D)*, P *(E)*, than under tachistoscopic conditions. Under t-scope presentation, the subject has a much higher probability of being in the intermediate confusion state (i.e., the *BD* or the *CE* confusion set). This pattern of data strongly suggests that the t-scope condition emphasizes the utilization of partial information by the subject. In other words, the subject rarely has either very little information or complete information but invariably has enough information to tell whether or not a *BD* or a *CE* was presented.

The deadline procedure, by contrast, is more capable of indicating the transition from one state to the next, because at any given time there is a higher probability of completing the necessary processing. Difference in error patterns of

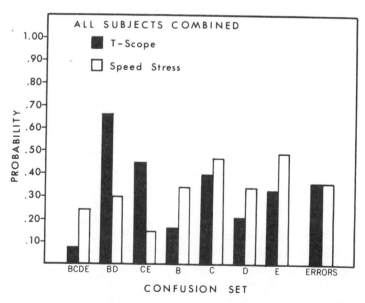

FIG. 7   Comparison of confusion set probabilities generated by *t*-scope and speed stress matched for error rate.

this type have been characterized by Garner (1970, 1974) as the result of state limitation in the former case or process limitation in the latter case. In other words, t-scope studies involve the question of whether or not certain information gets into the system for further processing; the deadline procedure investigates the chances for completing processing given that the information has gotten into the system.

GENERAL DISCUSSION

The experiments described in this chapter are intended to be representative of the paradigm described in the first three sections. The problems for which this paradigm holds the most theoretical value are those that involve the fundamental properties that distinguish stimulus-encoding processes from cognitive, decision, and response processes. Problems of this type have had extensive development throughout the history of experimental psychology. Theories concerning the mechanisms of selective attention and the nature of perceptual set, as well as probability effects, context effects, and word frequency effects, have all at one time or another necessitated the distinction between those processes that extract information from the presented stimulus and those that are involved in the interpretation, classification, and utilization of those cues, once extracted. Distinctions of this type have been an integral part of psychological theories at least since the time of Structuralism.

Sophisticated guessing theories, in the context of identification experiments, represent the simplest form of such a distinction. These theories, even though extremely simple, partition mental processing into those events that allow for the elimination of possible stimulus alternatives on the basis of sensory or input information and those that involve generating a response on the basis of what is otherwise equivalent information. It should be possible, therefore, to take the paradigm and analyses presented here and develop simple analogs of the complex questions mentioned previously for the purpose of empirical testing. What can be envisioned is a series of experiments that manipulate various experimental factors in order to see how they partition themselves across the classification of mental processes implied by the theory. This partitioning of factors as well as the interrelations among them at each level are valuable in developing models of the substantive problems and serve to demonstrate the inadequacies of structuralist-type theories exemplified by the present paradigm. Experiment II might constitute a first step in such an endeavor.

A second function of multifactor experiments, such as those alluded to previously, involve the manner in which the model-types described in the third section partition their effects.

The question here involves the concept of identifiability. As noted earlier, the Luce Biased Choice Model and the Informed Guessing Model are each variants of a class of models that can be characterized by Eq. (5). Thus each model-type gives identical fits to any particular confusion matrix. However, the models are not identical. The parameters of each model partition the variability of a given confusion matrix differently. Each parameter of each model-type is a function of both parameters of the other model. Thus, given a manipulation, such as stimulus contrast, the two model-types do not account for the additional errors as contrast is reduced in the same manner (even though both models account for the additional errors equally well). Comparing the two models across an entire set of manipulations from multifactor experiments then constitutes a fundamental test of the construct validity of the two models.

Construct validity (Cronbach & Meehl, 1955) in some sense supersedes the question of identifiability. For the purposes of developing theories, the parameters of a model ought to partition a set of independent variables in a meaningful way. That is, variability in the stimulus parameters should be correlated with variability in obvious stimulus factors, and variability in response parameters should be correlated with obvious response factors regardless of the quantitative fit of the models to particular confusion matrices. Another way of expressing this concern is to note that across a *set* of confusion matrices, such as those defined by the manipulation of stimulus contrast, if we are concerned with the theoretical question of the manner in which the parameters of the models account for this variability, then the models are, in fact, identifiably different: One or the other of the models will more efficiently partition the set of independent variables among its parameters. Experimental work, of the type presented here, in conjunction with analytic procedures for fitting sets of matrices, allows for the assessment of this efficiency.

Finally, a note of optimism needs to be stated regarding the potential impact of the present research on the logical and empirical problems that were described in the introduction. One of the motivations for the present work is the desire to understand the nature of the errors that occur in reaction-time paradigms. The presence of these errors makes difficult the interpretation of reaction-time measures, and there is an important need to place this class of methodology on a firm theoretical footing. The present situation is quite analogous to that which existed 30 years ago with regard to psychophysical methodology and the interpretation of threshold measurements. In that case, the presence of false alarms made difficult the interpretation of the rate of correct detections. The development of Signal Detection Theory greatly improved the theoretical understanding of sensitivity measurement techniques. However, perhaps one of the most important contributions of Signal Detection Theory was the demonstration that the measurement of thresholds, even with all of its logical and theoretical problems, nevertheless represents a reasonable approximation to the measurement of sensitivity. For most practical purposes, criterion variability poses no serious problem in the study of sensory psychophysics, and for those cases where problems seem to arise, the more complex methods of signal-detection theory can then be applied as a check on results.

So it will hopefully be the case with reaction-time methodology. One possible outcome of research of the type represented here is the demonstration that reaction-time methodology, with all of its *potential* problems, nevertheless does a good job of approximating the measurement of the duration of mental processing. Such a demonstration, however, necessitates the broad-scale application of alternative techniques, such as those described in this chapter, to a wide class of substantive problems. An empirical correspondence of the results between the experimentation with these new techniques and the simpler reaction-time methodology will greatly enhance the confidence with which the older techniques can be applied and interpreted.

REFERENCES

Bishop, Y. M. M., Fienberg, S. E., & Holland, P. *Discrete multivariate analysis: Theory and practice.* Cambridge, Mass.: MIT Press, 1975.

Broadbent, D. E. Word-frequency effect and response bias. *Psychological Review,* 1967, *74,* 1-15.

Cronbach, L. J., & Meehl, P. E. Construct validity in psychological tests. *Psychological Bulletin,* 1955, *52,* 281-302.

Falmagne, J. C. Stochastic models for choice reaction time with applications to experimental results. *Journal of Mathematical Psychology,* 1965, *2,* 77-124.

Fitts, P. M. Cognitive aspects of information processing: III. Set for speed versus accuracy. *Journal of Experimental Psychology,* 1966, *71,* 849-857.

Garner, W. R. The stimulus in information processing. *American Psychologist,* 1970, *25,* 350-358.

Garner, W. R. *The processing of information and structure.* Potomac, Md.: Lawrence Erlbaum Associates, 1974.

Jennings, J. R., Wood, C. C., & Lawrence, B. E. Effects of graded doses of alcohol on speed-accuracy trade-off in choice reaction time. *Perception and Psychophysics,* 1976, *19,* 85-91.

Link, S. W. Applying RT deadlines to discrimination reaction time. *Psychonomic Science,* 1971, *25,* 355-358.

Link, S. W. The relative judgment theory of two choice response times. *Journal of Mathematical Psychology,* 1975, *12,* 114-135.

Luce, R. D. Detection and recognition. In R. D., Luce, R. R. Bush, & E. Galanter (Eds.), *Handbook of mathematical psychology* (Vol. I), New York: Wiley, 1963.

Miller, J. O., & Pachella, R. G. Encoding processes in memory scanning tasks. *Memory and Cognition,* 1976, *4,* 501-506.

Ollman, R. T. Fast guesses in choice reaction time. *Psychonomic Science,* 1966, *6,* 155-156.

Ollman, R. T. *Discovering how display variables affect decision performance.* In S. Dornic (Ed.), *Attention and performance VI.* Hillsdale, N.J.: Lawrence Erlbaum Associates, 1977.

Pachella, R. G. *Memory scanning under speed stress.* Paper presented at the meeting of the Midwestern Psychological Association, Cleveland, Ohio, May 1972.

Pachella, R. G. Interpretation of reaction time in information processing research. In B. Kantowitz (Ed.), *Human information processing: Tutorials in performance and cognition.* Potomac, Md.: Lawrence Erlbaum Associates, 1974.

Pachella, R. G., & Fisher, D. F. Hick's law and the speed-accuracy tradeoff in absolute judgment. *Journal of Experimental Psychology,* 1972, *92,* 378-384.

Pachella, R. G., & Miller, J. O. Stimulus probability and same-different classification. *Percpetion and Psychophysics,* 1976, *19,* 29-34.

Pachella, R. G., & Pew, R. W. Speed-accuracy tradeoff in reaction time: The effect of discrete criterion times. *Journal of Experimental Psychology,* 1968, *76,* 19-24.

Pew, R. W. The speed-accuracy operating characteristic. *Attention and Performance II, Acta Psychologica,* 1969, *30,* 16-26.

Posner, M. I., Klein, R., Summers, J., & Buggie, S. On the selection of signals. *Memory and Cognition,* 1973, *1,* 2-12.

Rabbitt, P. M. A. Errors and error correction in choice response tasks. *Journal of Experimental Psychology,* 1966, *71,* 264-272.

Rabbitt, P. M. A., & Vyas, S. M. An elementary preliminary taxonomy for some errors in laboratory choice RT tasks. In A. F. Sanders (Ed.), *Attention and performance, III.* Amsterdam: North Holland, 1970.

Reed, A. V. Speed-accuracy tradeoff in recognition memory. *Science,* 1973, *181,* 574-576.

Reed, A. V. List length and the time course of recognition in immediate memory. *Memory and Cognition,* 1976, *4,* 16-30.

Rumelhart, D. E. *A multicomponent theory of confusion among briefly exposed alphabet characters.* Technical report 22, Center for Human Information Processing, University of California, San Diego, 1971.

Rumelhart, D. E., & Siple, P. Process of recognizing tachistoscopically presented words. *Psychologocal Review,* 1974, *81,* 99-1181.

Schouten, J. F., & Bekker, J. A. Reaction time and accuracy. In A. F. Sanders (Ed.), *Attention and performance.* Amsterdam: North Holland, 1967.

Stanovich, K. E., Pachella, R. G., & Smith, J. E. K. An analysis of confusion errors in naming letters under speed stress. *Perception and Psychophysics,* 1977, *21,* 545-552.

Sternberg, S. Memory scanning: An informal review of recent developments. In J. A. Deutsch (Eds.), *Short term memory.* New York: Academic Press, 1975.

Swensson, R. G. The elusive tradeoff: Speed versus accuracy in visual discrimination tasks. *Perception and Psychophysics,* 1972, *12,* 16-32. (a)

Swensson, R. G. Trade-off bias and efficiency effects in serial choice reactions. *Journal of Experimental Psychology,* 1972, *95,* 397-407. (b)

Theios, J. Reaction time measurements in the study of memory processes: Theory and data. In G. Bower (Ed.), *The psychology of learning and motivation: Advances in research and theory* (Vol 7). New York: Academic Press, 1973.

Theios, J. The components of response latency in simple human information processing tasks. In P. Rabbitt & S. Dornic (Eds.), *Attention and performance, V.* London: Academic Press, 1975.

Townsend, J. T. Theoretical analysis of an alphabetic confusion matrix. *Perception and Psychophysics,* 1971, *9,* 40-50.

Wickelgren, W. A. Speed-accuracy tradeoff and information processing dynamics. *Acta Psychologica,* 1977, *41,* 67-85.

Wood, C. C., & Jennings, R. R. Speed-accuracy tradeoff functions in choice reaction time: Experimental designs and computational procedures. *Perception and Psychophysics,* 1976, *19,* 92-101.

Yellott, J. I. Correction for fast guessing and the speed-accuracy tradeoff in choice reaction time. *Journal of Mathematical Psychology,* 1971, *8,* 159-199.

8

Methods of Modeling Capacity in Simple Processing Systems

James T. Townsend
F. Gregory Ashby
Purdue University

INTRODUCTION

The study of capacity, empirically and theoretically, is of considerable importance in cognitive psychology (see, e.g., Kahneman, 1973; Townsend, 1974a). Yet there are relatively few mathematical techniques within psychology designed to assess or analyze capacity, much less a systematic theory that interrelates the various and sundry uses of the concept.

Although we cannot hope to completely attain the latter goal in this chapter, we attempt to initiate development of some of the many possible branches that a mathematical knowledge-tree or theory-tree of capacity might possess.

One appropriate milieu in which to discuss and construct these branches could well be that of pattern recognition (Townsend, 1971) and multisymbol search situations (e.g., Sternberg, 1966; Townsend & Roos, 1973). The matching or comparison of patterned information from the environment with information that has previously been stored internally is a process that attracts a rather incredible amount of attention from psychologists as well as engineers and applied mathematicians. There is good reason for this interest. It is difficult to think of a psychological experiment that does not involve such processes in at least some phase of its conditions, although these may or may not be the target processes of significance to a particular study. Even the rote serial learning of a list of nonsense syllables necessitates the activation of comparisons of the input patterns with long-term and/or short-term memory. The burgeoning of the engineering and mathematical literature on pattern recognition in the last few years indicates the tremendous utility that diverse artificial recognizers can or will possess, affecting a broad spectrum of our existence in everything from biomedical devices (e.g., recognizers of disease syndromes and prosthetic reading aids for the blind) to high-altitude geophysical scanning techniques and foreign language translation.

Our goals in this chapter, then, are first to limn a theoretical perspective of pattern matching, concentrating on a linear correlational model of feature comparison and second, but with greater emphasis, to investigate some aspects of the architecture and dynamics of capacity. The pattern matching model allows us to give a detection-type analysis within which concepts of noise, capacity, and latency, can be introduced. The subsequent decision function is described only qualitatively, because it is discussed extensively elsewhere (e.g., Smith & Spoehr, 1974; Massaro & Schmuller, 1975; Townsend & Ashby, unpublished manuscript). Similarly, except as concerns the notion of capacity, remarks about matching a single target symbol with a multisymbol display or memory set are fairly cursory, because we are ready to add nothing especially novel about other issues (for an analysis of some of these, see Townsend, 1974a).

The analyses of capacity concentrate on two approaches. One takes a simple linear system point of view, and the other is developed within the confines of stochastic latency theory. The first approach concentrates on several interesting measures of capacity, of which some are relatively pure measures of expended "energy"; others are based on accuracy or accuracy plus latency. Results from the second approach may be directly employed when accuracy is high or when the errors are presumed to be unrelated to the process in question. They may be more indirectly employed in order to give the state of completion of a set of elements at any point of time and, hence, can be employed in conjunction with decision assumptions to produce latency-accuracy relationships in time-pressured or brief-display conditions.

Several of the new capacity measures that these approaches yield are primarily useful in model construction and in comparing the capacity structure of two or more models. Others are, in addition, observable, that is, computable from easily obtained statistics on accuracy and latency. These latter may prove helpful not only in relating internal model structure and dynamics to behavioral data but also in serving as summary capacity statistics.

It is not difficult to see that these capacity concepts have a natural interpretation in terms of the pattern-matching situation under discussion. However, they are much more general than this particular application might suggest. The pattern-matching milieu, though, is of interest in its own right and serves as a convenient vehicle to explicate our theorizing about capacity.

Some of the concepts we introduce (such as "power," "energy," and "linear filter") come from engineering theory and have been employed fruitfully by others, most particularly in modeling acoustical detection mechanisms, although linear system mathematics is now burgeoning in visual psychophysics (both spatially and temporally) and, naturally, in human performance as well. However, we seek to exploit these notions in more cognitive ways and to explore some new mathematical descriptions of capacity.[1]

Our attitude toward "capacity" is in line with the philosophy formulated earlier: that capacity is a construct that can and should be applied to different levels of processing and is one that can appear in various guises and possess somewhat different implications depending on the specific experimental and theoretical circumstances (Townsend, 1974a). It would be a mistake at this point, we think, to try to fit capacity into a narrow preconceived mold—such would appear to provide only a Procrustean solution. However, this attitude does not preclude the importance of investigation of relationships between differing conceptions of capacity; for example, between capacity as "power" and capacity as the ability to deal with computational complexity. Rather, we think such research is much needed.

A LINEAR SYSTEM MODEL OF FEATURE MATCHING

Before embarking on the theoretical development, it may be apposite to mention that there are characteristics that a full mathematical model or theory will ultimately have to possess, with respect to which the present model is mute. We have in mind particularly the possibility of hierarchical mechanisms that seem to be present in visual symbolic processing (e.g., Estes, 1972; Hoffman, 1975; Weisstein, 1973). For example, it may well be that location information is extracted relatively early, that presence of identical patterns in the display is detected soon thereafter, and so on. The development here does not exclude such mechanisms, which it is thought can be intercalated in later work. We do feel, however, that processing to the degree represented herein may be sufficient for elementary visual recognition tasks.

Hereafter we use the term *symbol* to refer to a pattern that has been assigned a response and learned by the organism, whom we shall call O. Our problem is to put down a plausible account of how O goes about recognizing one of the N possible symbols (it is convenient to take for granted that O knows the size and members of the presentation set). It would be possible but tedious for this particular enterprise to totally formalize the development. Instead, we work through the main ideas with emphasis on the mathematics that is requisite for getting across needed concepts and predictions.

For starting reference observe Fig. 1, which illustrates one version of a now familiar relatively coarse breakdown of processing subsystems germane to the present discussion. A subset of features is assumed to be extracted from the

[1]Some of Lappin's developments (chapter 6 of this text) also make use of linear system concepts.

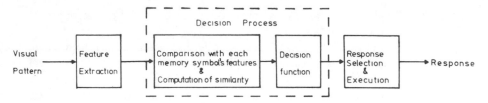

FIG. 1   Schematic of a model for feature matching.

symbol and then submitted to the decision process. Here two tasks are performed. First, this internal extracted feature list is matched in some way against the stored (presumably in long-term memory) list of all possible features. The fact that such a list exists follows from our assumption that O knows the size and members of the presentation set. We envision the second phase of the decision process as determining the identity of the presented symbol from the results of the matching phase by first assigning the various similarities a measure. This information is passed to response selection, which instructs the response execution phase as to the motor response to be associated with the presented symbol.

Townsend and Ashby (unpublished manuscript) explore a wide variety of models based on feature extraction principles. These models are very useful in the investigation of general properties of extraction, matching, and decision, but they are mute with regard to the question of exactly how the "seen" features are extracted from the stimulus, as well as to the question of how the extracted features are compared with the set of stored features that characterize the pattern set.

The extraction process is taken as a given here [but see, e.g., Weisstein (1973) for a discussion of issues at this level], and our present emphasis is on the comparison process.

To begin, we wish to propose to treat each feature as a separate signal, specifiable in principle by a waveform in time and space. The spatial representation of this waveform of course depends on the modality of the presented symbol. For example, in an auditory discrimination task, any presented symbol (e.g., any simple or complex tone) can be described as a function of time, with the dependent variable being amplitude. But the visual modality has two spatial dimensions, and thus the resulting waveform must be three-dimensional. Figure 2 shows a simple example. Assume that presentation of a straight line feature is characterized by a uniform intensity square-wave in two dimensions [as in Fig. 2 (A)], along with a time function indicating the entire temporal course of the waveform. Figure 2 (B) represents a hypothetical brief presentation of such a line. It must be remembered that the amplitude or intensity within the (x, y) plane is changing as a function of time. By taking infinitely thin slices orthogonal to the t axis, we can view this density at any desired point. Figure 2 (C) illustrates three such slices: one taken just after stimulus *presentation,* one just before, and one just after stimulus *offset.* It can be seen that $f(x, y)$, the amplitude surface, is initially small, increases, and then decreases following stimulus offset.

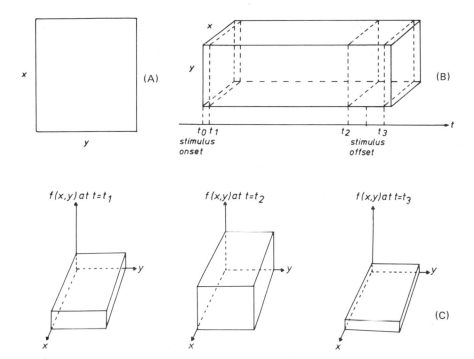

FIG. 2   An example of a three-dimensional visual waveform. (A) The characterization of a straight line feature as a square wave in two spatial dimensions. (B) The time course of a hypothetical brief presentation of this feature. (C) The amplitude surface within the (x, y) plane at three arbitrarily selected time points. These surfaces are obtained from (B) by taking slices orthogonal to the time axis at points t_1, t_2, and t_3 and then plotting amplitude, $f(x, y)$, as a function of position in the (x, y) plane.

Notice that in all cases the surface of $f(x, y)$ is flat; that is, the amplitude intensity is uniform and therefore independent of position in the (x, y) plane. In this respect Fig. (C) represents a perfect observer. In reality, we would expect some irregularities in the $f(x, y)$ surface, which could arise from such effects as neural lateral interaction and quantal fluctuations (with very weak signals).

To return to the feature-matching process, it seems reasonable to assume that O subjects this internal signal (feature) to comparisons with like signals, probably with whatever waveforms would exist in the same physical location (relative to the overall spatial extent of the symbol). We assume that O conducts this comparison by implementing a *cross-correlation* in two dimensions.[2] That is,

[2]Analogous notions of comparison arise when the pattern is represented as a Fourier (or other) transform of the original intensity function or in holographic models. For instance, comparison of holograms via interference patterns can be considered as a means of correlation or comparison (see, e.g., Smith, 1969). It is the logical structure with which we are primarily occupied here, not the ultimate resolution of the question of how visual input is coded.

we view O as taking a time series of spatial samples which are held in a visual operating memory, in the position of a given feature and then correlating these against the stored concomitants associated with the various memory symbols. Such a discrete series, sampled at the appropriate time interval, is capable of adequately describing virtually any real signal of finite duration.

From the sampling theorem of signal analysis, we know that the samples must be taken at time intervals no more than $1/2W$ seconds apart, where W is the signal bandwidth. Reconstruction of the signal using discrete sampling procedures can therefore only succeed with signals of finite bandwidth. However, this restriction appears in our case to be trivial, because it seems highly probable that O operates as a low-pass filter completely attenuating all frequency components of the input signal greater than some finite value W_0 (Cornsweet, 1970).

In such a model, reasonably long display times primarily provide for a lengthened comparison period (i.e., more samples), with the "figure" itself being quite stable except for "on" and "off" transient effects. That is, if the intensity is high and display period lengthy, the time course of the feature signal is pretty much the same. This state of affairs may be compared with that in audition where the main variation of interest is always in the time dimension (excluding spatial localization). However, it is to be expected that with short exposure times, low intensities, or small visual angles, noise will undoubtedly depend on the characteristics of the symbol, background, and any attendant mask. In the present development, we assume the standard white noise description.

It can now be assumed that the correlation comparisons within features are performed serially, although a limited capacity parallel mechanism would do as well and is no less viable presently. It is to be expected, however, that processing *across* features is parallel.

Let the simple feature sample be designated by $r_i = r_{i1}, ..., r_{iK}$, where r_{ij}, $j = 1, K$ is the jth of K samples (equally spaced every Δt time units) for the input from feature position i. The correlation result for memory feature s_r is, of course,

$$y_K = \sum_{j=1}^{K} r_{ij} s_{rj} . \tag{1}$$

In the continuous analogue to (1), we would have

$$y(T) = \int_0^T r_i(t) s_r(t)\, dt , \tag{2}$$

with T as the total interval of sampling. Note that to improve readability, we have treated r_{ij} as a single value rather than the two dimensional array we earlier argued for. A more detailed representation of (2) is

$$y(T) = \int_0^T \int_{[x]} \int_{[y]} r_i(x, y, t) s_r(x, y, t)\, dy\, dx\, dt .$$

In the discussion that follows, this more precise description of the cross-correlation device provides, in general, no added insight over the form of Eq. (2) and thus is dropped in favor of the simpler notation.

The correlation mechanism of (1) or (2) can easily be pictured as the result of (optimal) matched filtering. Without getting into the details of linear system theory (e.g., Padulo & Arbib, 1974), it can be noted that the output $y(T)$ of a real linear filter at time T can be written as

$$y(T) = \int_{\tau=0}^{T} h(T - \tau)r(\tau)\,d\tau\,, \tag{3}$$

where r is again the input, and h is the weighting the system gives the input back, from when it began [at time $\tau = O$: $r(O)$ was the input, and $h(T)$ is the importance it has T time units later] up to the present [at time $\tau = T$: $r(T)$ is the input, and $h(O)$ is the weighting given this present input in determining the output].

When this filter is "matched" for a certain signal s_i, $h(T - \tau)$ becomes $s_i(\tau)$ or, in the discrete sampling case, s_i; and the correlation mechanism is obtained. Of course, we are likening s_i, or $s_i(\tau)$, to a tape between times O and $T = K\Delta t$, which is then compared with a similar memory tape; although the possibility should not be entirely discounted that the correlation is done in real time rather than later as our iconic-like tape.

Now, given the present setup, it is easy to show that with white Gaussian noise $n(t)$ or n_j is introduced, where $\mu = O$ and $\sigma^2 = 1$ [i.e., written $N(O, 1)$], then

$$r_{ij} = \begin{cases} as_{ij} + n_j & \text{if feature } i \text{ is present, } a > 0, \\ n_j & \text{if feature } i \text{ is absent,} \end{cases} \tag{4}$$

where the separate n_j, $j = 1, K$ are uncorrelated and normally distributed, and a represents the strength of the input signal relative to the internal memory signal. The correlation result (alternatively the distribution of output y) is then

$$y_K = \sum_{j=1}^{K} r_{ij}s_{ij} \sim \begin{cases} N(a \sum_{j=1}^{K} s_{ij}^2, \sum_{j=1}^{K} s_{ij}^2) & \text{if feature } i \text{ is present,} \\ \text{or} \\ N(0, \sum_{j=1}^{K} s_{ij}^2) & \text{if feature } i \text{ is absent,} \end{cases} \tag{5}$$

where the symbol $\sim$ means "is distributed as."

From this familiar type of description, predictions of signal-to-noise ratio, selection of an optimal decision criteria, and hit and false-alarm frequencies can be computed. The reader should keep in mind those aspects of the foregoing structure contained in the input symbol and also in a given memory symbol.

The previous cases [Eq. (5)] were only those when the feature i was present in the memory symbol and was or was not in the input symbol. The other two cases, where there is no feature present in the memory symbol, are not so obvious. Assumptions must be made as to what happens when the input (with or without the feature) is correlated with "nothing." Although there are a number of possible tacks one could take, let us presume that "nothing" is representable as a constant background effect (or gain) and therefore as a constant factor b in the correlation; that is, $h\,(t) = bs_i$, or $h\,(t) = b$, depending on whether feature i exists in memory or does not.

Then, we acquire the complement to Eq. (5), which completes the set of four possibilities:

$$y_K = \sum_{j=1}^{K} h(K\Delta t - j\Delta t) r(j\Delta t) \sim \begin{cases} N(ba \sum_{j=1}^{K} s_{ij}^2, b^2 \sum_{j=1}^{K} s_{ij}^2) & \text{if present} \quad \bigg| \quad \text{present (6a)} \\[2ex] N(0, b^2 \sum_{j=1}^{K} s_{ij}^2) & \text{if absent} \quad \bigg| \quad \text{present (6b)} \\[2ex] N(ba \sum_{j=1}^{K} s_{ij}, Kb^2) & \text{if present} \quad \bigg| \quad \text{absent (6c)} \\[2ex] N(0, Kb^2) & \text{if absent} \quad \bigg| \quad \text{absent (6d)} \end{cases}$$

Feature i: *Input* | *Memory*

A b is now also a part of the formulas where the memory letter contains feature i and represents the arbitrary but nonzero gain or indiscriminate amplification (i.e., the DC component).

The signal-to-noise ratio is highest, of course in (6a), but interestingly there is a nonzero "signal" output in case (6c), although not in (6b). However, whether case (6b) or (6c) produces the most correlation results greater than a decision criterion c, also depends on the variances, $b^2 \Sigma s^2$ and KB^2, or in particular, on Σs^2 versus K.

If the average power in the signal feature $(\Sigma s^2)/K = 1$, then the variances are equal, and the frequency that feature i is detected to be present is greater in (6c) than in (6b) for any value of c. Notice also that (6b) and (6d) also depend on the variance (or equivalently, the total energy in the noise). If $(\Sigma s^2)/K = 1$ then they predict equal detection ratios.

The foregoing is highly tentative. In some cases it may be that an additional noise source should be associated with the correlation processor. This would lead to a greater symmetry in (6) with respect to cases (6b) and (6c). However, also attendant would be minor mathematical complications in that the resultant noise would not be Gaussian; and in any event, with well-learned memory symbols, (6) may be reasonable.

A quite different approach would be to posit a simple neural setup with a counter neuron being fed by a central memory-feature "i" neuron (member of a set of neurons associated with a given letter) and an input neuron from the periphery. The memory neuron would fire faster when feature i was contained in the memory letter, and the input neuron would fire faster when feature i was contained in the letter presented. Impulses from the two neurons could be additive with regard to the counter neuron. In this way, additive sources of noise could come from both types of neuron and affect overall accuracy. However, this additive approach loses the well-documented structure of detection within a linear filter framework that the former description possesses. McGill (unpublished manuscript) has shown that additive analogues can be worked out. Nevertheless, there is yet to appear an adequate account of spatial frequency effects in terms of counter theory. Anderson (1973) has explored a neural theory closely aligned with linear system theory.

At any rate, it is time to think about what happens regarding the decision function. We cannot go into it in much depth here; as noted earlier a number of current and new decision models are discussed in a recent report on letter recognition (Townsend & Ashby, unpublished manuscript). Suffice it to say that we may think of the decision function as exacting a probability measure on the matching and nonmatching features occurring with each memory symbol.

The result of the feature comparisons on *each* memory symbol can be characterized by three sets of features made up of: (1) those overlapping the particular memory symbol and the input set; (2) those in the memory symbol but not in the input set; and (3) those in the input set but not in the memory symbol. Potentially, each unique set of features in (1), (2), and (3) in combination with each specific memory symbol can have different effects on the decision function. Basically, we conceive of the first part of the decision function as exacting a measure on these sets that determines their weight in the final selection of a response.

In typical instances the process is simplified by assuming that the three types of matches have uniform effects on the measure, independent of the unique extracted-set-memory-symbol combinations. For example, in several current models, a single feature of type (3) is sufficient to deliver the memory symbol to the second part of the decision stage (see Fig. 1) with an assigned measure of zero; that symbol will than have no chance of being reported unless all other symbols also have measure zero attached to them on that trial.

The second phase of the decision function process maps the memory symbols, on the basis of the assigned measures, to a guessing set. The response is then selected from this set by use of response bias probabilities.

We have thus far developed our general feature matching model for the situation when only a single symbol is presented. Before presenting our results on mathematical capacity theory, we expand our discussion to include multisymbol search experiments.

Multisymbol search paradigms typically designate a single symbol as the target and, on some proportion of the trials, embed it in a set of other symbols; on the remainder of the trials, the target is absent. The multisymbol set may appear in a display after a target has been designated [*early target* (ET) design, e.g., Atkinson, Holmgren, & Juola, 1969, Townsend & Roos, 1973], or it may be in a short-term memory and the target or probe display after the multisymbol memory set [*late target* (LT) design, Sternberg, 1966]. In either case the task of the observer is to indicate, usually with a button press, whether or not the target was present. Of course, it is a short step to situations where one of a set of possible targets is always in the multisymbol set with a forced choice among the critical set of symbols (e.g., Estes & Taylor, 1964) and to situations where various aspects of the irrelevant symbols and targets are manipulated.

We discussed single symbol pattern recognition in terms of feature extraction via a filtering or matching of the input with the feature sets of the symbols in memory, presumably a long-term memory in the case, for example, of recognizing letters from one's native alphabet. The generalization of our model to multisymbol paradigms is straightforward. For LT tasks the details are analogous to those we have developed, because we assumed that O recognizes a present symbol by comparing it to N symbols stored in memory, although of course the LT set is presumably contained in a short- rather than long-term memory. When an ET task with visual display is considered, it may be that the target symbol acts as a filter against all the incoming symbols, most likely in parallel after which a decision is made on the basis of overall feature similarity, just as in the case of single symbol recognition. Here, however, the decision is made on the basis of similarity with the target symbol. In LT tasks, if comparisons were carried out in an acoustic form system (see Townsend & Roos, 1973), the matching would be between acoustic features, but if the comparisons were made in a visual form system, the matching would again be among visual features. As in the earlier case, it may be that the decision function proceeds in a more or less automatic fashion. For instance, the measures of similarity (based on feature overlap and differences) could be accruing continuously, and when (and if) one of them mounts higher than some criterion, a "yes" response is made. Alternatively, the decision function could be calculated after all feature matching is completed and all similarity measures computed.

We turn now to the dynamic description of capacity in pattern-matching tasks.

THE ARCHITECTURE OF CAPACITY

Capacity as Power or Energy

As is well known and as we saw earlier in the present context, capacity can be expressed in terms of the output signal-to-noise ratio, which in turn reflects the quality of the filter. If the filter is exactly the signal, which is correlated against the input, then the signal-to-noise ratio is maximized and is in fact the *input* signal-to-noise ratio accumulated over the sampling interval and the bandwidth of the signal.

We return to the signal-to-noise ratio (which is, of course, just the d' of signal detectability theory) later. Now, however, we wish to employ the correlational linear system model to go beyond d'. That is, we attempt to represent capacity at the microlevel of the correlator, unperturbed by noise, by developing the constructs of power and energy.

Power and energy, as defined in the following, although apparently not heretofore exploited in cognitive contexts (as opposed to uses in ideal detector theory as, for example, in acoustic psychophysics), are, of course, tried and true constructs from electrical and communications engineering. A cognitive development of these concepts seems potentially useful. For instance, individuals may differ in the power or energy of their systems rather than in the amount of noise present. Further, in some cases, notions of power and energy may be helpful in modeling variations in capacity devoted to a detection or recognition task (as in shared-attention experiments, e.g., Kantowitz & Knight, 1976). Some altered or expanded form of certain of these ideas may also find employment in the study of capacity in simple and complex motor performance situations (e.g., see Pew, 1974).

Here, though, we are concerned with pattern matching, where we feel capacity is closely related to latency. In order to bring latency into our deliberations, we find it necessary to invent some new potential measures. The first that we suggest are primarily for model building and comparison, as are power and energy, and our measures utilize these quantities again. Then, in the next subsection, the possibility that power and energy might affect the time taken by the system to perform its function is entertained, and a way in which this might be effected stochastically is presented. Finally, some summary measures of *effective* capacity, which attempt to capture accuracy and latency factors when the capacity supply is constant and which should often be observable, are developed.

First, we want to make some cursory remarks on time- and event-limited sampling. Let us consider the situation when O is forced by the experimenter to limit the latency of responses by deadline procedures. There seems to be basically two ways in which this might be accomplished (with many possible variations on these themes). First, O might directly fix the time in which he or she processes, or he or she might limit the amount of information he or she acquires (e.g., Luce & Green, 1972). In terms of the correlation scheme previously presented, both kinds of control could possibly limit the number of the time samples (e.g., to be less than K in the formulas in the second section).

In time-varying signals, this would have the effect of disallowing a complete correlation with the signal component of the input and thus lead to increased error. On the other hand, in basically stationary visual patterns with reasonably long display intervals, as when the rise and decay times shown in Fig. 2 are brief compared to the length of the signal, longer sampling intervals essentially permit repeated observations of the same information (although with varying noise intensity, of course). Therefore, increasing the time of observation in this case would lead to increment in detectability according to well-known formulas (e.g., Green & Swets, Chap. 9, 1966). We must truncate our discussion of these points in order to address the more neglected question of how to represent capacity of the functioning system per se, but we return to the relation of accuracy to processing duration in the next subsection.

As noted earlier, a system or subsystem employing a correlation function is optimal under rather wide conditions. Furthermore, once the so-called impulse response function $h(t)$ takes on the form giving the correlation result, additional amplification, for example by means of increasing b in Eq. (6), does not lead to any improvement in signal-to-noise ratio, because the noise is amplified also. Hence, a major part of any capacity allotment to a specific subsystem, as to one of the feature detectors (whether the capacity allotment is manipulable or not), must be the setting up and maintenance of the correct form of $h(t)$. It is clear, though, that below some lower limit of amplification, the system must fail to perform its work adequately. The best way to formally represent the capacity required for maintenance of $h(t)$, or how performance should suffer when the capacity allocated to amplification falls below the acceptable limit, is not at all obvious presently.

However, we may for the moment set aside the problems of how (and how much of) the available capacity is allocated to the maintenance of $h(t)$, what the lower limits of amplification are, and the consequences of not meeting these lower limits. We may still ask if there exists any potentially useful measure of the capacity used in the correlator. The answer is in the affirmative.

One measure of possible interest is the *power* or rate of energy disbursement. The power applied at a particular time can be found from $[h(t)]^2$ (which we sometimes write $h^2(t)$ to lessen the number of parentheses) for any t from O to T. For some purposes the power allocated to a particular frequency might be of interest, in which case $|H(f)|^2$ would be appropriate, where $H(f)$ is the Fourier transform of $h(t)$ and is known as the *system function* (e.g., Padulo & Arbib, 1974, p. 426).

If the *total* capacity used up during the entire correlation period (i.e., the energy) is of interest, then we must sum or integrate the power dissipated over the observation interval or frequency bandwidth covered by the correlator. Thus the total capacity in the type of system developed in the preceding can be described in "energy" terms as

$$C(T) = \int_0^T h^2(t)\, dt = \int_{-WT}^{WT} |H(f)|^2\, df.$$

One of the nice properties of the "System function" approach is that the system function of a serial system consisting of n linear subsystems can be written as the product of the component system functions. Thus, if $H_n(f)$ denotes the overall system function, and $H (f, i)$ is the individual system function i of the ith subsystem, then

$$H_n(f) = \prod_{i=1}^{n} H(f, i).$$

The power applied to frequency $f = f'$ then, for example, would be

$$H_n^2 (f') = \left[\prod_{i=1}^{n} H(f', i) \right]^2$$

and the total capacity in energy terms would be the integral of this expression over the appropriate bandwidth. Further, note that the power in terms of the time dimension can be obtained by taking the inverse Fourier transform of $H_n (f)$ and squaring. We should remark in passing that there are analogous structures for discrete-time linear systems as well.

We reemphasize here that the usefulness of say, $[h (t)]^2$, does not depend on there being a "real" power open to our inspection. Rather, $[h (t)]^2$ is a hypothetical process or function (what used to be called an *intervening variable*). This function represents the magnitude of the proposed hypothetical correlation mechanism at any point in time, in a way that allows us to employ some of the logic, intuition, and mathematical relationships of analogous concepts in physics and engineering.

Suggested Measures That Include Speed and Accuracy[3]

We as yet have no structure to reflect the type of *latency* changes that might stem from allocations of more or less capacity to the system given by $h (t)$ or $H (f)$. At any particular level of analysis, an observer might or might not be able to alter the allocation of capacity to a system (e.g., the feature-within-a-letter level may be too fine to permit such control), but even if the capacity is constant, the effect on latency must be shown for a complete system description. Although latency structure of a deterministic nature could be constructed, we may as well begin with the more interesting general problem where for a given allocation or amount of capacity, the latency varies probabilistically from trial to trial.

We want: (1) to have a measure of capacity that reflects not only, say, the power or energy applied on a particular trial (as we have previously) but also the

---

[3]The measures incipiently explored in this section are oriented around power, energy and signal-to-noise ratio interleaved with notions of stochastic latency theory. We refer the reader to other recent mathematical approaches to speed-accuracy relations, particularly Green and Luce (1973), Link (1975), Pike (1973), Swensson and Thomas (1974), Theios et al. (1973), and Thomas (1971). The chapters by Joseph Lappin, Stephen Link, and Robert Pachella, Keith Smith, and K. Stanovich, in the present text are all related to speed-accuracy issues.

speed with which it was applied; and (2) to have in hand a means of describing how capacity affects the latency of a system.

We must wade through some mathematical detail, even though our treatment is restricted to outline form, in order to develop a rationale for objective (1). So as not to lose sight of the forest for the trees, let us set down the suggested measure for (1) and then return to a slightly more specific justification. The measure investigated is Q/T, the total energy produced by a certain system, relative to the duration of time taken to produce it. Note that this measure increases with energy and with speed. As we shall see, in stochastic systems, it makes sense to think of Q as a random quanitity, for any given time T, and also, though less obviously perhaps, to consider T as a random variable for any given energy Q. Thus we wish to define, in general, the notion of an average or expected value of the ratio Q/T. In a particular psychological experiment, on each trial O is confronted with a task requiring some energy Q in order to be completed. The time variable T is immediately useful in expressing how long any particular system takes to produce the requisite energy Q.

An approach to this probelm that presents itself is to start with the time course $h(t)$ of the particular system under discussion. Now, in general, because we consider stochastic systems, there is a *set* or *ensemble* of such functions and a distribution describing the frequency with which one or more particular $h(t)$s actually occurs. This frequency distribution may be called $f[h(t)]$. What we are really interested in, however, is the power, and later, the energy, so we ask about $[h(t)]^2$ as a function of time, which is, as we saw earlier, the power curve of a deterministic system with impulse response function $h(t)$. The frequency distribution on $h(t)$ in a stochastic system immediately generates a new distribution on the power curves as functions of time, so that we also have the distribution $f[h^2(t)]$ (obviously this is a new f, not the old one for $h(t)$; we use f to keep the notation simple). For brevity, let $h^2(t) = P(t) =$ power, and $f[h^2(t)] = f[P(t)]$.

Let us return to consider our potential capacity measure Q/T. We would like to develop it stochastically from the preceding distribution on $P(t)$. Now, the amount of energy Q produced by our stochastic system at a particular time T is a random quanitity. Similarly, the duration T taken by the system to produce some amount of energy Q is also random or probabilistic. Hence, in order to achieve something like an average of Q/T over all possible values of Q and T, we require knowledge about the probability distribution on Q and T.

To begin, we define a necessary and important quantity

$$\bar{f}(Q, T) = \int_{[P']} f(P) \, dP,$$

where P' is the set of power curves that integrate to exactly energy Q in exactly time T. This formula clearly gives the total frequency with which the system has produced energy Q at time T. Note that we have suppressed the argument t in $P(t)$ in the main integral, because it is the probability density on the set of *functions* P, which is of interest there. We have placed a bar over f because it is not a true joint probability function, because it will not be 1 when integrated over all possible values of Q and T, each going from O to infinity.

On the other hand, by holding one variable fixed (either Q or T), we can define a conditional probability function on either Q or T that is always positive and integrates to one. For instance, when T is fixed and Q can vary, we can generate $f(Q|T)$ by sweeping out the variable Q in $\overline{f}(Q, T)$. For any value $Q = Q'$ that we choose, $f(Q', T)$ is the probability function (either a density or mass) of $f(Q|T)$ at the point $Q = Q'$; that is, $f(Q = Q'|T)$ is the "frequency" that, given processing is completed at time T, the system has produced energy Q' (or more precisely that it has produced energy between $Q' - \Delta Q$ and Q', where ΔQ is arbitrarily small).

Analogously, by holding Q fixed and sweeping out T, we can produce $f(T|Q)$, which is the density on the finishing times given that the system has expended exactly energy Q. This density is, of course, determined by the ensemble of power curves, because different curves produce energy Q at different times. In fact, if Q is large, there may exist curves that never produce it. It is obvious that such curves can not contribute to $f(T|Q)$. Hence $f(T|Q) = \overline{f}(Q, T)$ is defined (Q fixed and T varying) if and only if *every* power curve in the ensemble $P(t)$ of the system produces Q at *some* time point T.

Having now developed the necessary tools, let us, via some simple examples, see how a system's ensemble of power curves can affect its capacity as reflected in the statistic $E(Q/t)$, the expectation of the ratio of Q to T. First consider a system A that has but one power curve in its ensemble, $P(t) = P$. Thus in this system instantaneous power is always constant.

It may be assumed that the experimenter determines the processing load L of the system and that the total energy Q, which the system expends during processing, is some function of this load. For simplicity we assume $Q = L$ in these examples, but in reality it may be necessary to assume that L determines, say, some probability distribution on expended energy. Now processing is completed when energy, Q, is expended, and because system A has only one power curve, for any given Q, we will always be able to specify the completion time, T_A, exactly. T_A is just the time when the accumulated energy under the power curve, $P(t) = P$, is exactly Q:

$$\int_0^{T_A} P\,dt = Q,$$

or

$$PT_A = Q,$$

and finally

$$T_A = \frac{Q}{P}.$$

Thus for any Q we can quickly calculate T_A.

We can now determine $E(Q/T)$. Because $Q = L$, Q is a constant, and thus $E(Q/T) = QE(1/T \mid Q)$, and therefore

$$E(\tfrac{1}{T} \mid Q) = \int_0^\infty \tfrac{1}{T} f(T \mid Q) \, dt.$$

However, once we are given Q, we know that $T = T_A$ is certain. Therefore $f(T \mid Q)$ must have all of its mass at the point $T = T_A$; that is, $f(T \mid Q) = \delta(T - T_A)$, where $\delta(T)$ is the Dirac delta function at time T. The calculation of the preceding expectation is thus trivial:

$$E(\tfrac{1}{T} \mid Q) = \int_0^\infty \tfrac{1}{T} \delta(T - T_A) \, dt = \tfrac{1}{T_A}$$

Substituting in $T_A = Q/P$ yields $E(1/T \mid Q) = P/Q$, and therefore our measure of capacity is $QE(1/T \mid Q) = P$. The capacity of system A is, then, constant and thus independent of both expended energy and processing time.

To contrast this, consider system B, also with only one power curve, but one that is not a constant but that decays exponentially over time; $P(t) = Pe^{-t}$. For a given Q, we again know the completion time, T_B, exactly. Specifically, T_B is such that

$$\int_0^{T_B} Pe^{-t} \, dt = Q$$

and therefore

$$1 - e^{-T_B} = \frac{Q}{P}$$

or

$$e^{-T_B} = 1 - \frac{Q}{P}$$

Taking natural logarithms of both sides yields

$$T_B = \ln\left(\frac{P}{P - Q}\right).$$

Now again $f(T \mid Q)$ has all its mass at a single point in time; this time at $T = T_B$ [i.e., $\delta(T - T_B)$]. Thus $E(1/T \mid Q) = 1/T_B$, and, hence

$$QE(\tfrac{1}{T} \mid Q) = \frac{Q}{\ln\left(\dfrac{P}{P - Q}\right)}$$

First, note that this funciton is undefined for $Q \geq P$. This is not surprising when we note that if the system were to run for infinite time, it would only expend energy $Q = P$, because

$$\int_0^\infty Pe^{-t} \, dt = P.$$

Hence $f(T \mid Q)$ is not defined for $Q > P$, and, in fact, such a system could not process loads requiring energy greater than P.

Second, we note that as Q approaches zero (from the right), the measure approaches P. Alternatively, as Q gets large, the measure generally decreases toward zero. Therefore, without a doubt, capacity is greater in system A as measured by $Q \cdot E \, (1/T)$.

Notice, too, that the capacity in system B decreases because of its power curve; for larger values of Q, system B takes disproportionately more time to produce that Q than does system A. Thus system Bs capacity is less for larger Q than for smaller Q. This corresponds to the decreasing behavior of $QE \, (1/T)$ as a function of Q.

Finally consider system C, with two power curves in its ensemble. With probability 2/3, the curve $P(t) = Pe^{-t}$ (system Bs power curve) is selected, and with probability 1/3, the curve $P(t) = P$ is selected (system As curve). In this case $f(T \mid Q)$ is composed of two points, one of mass 2/3 at $T = T_B$ and one of mass 1/3 at $T = T_A$. Thus

$$E\left(\frac{1}{t} \mid Q\right) = \int_0^\infty \frac{1}{T}\left[\frac{1}{3}\delta(T-T_A) + \frac{2}{3}\delta(T-T_B)\right] dt = \left(\frac{1}{3}\cdot\frac{1}{T_A}\right)+\left(\frac{2}{3}\cdot\frac{1}{T_B}\right)$$

Once a power curve is selected, Q determines the completion time in exactly the same manner as it does in systems A and B. Our measure of capacity is therefore

$$QE\left(\frac{1}{T} \mid Q\right) = \left(\frac{1}{3}\cdot P\right) + \left(\frac{2}{3}\cdot\frac{Q}{\ln\left[P/(P-Q)\right]}\right)$$

just a weighted average of the capacities of systems A and B. More complex examples are easy to construct. The reader is invited to investigate the case where: (1) Q, the processing energy required, is distributed exponentially given the load L, that is, $g(Q \mid L) = (1/L)e^{-Q/L}$; and (2) there are two power curves in the ensemble—P, a constant that occurs with probability r, and the other being Pt which occurs with probability $(1 - r)$. From these facts a joint density on Q and T can be generated and $E(Q/T)$ and other statistics computed.

In the foregoing example, the quantity $E(Q/T)$ reduced to $Q \cdot E(1/T)$, because Q was viewed as being determined by the task load selected by the experimenter. Two other measures may often be preferable due to their easy computability, and although they may not always give equivalent answers, they do tend to represent the same kind of information. One of these measures simply employs $Q/E\ (T) = Q/\overline{T}$, that is, the fixed value of energy over the mean of the time taken to produce that energy (strictly speaking, we should have written $E\ (T\ |Q)$ in the denominator). The other related measure uses the median of T conditional on Q in the denominator, med $(T\ |Q) = T^*$.

As a simple example of these latter measures, suppose that $f\ (T\ |Q)$, determined from $\overline{f}\ (Q,\ T)$ by holding Q fixed and generating the distribution on T, turned out to be exponential: $f\ (T\ |Q) = a\ (Q)\ e^{-a\ (Q)\ T}$, where $a\ (Q)$ is the exponential rate parameter, which, in general, depends on Q but is of course fixed for a given Q. We then have immediately

$$\frac{Q}{\overline{\overline{T}}} = a(Q) \cdot Q \qquad \text{and} \qquad \frac{Q}{T^*} = \frac{a(Q) \cdot Q}{\log 2}$$

Note that these two measures are linearly related to each other. Note also that, in general, we can expect $a\ (Q)$ to decrease as a function of Q, because we believe longer times are needed to produce larger values of Q. As in the earlier examples of Systems A, B, and C, exactly how these measures act as Q varies depends on how the energy-producing ability of the ensemble of power curves changes with Q. This ability is summarized in this example in $a\ (Q)$. Thus, if $a\ (Q) = 1/Q$, then our present capacity measures are constant, indicating that the energy producing capacity of our system keeps up with increased needs as expressed by Q.

Before passing to the next topic, the possibility should be mentioned again that a (a priori) distribution may be placed on Q. This makes sense whenever the experimenter is varying the load and the dependent variables are not segregated according to load. As mentioned earlier, in some circumstances it might instead be that there is an internal distribution on the energy required for processing a given load from trial to trial even though that load is constant. In any case, such a distribution on Q immediately induces a true joint distribution on Q and T and allows the computation of such capacity statistics as $E\ (Q/T)$ and $E\ (Q)/E(t)$.

Furthermore, in some cases, there may exist an a priori distribution $f\ (T)$, on T. As we shall see, such a distribution could be generated by inherent randomness in the human processing system or by trial-to-trial variations in Os criterion on time or information sampling. In fact, it turns out that postulation of an $f\ (T)$ is necessary to predict speed-accuracy trade-offs when a single power curve is assumed and the processing load and externally imposed accuracy-time constraints are fixed. This necessity arises, for example, in certain interpretations of the Lappin and Disch results (1972).

We finally mention, in anticipation of discussion in the following on speed-accuracy trade-off, that the foregoing examples have been constructed with the idea of processing a given load exactly once. We consider further the possibility that the load may be processed more than once, or, in general, that more information can be gained with longer processing.

Lest we forget, at the beginning of this section, we cited *two* requirements for our study of the effects of both speed and accuracy on capacity. As of now we have only considered the first of these, which was to find measures of capacity that take into account both the energy produced as well as the time occupied in producing it. The second requirement, which is in a sense the obverse of the first, is to find a means of exhibiting the influence of capacity on the latency probability distribution. It is to this problem that we now turn.

Keeping in mind that we are discussing energy and the speed with which the system produces it, rather than effective capacity, which includes an observable accuracy component (to be taken up later), it becomes clear that we can represent increased capacity by way of a general increase in the height of the power curves in the ensemble of a given system. For instance, P could be elevated in the preceding examples (Systems A, B, and C). This naturally increases the average speed with which any particular energy is output. However, it may be that in some cases, it will be possible to describe the effect on the distribution of T *directly* by some means.

There are a number of possibilities that come to mind, but our present conception, one that seems to offer some insight and intriguing results, is to enter a capacity factor into the probability distribution by way of the so-called intensity function (Gumbel, 1958), also known as the hazard function, the age-specific failure rate, and the conditional density function (e.g., McGill & Gibbon, 1965; Cox, 1962). The intensity function gives the likelihood that something being processed will be completed in the immediate future, given that it has not yet been completed up to the present time; it can be written as

$$I(t) = \frac{f(t)}{1 - F(t)} = \frac{f(t)}{\overline{F}(t)}$$

where $f(t)$ is the density function of the processing distribution, and $F(t)$ is the cumulative distribution function. The quantity $1 - F(t) = \overline{F}(t)$ also goes by various names, the most common of which is probably *survivor function*, due to its use in failure theory. There, $\overline{F}(t)$ is the probability that a component has not yet failed, or, synonomously, that it has "survived" to time t.

Let us suppose that the capacity factor enters into the intensity function as a multiplicative factor so that

$$I(t; c) = cI(t),$$

where $I(t)$ is the intensity function when $c = 1$. The interesting result follows immediately that the survivor function is

$$\overline{F}(t; c) = \exp[-\int_0^t I(t; c)\, dt] = \exp\left\{\ln[\overline{F}(t)]^c\right\} = [\overline{F}(t)]^c,$$

that is, the survivor function is a power function with exponent c. This means that the family of survivor functions, or, equivalently, the family of distribution functions $F(t; c) = 1 - \overline{F}(t; c)$, are ordered according to c:

$$\overline{F}(t; c_1) > \overline{F}(t; c_2) \qquad \text{if and only if } c_2 > c_1$$

or

$$F(t; c_1) < F(t; c_2) \qquad \text{if and only if } c_2 > c_1$$

Thus it can be seen that a larger c means shorter latencies. It is obvious that the foregoing relation implies a consequent ordering of the means and medians of the distributions. In the case of the median, for instance, the dependence of the median on the gain is represented by

$$T^*(c) = \overline{F}^{-1}(\sqrt[c]{.5}).$$

so the median is the inverse survivor function of the cth root of ½. Clearly, the median moves to the left (decreases) as c increases, in a way that can be trivially calculated once the distribution or survivor function is known.

It is pertinent to note here that the intensity function is stronger or more elemental than the survivor or distribution functions in the sense that an ordering of the intensity functions implies an ordering of the distribution or survivor functions, but the reverse is not true; one distribution function may always (for any t) be greater than another without the same being true for their associated intensity functions (a formalization follows in the next section).

Now we can see that with the energy Q set at some value, but possibly also dependent on c, the measure of capacity given by the ratio of Q to the median time T^* is

$$\frac{Q}{T^*} = \frac{Q}{F^{-1}(\sqrt[c]{.5})},$$

The intensity function of exponential distributions is just the rate of the distribution, so that in our especially simple example of a system producing $f(T \mid Q)$ as an exponential function of T, seen previously, the new distribution, including the influence of capacity via a multiple of the intensity function, becomes

$$f(T \mid Q) = ca(Q)e^{-ca(Q)T}$$

Following from this, the capacity measure taken as the ratio of Q to the median of T is given as

$$\frac{Q}{T^*} = \frac{c \cdot a(Q) \cdot Q}{\log(2)}$$

This quantity increases linearly with c as it stands, indicating that capacity is improving, just as it increases with Q if $a(Q) = a$ and c are constant. The former reveals capacity improvement because of faster speed, the latter because of increased energy production for given average speed.

Of course, although the effect of capacity on latency through the intensity function can be quite helpful, the circumstances under which manipulations of the distribution on the power curve ensemble (or the ensemble itself) produce changes in the intensity function, particularly multiplicatively, are unknown. It is likely that a fairly narrow class of transformations on the ensemble lead to intensity function orderings. To be sure, it is not even clear what class of ensembles and associated distributions leads to particular $f(T \mid Q)$s, for example, the exponential.

We have thus far considered capacity as a function of expended energy and of processing time. We now turn our attention to possible measures that might reflect what we call *effective capacity*. These are typically based on observable reaction times and an accuracy statistic. It may be anticipated that such measures can also be closely related to trade-offs of speed and accuracy.

The approach taken here is a special case of the foregoing general development, with additional assumptions linking capacity as energy to observable accuracy statistics. Specifically, suppose that the power curve ensemble consists of a single function that is constant at power P over all time. Strictly speaking, $h^2(t)$ is not exactly constant, of course, but, in general, we can write

$$\frac{1}{T} \int_0^T s^2(t)\, dt = \overline{P}$$

and hence the total signal energy equals $\overline{P}T$, that is, the (average power) $\cdot$ (time). Actually, in the ideal visual situation, where in each time interval ΔT, a spatial correlation is performed on the constant pattern (with independently varying Gaussian noise), the variations in h are *spatial*, but h is constant in time for each ΔT. This ideal situation produces $h^2(t) = P(t) = P$; that is, the power allotted to the cross-correlation between the input and the memory item is constant for each correlation.

Under these assumptions we can write an expression for the expended energy in terms of time T:

$$Q_h(T) = P \cdot (T - t_0)$$

where $Q_h(T)$ represents the energy produced by the filter $h(t)$ up to time T, P is the constant power, and t_0 is the dead time before the system can produce any effective energy. It may be reasonable to identify the effect of this power with the well-known quantity $(d')^2$, which in matched filtering, such as we are considering, is defined as the total signal energy relative to the noise power density. This is due to the well-known aforementioned relation (Green & Swets, Chap. 9, 1966) between repeated observations of a constant stimulus in Gaussian noise and increases in detectability. More precisely, it is easy to see that

$$[d'(T)]^2 = \frac{\int_0^T s^2(t)\, dt}{\frac{N_0}{2}} = \frac{Q_h}{\frac{N_0}{2}}$$

where $N_0/2$ is the noise power per unit frequency, which with white Gaussian noise is constant. Substituting in $Q_h = P \cdot (T - t_0)$, we arrive at

$$[d'(T)]^2 = \frac{2}{N_0} P \cdot (T - t_0) = (A \cdot P \cdot T) - (A \cdot P \cdot t_0)$$

Where A is the reciprocal of the constant noise power. Hence $[d'(T)]^2$ is a linear function of time with a slope that is proportional to the power. Note that all three terms $(A, P,$ and $t_0)$ that determine the intercept must always be nonnegative. Hence we have an additional test of the foregoing assumptions; not only must $(d')^2$ be a linear function of T, but also the $(d')^2$ intercept must be negative.

Note that we actually plot $(d')^2$ against RT rather than T and that in general RT is unequal to T. Specifically, we assume RT $= T + t_1$, where t_1 is the time contributed by all other stages in the entire processing system (e.g., response selection and execution). This inconvenience causes us no great problems, because it means only that $[d'(t)]^2$ lifts off the time axis when RT $= t_1 + t_0$ rather than when $T = t_0$. Thus we can consider the $(d')^2$ plot against RT as a simple shift of the "true" plot against T.

One interpretation of the speed-accuracy curve $[d'(T)]^2$ as a function of T (or RT) is that a suitable transformation of the curve should yield capacity viewed as power or something proportional to power. In the present instance, the appropriate transformation is of course

$$\frac{[d'(T)]^2 + APt_0}{RT} = AP$$

where APt_0 is the intercept and A is a constant of proportionality from the foregoing formula of $[d'(T)]^2$.

The simple form of this function suggests a transformation to attempt to get at the underlying capacity expressed as power, or at least something that is proportional to this power. This "power" measure can be considered as a measure of effective capacity per unit time. In the present case, it is the slope of the $[d'(T)]^2$ curve.

These concepts have some general validity: If the power of a system, expressed in terms suitable to that system, is constant over time, and if accuracy increases as a function of increased time, then it is always possible in principle to *transform* the resulting speed-accuracy curve to a measure reflecting the constant underlying "power." However, it is critical to note that if the cognitive or perceptual power $P(t)$ is *not* constant over time, then such an attempt to find a constant measure of capacity is fruitless. Indeed, a speed accuracy curve then represents the variation in $P(t)$ as well as the more often assumed variation in an internal criterion on time or information. It still may be possible, with a suitable model, to uncover $P(t)$ as a function of time.

Despite the foregoing caveats, it might nevertheless be of interest to look for accuracy measures that are linear functions of time. Some other investigators have proceeded in this or an analogous fashion. That is, under the assumption of a constant system, discriminability per unit time (this implies the assumption of but one power curve in the ensemble for a given experimental condition), a measure proportional to this discriminability should be a linear function of reaction time. The results of these studies, which have plotted accuracy measures, such as $(d')^2$, as functions of reaction-time data, are overall rather encouraging.

Taylor, Lindsay, and Forbes (1967) have studied, in a series of experiments, the relationship between $(d')^2$ and reaction time. These studies involved detection tasks embedded in a 2 X 2 design. In the most conclusive of these, they transformed data of Schouten and Bekker (1967) to $(d')^2$ versus mean reaction time. The results strongly supported linearity.

Lappin and Disch (1972), instructing their subjects to respond to two easily discriminable stimuli at a speed that maintained a 25% error rate, studied the relationship of median RT to five different accuracy measures, including d' and $(d')^2$, each coming from a distinct model of the system. All of these measures provided reasonably good linear fits to the data, and in every instance the Q_h intercept was indeed negative. On the other hand, it may strike one as curious that none of the measures were strongly falsified, because they arose from separate theoretical hypotheses. Several potential explanations for this state of affairs come to mind.

First, it is possible that there was too much variability or noise in the data to separate the predictions of the models. Second, it could be that these measures are really similar functions of the data. For instance, one of the measures was $(-\ln \eta)$, where η is the stimulus similarity parameter of Luce's choice theory. Luce (1963) has shown this parameter is quite similar to d' of signal detectability theory. Also tested by Lappin and Disch (1972) was transmitted information that Taylor, Lindsay, and Forbes (1967) have pointed out is related to $(d')^2$.

The third possibility is that all of the functions are approximately linear only over the restricted range of the experiment. The set of RT data collected by the authors ranged from about 100 msec to about 300 msec, and thus the fitted linear curves were quite steep. Possibly, if widely varying experimenter-imposed deadlines had been employed, there would have been greater predictor variation.

The Lappin and Disch study can be considered a micro-trade-off experiment, where the speed variation arises out of internal processing variations rather than direct experimenter manipulation. As anticipated earlier, it is exactly in this type of situation that it is necessary to assume the existence of an a priori distribution $f(T)$, because a power ensemble of one curve can produce no variation in reaction time related to accuracy. Note that $f(T)$ does not enter into the $[d'(T)]^2$ plots directly; it only provides for variation in T, which is accompanied by more or less energy acquired from the (single) power curve. The distribution $f(T)$ could be generated by a varying criterion on the part of O on how much time or information he or she employs each trial. Another possibility is that $f(T)$ might be generated by assuming that the time the stimulus is available is distributed as $f(T)$, and that for any given time T, the information is of a constant integrity.

Green and Luce (1973), by varying response deadlines in a yes-no detection task, generated d' versus $\bar{T}$ curves, which appear quite linear over a larger RT range (ca. 200 to 1200 msec). Again, in all cases, the d' intercepts were negative. In one condition deadlines were placed on both signal and noise trials; in another condition a deadline was placed only on signal-present trials. On noise trials Os were not penalized for long response times. Results indicated that the d' versus $\bar{T}$ slopes were consistently much steeper in the signal-only deadline condition. This is perhaps interpretable as an increase in P due to release of capacity from elsewhere in the total system.

If, according to our earlier development, we can write an approximate relation of the form [rather than the exact relation in terms of $(d')^2$] as,

$$d'(T) \doteq (A \cdot P \cdot T) - (A \cdot P \cdot t_0),$$

we see at once that Ps increase should not alter the $d'(T) = 0$ intercept. In fact, the points where the d' curves cross the time axis appear little changed across the two conditions. In addition, increasing P should push the $d'(T)$ intercept (the $T = 0$ intercept) farther away from zero, because the term APt_0 increases. This prediction also was clearly supported by the Green and Luce data.

As the duration and/or intensity of the display is turned up and the signal-to-noise ratio increases to where performance approaches perfection, a measure based on speed and accuracy may become less adequate; for example, errors may be largely unrelated to the perceptual and decision processes under study. It may then be preferable to employ one or more quantities to measure capacity related to latency only rather than to both latency and accuracy.

CAPACITY MEASURES AND DYNAMICS BASED ON SPEED ONLY

General Introduction

In this section we consider approaches to pattern-matching tasks that emphasize speed alone and are broad in the sense that they are based on nonparametric properties of the processing distributions. One can utilize these characteristics or derivative properties in tests of fundamental principles of processing and in delimiting the range of potential explanatory models. One of the first attempts at such a development was by Sternberg (1973), who proposed a test of self-terminating models based on some properties of the RT distribution. Sternberg proceeded by way of assumptions about how search or comparison varies with the location of an item in a hypothetical internal storage array and by then deriving predictions about how the RT distributions should be affected by changes in this array size.

Although Sternberg apparently derived these properties with the idea of seriality in mind, his assumptions are not necessarily confined to this class of models. However, predictions emanating from those assumptions are contrary to many plausible parallel models. Specifically, Sternberg assumes that the processing system consists of a series of stages, each acting as though it has its own source of capacity that is unaffected by how many other stages are in the chain. This is essentially an assumption of unlimited capacity within each stage (see Townsend, 1974a, 1974b), and his method is therefore applicable to only a limited subset of the class of potential models.

Our own view is that a prediction about the ordering of distributions is first and foremost a prediction that arises from the architecture of capacity and only secondarily concerns issues such as self-terminating versus exhaustive or parallel versus serial. Thus we present what we hope is a more general theoretical approach. It is based on the examination of capacity effects at different levels of processing: in terms of hazard functions, distribution functions, and a measure of central tendency.

We take special care to make clear that although we discuss these approaches in terms of the multisymbol matching task, the notions are much more general; in fact, they can be applied to any situation in which a system is processing some finite number of things. That is, we are concerned with the effect of increasing the number of elements on reaction time, and although we speak here of these elements as symbols (e.g., letters), they are in no way restricted to symbols. Rather, they could be features within letters, as in the work of Taylor (1976), or each element could conceivably be a group of letters (e.g., words).

Throughout this discussion it is assumed that error rates are low and that those errors that do occur are independent of the comparison process and hence can be ignored. There are several germane points in this regard. The first is that in some cases conclusions are unchanged or strengthened when errors change. For instance, if error rate and latency both increase when the number of symbols increases, then obviously evidence of limitations in capacity is obtained. Only when latency and error information go in opposite directions will ordinal conclusions about capacity be ambiguous.

The second point is that it is still not clear that the errors acquired in a typical memory or brief visual display search experiment with very high accuracy are intimately connected to the comparison process itself. Such intuitions are supported by findings such as those of Swanson and Briggs (1969) and Pachella

(1974) that an 8% or 9% error increase in an LT task revealed only a change in intercept (i.e., slope remained constant). Changes in intercept but not slope have been said to imply corresponding changes in base time (stimulus encoding, response selection, and response execution) but not comparison time (e.g., Swanson & Briggs, 1969; Sternberg, 1967). Thus it may be that error rates up to about 10% (with error rates greater than 10%, Pachella, 1974, began finding slope changes) do not greatly influence the comparison process and therefore may be safely ignored when modeling this stage.

Third, the type of structure developed here (in addition to that introduced in the previous sections) can itself be of aid in predicting accuracy changes in certain cases. For example, the derivations in the following yield probability distributions for completion times, so that if the time allowed for processing is abbreviated, either by experimenter control (as with shortened display times in the case of visual search) or by observer-determined deadlines, the latency and accuracy effects can be predicted.

We make these remarks not because we are unconvinced of the importance of empirical and theoretical work in the relations of speed to accuracy, quite the contrary, as the earlier sections should demonstrate. It is only by continued work in these regions that a fuller understanding of the precise relationships will be achieved.

Development of the Stochastic Inequalities

A peculiarly intriguing approach to the study of stochastic systems is the analysis (or development) of the time intervals between successive completions (the intercompletion times) in terms of capacity written via the intensity function on the intercompletion time. The overall intensity function for a given stage (and therefore a given intercompletion time) is just that of a given symbol in serial processing but in parallel processing and some hybrid models will be itself a combination of intensity functions of individual symbols undergoing processing. Of course, qualitative or quantitative differences in capacity can be embedded in the orderings of the respective intensity functions.

It is useful to compare the use of the intensity function to represent capacity differences with two other candidates. One places orderings directly on the distribution functions and another on an inequality of random times. It is easy to show that if, say, the intensity function for symbol A is always greater than that for symbol B, then the distribution function for symbol A (or A and B may be intercompletion times or subsystems, etc.) is always greater than that for symbol B. Suppose that

$$I_A(t) = \frac{f_A(t)}{\overline{F}_A(t)} > \frac{f_B(t)}{\overline{F}_B(t)} = I_B(t)$$

then

$$\int_0^t \frac{f_A(t)}{\overline{F}_A(t)} \, dt = -\int_0^t \left[\frac{d \log \overline{F}_A(t)}{dt} \right] dt > -\int_0^t \left[\frac{d \log \overline{F}_B(t)}{dt} \right] dt$$

$$= \int_0^t \frac{f_B(t)}{\overline{F}_B(t)} \, dt$$

which by integration leads to

$$-\log \overline{F}_A(t) > -\log \overline{F}_B(t),$$

and by exponentiation implies

$$\overline{F}_A(t) < \overline{F}_B(t) \qquad \text{i.e.,} \qquad F_A(t) > F_B(t),$$

which was the claim. This is natural, because the intensity inequality states that at any time t when A is not yet completed, the likelihood that it is completed in the next instant is greater than the comparable likelihood for B. The inequality in the distribution functions makes the weaker statement that for any t the probability that A was completed at some time less than or equal to t is greater than the comparable probability for B. Put succinctly, an ordering of intensity functions orders the distribution functions, but not conversely; if the distribution functions are ordered, the intensity functions may or may not be.

As an example of this latter proposition, consider the two density functions illustrated in Fig. 3, where the random variable A is distributed Rayleigh (i.e., $f_A(t) = te^{-t^2/2}$ for $t > 0$ and zero otherwise), and B is distributed exponential with rate $\lambda = 60$ but displaced $t = 40$ units to the right (i.e., $f_B(t) = 60e^{-60(t-40)}$, $t > 40$; zero otherwise). We might think of this 40-unit time lag as a dead time or an irreducible minimum response time. Now our first requirement is that the distribution functions are ordered; thus we ask,

$$F_A(t) \overset{?}{>} F_B(t) \qquad \text{for all } t > 0,$$

which is equivalent to asking

$$1 - e^{-t^2/2} \overset{?}{>} 1 - e^{-60(t-40)}$$

or

$$e^{-t^2/2} \overset{?}{<} e^{-60(t-40)}$$

Taking natural logarithms of both sides yields

$$\frac{-t^2}{2} \overset{?}{<} -60(t - 40)$$

and finally

$$t^2 - 120t + 4800 \overset{?}{>} 0 \qquad \text{for all } t > 40.$$

This expression obviously describes a parabola opening upward. Setting the derivative equal to zero and solving for t implies that its minimum is at $t = 60$. But we see that the value of the parabola as it crosses $t = 60$ is

$$(60)^2 - (120)(60) + 4800 = 1200 > 0.$$

Because the minimum is greater than zero, we know all other points must be, and therefore, as desired,

$$F_A(t) > F_B(t) \qquad \text{for all } t > 0.$$

Now the intensity function of A is given by

$$I_A(t) = \frac{te^{-t^2/2}}{e^{-t^2/2}} = t \qquad \text{for all } t > 0$$

and

$$I_B(t) = \frac{60e^{-60(t - 40)}}{e^{-60(t - 40)}} = 60 \qquad \text{for all } t > 40.$$

Thus, when $40 \leqslant t < 60$, we see that $I_B(t) > I_A(t)$, and thus the counterexample

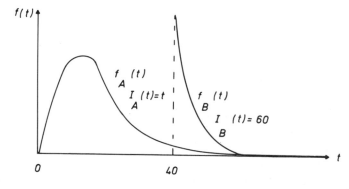

FIG. 3   Counterexample to the proposition that $F_A(t) > F_B(t) \Rightarrow I_A(t) > I_B(t)$, for all $t > 0$.

is complete. An ordering on the distributions does not imply an ordering on the intensity functions.

Yet a third type of ordering can easily be stated in terms of the underlying random variables. Let t_B and t_A be the respective random variables for As and Bs completion. Then this type of ordering can be put as

$$P(t_A < t_B) > \frac{1}{2}$$

That is, the probability that the time to complete A is less than that to finish B is greater than ½. This type of ordering is the basis of several nonparametric tests, which are probably often employed with little thought to exactly what a significant statistical result really has to say about the underlying populations.

As it happens, this inequality is implied by an inequality in the distribution functions and therefore by an inequality in the intensity functions. The proof is quick. If $F_A(t) = F_B(t)$ for all $t \geqslant 0$, then we see that

$$P(t_A < t_B) = \int_0^\infty f_B(t)F_A(t)\,dt = \int_0^\infty f_B(t)F_B(t)\,dt = \frac{1}{2} \, .$$

When $F_A(t) > F_B(t)$ for all $t > 0$ as assumed, we can compare

$$P(t_A < t_B) = \int_0^\infty f_B(t)F_A(t) \qquad \text{versus} \qquad \int_0^\infty f_B(t)F_B(t)\,dt = \frac{1}{2}.$$

This is easily transformed to

$$\int_0^\infty f_B(t)F_A(t)\,dt - \int_0^\infty f_B(t)F_B(t)\,dt \quad \text{versus} \qquad 0,$$

or

$$\int_0^\infty f_B(t)[F_A(t) - F_B(t)]\,dt > 0,$$

by virtue of our assumption $F_A(t) > F_B(t)$ for all positive t, and we are done, because if the last expression is greater than $0, P(t_A < t_B) > $½.

On the other hand, such an ordering on the random variables does not imply an ordering on the distributions. An appropriate counterexample is found when both distributions are normal, with the mean of the A-distribution being less than that of the B-distribution. Because $P(t_A < t_B) > $½ is equivalent to $P(t_A - t_B < 0) > $½, we see from symmetry, and the fact that the mean of the difference variable $(t_A - t_B)$ is less than 0 and its mean equals its median, that the inequality $P(t_A < t_B) > $½ holds. However, we can set the variance of the A-distribution sufficiently large (relative to the B-variance) that an obvious cross-over in the distribution functions occurs, therefore violating an inequality in the latter.

This random-variable (or probability) ordering is moreover even weaker than the foregoing indicates, because it does not imply an ordering on either the means or the medians. For instance, assume that t_A is distributed Cauchy for $t > 0$ (i.e., $f_A(t) = 2/[\pi(1 + t^2)]$ for $t > 0$ and 0 elsewhere) and that $f_B(t)$ is any distribution with a finite mean and displaced far enough to the right so that $P(t_A < t_B) > \frac{1}{2}$. Now the expected value of A is infinite, and therefore

$$P(t_A < t_B) > \frac{1}{2} \;=\!\!\!\!/\!\!\!\Longrightarrow\; E_A(t) < E_B(t).$$

As for the medians, consider the discrete case in Fig. 4. Here

$$P(t_A < t_B) = (.49) \cdot (1.0) + (.02) \cdot (.49) + (.49) \cdot (.49) = .73$$

and therefore $P(t_A < t_B) > \frac{1}{2}$. Now it is obvious that $\text{Med}(t_A) > \text{Med}(t_B)$, and thus

$$P(t_A < t_B) > \frac{1}{2} \;=\!\!\!\!/\!\!\!\Longrightarrow\; \text{Med}(t_A) < \text{Med}(t_B).$$

We have thus established the following dominance relationship in the three types of "stochastic" inequalities

$$[I_A(t) > I_B(t)] \;\Longrightarrow\; [F_A(t) > F_B(t)] \;\Longrightarrow\; [P(t_A < t_B) > \frac{1}{2}]$$

for all t in the domain of the probability functions. We refer to these, from strongest to the weakest, as a "intensity," "distribution," and "probability" inequality

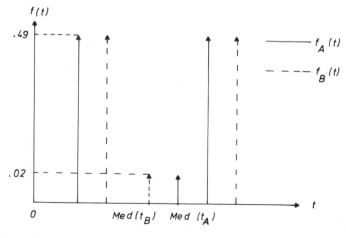

FIG. 4   Counterexample to the proposition that $P(t_A < t_B) > \frac{1}{2} \Rightarrow \text{Med}(t_A) < \text{Med}(t_B)$, for all $t > 0$.

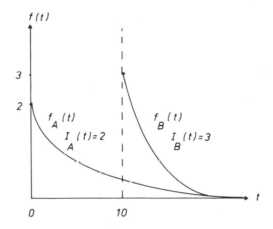

FIG. 5   Counterexample to the proposition that $P(t_A < t_B) > \frac{1}{2} \Rightarrow I_A(t) > I_B(t)$, for all $t > 0$.

or ordering. The rubric of the last leaves something to be desired in terms of specificity but perhaps will suffice for now.

Further, via counterexamples, we have seen that

$$[P(t_A < t_B) > \frac{1}{2}] \;\Longrightarrow\!\!\!/\!\!\!\Longrightarrow\; [F_A(t) > F_B(t)] \;\Longrightarrow\!\!\!/\!\!\!\Longrightarrow\; [I_A(t) > I_B(t)]$$

In this reverse case, the transitivity [that $P(t_A < t_B) \geq \frac{1}{2} \not\Rightarrow I_A(t) > I_B(t)$] must be demonstrated. As one would expect, the counterexample is easily constructed.

Assume that t_A and t_B are both distributed exponentially with rates two and three, respectively, but that $f_B(t)$ is displaced to the right $t = 10$ units as in Fig. 5. Now $P(t_A < 10) \cong 1$, and therefore it is obvious that $P(t_A < t_B) > \frac{1}{2}$. But $I_A(t) = 2$, and $I_B(t) = 3$, and hence $I_A(t) < I_B(t)$, which completes the counterexample.

It is to be emphasized that the foregoing dominance relationship does not rule out that, for instance, $I_A(t) > I_B(t)$ and $F_A(t) > F_B(t)$ both hold simultaneously. Instead, this may frequently occur; but if one knows only that $F_A(t) > F_B(t)$, one must check $I_A(t) \overset{?}{>} I_B(t)$ to be sure that the ordering holds there also.

CONSTRUCTION AND ANALYSIS OF MODELS VIA INTENSITY FUNCTION DYNAMICS

In the rest of the chapter, we utilize some of the theoretical developments of the preceding section to study microscopic capacity influences on the stage of some very general classes of models. The focus is on intensity functions as measures of capacity, although one can, of course, start instead at the weaker levels associated with the distribution or probability inequalities. We begin by positing a common variety parallel model and then generalizing our results to a much broader class of systems.

Suppose as noted that processing is parallel and also independent on total completion times of the individual symbols (see Townsend, 1974a). This means that the processing times on the various symbols are independent events, which of course has different ramifications in parallel as opposed to serial systems. As we shall see, the investigation of the capacity question, which arises as the number of symbols is varied, places no constraints on the rates at the various individual symbol positions. In general, they may all be distinct.

Consider, then, the intensity functions that describe the capacity of the system during the *first* stage of processing. For various possible numbers of symbols, we have

$$I_1(t) = \frac{f_{11}(t)}{\bar{F}_{11}(t)}$$

$$I_2(t) = \frac{f_{21}(t)\bar{F}_{22}(t) + f_{22}(t)\bar{F}_{21}(t)}{\bar{F}_{21}(t)\bar{F}_{22}(t)} = \frac{f_{21}(t)}{\bar{F}_{21}(t)} + \frac{f_{22}(t)}{\bar{F}_{22}(t)} \tag{7}$$

$$= I_{21}(t) + I_{22}(t),$$

$$\vdots$$

$$I_n(t) = \frac{\sum\limits_{i=1}^{n} f_{ni}(t) \prod\limits_{\substack{j=1 \\ j \neq i}}^{n} \bar{F}_{nj}(t)}{\prod\limits_{i=1}^{n} \bar{F}_{ni}(t)} = \sum\limits_{i=1}^{n} \left[\frac{f_{ni}(t)}{\bar{F}_{ni}(t)}\right] = \sum\limits_{i=1}^{n} I_{ni}(t),$$

where the first subscript denotes the value of n (display size) and the second the serial (spatial or temporal) position of a symbol. These intensity functions reveal the likelihood that a symbol is completed at the instant after time t, given that it is not yet finished (at time t). There are several things to notice about (7). One is that the preceding expression for a fixed value of n determines the capacity of the individual symbols (during *all* stages of processing), because independence necessitates that the f_{ni} do not change during a single trial, and also that the overall capacity of the system is therefore given. Another aspect of (7) is that this overall capacity, as designated during Stage 1, before any symbols have been completed, can be written as the sum of the individual intensity functions and therefore the sum of the individual capacities. This seems to be an exceedingly felicitous and natural property of representation of capacity by way of the intensity functions. However, it is important to take note that when the "excess" survivor functions, the $\bar{F}_{nj}(t)$, $(j \neq 1)$, are cancelled out of the numerator and denominator, the resultant expression is no longer a true intensity function, because it integrates to n instead of to 1.[4] This should cause no difficulties as long as properties of intensity functions are not inappropriately applied to the simplified versions of (7). Comparisons of overall capacities during Stage 1 can be made between the models of different systems by employment of the sums of the individual intensities.

We emphasize the capacity for Stage 1, even though all capacity consequences are fixed by stating (7), because the orderings for potentially observable reaction times are in general implied only for the Stage 1 intercompletion time, which is, of course, equivalent to the minimum finishing time for the n symbols (processing time of first element finished). Following the development from an earlier paper (Townsend, 1974b), and assuming an inequality in the overall intensity of capacity as suggested in (7), for two systems working on n_1 and n_2 symbols, respectively, we have, as earlier

$$I_n^{(1)}(t) = \sum_{i=1}^{n_1} \frac{f_{n_1 i}^{(1)}(t)}{\bar{F}_{n_1 i}^1(t)} > \sum_{i=1}^{n_2} \frac{f_{n_2 i}^{(2)}(t)}{\bar{F}_{n_2 i}^2(t)} = I_n^{(2)}(t)$$

[4] To be precise we should write

$$I_n(t') = f(t' \mid t' \geqslant t) = \frac{\sum\limits_{i=1}^{n} f_{ni}(t') \prod\limits_{\substack{j=1 \\ j \neq i}}^{n} \bar{F}_{nj}(t')}{\prod\limits_{j=1}^{n} \bar{F}_{nj}(t)}$$

Now we can see that when $t' = t$, cancellation is perfectly legitimate, at that time point t. And, $I_{in}(t)$ *does* equal the intensity function of the ith position being processed alone at time t. However, for actual description of $I_n(t)$ as t' varies over values greater than t, both $I_n(t)$ and $I_{ni}(t)$ must contain the entire probability measure, i.e.,

$$I_{ni}(t') = \frac{f_{ni}(t') \prod\limits_{\substack{j=1 \\ j \neq 1}}^{n} \bar{F}_{nj}(t')}{\prod\limits_{j=1}^{n} \bar{F}_{nj}(t)} = I_{ni}(t' \mid t).$$

In any case, the instantaneous rate description, which is given when $t' = t$, is properly written as the sum with cancellations included and so validly represents a summing of capacity at $t' = t$. Further, the minimum completion time distribution predictions (or any others for that matter) do not depend on this mode of expressing capacity.

By integration we achieve

$$\int_0^t I_n^{(1)}(t)\,dt = -\sum_{i=1}^{n_1} \log \overline{F}_{n_1 i}^{(1)}(t) > -\sum_{i=1}^{n_2} \log \overline{F}_{n_2 i}^{(2)}(t) = \int_0^t I_n^{(2)}(t)\,dt$$

which leads to

$$\overline{F}_{n_1}^{(1)}(\min t) = \prod_{i=1}^{n_1} \overline{F}_{n_1 i}^{(1)}(t) < \prod_{i=1}^{n_2} \overline{F}_{n_2 i}^{(2)}(t) = \overline{F}_{n_2}^{(2)}(\min t)$$

or

$$F_{n_1}^{(1)}(\min t) > F_{n_2}^{(2)}(\min t).$$

As indicated by the notation, these products are just the survivor functions for the respective minimum completion (or Stage 1 intercompletion) times, and so it is ascertained that for any value of t, it is always more likely that System 1 has completed its first symbol than that System 2 has.

On the other hand, this measure of overall capacity is not very general, because it holds no strict implications for other processing times. For example, an inequality may hold in the foregoing measure, yet the distribution functions for the *exhaustive* processing times need not be ordered such that the System 1 times are (in terms of distribution) shorter than those for System 2. To end up with distribution or probability inequalities to any particular level of processing (e.g., minimum processing time, as in the foregoing, self-terminating with a single target, and exhaustive are the most commonly used), one must write the intensity function for that level. Thus, for *exhaustive* processing in the present independent parallel model, the intensity function is just

$$I_n(\max t) = \frac{\sum\limits_{i=1}^{n} f_{n_i}(t) \prod\limits_{\substack{j=1 \\ \neq i}}^{n} F_{nj}(t)}{1 - \prod\limits_{i=1}^{n} F_{ni}(t)}.$$

On the other hand, the *self-terminating* intensity when the target is specified to be in position j, is simply $[f_{nj}(t)/\overline{F}_{nj}(t)]$. Interestingly, the average of the self-terminating intensities is *not* the intensity function of the self-terminating processing time. Rather, the latter, which is the quantity we need, is

$$I_n(S - T, t) = \frac{\dfrac{1}{n} \sum\limits_{i=1}^{n} f_{ni}(t)}{1 - \dfrac{1}{n} \sum\limits_{i=1}^{n} F_{ni}(t)}$$

which brings with it the necessary implications for the self-terminating distribution function, which is, of course,

$$F_n(S - T, t) = \frac{1}{n} \sum_{i=1}^{n} F_{ni}(t).$$

The intensity function can be written for any given level of processing in which one has interest. But the mathematics developed in the preceding for the minimum completion time turn out to be more general in the sense that at any stage of processing, we can conditionalize on the past events (e.g., items completed) and times (e.g., times of completion of the items), and then the basic structure of the minimum completion time lifts over into the conditional *intercompletion time*. Thus one can investigate the capacity at any stage of processing, given any particular previous set of completions and times (on that trial), and *compare* two or more models at that processing stage. Alternatively, one can *build* any particular capacity architecture, in the fullest possible sense, by considering each possible stage (or class of stages) and imposing his or her capacity specifications there.

As a simple example of this *comparison* property, consider the standard serial model (with a single order of processing) based on a gamma distribution with k stages at each symbol versus a standard independent parallel model whose distributions are gamma with k stages each, and assume that all rate parameters are equal. Then, a comparison of the intensity functions shows that the one for the serial model's successive stages remains constant, whereas the one for the parallel model decreases. A manifestation of this is the lengthening intercompletion times (probabilistically) in the parallel case as opposed to the constancy of the intercompletion times of the serial model.

As an example of the *building* concept, we may note that many, perhaps most, of the models we might think up on the spur of the moment to attempt to represent psychological phenomena probably would possess constant or decreasing intensity functions, for reasons associated with the two models immediately preceding. Suppose, though, that because of warm-up effects in serial processing, for instance, that it was expected that intercompletion times (which are equivalent to processing times in serial models) should actually decrease in a certain fashion. This property could be incorporated directly into the model by specification of the pertinent intensity functions. Or assume a series of problems, each successive member of which is composed of an increasingly smaller set of subproblems. Again, this structure could be implemented by way of the intensity functions—as a reduction in the number of stages in successive gamma processes, for instance. Of course, such a description is by no means restricted to gamma processes—stage mechanisms (or successive intercompletion time distributions) can be associated with any set of distributions whatsoever.

Let us briefly take up a special case of a conditional intensity function in intercompletion times. Consider a parallel model that assumes within-stage independence (e.g., Townsend, 1976). Suppose that $n = 2$ and that we wish to peruse the intensity for the intercompletion time for item a conditioned on b having been completed at time $t'_{b1} = t_{b1}$. Let the state of as processing at time t_{b1} be designated by $S_a = j$, where the state of being completed for a is $k > j$ (e.g., k may be the number of features making up a and j the number completed by time t_b). Let τ_{a2} (τ_{b1}) be the second (first) intercompletion time when b is completed first (note that t_{b1} is the same as τ_{b1}; that is, the first intercompletion time is equal to the first processing time). For the moment, let f_{ij}, $\bar{F}_{ij}$ be the density and survivor functions for the *intercompletion times* (of item $i = a, b$, during stage j), and let g_i, $\bar{G}_i$ be the density and survivor functions for the *processing times* per se (for item i). The intensity function we wish to observe is

$$I(\tau_{a2} \mid S_a = j \quad \text{at time } t'_{b1} = t_{b1}) = \frac{f(\tau_{a2} \ \& \ S_a = j \ \& \ t'_{b1} = t_{b1})}{P(\tau'_a \geqslant \tau_a \ \& \ S = j \ \& \ t'_{b1} = t_{b1})}$$

$$= \frac{f_{a2}(\tau_{a2} \mid S_a = j \quad \text{at } t_{b1})P_{a1}(S_a = j \quad \text{at } t_{b1})g_{b1}(t_{b1})}{P_{a1}(S_a = j \quad \text{at } t_{b1})\bar{F}_{a2}(\tau_{a2} \mid S_a = j \quad \text{at } t_{b1})g_{b1}(t_{b1})}$$

$$= \frac{f_{a2}(\tau_{a2} \mid S_a = j \quad \text{at } t_{b1})}{\bar{F}_{a2}(\tau_{a2} \mid S_a = j \quad \text{at } t_{b1})}.$$

The first fs (without subscripts) are, of course, meant to represent the appropriate general probability functions.

The very last formula gives the intensity function in terms of the Stage 2 conditional intercompletion time density (in the numerator) and the Stage 2 conditional survivor function for as intercompletion time. Note that we have a general case here where the second stage intercompletion time distribution can depend not only on the state the uncompleted item was in at time t_b but also on the exact time that item b finished. Clearly, by manipulation of this expression for the different stages and times and order of completion, any conceivable stochastic capacity structure can be embedded in the model.

If grosser intensities are desired, these can be obtained by averaging. For example, suppose that one would like to have the above intensity conditioned on t_b but *not* on the state j. Then we could derive

$$I_{a2}(\tau_{a2} \mid t'_{b1} = t_{b1}) = \frac{f(\tau_{a2} \ \& \ t'_{b1} = t_{b1})}{P(\tau'_{a2} \geqslant \tau_a \ \& \ t'_b = t_b)}$$

$$= \frac{\sum\limits_{j=0}^{k-1} P_{a1}(S_a = j \quad \text{at } t_{b1})f_{a2}(\tau_{a2} \mid S_a = j \quad \text{at } t_{b1})}{\sum\limits_{j=0}^{k-1} P_{a1}(S_a = j \quad \text{at } t_{b1})\bar{F}_{a2}(\tau_{a2} \mid S_a = j \quad \text{at } t_{b1})}.$$

A special case of this model is when both g_a and g_b are gamma with k features and parameter v, and v does not change across stages. The two intensity functions (conditioned and not conditioned on state S_a, respectively) are then elementary:

$$I_{a2}(\tau_{a2} \mid S_a = j \ \text{ at } t'_{b1} = t_{b1}) = \frac{\dfrac{v(v\tau_{a2})^{k-j-1} \, e^{-v\tau_{a2}}}{(k-j-1)!}}{\displaystyle\sum_{i=0}^{k-j-1} \dfrac{(v\tau_{a2})^i \, e^{-v\tau_{a2}}}{i!}}$$

and

$$I_{a2}(\tau_{a2} \mid t'_{b1}) = \frac{\displaystyle\sum_{i=0}^{k-1} \dfrac{(vt_{b1})^i \, e^{-vt_{b1}}}{i!} \cdot \dfrac{v(v\tau_{a2})^{k-i-1} \, e^{-v\tau_{a2}}}{(k-i-1)!}}{\displaystyle\sum_{i=0}^{k-1} \dfrac{(vt_{b1})^i \, e^{-vt_{b1}}}{i!} \sum_{j=0}^{k-i-1} \dfrac{(v\tau_{a2})^j \, e^{-v\tau_{a2}}}{j!}}$$

A more general model than this parallel gamma model is obtained by allowing v to be dependent on the stage and on the item, so that v in the numerator of $I_{a2}(\tau_{a2} \mid S_a = j \ \& \ t'_{b1} = t_{b1})$ would become $v(a; 2) = v_{a2}$, and the rate in the denominator (representing the processing rate during Stage 1 for a) would be $v(a; 1) = v_{a1}$. A very general model would result from allowing v to be also dependent on the times of completion and on the state the item is in, thus turning the v for a at Stage 2 into $v(a; 2; j; t_{b1})$.

The discussion has been emphasizing the description of the intensity function by way of the associated densities, survivor functions, etc. We can, however, choose to take the intensity function as the "given" and derive the other ways of describing the distribution (distribution function, density function, etc.) from the intensity function. The nice aspect of this is that almost *any* function of time, $u(t) > 0$ for all $t \geqslant 0$, can be *defined* as an intensity function and the associated distribution function produced by

$$F(t) = 1 - e^{\int_0^t u(t')dt'}$$

or the survivor function simply as

$$\overline{F}(t) = e^{-\int_0^t u(t')dt'}$$

It is clearly necessary that $\lim_{t \to +\infty} \int_0^\infty u(t') \, dt' = +\infty$. Of course, we can also make $u(t) = I(t)$ depend on the state of processing as well as previous processing times. Thus, if in our present developments, $I_{a2}(\tau_{a2} \mid t'_{b1} = t_{b1})$ is specified, then the survivor function is $\exp\left[-\int_0^{\tau_a} 2I_{a2}(\tau_{a2}|t'_{b1} = t_{b1})d\tau'_{a2}\right]$, and the density function for this particular intercompletion time is just

$$I_{a2}(\tau_{a2} \mid t'_{b1} = t_{b1}) \; \exp \; \left[- \int_0^{\tau_{a2}} I_{a2}(\tau'_{a2} \mid t'_{b1}) \, d\tau'_{a2} \right]$$

One way of viewing the latter expression is that we can conceive of any stochastic process (e.g., on intercompletion times) as a sort of time-varying exponential process. Of course, the distribution is truly exponential if and only if the intensity function I is constant (not varying with time).

Using the intercompletion time distributions is particularly appropriate when the successive intercompletion times are independent. This occurs with exponential distributions but is by *no means* confined to them. To be sure, some systems or their models may be more easily described by the intensity functions on the completion times themselves, and capacity can still be compared between two models, for example, by selecting the analogous states of processing in the two models. We find in this connection, not surprisingly, that independent parallel models are nicely depicted by intensity functions of the individual *total completion time* (this is the time from $t = 0$, when the system begins processing anything, to when the item under study is completed; Townsend, 1974a). Such intensity functions for an element may depend on time and state for that element but cannot depend on what is going on within the other items. Serial systems, on the other hand, are usually more simply described via the intercompletion time distributions, because in serial processing the intercompletion times are the actual processing times on individual items.

SUMMARY OF MAJOR RESULTS

We first developed a feature-matching and letter-recognition model based on a linear correlator with output

$$y_K = \sum_{j=1}^{K} r_{ij} s_{rj}$$

where r_{ij} is the jth discrete sample of feature i, and s_{rj} represents the analogous sample from memory feature s_r. Distributions of y_K were then obtained when the input signal contained white Gaussian noise and the memory signal was riding a DC component of amplitude b. There it was found that y_K is distributed as

$$
\begin{cases}
N(ba \sum_{j=1}^{K} s_{ij}^2,\, b^2 \sum_{j=1}^{K} s_{ij}^2) & \text{if present} \quad \text{present} \\[2em]
N(0,\, b^2 \sum_{j=1}^{K} s_{ij}^2) & \text{if absent} \quad \text{present} \\[2em]
N(ba \sum_{j=1}^{K} s_{ij},\, Kb^2) & \text{if present} \quad \text{absent} \\[2em]
N(0,\, Kb^2) & \text{if absent} \quad \text{absent}
\end{cases}
$$

Feature i
Input   Memory

where a represents the strength of the input signal relative to the memory signal. Signal-to-noise ratios for these cases were discussed.

The concepts of power and energy were developed within both the time and frequency domain. The notion of a set or ensemble of power curves and a distribution on these as representing the ability of a system to produce energy played a central role in these parts of the chapter. Some measures of capacity were suggested that included both the energy, Q, consumed by the system, and the time, T, taken by the system to expend that energy. These measures were of the form Q/T. Note that increasing either the energy or the speed increases these measures. Also suggested as a possible measure of effective capacity, which is proportional to the power, P, allocated to the filter, was

$$
\frac{[d'(T)]^2 + APt_0}{RT} = AP
$$

where APt_0 is the intercept of $[d'(T)]^2$ as a function of RT, and A is a constant of proportionality. These results were discussed in light of some recent empirical studies.

Then emphasizing speed alone, we developed three very general measures of capacity; that is, the measures were in the form of orderings on intensity (hazard) functions, distribution functions, and the underlying random variables. It was shown that a dominance relationship exists among these measures, that is

$$
[I_A(t) > I_B(t)] \implies [F_A(t) > F_B(t)] \implies [P(t_A < t_B) > \tfrac{1}{2}] \qquad \text{for all } t > 0
$$

but that the reverse ordering does not necessarily hold. It was then demonstrated (using the intensity function ordering) how one can use these measures to: (1) investigate the capacity at any stage of processing; and/or (2) construct any particular capacity architecture in a model one wishes.

ACKNOWLEDGMENTS

The final stages of preparation of this manuscript were completed at the Technical University of Braunschweig during a Visiting Professorship of the first author sponsored by the Deutsche Forschungsgemeinschaft. Both authors were on leave there and are indebted to the Deutsche Forschungsgemeinschaft and the Institute for Psychology. Joseph Lappin provided a critical reading, and John Castellan and Stephen Link gave helpful editorial assistance. We also thank Leslie Waugh Townsend for assistance in preparation of this chapter.

REFERENCES

Anderson, J. A. A theory for the recognition of items from short memorized lists. *Psychological Review*, 1973, *80*, 417-438.

Atkinson, R. C., Holmgren, J. E., & Juola, J. F. Processing time as influenced by the number of elements in a visual display. *Perception & Psychophysics*, 1969, *6*, 321-326.

Cornsweet, T. N. *Visual perception*. New York: Academic Press, 1970.

Cox, D. R. *Renewal theory*. London: Methuen, 1962.

Estes, W. K. An associative basis for coding and organization in memory. In A. W. Melton & E. Martin (Eds.), *Coding processes in human memory*, New York: Winston-Wiley, 1972.

Estes, W. K., & Taylor, H. A. A detection method and probabilistic models for assessing information processing from brief visual displays. *Proceedings of the National Academy of Sciences*, 1964, *52*, 446-454.

Green, D. M., & Luce, R. D. Speed-accuracy trade-off in auditory detection. In S. Kornblum (Ed.), *Attention and performance, IV*, New York: Academic Press, 1973.

Green, D. M., & Swets, J. A. *Signal detection theory and psychophysics*. New York: Wiley, 1966.

Gumbel, E. J. *Statistics of extremes*, New York: Columbia University Press, 1958.

Hoffman, J. E. Hierarchical stages in the processing of visual information. *Perception & Psychophysics*, 1975, *18*, 348-354.

Kahneman, D. K. *Attention and effort*. Englewood Cliffs: Prentice-Hall, 1973.

Kantowitz, B. H., & Knight, J. L., Jr. Testing tapping timesharing, II: Auditory secondary task. *Acta Psychologica*, 1976, *40*, 343-362.

Lappin, J. S., & Disch, K. The latency operating characteristic: I. Effects of stimulus probability on choice reaction time. *Journal of Experimental Psychology*, 1972, *92*, 419-427.

Link, S. W. The relative judgment theory of two choice response times. *Journal of Mathematical Psychology*, 1975, *12*, 114-135.

Luce, R. D. Detection and recognition. In R. D. Luce, R. B. Bush, & E. Galanter (Eds.), *Handbook of mathematical psychology* (Vol. I). New York: Wiley, 1963.

Luce, R. D., & Green, D. M. A neural timing theory for response times and the psychophysics of intensity. *Psychological Review*, 1972, *19*, 14-57.

Massaro, D. W., & Schmuller, J. Visual features, pre-perceptual storage, and processing time in reading. In *Understanding Language*. New York: Academic Press, 1975.

McGill, W. J. *Introduction to counter theory in psychophysics*, Unpublished manuscript, 1966.

McGill, W. J., & Gibbon, J. The general-gamma distribution and reaction times. *Journal of Mathematical Psychology*, 1965, *2*, 1-18.

Pachella, R. G. The interpretation of reaction time in information-processing research. In B. H. Kantowitz (Ed.), *Human information processing: Tutorials in performance and cognition*. Potomac, Md.: Lawrence Erlbaum Associates, 1974.

Padulo, L., & Arbib, M. A. *System theory*. Phila., Pa.: Saunders, 1974.

Pew, R. W. Human perceptual-motor performance. In B. H. Kantowitz (Ed.), *Human information processing: Tutorials in performance and cognition*. Potomac, Md.: Lawrence Erlbaum Associates, 1974.

Pike, R. Response latency models for signal detection. *Psychological Review*, 1973, *80*, 53-68.

Schouten, J. F., & Bekker, J. A. M. Reaction time and accuracy. *Acta Psychologica*, 1967, *27*, 223-229.

Smith, H. M. *Principles of holography*. New York: Wiley-Interscience, 1969.

Smith, E. E., & Spoehr, K. T. The perception of printed English: A theoretical perspective. In B. H. Kantowitz (Ed.), *Human information processing: Tutorials in performance and Cognition*. Potomac, Md.: Lawrence Erlbaum Associates, 1974.

Sternberg, S. High-speed scanning in human memory. *Science*, 1966, *153*, 652-654.

Sternberg, S. Two operations in character recognition: Some evidence from reaction-time measurements. *Perception & Psychophysics*, 1967, *2*, 45-53.

Sternberg, S. *Evidence against self-terminating memory search from properties of RT distributions*. Paper presented at the annual meeting of the Psychonomic Society, St. Louis, November, 1973.

Swanson, J. M., & Briggs, J. E. Information processing as a function of speed versus accuracy. *Journal of Experimental Psychology*, 1969, *81*, 223-239.

Swensson, R. G., & Thomas, R. E. Fixed and optimal stopping models for two-choice discrimination times. *Journal of Mathematical Psychology*, 1974, *11*, 213-236.

Taylor, D. A. Holistic and analytic processes in the comparison of letters. *Perception & Psychophysics*, 1976, *20*, 187-190.

Taylor, M. M., Lindsay, P. H., & Forbes, S. M. Quantification of shared capacity processing in auditory and visual discrimination. *Acta Psychologica*, 1967, *27*, 223-229.

Theios, J., Smith, P. G., Haviland, S. E., Traupmann, J., & Moy, M. C. Memory scanning as a serial self-terminating process. *Journal of Experimental Psychology*, 1973, *97*, 323-336.

Thomas, E. A. C. Sufficient conditions for monotonic hazard rate. An application to latency-probability curves. *Journal of Mathematical Psychology*, 1971, *8*, 303-332.

Townsend, J. T. Theoretical analysis of an alphabetic confusion matrix. *Perception & Psychophysics*, 1971, *9*, 40-50.

Townsend, J. T. Issues and models concerning the processing of a finite number of inputs. In B. H. Kantowitz (Ed.), *Human information processing: Tutorials in performance and cognition*, Potomac, Md.: Lawrence Erlbaum Associates, 1974. (a)

Townsend, J. T. *Analysis of search reaction time distributions and independent parallel models*. Paper presented at seventh annual Mathematical Psychology Meeting, Ann Arbor, August, 1974. (b)

Townsend, J. T. A stochastic theory of matching processes. *Journal of Mathematical Psychology*, 1976, *14*, 1-52.

Townsend, J. T., & Ashby, F. G. *Toward a theory of letter recognition: Testing contemporary feature models*. Unpublished manuscript, 1976.

Townsend, J. T., & Roos, R. N. Search reaction time for single targets in multiletter stimuli with brief visual displays. *Memory and Cognition*, 1973, *1*, 319-332.

Weisstein, N. Beyond the yellow-Volkswagen detector and grandmother cell: A general strategy for the exploration of operations in human pattern recognition. In R. L. Solso (Ed.), *Contemporary issues in cognitive psychology: The Loyola Symposium*, New York: Winston-Wiley, 1973.

Part **III**

ENCODING AND RETRIEVING
ORDERED RELATIONSHIPS

9

Encoding and Retrieval in Comparative Judgments

George R. Potts
University of Denver
William P. Banks
Pomona College
Stephen M. Kosslyn
Harvard University

Robert S. Moyer
Bates College
Christine A. Riley
University of Iowa
Kirk H. Smith
Bowling Green State University

The teacher of experimental psychology often finds himself in the uncomfortable position of knowing a multitude of "facts" (usually taking the form of experimental results) but being unable to answer the key question "What about this area is sufficiently general and basic that it is important for an undergraduate to know?" "Facts" in experimental psychology tend to be specific to very limited paradigms, and most models fall apart when extended beyond the limited paradigm they were initially designed to deal with.

In view of this, when an effect is observed concurrently but independently in a wide variety of situations, it is worthy of close examination. One such effect is the *distance effect* in comparative judgments. When comparing two items on a particular dimension such as size, the more discrepant the two stimuli, the easier the comparison. This effect was first observed in perception experiments but has since become an integral part of the memory literature as well. The generality of the distance effect suggests that it may represent one of those critical phenomena that reflect basic psychological principles. This being the case, it seemed desirable to establish an active dialog among the various groups of people working on the problem. The Indiana Conference provided a suitable vehicle for establishing such a dialog. The workshop from which this paper sprang was organized by Kirk Smith and George Potts, and the authors of this paper were the participants. Tom Trabasso was also scheduled to participate but unfortunately had to cancel due to illness. We are grateful to the members of the audience, many of whom have done important work on these issues, for providing necessary stimulation for the discussion, and we are particularly grateful to Susan Dumais who somehow managed to take organized notes during the free-ranging discussion and provided those notes to help in the organization of this paper.

To say that not all the participants held the same viewpoint would be the ultimate in understatement. In writing this article, we tried to be careful to credit each participant with his own point of view. The first author took responsibility for editing the various positions into a more-or-less unified article. The authorship among the remaining participants is listed in alphabetical order.

Distance effects have been an important part of the perception literature for a very long time. Thus it is appropriate to begin with a review of that literature. This review is followed by a brief overview of the distance effects that have been reported in the memory literature. This memory literature constitutes the primary focus of this chapter.

DISTANCE EFFECTS IN PERCEPTION (MOYER)

Consider Fig. 1A. Which of the two circles is larger? Now make the same judgment for the pair depicted in Fig. 1B. Such perceptual comparisons nearly always require more time when the physical difference between the two stimuli is small than when it is large. This perceptual phenomenon is quite general and has been observed using a wide variety of stimuli.

Cattell (1902) had people make pair comparisons of gray squares that reflected different amounts of light. The stimuli were mounted side by side, and on each trial, subjects chose the brighter gray by responding with the appropriate hand. A few years later, Henmon (1906) used chromatic stimuli in a similar experiment. In this study subjects responded with the hand on the same side as a designated color (e.g., "red"; or "green"). Henmon (1906) and Johnson (1939) used

A   B

FIG. 1   Demonstration of the perceptual distance effect.

Cattell's (1902) method to study the time needed for comparing line lengths, and subjects in an experiment by Birren and Botwinick (1955) indicated the location of the longer of two lines with a vocal response ("left" or "right"). Curtis, Paulos, and Rule (1973) also investigated reaction time for visual size comparisons in an experiment where circles of different sizes served as stimuli. In all these studies, reaction time increased systematically with increases in the physical similarity of the stimuli compared. The same finding has consistently emerged from experiments that require people to make comparisons of visual numerosity. Lemmon (1927) and Buckley and Gillman (1974), for instance, employed Cattell's (1902) method in studies where subjects decided which of two stimuli contained the larger number of illuminated light bulbs or printed dots, respectively; and Crossman (1955) also observed reaction time to be inversely related to differences in perceptual numerosity in a card-sorting task. This pattern of results characterizes comparisons in other perceptual modalities as well, although the data are not as abundant. Henmon (1906), for example, sounded a standard tone, followed two seconds later by a comparison tone (4, 8, 12, or 16 Hz higher or lower than the standard). Subjects responded with one hand if the second tone was of a higher pitch than the standard and with the other hand if the second tone was of a lower pitch. The latency of the decision in this successive comparison task was directly related to the physical similarity between the standard and comparison tones. Finally, Crossman (1955) found a similar result in a kinesthetic task in which people shoved cans into two different piles according to weight.

Thus the effect of physical stimulus difference on reaction time is quite reliable and general; in fact, in a well-known review, Smith (1968) concluded that, for a given number of alternatives, "decreasing discriminability unequivocally results in longer CRTs [p. 83]." The exact functional relationship between reaction time and stimulus difference has been the source of some debate (see Buckley & Gillman, 1974; Crossman, 1955; Curtis et al., 1973; Welford, 1960) and is not pursued here. We do note that reaction time generally increases (in a proper Weber-Fechner fashion) as the ratio of the physical differences decreases, even when the absolute difference is held constant, and that a small effect of absolute difference is sometimes observed, even when the ratio is constant (see, e.g., Crossman, 1955; Henmon, 1906).

THE DISTANCE EFFECT IN MEMORY EXPERIMENTS (POTTS)

Clearly, the perceptual distance effect is quite general and is not restricted to one or two particular dimensions. A similar distance effect is observed even when the actual physical stimuli are not present and subjects are required to make a comparison of two stimuli stored in memory. This was first observed by

Moyer and Landauer (1967) when they measured the reaction time for deciding which of two simultaneously presented digits (1-9) was the larger. This is a simple task. Error rates are low, and subjects report that all decisions are equally trivial. However, the reaction times show consistent differences in difficulty among the pairs. Moyer and Landauer reported a significant decline in reaction time as the difference between the digits in a pair increased. Their subjects took a mean of about 620 msec to decide which digit was larger when the two digits differed by one. As the difference between the digits increased to eight, the reaction time decreased monotonically to about 500 msec. A similar distance effect was observed by Moyer (1973), when he presented subjects with all possible pair-wise combinations of seven animal names and required them to indicate which of the animals was the larger. Again, reaction time decreased as the size difference between the animals increased. Both Paivio (1975) and Banks and Flora (1977) showed that this result did not depend on the repeated testing of a small set of items. They used names of objects whose perceived size was determined by ratings. Pairs of these names were presented to subjects for comparative judgments, with each name being presented only once. The reaction time to select either the larger or the smaller member of the pair declined sharply with increases in the difference between the perceived size of the items.

All of the above tasks can be categorized as semantic memory tasks, because they test information stored as part of a person's generalized world knowledge. It was not necessary to explicitly teach the true relation between the terms employed. Distance effects are also routinely obtained even when people are taught to assign physical referents to previously nominal stimuli. In these cases, subjects are given information necessary to arrange these previously nominal stimuli into an ordinal (or higher) scale. This has been accomplished in two ways. In one case subjects are given pairs of nominal stimuli and are taught the relation between the two stimuli comprising each pair. For example, Trabasso, Riley, and Wilson (1975) presented subjects with pairs of colored sticks that differed in length and required them to learn which color corresponded to the longer (or shorter) stick. If the underlying ordering of the sticks is characterized as $A > B > C > D > E > F$ (for a six-term ordering), then subjects were taught the relations between the five adjacent pairs $A > B, B > C, C > D, D > E, E > F$. After training to criteria on these adjacent pairs, all possible pairs of colors (five adjacent and ten remote for a six-term ordering) were presented, and subjects were required to indicate which color of each pair corresponded to the longer (or shorter) stick.

A second procedure was used by Moyer and Bayer (1976). Instead of presenting pair-wise information (i.e., training on the set of adjacent pairs), they taught subjects the "names" of each of four circles that differed in size. Nonsense syllables were used for the names. Subjects were trained until the CVC-circle associations were overlearned; they were then tested on all possible pair-wise combinations of names. As in the previous paradigm, subjects were presented with a pair of names and were required to indicate which name referred to the larger circle. Regardless of whether subjects were trained on pair-wise relations between items (e.g., Trabasso et al., 1975) or were taught specific information about individual items (e.g., Moyer & Bayer, 1976), the results were the same. Both procedures yielded strong distance effects; the larger the difference between the two referents being compared, the shorter the reaction time.

Finally, distance effects can be observed even when there is no simple perceptual referent, (Potts, 1972, 1974; Riley, 1976; Banks & Flora, 1977, Experiment 2; Friedman, 1976). For example, Potts (1972, 1974) presented subjects with a paragraph that employed sentence frames to present the relations between the adjacent terms in an ordering. Thus subjects might be told that "a fish is friendlier than a frog, a frog is friendlier than a duck," etc. When tested on their knowledge of all possible pairwise relations, subjects still showed the typical distance effect; the farther apart two stimuli were on the induced scale, the shorter the reaction time.

It should be clear from this brief overview that distance effects are consistently observed in a wide variety of memory experiments. Can all these results be accounted for by a single set of basic psychological principles? What are these principles? What is the relation between the perceptual distance effects described earlier and the distance effects obtained in memory experiments? It is to questions such as these that this chapter addresses itself.

Because the number-comparison literature represents one of the initial observations of the distance effect in memory experiments, it is appropriate to begin by reviewing this literature. The effects and models comprising the number-comparison literature, it turns out, are precursors of the effects and models that developed later in other paradigms.

REVIEW OF THE NUMBER-COMPARISON LITERATURE (BANKS)

As noted previously, Moyer and Landauer (1967) measured reaction time for deciding which of two simultaneously presented digits was larger and observed that reaction time decreased monotonically as the difference between the two numbers increased. Following Parkman (1971), we refer to the numerical difference between members of a digit pair as the *Split* for that pair, to the smaller member as the *Min*, and to the larger as the *Max*. In these terms, the Moyer and Landauer (1967) finding is that reaction time declines as Split increases. We note later that reaction time also declines as Min decreases.

Moyer and Landauer point out that their findings disconfirm at least two models of how subjects decide which digit is larger. The first of these contends that subjects initially locate one of the digits in memory and then count up or down to the other digit to make the decision. Such a process would be plausible if, for example, subjects had the relative size of each adjacent number encoded propositionally ($1 < 2, 2 < 3, 3 < 4$, etc.) and then computed other nonadjacent pairs from these. A system like this would be economical in terms of memory requirements, but it predicts that reaction time will increase with Split, in clear contradiction of the data. The second model is simply a less economical version of the first one; all relations among digits, not just those among adjacent ones, are stored, and the decision is based on retrieval of the pair in question. This model has no reason to predict the decrease in reaction time with Split and is thus not confirmed.

Moyer and Landauer's own interpretation of the data is that reaction time for deciding which digit is larger declines with Split for the same reason that reaction time declines as the difference in physical quantities increases. They suggest that: "The displayed numerals are converted to analogue magnitudes, and a comparison is then made between the magnitudes in much the same way that comparisons are made between physical stimuli [p. 1520]." This theoretical approach has motivated much of the subsequent research on digit inequality judgments, and I use it as an organizing principle for the remainder of this section.

Figure 2 shows the reaction time for choosing the larger member of all the 36 different pairs of digits. This figure is derived from Gillman, Buckley, and Theios (1973; see also Buckley & Gillman, 1974), but the general pattern of data shown here is typical. Digit pairs are arranged in the figure with Min along the x-axis and with separate plots for each Split. This plotting illustrates two important effects in addition to Split, these being the Min effect and the Mix x Split interaction. As can be seen, Min has a strong effect on reaction time, and Split has more of an effect on reaction time when Min is large than when it is small (Min x Split interaction).

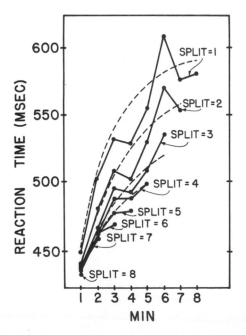

FIG. 2   Reaction time as a function of Min for Split = 1 through 8 (see text for definition of Min and Split). These points are derived from a figure presented by Gillman, Buckley, and Theios (1973). The dashed lines depict idealized approximations to the function for Splits 1, 2, 3, and 4.

Both the Min and the Min x Split effects follow from Moyer and Landauer's model if the internal "analogue magnitude" is assumed to be a nonlinear, compressed (e.g., logarithmic) function of the magnitude of the digit. In such a compressive spacing, 8 and 9 would be closer together on the internal scale than 7 and 8, 7 and 8 closer together than 6 and 7, and so on. The Min effect emerges because pairs at the lower end of the continuum, for any given Split, are more discriminable than pairs at the upper end. Consider, for example, the set of pairs with Split = 1. These are 1 and 2, 2 and 3, and so on. Clearly, reaction time increases with Min for these pairs, because 1 and 2 are most different, 2 and 3 next most, and 8 and 9 least different in the sizes of the corresponding internal magnitudes that subjects are assumed to compare in making their choice. Likewise, reaction time increases with Min for any other Split.

Moyer and Landauer (1967, 1973) showed that Welford's (1960) general equation for predicting reaction time for psychophysical discriminations predicts reaction times for digit discriminations very well. The equation they used is RT = a + b log (Max ÷ Split). This equation can be rewritten as RT = a + b log (Min ÷ Split + 1) to correspond better to the plot in Fig. 2. Note that reaction time increases with Min and decreases with Split in this equation. The prediction of the Split x Min interaction is best seen in intuitive terms in the latter equation, because there Split is a multiplicative scaling factor. It therefore has more of an effect when Min is large than when it is small. Thus, when Min is small, the quantity (Min ÷ Split) varies less, absolutely, with changes in Split than when Min is large, and the Min x Split interaction emerges.

Shepard, Kilpatric, and Cunningham (1975) point out that Welford's equation can be written as

$$RT = a - b \log (1 - e^{-D}),\tag{1}$$

where a and b are arbitrary constants, and D is defined as

$$D = \log (\text{Max}) - \log (\text{min})\tag{2}$$

In other words, D is a kind of Split. It is "Split" defined in terms of the logarithmic psychological continuum rather than the digits. Equations (1) and (2) do have an advantage over the simpler equation of Welford, because they reduce the independent variables from two (Min and Max, or Min and Split) to one, D, which is a kind of "psychological split" on the nonlinear subjective scale.

There is a great deal of independent evidence for the notion that people have available to them a nonlinear psychological scale of number, one that gives them a quick, intuitive "feel" for the size of a number. Banks and Hill (1974) review several lines of evidence on this point, and Shepard et al. (1975) add some more recent evidence of their own. It is clear that people *can* use numbers in a linear fashion, of course, because they can perform linear operations such as addition perfectly accurately. The situations in which subjects seem most likely to use a nonlinear subjective scale of number are ones in which an intuitive judgment or a speeded response is required. Restle (1970), for example, showed that subjects in a speeded addition task gave results consistent with an analog operation on a nonlinear subjective number line rather than any purely digital algorithm. Banks and Hill's (1974) evidence for a nonlinear subjective scale of number is, on the other hand, based on various methods for obtaining intuitive judgments from subjects about their impressions of numerical size. When subjects do not use arithmetic algorithms to compute the "right" answer, their intuitive judgments generally conform to a nonlinear scale of numerical magnitude.

Returning to the digit inequality judgments, we should consider one possible artifact that could contribute to the Split effect, and one model of processing in the task that differs radically from Moyer and Landauer's. The possible artifact was first considered by Moyer and Landauer (1967). They pointed out that in their task, which used all nonrepeating pairs of the digits 1 through 9, the digit 9 was always the appropriate choice, no matter what other digit it was paired with. The digit 1, on the other hand, was never the appropriate choice. The digits in between have intermediate probabilities of being the choice, and so there is a strong confounding between digit size and probability of choice of a digit. This confounding could create, artifactually, a Split effect if reaction time is systematically related to uncertainty of choice. Consider, for example, all pairs that contain the digit 9. Responses to these should be very fast, because the subject need only see the 9 and immediately choose it. Likewise, pairs containing the digit, 1 might also lead to very fast responses. The Split effect would then emerge, because pairs containing 1 and 9 have, on the average, a larger Split than the pairs containing intermediate digits.

The data indicate that the artifact contributes little, if anything, to the Split effect. First, the pattern of data in Fig. 2 is exactly counter to the pattern to be expected from the artifact. We should expect either a set of U-shaped functions, with 9 and 1 being members of all the fastest pairs, or possibly a Min effect the opposite of what is seen. The opposite Min effect would occur if subjects were able to use only the predictability given by the larger digits. Second, the Split effect holds up even if only pairs containing 9 are considered. That is, the choice between 9 and 8 is slower than that between 9 and 7, which is slower than 9 and 6, and so on. All these would be equal if the artifact determined the reaction time.

Several experimental tests have been explicitly directed at this artifact, and they have generally shown that it has a negligible influence on reaction time. Moyer and Landauer (1967), Parkman (1971), and Banks, Fujii, and Kayra-Stuart (1976) all varied digit probability across conditions in order to vary the probability with which the digits were associated with the responses, and these variations did not influence the Split or Min effects in any systematic way. Sekuler, Rubin, and Armstrong (1971, Experiment II) conducted an ingenious experiment that eliminated the artifact altogether yet still gave a sizeable Split effect. In this experiment the subject decided whether singly presented comparison digits were larger or smaller than a constant digit, which was always 5. Because there are four digits smaller and four larger than 5, and all were presented with equal probability, there was no way for the subject to predict the correct response without processing the comparison digit, but RT still declined with Split.

Parkman (1971) has proposed an alternative to Moyer and Landauer's theory (see also Parkman & Groen, 1971; and Groen & Parkman, 1972). This theory treats the Split effect as a byproduct of the Min effect and thus as something on the order of an artifact. Parkman's theory assumes that the digits are identified by an analysis-by-synthesis process that generates "internal digits" very rapidly and rapidly compares them one at a time with the digits presented; when a match is made between an internally generated and experimentally presented digit, the presented digit is identified. Parkman assumes that in the comparative judgment task, the internal generation process begins with zero or 1, produces trial digits in numerical order, and stops when the Min is reached. The correct choice can then be made. The increase in reaction time with Min is a natural prediction of this model. The Split effect emerges because Split and Min are confounded. This confounding is a result of the constraints dictated by the fact that the set of digits is limited. If the full set of 36 different pairs is used, a Split of 1 consists of the pairs 1 and 2, 2 and 3, . . ., 8 and 9. The mean Min for this set of pairs is 4.5. The mean Min for the pairs with Split of 2 (1 and 3, 2 and 4, . . ., 7 and 9) is 4, and Min continues to decline linearly with Split until it reaches 1 at a Split of 8. Reaction time therefore declines with Split, according to Parkman's model, because Min declines with Split.

The difficulties for Parkman's model are very great. The Min effect has a very strong nonlinear component, as can be seen in Fig. 2 (cf. Moyer & Landauer, 1973). Furthermore, when Min is held constant, there is still a Split effect, as is seen in Fig. 2 and in Parkman (1971, pp. 196 and 200, Figs. 2 and 5). The results of Sekuler et al.'s (1971) Experiment II, where 5 was held in memory and compared with other digits, seem impossible to account for with such a model. Reaction time in this experiment declined as the comparison digits were further from 5, for both larger and smaller comparison digits. The "counting up" process that Parkman's model uses to identify digits should cause RT to increase for comparison digits larger than 5, but reaction usually decreases by about the same amount for comparison digits on both sides of 5. Still other problems for Parkman's model are discussed in Banks et al. (1976), where the model is shown to be unable to account for the semantic congruity effect (discussed in the following).

Semantic Congruity in Digit Choices

The semantic congruity effect in digit choices, recently demonstrated by Banks et al. (1976), necessitates a basic modification in our model of how numerical information is encoded and processed by subjects. The semantic congruity effect is an interaction between the choice specified by the instructions ("choose larger" versus "choose smaller") and the overall size of the digits being compared.

252   POTTS, BANKS, KOSSLYN, MOYER, RILEY, SMITH

Several examples of semantic congruity effects are seen in Fig. 3. A congruity effect is observed when, for example, the choice between the members of a pair of small numbers (e.g., 1 and 2) is made faster under "choose smaller" instructions than under "choose larger" instructions, and the choice between a pair of large numbers (e.g., 8 and 9) is made faster under "choose larger" instructions than under "choose smaller" instructions. This is termed a *congruity effect*, because the pair 1 and 2 is at the small end of the continuum and 8 and 9 is at the large end, and the pairs are processed faster when they fall at the end of the continuum specified by the instructions, i.e., when their size is congruent with the size specified by the instructions. It is a *semantic* congruity effect, because the congruity in question is congruity of position on a semantic scale.

Figure 3 plots semantic congruity effects obtained by Banks et al. (1976), where 1, 2, 3, and 4 are small digits and 6, 7, 8, and 9 are large digits. The plots show semantic congruity effects separately for Splits of 1, 2, and 3 (left, middle, and right functions, respectively). The points are means of data obtained in Banks et al.'s (1976) Experiments 1 and 2 for the pairs shown in the figure. Note that both Split and Min effects are apparent in these plots: The Split effect can be seen in the progressive lowering of the three functions from left to right, and the Min effect is seen in the overall longer RTs for the larger than the smaller

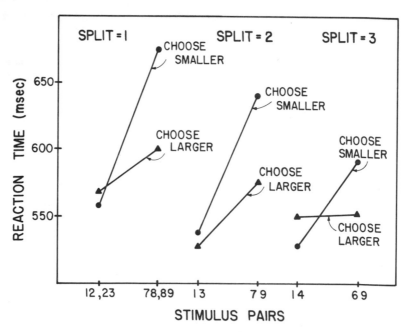

FIG. 3   Reaction time for discriminating pairs of small or large digits under "choose larger" or "choose smaller" instructions. These are semantic congruity effects for splits of 1, 2, and 3, averaged over the two experiments in Banks et al. (1976).

pairs in each of the three functions. The semantic congruity effect is the interaction between instructions and digit size in each plot, and as can be seen, it is a strong effect.

Now that the semantic congruity effect has been shown to be a reliable phenomenon, it seems likely that congruity effects may have been present in a number of previous studies but were not interpreted or analyzed as such. Parkman (1971), for example, found an approximately 50% steeper Min effect for "choose smaller" instructions (Experiment II) than "choose larger" instructions (Experiment I). This difference in slope indicates that large digits were processed faster under "choose larger" than "choose smaller" instructions, but the two instructions were about equal for small digits. Thus there was probably a congruity interaction in the data, but Parkman did not analyze the data in a way that would show it definitely. Likewise, Fairbank found a number of phenomena in his doctoral dissertation (Fairbank, 1969) that we would interpret as semantic congruity effects. Fairbank and Capehart (1969) also reported a phenomenon that is best interpreted as a semantic congruity effect.

According to Banks et al. (1976) the semantic congruity effect indicates that processing of the digits is done in terms of size codes rather than analog representations. The congruity effect emerges at the stage of processing at which the size codes for the digits are matched to the codes for the instructions. The members of a pair of large digits like 8 and 9 are, in their model, most likely both to be coded as *large*, and members of a pair of small digits like 1 and 2 are most likely to be coded as *small*. The instructions "choose larger" are assumed to be coded as *large* and the "choose smaller" as *small*, and the choice of the correct digit is assumed to be made by an identity match. Thus the choice of the correct digit in the pair 8 and 9 is made faster for "choose larger" than for "choose smaller" instructions, and the reverse is true for the pair 1 and 2.

The complete processing model of Banks et al. explains both the Split and Min effects (as well as the Split x Min interaction) in terms of code processing. The model is based on code processing (rather than analog processing, imagery, internalized perception of analog quantitites, etc.), because the semantic congruity effect indicates that coding operations occur at some point in the decision process, and it seemed most parsimonious to explain the other effects also in terms of semantic coding. The way the model predicts the various effects is described in the section on discrete semantic code models.

What generalizations does the literature on comparative judgments among digits allow us to make about processing numerical information? First, it seems that Moyer and Landauer's (1967) suggestion that numbers are perceived initially as quantities is still the best approach to the problem. It also seems, however, that processing is not done completely in terms of finely graded quantitative intuitions about the relative sizes denoted by the numbers. Rather, very early in processing, the quantitative intuitions get converted to discrete semantic codes, and the major part of processing is devoted to operating on the semantic codes. Once the sizes of the digits to be compared have been encoded, the processing is very similar to the processing of comparatives with other types of stimuli. Moyer and Landauer's analogy between digit comparisons and other comparative judgments is supported, but in a curious way. The similarities between the processing of comparisons among digits and among other sorts of stimuli derive from a common discretely encoded form into which they are translated rather than from a common analog medium in which they are processed.

THE REPRESENTATION AND RETRIEVAL OF ORDERED INFORMATION

Banks' review of the number comparison literature indicated the existence of three interrelated effects and two viable alternative models for comparative judgments. The *split effect*, which we also refer to as the *distance effect*, is of prime interest to us. Moyer argues strongly that this effect indicates that ordered information is represented by an analog code. According to this *Analog Code Model*, comparisons among items stored in memory reflect comparisons among the appropriate memorial analogs and are similar to comparisons among actual perceptual stimuli.

The other two effects are important because of their relevance to the proposed models. The *min effect* is closely related to the *end-term effects*, which are discussed later. Both indicate a superior performance on pairs containing at least one term that is at or near one of the extremes of the ordering. The *congruity effect* refers to the fact that pairs are processed faster when the terms of that pair fall at the end of the continuum indicated by the adjective used in the question. For example, the question "Which is larger?" yields shorter reaction times when comparing large terms, and the question "Which is smaller?" yields shorter reaction times when comparing small terms. This congruity effect is most easily explained by the *Discrete Semantic Code Model* espoused by Banks.

In the following three subsections, Moyer provides evidence for his analog model and discusses how such a model can be expanded to account for congruity effects. Banks discusses his discrete model and how it accounts for distance effects. Finally, Kosslyn presents evidence for a dual coding model.

Analog Code Models (Moyer)

A parsimonious explanation for the distance effect (proposed by Moyer & Landauer, 1967; Moyer, 1973; Moyer & Bayer, 1976) posits an analog representation for each item in the experimental series. These analogs preserve the value of each symbol along the dimension in question, and when the symbols are presented on a test trial, the appropriate analogs are retrieved and compared. Reaction time is supposed to vary inversely with the difference between these internally represented analogs, just as it does when different stimulus values are actually presented, as in the perceptual experiments previously described.

Now in nearly all the linear order experiments, the subject is presented with only ordinal information, as in Potts' studies (the fish is friendlier than the duck, the duck is friendlier than the frog, etc.), or else ordinal and interval information are completely confounded, as in the Trabasso and Riley studies, where the subjects compare sticks of different lengths, and in the digit- and letter-comparison work. Although the analog model has no trouble with these data, it also naturally predicts that the internal analogs preserve more than ordinal information when quantitative information is available and that mental comparison time ought to be predictably influenced by this quantitative information (e.g., long reaction time if the difference between adjacent items in a series is small, short reaction time if the difference is large). But would reaction time indeed be sensitive to different intervals between items when ordinal distance was constant? This struck Richard Bayer and myself as a fundamental question about the nature of mental comparison; and, clearly, a negative answer would give no comfort to the analog model. In an experiment (Moyer & Bayer, 1976) designed to examine this question, some subjects made perceptual comparisons of circles like those depicted in Fig. 1; other subjects learned arbitrary names for the same circles and later decided, from memory, which of two names stood for the larger circle. There were two *perceptual* groups; a small range group compared circles of diameters 11, 13, 15, and 17 mm, and a large range group compared circles of diameters 11, 15, 19, and 23 mm. Figure 4 shows that in all cases the

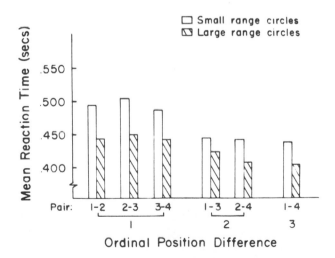

FIG. 4   Reaction time (for correct responses) for individual pairs (perceptual groups). (Reproduced from Moyer & Bayer, 1976, p. 235.)

large-range circles were perceptually compared more quickly than the small-range circles. This difference is highly reliable, and, although not unexpected, it is gratifying to obtain perceptual range effects with exactly the same stimuli that other, randomly assigned, subjects compared from memory. Subjects in the small- and large-range *memorial* groups first overlearned names (low association value CVCs) for the same circles that the perceptual subjects compared and then returned one day later to make pair comparisons of these names. Each pair of names was presented, and subjects were required to indicate which name stood for the larger circle. The circles themselves were not presented during the test. Figure 5 shows that every name pair was more quickly compared when the referents belonged to the large-range circle series than when the referents belonged to the small-range circle series, even though ordinal position difference was constant at each contrast. Furthermore, detailed tests showed that these differences could not be attributed to differences in ease or degree of learning the

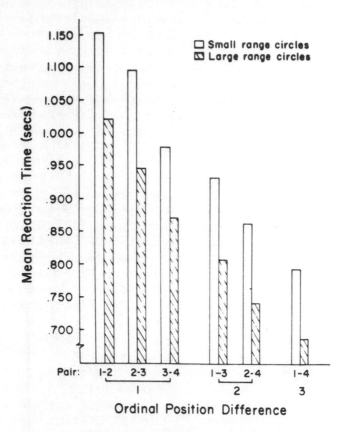

FIG. 5   Reaction time (for correct responses) for individual pairs (memorial groups). (Reproduced from Moyer & Bayer, 1976, p. 235.)

circle names, differential forgetting over the retention interval, or differential availability of the names (as measured by latency of naming in an absolute judgment task conducted after the reaction-time comparisons on Day 2). These data therefore appeared to force the conclusion that our subjects retrieved more than ordinal information about the symbols that they compared, and the parallel to the perceptual data (Fig. 4) cannot be ignored.

But the memorial data clearly reveal an additional effect not present in the perceptual data; at each ordinal position difference, the closer a name pair is to the "large" end of the series, the quicker the comparison. These differences are statistically reliable and characterize both memorial groups. We believe that this feature of the memorial data points to an important difference between perceptual and memorial mental comparisons—namely, that values for the stimuli must first be retrieved in a memorial task but are given when a perceptual comparison is required (value and stimulus are synonymous in the perceptual task). A fairly simple retrieval model that can accommodate these memorial data supposes that subjects order the circle names in memory according to size; in this respect small-range and large-range subjects have the same internal representation. When two names are presented and the subject must select the one that stands for the larger circle, he or she begins at the larger end of this series and executes a self-terminating search for either of the displayed names. Because names of larger circles are stored closer to the place where the search begins, they are encountered sooner and, *ceteris paribus*, therefore enjoy the reaction-time advantage evident in Fig. 5. Having found a name match, the subject retrieves the associated circle's absolute value (the two memorial groups do differ, of course, in the values they have associated with each name), searches for the other name, retrieves its internal analog, and then compares these two values. For every name pair, these absolute values differ by a larger amount for the large-range than for the small-range subjects (cf. Moyer & Bayer, 1976, pp. 236-240 for details). Congruity effects (see Banks' section) follow naturally from this retrieval model if we simply assume that the subject begins his or her search from the end of the array congruent with the instructions. Thus, if the subject were asked to choose the name of the *smaller* circle, he or she would begin the search from the "smaller" end of the array, producing reaction-time advantages for pairs near that end (i.e., in Fig. 5 the sign of the linear effects within each ordinal position difference should now be positive instead of negative). Although our experiment was not designed to test for this sort of congruity effect, this pattern of results was reported in three experiments, using different materials, by Holyoak and Walker (1976).

We must note, however, that these *linear* congruity effects are not always observed. In fact, it is quite common to find serial position effects in which a reaction-time advantage accrues to pairs near both ends of the series (Trabasso & Riley, 1975). With an additional assumption, the linear- and serial-position congruity effects can both be handled by the scanning model (see Moyer & Bayer, 1976, appendix 1.2), but Banks' semantic code models also accommodate both kinds of effects well, and at present writing, we don't appear to know enough about these phenomena to decide between these alternative explanations.

But our experiment was not really designed to explore congruity effects, and the question it was designed to ask—does the interval distance between the referents of symbols affect mental comparison time—appears to have been answered in the affirmative. When our article was in press, Paivio (1975, Experiment 1) independently reported a study that showed essentially the same effects in a within-subject design that used entirely different materials. He first had one group of subjects make size ratings (on a scale of 1 to 9) of names of various animals and inanimate objects (e.g., flea, prune, hairbrush, tuba, tractor, whale). Paivio then constructed pairs of these names such that the range of rated size was either small, medium, or large (2.99, 4.99, or 5.99 ratings scale points, respectively). A separate group of subjects made comparisons in which they chose the (conceptually) larger item in each pair. The results showed a highly reliable effect of absolute size range—memory comparisons were quicker, the larger the size range. It is extremely unlikely that these data simply reflect some sort of ordinal effects, because no subject saw any item more than once, and no "series" was ever presented.

Taken together, these two experiments strongly suggest that absolute size differences between the referents of symbols have functional significance for memorial comparisons, and the results are quite consistent with the analog model. We don't yet know whether comparisons on dimensions other than size will show similar effects, and experiments are now under way to explore the generality of these findings.

Discrete Semantic Code Models (Banks)

The discrete modeling approach is characterized by the assumption that processing is done in terms of internal codes for the elements of the task. Although the semantic coding approach could allow analog processing at various points (as it does in the Banks et al., 1976, model of comparisons), it assumes that the choice in comparative judgment is made in terms of the same contrastive, discrete, "componential" codes that carry meaning in natural language (cf. Leech, 1974, pp. 28-46 and 95-125). Consequently, the model predicts in a natural way a number of phenomena related to the role of language in processing that are difficult for other models to deal with. In the discussion that follows, it should become apparent how this model predicts the other phenomena of comparative judgment as well.

To prevent misunderstanding, we should make it clear at this point that the discrete model is being proposed only for tasks in which processing is done in a linguistic medium. An exhaustive definition of such tasks is not possible at present, but the comparative judgment tasks under discussion here do seem to fall into this category, because they require subjects to indicate which member of a pair of stimuli is the one specified by a common English adjective. There are also a large number of tasks in which the important processing does not seem to be done in a linguistic, discrete-coded medium. These include mental rotation (Cooper, 1975) and many visual-imagery tasks (cf. Kosslyn, 1975).

A homely example of discrete coding of continuous attributes would be the pronouncement that the coffee is "too cold." The temperature of the coffee is surely a continuous attribute, yet we encode for later use only a few levels of the coffee's temperature, perhaps levels forming a series like "too hot," "a little on the warm side," "just right," "a bit too cool," and "too cold." More subtle temperature differences within these categories are usually not lost on us, but we do not encode them, remember them, or communicate them to others unless there is some reason to do so. When we do encode or remember the within-category differences, a strict discrete approach still models the use of the finer information in terms of categorical codes. According to this approach, an appreciation of a subtle distinction in temperature within, say, the "a bit too cool" category would need a new category boundary, or a shift of an old one, before it could be encoded and remembered.

The coffee example is related to the topic known as *absolute judgment*. In an absolute judgment experiment, one is called on to recognize absolute levels of stimulus attributes. The general finding is that, whatever the stimulus attribute in question, subjects can recognize only a limited number of absolute levels. The number seems to be about 7 ± 2 (Miller, 1956). Thus, even if we could store raw analog sensations of, say, degrees of warmth of the coffee, we could only store 7 ± 2 different levels. The memory representation is thus not semantically dense (see Kosslyn's section) and is therefore, for all practical purposes, discrete.

The literature on absolute judgment also indicates in another way that the internal representation or "memory trace" of an absolute level on a continuum is not a literal image of the sensation. If subjects stored sensory images of the stimulus levels, memory performance for levels of the continuum should show the same confusability and discriminability effects as does sensory discrimination on that stimulus continuum. However, memory-based performance is subject to effects very different from those that govern sensory discrimination. As Gravetter and Lockhead (1973) and Pollack (1952) have shown, accuracy of memory performance is not much affected by bunching the stimulus levels to be remembered close together on the continuum or by spreading them very far apart. Such manipulations of stimulus discriminability have, of course, a very strong effect on discrimination performance in a purely sensory task. The number of stimulus levels to be remembered seems to be a much more important factor in memory than the absolute spacing of the levels, and the limiting numbers of levels that can be processed accurately is fairly constant across stimulus continua (Miller, 1956). The clear implication of these findings is that our ability to recognize absolute stimulus levels is not based on retained literal images of the stimulus levels involved. Some analog knowledge of the range of the stimulus continuum may be necessary for memory performance, but the memory itself seems to be represented in symbolic terms.

Bower (1971) has reviewed a number of transfer experiments in which labels were associated with absolute stimulus levels, and then, once the associations were learned, the labels were repaired with different absolute levels. The results show that systematic shifting of the stimulus levels on the continuum such that the ordinal positions of the labels are preserved leads to very good transfer performance. Transfer is much worse when the reassignment of stimuli to the labels is not simple or systematic. The crucial experiments reviewed by Bower compare transfer in the case where some labels are kept with the *same* stimulus levels in transfer to cases where all labels are assigned to *new* stimulus levels. These experiments show that keeping as many as half of the labels paired with the same stimuli in transfer does not help performance if the ordinal positions of the other labels are rearranged, whereas changing *all* of the label-stimulus associations gives good transfer if the changed ordinal positions of the labels are a simple transformation of the original ones.

These and other findings led Bower (1971) to conclude that memory for the stimulus levels is not mediated by "mental images of specific referents [p. 194]." He concluded that a general cognitive structure underlies use of the category labels in an absolute judgment task, whatever the stimulus modality. This structure is an abstract, amodal linear order that allows relations as "between" or "greater than" among its members but that does not express anything more than ordinal information. The linear order has the same structure for different continua, because it is actually the same cognitive structure being applied in the different cases, a kind of "scaffold" to which tags for levels in any modality may be hooked. Bower states that the underlying cognitive structure could be either a set of verbal labels or else a more purely conceptual semantic framework. In either case it conforms to the same type of semantic coding that the discrete approach uses.

The discrete modeling approach has the task, in any given situation to be modeled, of spelling out how codes are generated on each trial and how they are processed to satisfy the requirements imposed on the subject. When applied to predicting reaction times in comparative judgments, the model generally has three phenomena it (and any other model) must account for. The first is the Distance or Split effect, which refers to the decline in reaction time as the distance between the items on the dimension of comparison increases. The second is an end-anchor effect, in which reaction time is faster for end terms than middle terms. The third is the semantic congruity effect, which is an interaction between the polarity of the comparative judgment to be performed and the position of the items on the scale in question (cf. Fig. 3).

The semantic coding model approaches comparative judgment as a problem-solving task. The subject knows a lot of things about the two objects being compared, must use whatever information available to make his or her decision, and tries to respond as quickly as possible and still be accurate. The information the subject knows can be referred to as the *data base* for the task. A special data base may be set up for the task if a well-learned series is tested, or the data base may be as large as all of memory if items are never repeated (cf. Paivio, 1975; Banks & Flora, 1977). The first step in the model is the generation of codes for the stimuli to be compared. The data base may be used for code generation, but it is not necessarily the case that the codes are simply retrieved from the data base. The codes used in processing could be very different in form from those stored in the data base. The model operates on the codes, once they are generated, until one and only one correctly matches the previously coded instructions.

Two different types of data base seem likely for the case when a small, well-learned set of items is used. One is a "scaffold" structure like that which Bower (1971) discussed. He used it to account for transfer and absolute judgment, but it could easily be modified for comparative judgment. Banks et al. (1976) assumed a different sort of data base for comparative judgments of numerical magnitude among pairs of the digits 1 to 9. Theirs was analog in the sense that distances between adjacent digits varied, but the representation was also discrete, in the sense that there were only nine different levels. Perhaps the nearest analogy to this representation for the digits is the diatonic scale in music, which has an exactly fixed number of steps and different (but also exactly fixed) distances between the steps.

When the testing situation does not allow subjects to set up a "scaffold" or other sort of special data base for the experiment, they must rely on their linguistic or real-world knowledge. The data base thus falls into the realm of semantic memory and could have any of a variety of structures, depending on which model of semantic memory ultimately proves to be correct. Paivio (1975) has shown some limitations on semantic memory models postulating storage of attributed information within categories, because he showed that size comparisons between the categories of animals and objects are as fast as those within them. However, Paivio's own model, that size information is stored as an absolute analog quantity in semantic memory, seems doubtful. First, this notion implies that absolute size information *exists* to be *found* in memory and thus that subjects must have accurately precoded and stored the sizes of all things whose sizes they can decide on in a comparative judgment task. It seems unlikely that we store such literal information, and our knowledge of range (Walker, 1975) and contextual variations (Halff, Ortony, & Anderson, 1976) is difficult to model with an absolute memory representation. Second, the 7 ± 2 limitation on the number of discriminable absolute levels in a memory representation of a unidimensional continuum holds as well for items in long-term memory as for briefly retained memories. The only exception is the unusual and poorly understood phenomenon of absolute pitch. Third, it seems unparsimonious to have a special analog, perceptually based representation for size, when other dimensions, for which there are no equivalent perceptual origins, show the same phenomena as does size in comparative judgment experiments (Banks & Flora, 1977; Riley, 1976; Friedman, 1976).

The semantic coding model begins by generating codes from information stored in the data base; then it operates on these codes to obtain a match with the instructions. The representation of information assumed by the model is, then, two-part: (1) a data base (that holds the information needed for the task); and (2) semantic codes generated from the data base and used in processing. In the "scaffold" type of data base, with a small, well-known ordering, the semantic codes generated may be very similar to the tags for the positions in the scaffold. That is, they may be represented as "largest," "smallest," "small medium," and so forth in both cases. In the cases where semantic memory must be consulted, the code for processing could come from gross category labels retrieved from memory or from fairly complex processes of deduction based on pieces of information retrieved from semantic memory.

Figure 6 illustrates how coding operates in the Banks et al. (1976) model for comparative judgments of digit magnitudes. The model assumes that subjects can use an analog data base for rapid generation of a code for the size of each digit in a pair presented for comparative judgment. The codes are sometimes sufficient for a quick solution to the comparative judgment; when they are not, an additional process of code-manipulation must be entered into. The rapidly generated codes are based on an analog perception of digit size. The analog subjective scale of number was assumed to be a decreasing (compressed) function

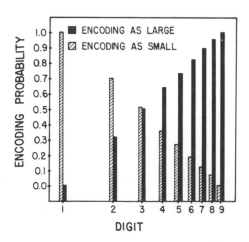

FIG. 6   Encoding probability for the digits 1 through 9 in the Banks et al. (1976) model. The encoding function is assumed to be subjectively "even" over a compressed subjective scale of numerical magnitude. In this case the compressive function is logarithmic.

of numerical magnitude, such that 1 and 2 were further apart than 2 and 3 in subjective size, and 8 and 9 were closest together on the scale. Figure 6 assumes a logarithmic subjective scale for the digits and assumes further that subjects distribute the codes "evenly"—in a subjectively linear manner—over this scale. Here it is seen that subjects make a binary decision in coding. It is either a "larger" digit (symbolized as L+) or a "smaller" one (S+). Binary coding is necessary eventually, because the choice codes are stored as L+ or S+, and the model puts the binary stimulus coding right at the start. Note that Fig. 6 has subjects feeling that 3 is about a middle-sized digit and that most digits are large; such a situation agrees with evidence from other sources on the subjective scales of numbers. (See the third section, Review of Number-Comparison Literature).

The semantic congruity effect is naturally predicted by this model, because large digits are most likely to get coded as L+. If the instructions are L+ ("choose larger"), a match can be made easily, but if they are S+ ("choose smaller"), a time-consuming transformation of codes is necessary to effect the match. Thus the larger choice is faster than the smaller choice for relatively large digits. The reverse is true for small digits by the same reasoning, and the congruity effect is predicted.

How about the Min effect and the Split effect? (See Fig. 2 for the form of these effects.) These effects come out of stages of processing prior to the congruity-ensuring stage that generates the congruity effect. Both Split and Min effects arise from the fact that sometimes the codes for both digits are the same: both S+ (symbolized as S+/S+) or both L+ (symbolized as L+/L+). When the codes for the two digits are the same, a time-consuming process of disambiguation is necessary; this process converts S+/S+ to S/S+ and L+/L+ to L/L+. The closer two digits are to each other (the smaller the Split), the more likely they are to be given the same code (see Fig. 6), and thus the more likely they are to take longer to process.

The Min effect results from the compressive subjective scale of numerical magnitude (see Fig. 6 again). The larger a pair of numbers is (for a constant Split), the more likely they are both to have the same code (this being L+). Consequently, the larger they are, the more likely they are to require time-consuming disambiguation, and the Min effect is thus predicted. The compressive encoding scale also explains the form of the congruity effect (see Fig. 3). Pairs of small digits are more likely to be coded differently (that is, as S+/L+) than large digits, which are usually coded L+/L+. The congruity-ensuring transformation is not necessary when the code is S+/L+, because one of these codes matches the instructions, whatever they are. Consequently, there is less congruity effect—less difference in RTs for the different instructions—for small digits than large digits, as is seen in Fig. 3. Incidentally, the code generation process described by Banks et al. (1976, p. 437) does not generate S+/L+ codes that are wrong.

Previous models of digit comparison predict neither the congruity effect nor a decline in the congruity effect as Split increases. The decline is predicted because increasing Split increases the probability of S+/L+ coding, which in turn decreases the probability of a congruity-ensuring transformation. Banks et al. (1976) report some evidence for such a decline, and the data of Banks and Flora (1977) and Jamieson and Petrusic (1975) show it very strongly.

The Banks et al. (1976) model for digit comparison can be modified in several ways for use with a discrete serial-order schema rather than an analog continuum at the code generation stage. One possibility would be to have a stage that checks for end terms in the stimulus codes and passes the codes on to the instruction-matching stage if either code is an end code. This would be an efficient strategy if the instructions and corresponding ends are given the same codes, such as L+ and S+. If neither stimulus code is an end code, then this stage manipulates the codes until one of them is an end code and then passes them on to the matching stage. The matching stage has the job of manipulating the codes a second time if they are not congruent with the instructions. Potts (1972) showed how a model very similar to this could handle end-term effects. It could also handle the congruity effect, the symbolic distance effect, and the decline in the congruity effect as symbolic distance increases. Data like Trabasso, Riley, and Wilson's (1975) encourage such an end-term processing strategy, because they obtained very strong end-term effects and had a semantic congruity effect that showed itself largely at the end points of the scale.

The semantic coding model can also predict the various reaction-time effects (particularly, the distance effect and the semantic congruity effect) when the comparative judgment task must use semantic memory information. There seem to be only two experiments (Paivio, 1975; Banks & Flora, 1977) that have studied comparative judgments using a paradigm in which subjects could not set up a temporary data base but had to consult semantic memory on every trial. Both showed a strong distance effect, and Banks and Flora showed, in addition, a strong semantic congruity effect. Thus these effects clearly do not depend on repeated testing of a small set.

The distance effect in judgments that require semantic memory is probably best explained as the time taken to find discriminating information in the semantic memory data base. On any continuum of comparative judgment, the more similar two items are to each other on the continuum, the longer it will take to find information that gives their relative positions on the continuum. The distance effect is thus predicted by what I call an *availability principle*: The greater the distance, the more available is the information that discriminates the objects. In the following section, Kosslyn suggests one mechanism that would predict the distance effect by an availability principle. This mechanism is one in which subjects first seek to discriminate the objects by using gross category information; then, if this information does not help, they search for other more specific facts about the objects that may discriminate them. Clearly, this process leads to a distance effect, because more distant items are more likely to be discriminated on the basis of the quickly obtained gross information. The availability principle should apply to search for more specific facts, as well. If two things are both large, there should still be more facts, on the average, that distinguish them if they are far apart in size than if they are close together.

The availability principle can probably not be proved to hold in general, but it holds for every strategy of fact retrieval I can think of. Consider, for example, a case in which two items are presented for comparative judgment of size, and the subject does not know immediately which is larger. One strategy for solving the problem is to find a third item whose relation to both of the two items to be compared is known. Such a third item cannot, however, be of help if it is either larger or smaller than both of them. It must fall between them if it is to establish their relative positions. The farther apart the items to be compared are, the larger is the proportion of the total population of items that fall between them, and the faster, on the average, one of these items will be found. The distance effect then follows from the availability principle if a search for a "third item" is used to determine the relation between the first two.

The semantic congruity effect comes about in the semantic memory case for the same reason as in the other cases. Once the codes are generated, they may or may not match the codes for the instructions, and the congruity effect comes from the code-matching process. It does not matter whether the stimulus codes were derived from a semantic memory data base or a temporary data base. Code generation is over before the stage responsible for the congruity effect.

Differences between the models. The following paragraphs on the discrete semantic coding model are sandwiched between sections describing two rival approaches, and I should try to describe the crucial differences between my approach and the other two.

The analog approach (Moyer's section) is different from the discrete approach in many ways, but two seem crucial. The analog approach assumes: (1) that the data base contains interval-scale (or ratio-scale) analog information; and (2) that mental processing uses analog rather than discrete quantities to compute the correct response. (See Moyer's and Kosslyn's sections for discussions of the definition of "analog.") The semantic coding model permits limited analog coding in certain kinds of data base, but in general, it avoids analog data-base assumptions. Likewise, the model could permit some analog operations at the beginning of processing (code generation), but it assumes that the chief currency of thought in processing is discrete linguistic codes.

One experimental result that encourages the speculation that analog information is encoded in the data base is the reaction-time difference between the large-range and small-range groups of Moyer and Bayer (1976; see Moyer's section for a discussion of this experiment). As Moyer mentions in his section, however, there are ways of modeling the data base perfectly well with discrete codes. The experiment of Moyer and Bayer does not, therefore, disconfirm the discrete approach. I have twice tried, in my laboratory at Pomona, to perform an experiment that would test whether the analog or discrete approach better accounted for the form of the semantic congruity effect one would obtain in Moyer and Bayers' experiment. Unfortunately, my efforts have been stymied by what seems to be a lack of robustness in the Moyer-Bayer effect. I have been unable to obtain the same small-range versus large-range difference they obtained, and my reaction-time functions show end-anchor effects rather than the linear serial position effects found by Moyer and Bayer (Fig. 5). My attempted test between the two models will have to wait until the conditions necessary for replicating the Moyer-Bayer effects are found. In the meantime, all I can say is that I do obtain congruity effects, and they are not of a form that the Moyer-Bayer model predicts. The nonreplication of the small-range/large-range difference is, however, just as important as the form of the congruity effect obtained in these experiments.

Holyoak (1977) has tested analog versus discrete models of the processing functions in comparative judgment. He used what could be considered diagnostics of image processing derived from Kosslyn's (1975) work on imagery. Holyoak's results showed evidence for image processing in comparative judgments only when subjects were specifically instructed to use imagery. It seems clear from Holyoak's results that subjects can use imagery to do the processing, but it is just as clear that they do not normally use it. Of course, not all analog models postulate the sort of internalized perceptual processing Holyoak was testing for, and so his results affect only a subset of the general class of analog models.

The discrete modeling approach has more in common with Kosslyn's hybrid approach than with the pure analog approach. The Banks et al. (1976) model of digit comparisons is, in fact, a hybrid model, with an analog encoding process and a discrete choice stage. The parallel versus serial processing assumptions do not in themselves distinguish the hybrid and discrete models. Probably the only real difference is the assumption of the hybrid model that the choice stage itself sometimes uses analog codes. The discrete model does not admit this possibility.

Experimental tests of hybrid versus discrete models in the future will probably concentrate on the same issues that distinguished the discrete and analog models. However, as Kosslyn's section shows, the nature and use of discrete codes can be an important issue within the hybrid model. The research he reports puts some important constraints on the use of one particular type of discrete code, a category tag.

My own hope for the future of theory in this area is that, as more information about comparative judgments is assimilated, advocacy of analog or discrete approaches per se will diminish. Global and philosophically motivated issues such as "analog versus discrete" are a sign of health in the youthful stages of a new area of study. If the area matures, such issues will be traded for more specific ones that are related directly to models and that are subject to conclusive empirical testing. It is an unfortunate characteristic of youth that the form maturity will take is not known. We will just have to wait.

Hybrid Models (Kosslyn)

Theorists have tried to account for the "symbolic distance effect" by hypothesizing "analog" (also spelled "analogue") or "discrete" processes but usually not both. Moyer and Landauer (1967, 1973), for example, appeal to the notion that analog representations are processed in memory as in perception; Banks et al (1976), in contrast, account for the symbolic distance effect by positing purely discrete processes, involving the comparison of symbolic codes. Kosslyn et al. (in press) discuss several sorts of "mixed" models, incorporating both analog and discrete processes. Before discussing these hybrid models and the support for them, let us first consider what we mean by the terms "analog" and "discrete."

Analog representations in memory are characterized by three properties:

1. They are "continuous" in two senses: (a) they are so dense syntactically as to be practically undifferentiated (see Goodman, 1968). "Syntactic" differentiation entails some sort of marking system wherein discrete units are defined. For example, the marks on a thermometer produce a syntactic differentiation; if the thermometer had an infinite number of marks, it would be extremely dense syntactically. (b) In addition, analog representations are so dense semantically as to be almost undifferentiated in this regard. "Semantic" differentiation implies that the meaning of portions or subunits of an object fall into equivalence classes. For example, if every reading on a thermometer was meaningful, it would be extremely dense semantically; if the readings are meaningful only to the nearest degree, however, the thermometer is more semantically differentiated.

2. Analog representations in memory also bear a 1:1 structural isomorphism (an "abstract first-order isomorphism"; see Kosslyn, 1973, and Shepard, 1975) to the internal representations underlying perception of the referent. That is, the organization of the parts and their relationships is the same in the analog memory representation and in the representation evoked while actually perceiving the object (more precisely, the representation that underlies experience of perceiving the object, not representations concomitant with perception—e.g., those underlying emotional reactions to the percept, etc.).

3. Analog representations in memory may be appropriately processed by mechanisms usually recruited only during like-modality perception. That is, the representations that underly the experience of perceiving an object themselves are presumed to be analog, and mechanisms specifically used in processing such representations (e.g., comparing them along some dimension) also may be applied to analog representations in memory. This sort of "analogous" processing is called *analog processing.*

Finally, for these three properties to be meaningful, we must also assume that the interpretive mechanisms are sensitive to these characteristics of the representation. If this were not the case, then these properties could have no impact on cognitive functions (see Kosslyn & Pomerantz, 1977; Pylyshyn, 1975).

Discrete representations, in contrast to analog representations, have the following three properties:

1. They are both syntactically and semantically differentiated (not very dense). Every reading of a digital clock, for example, is practically unambiguous with regard to both its identity and its meaning.

2. Discrete representations bear no necessary structural isomorphism to representations underlying perception of the referent; the correspondence between a discrete representation and the represented object may be established on entirely arbitrary grounds (e.g., as occurs with English nouns).

3. Discrete representations cannot be processed by mechanisms specialized for dealing with perceptual representations.

Although no representation will exactly be described by these three criteria, or the three discussed in connection with analog representation (see Sloman, 1975; Wittgenstein, 1953), linguistic/propositional representations seem primarily discrete, whereas visual images seem primarily analog.

How might analog and discrete representations be used in performing mental comparisons of size? Consider the following questions: Which is larger, a tree or a stone? Which is larger, a tennis ball or a pear? In the first case, most people report "just knowing" that a tree is larger; a tree is reportedly thought of as being "large," whereas a stone is "small." These sorts of discrete labels could be compared and a decision based on the outcome of this comparison. But consider the second query; a tennis ball and a pear are both usually thought of as being relatively "small." If so, then comparison of category labels would not allow one to assess relative sizes. In this situation many people report that they mentally image the two objects and then compare the images before they decide that a pear is larger. The images more or less capture the continuity of size and shape of the objects, incorporate a structural isomorphism to the perceptual representations of the subjects, and are compared as if the objects themselves were being perceived. In other words, this imagery comparison seems to be an analog process.

Two questions arise from this sort of introspective exercise: First, how does one use linguistic and analog representations? In particular, does one access the two sorts of representations in a specified order, or simultaneously? Second, can we really demonstrate that imagery is in fact functional in this situation? The experience of having to use imagery for the second sort of query could be merely epiphenomenal, an unnecessary correlate to more abstract processes (see Kosslyn & Pomerantz, 1977; Pylyshyn, 1973). These questions are considered in some detail in Kosslyn et al. and are only briefly discussed here.

First, let us consider what I take to be the two most plausible models of how discrete and analog representations might be accessed and used in performing mental comparisons of size. According to one conception, one always accesses discrete information first and then consults analog representations if necessary. According to another conception, however, both types of representations are processed at the same time. In an attempt to test these models, we conducted a reaction-time experiment requiring mental comparisons of the sizes of learned drawings. We first asked people to learn to draw six different-colored, different-sized "stick men." After subjects could draw each figure at the correct size when told its color, these people than learned to classify the figures into two categories. The three smallest figures were to be considered as "small," and the three largest figures were to be considered as "large." The critical variable in this experiment was the amount of overlearning subjects received when associating the figures with the category labels: One group of subjects was tested until the category labels were 200% overlearned; the other group of subjects was tested until the labels were 500% overlearned. We then presented subjects with pairs of color names and asked them to indicate as quickly as possible which color characterized the larger figure. If people always access and compare discrete category labels first, then more overlearning should merely speed up decisions overall. If people simultaneously access analog representations and category labels, however, more overlearning of category labels should differentially speed up discrete processing. If discrete processing is fast enough, it will run to completion before analog processing is finished. If decisions are in fact based on label comparison, we reasoned, then there should be no symbolic distance-effect evidence in the decision times: It should take just as long to discover that the labels "small" and "large" mismatch when they are associated with very small and very large figures as when they are associated with figures less disparate in size. If analog processes finish first, in contrast, we expect effects like those found in perceptual comparisons: Decisions should be reached sooner when the stimuli being compared are of widely differing sizes than when they are of more similar sizes. Thus the critical data were from comparisons involving figures drawn from different categories. If the serial model is correct, then we do not ever expect a symbolic distance effect when people compare figures from different categories (and labels mismatch), providing—of course—that category labels are retrieved in about the same amount of time for the different figures (this factor was not responsible for the results, as is reported in Kosslyn et al., in press). This prediction holds for both amounts of overlearning. If the parallel analog-discrete "race" model is correct, however, amount of overlearning is crucial: For relatively small amounts of overlearning, the analog comparison processes may finish first, resulting in symbolic distance effects in the data. For relatively large amounts of overlearning, in contrast, the category-label comparison process ought to become increasingly likely to finish first, resulting in the absence of symbolic distance effects.

The results of this experiment were clearcut: Amount of overlearning was critical in determining whether symbolic distance effects were obtained. Only with large amounts of overlearning of category labels was the symbolic distance effect eliminated (and then only within a limited subset of the data). This result is consistent with the parallel model and is inconsistent with discrete-analog serial models. (The actual experiment, predictions, and results are considerably more complex than those just described, but this summary should convey the basic idea.) A number of other experiments reported in Kosslyn et al. produced results that converge in implicating some sort of simultaneous retrieval and comparison of both analog and discrete representations.

But what evidence do we have that imagery has anything to do with analog comparisons? Consider the following experiment: One is given a noun and asked to mentally image the named object. Further, one is asked to image it either at a subjectively normal size or at a seemingly very tiny size. Following this, one receives a second noun and is asked whether the object named is larger than the first object. If images of the two objects must be compared, we expected that more time would be required if a person starts off with a subjectively tiny image of the first object; in this case, one may have to "zoom in" (see Kosslyn, 1975) prior to comparing the objects—an operation that is not necessary if one begins with a normal-sized image of the first object. We used this basic technique, first used by Holyoak (1977), as a diagnostic for whether imagery was used to perform comparisons; if more time was required when people began with a tiny image instead of a normal-sized image, we assumed that this difference was due to manipulating the first image prior to comparison (as was in fact reported by subjects when queried after the experiment).

In this experiment we were primarily interested in the time to compare pairs composed of items of very similar sizes, which presumably fell into the same "natural" size category. Subjects were divided into two groups; one group was taught to classify the items into two categories, "large" and "small," whereas the other group did not categorize the items. The category-learning group greatly overlearned the category labels. As before, we expected that when pairs include items from different categories, and category labels were well overlearned, discrete processes would usually outrace analog processes. If so, then when category labels are different for two items, the initial subjective size of the first image should be irrelevant; in addition, the symbolic distance effect should be attenuated, as occurred in the first experiment described previously. When pairs include items from the same category (for the category-learning group, or any items from the no category-learning group), in contrast, comparison of category labels cannot result in a decision, and analog representations presumably must be compared before a decision can be reached. In this case, images presumably are compared, and the subjective size of the initial image should be important; in addition, we now expect to find symbolic distance effects in the data.

Although the results of this experiment (two experiments, actually, were performed to test these ideas) were somewhat complicated, the basic predictions were confirmed. Subjectively small initial images slowed down comparisons in the no category-learning group, in general, and in the category-learning group when pairs contained items from the same category. This result, coupled with the postsession self reports, seemed to implicate imagery in the comparison process in the role of an analog representation as described previously (but cf. Holyoak, 1977).

In summary, there is evidence that both discrete and analog representations are used in mental comparisons, and that verbal labels may serve as discrete representations, and that visual images may serve as analog representations. Further, these two sorts of representations seem to be accessed at the same time, not in a fixed sequence. If these inferences survive the test of time, they may have broad implications for the structure of models of other sorts of cognitive processes, particularly within the domain of "semantic memory."

THE CONSTRUCTION OF LINEAR ORDERINGS

One of the disagreements that arose during the discussion was the question of whether the representation of linearly ordered information was actually in the form of an ordered array in memory or represented simply quantitative information about each item. This question is orthogonal to the question of whether the representation is analog or discrete, because an ordered array can, but need not, contain analog information; and item information can be analog or discrete. In his section on analog code models, Moyer argued strongly that subjects retained in memory a perceptual analog of each item and "when the symbols are presented on a test trial, the appropriate analogs are retrieved and compared [p.254]." Riley, on the other hand, has assumed that, at least in her paradigm, subjects form an ordered array of items (which may preserve analog information by appropriate spacing of the items), and comparisons are made based on position in the array. No general agreement was reached regarding the conditions under which subjects actually organize quantitative information into an ordered array.

Most of the participants felt that it seemed unlikely that subjects carried around in their heads an ordering of all possible lexical items on all possible dimensions. Hence, most agreed that in a true semantic memory task, subjects probably accessed quantitative item information. (But see Potts, 1976, for a possible alternative). By the same token, there seems to be convincing evidence that in many interactions, subjects do indeed construct an ordering in response to the experimental task. Potts (1972) allowed subjects to take notes while studying the paragraph describing a linear ordering. Of the subjects, 86% did indeed take notes spontaneously, and of those who took notes, 73% did so by writing down the correct ordering of the terms. Further, as Riley notes, strong serial position effects are observed in her paradigm. Such effects constitute strong evidence that subjects are indeed constructing a linear ordering.

Given that, at least under certain circumstances, subjects do construct a linear array of terms, a question arises regarding the way in which this is accomplished. Smith has addressed this question by presenting an ordering in the form of a list of adjacent pairs and by examining the effect of the order of presentation of the pairs. He argues that such pairs are held in short-term memory until they can be linked, and he shows the effect of both storage load and the reordering of items required when pairs are not presented in natural order. Riley, on the other hand, argues that orderings are learned from the ends inward and that construction is facilitated when the premises are presented in an order that enables subjects to first isolate the end terms of the ordering. She then goes on to reconcile these apparently opposing positions by analyzing the differences in objectives and procedures employed in the two lines of research.

The Process of Constructing a Linear Order (Smith)

The foregoing sections have described several studies of the symbolic distance effect, in which the ordinal properties of a set of symbols were learned by subjects in the experimental situation. We have seen that the principal concern in these studies has been with two issues: the nature of the mental representation of the linear ordering and the processes by which the subject accesses this information. An equally interesting but generally neglected question concerns the mental representation of the linear order. How is it constructed? In most experiments the subjects are given information about previously unordered symbols in parcels that describe only one pair of items in the ordering. The two items are presented along with the relationship between them, and the subject is required to build a linear ordering of three, four, five, or more items from the pieces given him. The question is: How are the two or more pair-wise relationships combined to form a single, integrated representation of the ordering?

The problem of how ordinal information is integrated is not new, of course. The same question lies at the heart of the long history of experimentation on how transitive inferences are made. In typical experiments with adults, subjects are presented all at once with two premises and a question about a potential inference. For example, the problem might take the following form: "If Ann is better than Bill, and Bill is better than Cathy, is Ann better than Cathy?" Although all the information is present at once, it is still packaged in pair-wise relationships that must be combined in some way in order to draw the inference. The total process leading to the subject's response requires building a mental representation at some stage. Unfortunately, the procedures used shed very little light on the process of construction, because the latter is easily obscured by any number of other operations that must occur either before or after the inference is made. For example, the individual sentence parcels must be interpreted and represented before any inference can be drawn. And when the inference has been made, the question must be interpreted and the proper response formulated. The work of Clark (1969) has convincingly demonstrated that these ancillary processes play a central role in the standard experiments on transitive inference. However, a review by Johnson-Laird (1972) presents an equally convincing argument that the inferential process of combining information from the two premises cannot be understood without a theory of how a representation of the three-term series is built.

The developmental literature on transitive inference contains a similar limitation. In particular, most investigations have sought to determine whether children were capable of making inferences at a certain stage. The recent work of Riley and Trabasso (1974) suggests that the effort to eliminate possible artifacts and confoundings from these experiments has led to designs in which transitive inferences occur as part of the learning phase (see also Trabasso, 1975; and Trabasso & Riley, 1975). All the evidence indicates that the result of this learning is a mental representation of a linear ordering. As with the research on adults, the inferential process is buried under a considerable mass of input and output operations. (Riley provides an extensive review of these issues in the following section.)

In the investigations conducted by Smith and his associates, the central objective was to develop procedures that would lay bare the constructive or inferential process and to formulate a theory of how a mental representation of a linear ordering is achieved. In what follows, the procedural issues are first discussed, and then a theory is presented to account for the data obtained from experiments in which efforts were made to minimize the effects of both input and output variables. A final section examines a recent series of experiments that suggest that the nature of the representation as well as some of the details of the constructive process are influenced by the form in which the pair-wise relations between items in the ordering are presented. This conclusion is especially relevant to the earlier controversy over discrete versus analogue models of the symbolic distance effect, because it appears that conditions can be contrived to induce subjects to represent a linear order either as a string of verbal symbols or as an array of visual images.

Procedures for studying construction.   Consider a typical experiment in which subjects must learn an arbitrary linear ordering. Potts (1972) had subjects study paragraphs that contained sentences of the form, "The hawk is smarter than the deer" (or, in even more abstract form, $A > B$). The subjects received three sentences expressing the adjacent relationships that define a four-term linear ordering, $A > B, B > C, C > D$, and subsequently were required to verify a set of sentences that included both sentences that they had actually studied and new sentences, some of which were true and some of which were false. If the linear ordering is represented as $A > B > C > D$, then subjects were tested with the sentences they had studied, such as "The C is smarter than the D" (i.e., $C > D$), true sentences they had not studied ($A > C$), and false sentences ($D > A$, $C > B$). In such a study, the symbolic distance effect means that sentences expressing more remote relationships such as $A > D$ are verified more quickly and accurately than sentences expressing adjacent relationships ($B > C$), even though the remote pairs were not presented in training and the adjacent pairs were. This finding has been taken as evidence that the subjects combine information from the individual relational sentences to form a unified ordering.

A study by Barclay (1973) suggests that construction does not occur automatically. Barclay presented eight relational sentences one at a time for three learning trials. The sentences used both polar relational words, e.g., both "left of" and "right of," and included the four adjacent relations necessary to describe a five-term ordering, such as $A > B$ and $D < C$, as well as four remote relations, such as $B > E$ and $C < A$. One group of subjects was explicitly instructed that the sentences described an ordered array that was to be learned. A second group of subjects was told that their task was to remember the verbatim form of the sentences they were shown. After the learning phase, subjects in the first group were asked to write down an ordered list of elements describing the array, and most were able to do so without error. This demonstrated that they had constructed a linear ordering. These subjects were then given a surprise recognition test in which they were asked to indicate whether they had seen a given sentence in that exact verbatim form. They were unable to do this, although they were quite accurate in discriminating between sentences that agreed with the linear ordering and sentences that did not. The second group of subjects who were instructed to memorize the specific sentences also performed rather poorly in recognition of which sentences had actually been presented. However, these subjects also did not show any evidence of discriminating between true and false sentences. On a surprise test in which they were asked to produce an ordered list representing the information in the sentences, most were unable to do so.

Barclay's results show that the linear ordering is obtained from the individual relations by a voluntary cognitive process of construction. Forming a linear ordering is only one strategy available to the subject in this situation, and some of Frase's work (1972) suggests that it may not even be the most likely strategy adopted when instructions are simply to learn a passage. Thus any procedure designed to investigate constructive processes must make clear to the subject that the information is to be combined to form a single ordering. Otherwise, a failure to display symbolic distance effects or other diagnostic measures of linear-order formation cannot be unambiguously attributed to a failure of the constructive process.

In addition to manipulations of instructions, only one other variable appeared to affect the probability of success in constructing an ordering. This is the order in which the pair-wise relations between items is presented. For example, Potts

(1972) presented his pair-wise relational information in two different orders to different groups of subjects. One group received paragraphs in what seems intuitively to be the natural order, $A > B$, $B > C$, $C > D$. The second group received the information in a scrambled order, $C > D$, $A > B$, $B > C$. Subjects in the first group made fewer errors. Frase (1972), using quite different materials and procedures, arrived at similar results in that orders of presentation that seem more regular led to fewer errors. In both the Potts and Frase studies, however, the effect of different presentation orders was assessed only by different responding to various test items. There was no direct test of whether a complete linear order had been achieved.

A more detailed and systematic study of this phenomenon was carried out by Smith and Foos (1975), who presented the pair-wise sentences one at a time and then required the subject to respond with an ordered list of the items as implied in the pair-wise sentences. This procedure yields an explicit assessment of whether construction has been successful. Smith and Foos examined all six different orders of presentation that are possible in presenting the three adjacent pair-wise relations in a four-term linear ordering. The proportion of trials on which subjects produced the correct ordering was found to vary as a function of the order of presentation of the sentences. The six orders of presentation are shown in Table 1 along with the results from two experiments by Smith and Foos. The results are consistent with Potts (1972) insofar as construction was more likely to be successful with order 1 than with order 6. However, order 1 did not differ from orders 2, 3, and 4. From a statistical point of view, the only difference among orders is a comparison between the first four orders of presentation and the last two.

One simple theory of how the subject builds a linear ordering from pair-wise relationships is to suppose that the task is easy if the items are presented in the same order as they must appear in the constructed linear array and that it is more difficult if they are disordered or scrambled in order of appearance. However, this hypothesis will not account for the data in Table 1, since the information is disordered in all presentation orders except the first, and yet there are considerable differences among the various examples of disorder.

Smith and Foos (1975) proposed a model to give a more complete account of their results. The general idea is that the subjects build the linear ordering piecemeal as the sentences come in, to the best of their ability. The order information from the first sentence is stored in short-term memory so that it can be retained while the second sentence is processed. When the necessary order information has been extracted from the second sentence, the subject may be able to connect the second ordered pair of elements with the first by finding one element in each that is the same. For example, if the first sentence is $A > B$ and the second is $B > C$, then the subject can find that the same element B appears in both ordered pairs. He matches the two pairs with respect to this element and then can form the three-term linear ordering, $A > B > C$. Such a construction presumably

TABLE 1

Mean Proportion of Correctly Constructed
Strings as a Function of Presentation Order

Presentation order[a]	Sentences[b]		Pairs[c]
	Exp. 1	Exp. 2	
Match orders			
1. $A > B, B > C, C > D$	.67	.68	.91
2. $C > D, B > C, A > B$	.59	.61	.73
3. $B > C, C > D, A > B$	.57	.64	.73
4. $B > C, A > B, C > D$	.54	.61	.81
Nonmatch orders			
5. $A > B, C > D, B > C$	.44	.48	.68
6. $C > D, A > B. B > C$	.34	.47	.46

[a]The order to be constructed in every case is $ABCD$.

[b]Data from Smith and Foos (1975).

[c]Data from Foos et al. (1977).

takes up less short-term storage capacity than would the two independent, ordered pairs or two sentences complete and, therefore, makes the task easier.

In Table 1, notice that the last two orders of presentation, 5 and 6, are most
difficult. In both cases the first two sentences fail to have a common element,
and therefore the subject is unable to find a basis for matching elements. The
first two sentences cannot be reduced to a three-term linear ordering. Instead,
the order information from both of the first two sentences must be kept in
memory while taking in the third sentence. The equivalent of three independent
sentences must be held in memory while searching them for matching elements
and rearranging the elements into a unified ordering. The "Memory Load" hypothesis proposed by Smith and Foos holds that presentation orders 5 and 6
are more difficult because of this extra demand on memory capacity.

The order construction task devised by Smith and Foos (1975) provides a
way of getting at the constructive processes without the complexities of lengthy
testing sessions. However, Smith and Foos also reported that the measure of
successful construction is influenced by the linguistic form of the sentences presented. In general, such a finding could indicate that the linguistic properties of
the input event play an intimate role in determining how a linear order is constructed. It is, therefore, important to examine the exact nature of the linguistic
influence. In their second experiment, Smith and Foos used both "left" and
"right" to express the relationship between elements in the linear order to be

constructed. The sentences had the general form, "The farmer is to the left of the doctor," and the relational word varied systematically with respect to presentation orders. As can be seen in Table 1, the overall effect of presentation order was the same in this second experiment as in the first. The memory load hypothesis provides an adequate account of the data no matter how lexical entries vary. However, in the second experiment, there was an interaction between presentation order and the relation word used. Two different accounts of this interaction are possible.

In a study of transitive inference in the three-term series problem, Huttenlocher (1968) reported that the grammatical status of elements described in the second sentence influences the speed and accuracy of making transitive inferences. Suppose that the first sentence is "A is better than B" ($A > B$). The second sentence could be either "B is better than C" ($B > C$) or "C is worse than B" ($C < B$). In the first instance, the new element C enters the problem as the grammatical object of the sentence, whereas in the second instance, C enters as the grammatical subject. Huttenlocher's generalization was that the task was easier when the new element appeared as the grammatical subject of the sentence. She found that subjects made fewer errors and responded faster in answering questions that required the inference when the new information was related to old as subject to object (or topic to comment), respectively.

Smith and Foos (1975) examined the interaction of presentation order with relation words to see whether the pattern supported Huttenlocher's generalization. They noted that Huttenlocher's account only applied to the first four orders; in orders 5 and 6, the second sentence provides *two* new elements, and the third relates two old elements. However, in the first four presentation orders, Smith and Foos found that grammatical status did affect success in constructing the linear orderings. If the new element introduced in either the second or third sentence appeared as the subject of the sentence, performance was relatively good, and if the new element appeared as the object of one of the sentences, performance was worse. Furthermore, when errors were made, they tended to consist of failures to order properly those items that had first appeared as grammatical objects. However, the effect of grammatical status was not additive for the second and third sentence, and because Huttenlocher's generalization applies only to the first four orders, the value of this interpretation was inherently limited.

A hypothesis of greater generality can be derived from a recent study of the three-term series problem by Potts and Scholz (1975). The time subjects take on transitive inference problems was analyzed into two components. The first component is the time taken to study the two premises, and the second is the time required to answer the question. They found that the first component, premise study time, did not vary consistently with grammatical status, as would be predicted by Huttenlocher's hypothesis. Instead, study time was a function of whether or not the adjective used in each premise was congruent with the placement of the end-term item described in the premise. Consider the set of all possible pairs of premises that could be used to describe an array of elements with A on the left, B in the middle, and C on the right. The element A might be introduced in a congruent sentence, such as "A is to the left of B," in which the element A is placed on the left, and the adjective used is "left." Alternatively, A might be introduced in an incongruent sentence, such as "B is to the right of A," in which A is on the left, but the sentence uses the adjective "right." [It should be pointed out that Potts and Scholz use the term "congruence" in a different sense than Clark (1969). Clark's theory was also shown to be inconsistent with the premise study times.]

Potts and Scholz's (1975) congruity principle makes a complete set of predictions for all combinations of adjectives and presentation orders with four-term series, whereas predictions derived from Huttenlocher's (1968) grammatical status analysis covered only the first four of the six presentation orders. Thus Potts and Scholz's account is more general and, therefore, more likely, in the abstract, to be disconfirmed by the data. In fact, a reanalysis of the Smith and Foos (1975) study revealed that the congruity principle of Potts and Scholz accounted for a greater proportion of the interaction variance than the grammatical status principle of Huttenlocher. Thus it would appear that the relationship between what a sentence says about an element in a linear order and the ultimate placement of that element in the linear ordering plays a role in the construction of the ordering. The expression of a relationship that makes explicit the polar opposition of the underlying dimension seems to bias the constructive process in a subtle way.

The foregoing results clarify some of the problems with sentences as a medium for presenting pair-wise relationships between elements in a linear ordering. These problems are interesting in their own right, of course, and we return to them later. What should be apparent is the need for some method of presenting the pair-wise relationships that avoids the complexities of sentences. A technique for presenting pure order relationships was first conceived by Paul Foos. He simply presented the relations between adjacent elements in the linear ordering as ordered pairs, with no comparative adjective involved. The elements used were digits. The subject was instructed to construct a single linear ordering that preserved the orderings of all the pairs. On a typical trial, the subject might hear the pairs 37, 96, 63, in that order, and the correct response would be the single ordering 9637. Although the digit-string construction task might not eliminate all linguistic factors in the processing, at least it ensures that subjects use a consistent strategy when dealing with relational inputs. Because there is no possibility of incongruent relational words in this procedure, it is most appropriate for analysis of memory load factors and the processes by which pairs are assembled into longer linear orderings.

Foos has conducted several experiments with the digit-string construction task and has shown that the effects of presentation order are consistent with the earlier results with sentences (Foos, 1975; Foos et al., 1976). Overall performance is generally superior with pairs of elements, and this fact makes it possible to investigate longer orderings for which more complex orders of presentation exist. Foos also showed that the effect of presentation order remained the same when pairs of words were used instead of pairs of digits. In particular, he found that pairs of the profession names used in the Smith and Foos (1975) study yielded the same pattern of results as pairs of digits, although overall performance was slightly poorer with the word pairs.

A theory of linear order construction.   Foos et al. (1976) presented a model of how subjects construct linear orders in the context of the digit-string construction task. The model represents an attempt to extend the memory load hypothesis to account for the more subtle differences in the construction processes that arise when elements of a new relationship match with elements already processed, and also when the new pair does not have an element that matches with old information. The model assumes an ordered rehearsal buffer in short-term memory similar to that in the familiar Atkinson and Shiffrin (1971) memory theory. Each new pair is entered into this memory buffer, adjacent to the ordered information already present except that a marker is placed at the end of each pair as it is presented. In other words, if the subject heard the pairs 57, 25, he would first place the pair 57 in memory followed by a marker θ, and the second pair producing the memory content 57θ25θ.

Once this memory content is established, the subject searches the contents of the buffer to establish whether there are any matching elements and where they are. Under some circumstances, the matching elements are found on either side of the marker element, as when the input order 42, 25, results in a memory content of 42θ25θ in the rehearsal buffer. In this case, the subject can employ a deletion operation to remove one of the two matched elements and the marker, in the transformation 42θ25θ → 425θ. A sequence that permits this sort of operation directly must have the same element appearing last in the old memory content and first in the new relation. This is called a "Match 1" or M1 process.

A second possibility is that when searching the memory content, the subject will find a matching pair of elements, but they will not be adjacent to the same marker. This would happen, for example, if the input order is 58, 25, which will result in the rehearsal buffer containing 58θ25θ. The subject's task is to turn this into the ordering 258, but this cannot be accomplished by a simple deletion—the contents of the rehearsal buffer must first be rearranged. This requires a "Match 2" or M2 process.

Without specifying the precise process by which rearrangement occurs, we may predict that it will take time. This means that M2 sequences take more time to process than M1 sequences. It also appears likely that rearrangement may be an error-prone process, because the subject is forced to manipulate the basic order information held in the rehearsal buffer. The tendency to make errors in rearrangement would be especially likely when pairs are presented at a fixed rate with a limited amount of time between pairs (e.g., 3 sec in the Foos et al. experiment). This would mean that M2 sequences would result in more errors than M1 sequences. Both of these predictions have been confirmed experimentally; the processing of M2 sequences is both slower and less accurate than the processing of M1 sequences.

Foos et al. (1976) investigated the entire set of six presentation orders for four-digit orderings and 24 presentation orders for five-digit orderings. In both four- and five-term orderings, there are several instances in which new information is added to previous relations, and each of these additions may be of type M1 or M2; that is, they may or may not require rearrangement before the new information can be incorporated into the existing ordering. Foos et al. found that errors increased linearly as the number of M2 processes increased relative to the number of M1 processes. Moreover, the specific errors were associated significantly more often with pairs that required the reordering process (M2) than with pairs that did not (M1). For example, if the input pairs were 23, 12, 34 (so that the correct string was 1234), subjects who made an error were more likely to respond 2341, correctly performing the M1 process 23θ34θ → 234θ, than 4123 which results from performing the M2 process 23θ12θ → 123θ.

It appeared possible that the above results might be found when subjects were linking up pairs of digits to form a string but might not occur in experiments in which meaningful words were to be linked. However, Smith and Mynatt (1977) presented pairs of digits and pairs of profession names (such as "teacher" and "doctor") in a self-paced procedure that permitted the measurement of study times for each pair. For pairs of both types, they found that when reordering was required (M2), the pairs were studied significantly longer than when only deletion was required (M1).

The above results give a clear picture of the different processes that may be invoked when at least one element of the newly presented pair can be matched with information already in the rehearsal buffer. Generally, when the match involves elements surrounding a marker θ, so that mere deletion assembles the information into the linear ordering, performance is relatively rapid and accurate. If the match involves elements that are in separate places, so that the information must be rearranged before deletion can take place, then the process results in more errors and is slower.

Sometimes the new information given to the subject cannot be matched with old information in any way, because it involves an entirely new pair of elements. In this case the subject must hold the information and await further pairs that provide the basis for linkage. Foos et al. (1976) suggested that there would be differences in the mental operations performed with different nonmatch orders.

As an example of what can happen, suppose the experimenter presents 30, followed by 71. According to the preceding memory model, the subject assembles this into a rehearsal buffer in the form 30θ71θ. However, this cannot be reduced by deletion, nor is there any rearrangement of the elements that permits deletion. Now suppose that the next item presented is 07. This is first added to the original contents, yielding 30071θ07θ. A search for matching elements establishes matches for two elements, lying on either side of the first marker element. Thus the initial order is confirmed, and a deletion can produce the proper ordering. However, this search and deletion process can be specified in precisely the same terms for both the present situation and the M1 and M2 match discussed earlier.

In order to make the rearrangement process explicit, let us assume that the function of a rearrangement is always to place matching elements on either side of a marker element so that duplicate elements and the marker can be deleted. We can then characterize the five constructive situations (or processes) described by Foos et al. (1976) in terms of the set of five mental operations shown in Fig. 7. The operations, indicated by numbered boxes in the figure, are, as follows:

1. A search for a nonterminal marker, i.e., a marker not followed by a blank. This search proceeds from the first element in the buffer and terminates with the *first* nonterminal marker identified. If none is found, the constructive process is complete and is terminated. When the first nonterminal marker is identified, the second operation is initiated.

2. A comparison of the elements on either side of the marker identified by operation 1. If these elements match, operation 3 is initiated. If they do not match, then operation 4 occurs.

3. Deletion of one duplicate element and the marker. Deletion occurs whenever a nonterminal marker is surrounded by two matching elements and is always followed by reinitiation of operation 1, a search for additional nonterminal elements.

4. A search for matching elements not previously located in the buffer. Operation 4 is an ordered search that takes the first element in the buffer as a probe and searches each subsequent nonmarker element to determine whether it matches the probe. If the end of the buffer is reached without finding a match, the second element is taken as a probe, and the third, fourth, and remaining elements are searched. If no matches are present, this search cycle is repeated until all nonmarker elements in the buffer have served as probes for the elements that follow them in the buffer. The failure to find matching elements signifies that no construction is possible, and the constructive process terminates. If, however, a match is found, the rearrangement operation is initiated.

5. Rearrangement of pairs (or larger suborderings) so that matching elements are placed on either side of a marker. The rearrangement operation moves strings of nonmarker elements along with the marker that follows them. The string may be only two elements long, i.e., a pair. Because the rearrangement operation is always preceded by a search through the nonmarker elements of the buffer, we can characterize it as a movement of the

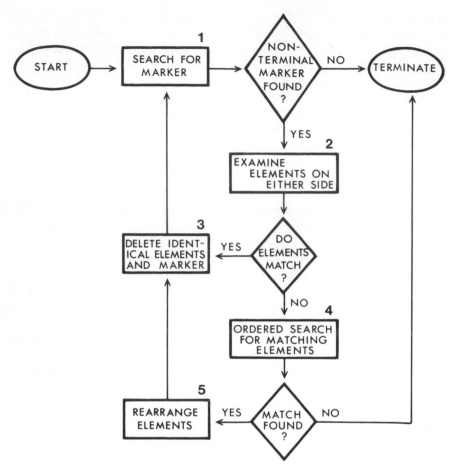

FIG. 7   A process model describing the sequence of mental operations that occur during construction of a linear ordering when the adjacent pairs are presented in varying orders.

string containing the matching element. This string necessarily appears toward the end of the elements in the buffer. The rearrangement moves the string forward in the buffer so that the element identified by the search (operation 4) is placed on either side of a marker. The rearrangement operation is always followed by operation 3, deletion of matching elements and the marker.

The foregoing process model can deal with any order of presentation for a set of pairs that contains an implicit linear order. (It will, of course, fail on sets such as 72, 29, 97, and 61, 64.) Consider again what happens in the M1 and M2 situations. When 42, 25, is presented (M1 situation), operations 1, 2, and 3 are executed and, upon recycling to operation 1, the process terminates. When 58, 25, is presented (M2 situation), all five operations are executed, as follows: The buffer content is $58\theta_1 25\theta_2$. (The markers are labeled for clarity of presentation; however, their identification plays no role in the model.) Operation 1 identifies the marker θ_1. In operation 2, the digits "8" and "5" on either side of θ_1 fail to match. In operation 4, a search begins with "5" and a match is found in the pair 25. In operation 5, the string $25\theta_2$ is moved forward in the buffer, yielding $25\theta_2 58\theta_1$. The situation is now formally identical to the M1 situation, and execution of operation 3 followed by operation 1 again leads to termination.

Two aspects of the account of match processes just given deserve comment. First, it should be noted that the search in operation 4 is not an exhaustive one. In fact, when the first element in the buffer is used as a probe to search the remaining elements, a match is found with the last nonmarker element in the buffer. Hence, the execution of operation 4 in this case might not be as time-consuming as compared to cases where several passes through the buffer are required (discussed later). Second, as already indicated, when there are multiple instances of M1 and M2 situations, the rearrangements in operation 5 move suborderings with three or more elements. Consider the presentation series 42, 25, 94. Following the second pair, the subject constructs the string 425, so that on presentation of the third pair, the buffer contains $425\theta_1\ 94\theta_2$. Operation 5 then interchanges $425\theta_1$ with $94\theta_2$ to yield $94\theta_2 425\theta_1$.

The foregoing model is now sufficiently specified that we can apply it to the situations that arise in the last two orders of Table 1. Foos et al. (1976) referred to these as "nonmatch" orders, because there are no matching or duplicate elements on which construction can operate following the presentation of the second pair. For example, when 30, 71, is presented, the buffer contains $30\theta_1 71\theta_2$, and operations 1, 2, and 4 are executed, leading to an exhaustive search of the contents of the buffer followed by termination. Foos et al. labeled this situation the "Nonmatch" or N process.

The presentation of the third pair following a nonmatch situation can lead to one of two types of double-match situations. Consider the previous example, 30, 71, 07, again. At the end of presentation, the buffer contains $30\theta_1 71\theta_2 07\theta_3$. Operations 1, 2, and 4 are executed. The search in operation 4, after determining that there is no matching element for the first digit "3," finds a match with "0" in the pair 07. In operation 4, this pair along with the marker θ_3 is moved forward (and interchanged with $71\theta_2$) to form a new buffer content $30\theta_1 07\theta_3 71\theta_2$. Upon recycling to operation 1, two deletions ensue. First, marker θ_1 is located by operation 2, and the deletion by operation 3 leaves $307\theta_3 71\theta_2$ in the buffer. Then marker θ_3 is located and deleted, leaving $3071\theta_2$ in the buffer. Foos et al. labeled the foregoing process (consisting of the sequence of operations 1, 2, 4, 5, 3, 1, 2, 3, 1) a double match of type 1, "Double Match 1" of D1. It applies specifically to what happens in order 5 of Table 1 when the third pair of the presentation series occurs.

The last order in Table 1 (order 6) presents a still more complex situation. An example of input in this order would be 45, 16, 64, which would leave $45\theta_1 16\theta_2 64\theta_3$ in the buffer after the third pair. A search for nonterminal markers (operation 1) could identify two, θ_1 and θ_2. It is assumed that the search for markers is serial, self-terminating, and always begins at the front of the buffer. (The basis for the decision to treat operation 1 in this fashion is discussed later.) Hence, the marker θ_1 is found, and operation 2 is executed followed by operations 4 and 5, because the digits on either side of θ_1, "5" and "1," do not match. In operation 5, the pairs are rearranged in the buffer to yield $64\theta_3 45\theta_1 16\theta_2$. Now, operations 1, 2, and 3 follow, leaving $645\theta_1 16\theta_2$ in the buffer. Upon recycling through operations 1, 2, 4, and 5, a second time, another rearrangement is performed in which a match involving the digit "6" is found in operation 4, and the buffer contents are $16\theta_2 645\theta_1$ following operation 5. Finally, operations 1, 2, 3, and 1 are executed to achieve deletion of the marker θ_2 and the repeated "6." The entire process (consisting of the sequence of operations 1, 2, 4, 3, 5, 1, 2, 4, 5, 3, 1) was labeled by Foos et al. a double match of type 2, "Double Match 2" or D2.

The decision to treat operation 1 as a serial, self-terminating search that always begins with the first element of the buffer was based on the findings of Foos et al. (1976) showing that orders requiring the D2 process, e.g., order 6 in Table 1, were consistently less likely to be constructed successfully than those requiring the D1 process, e.g., order 5 in Table 1. The formulation of the preceding model predicts that the D2 process involves executing operations 4 and 5 twice. If we assume that operation 5, the rearrangement of pairs and suborderings in the buffer, is a major source of errors and also consumes relatively large amounts of time, the prediction follows that order 6 takes more time and leads to more errors.

The foregoing model provides a good qualitative description of the results from the digit-string construction task. Foos et al. (1976) did not formulate the model quite as specifically as has been done in the foregoing. Instead, they isolated the five constructive situations labeled processes M1, M2, N, D1, and D2 and showed that a corresponding set of five additive parameters could account for roughly 92% of the variance due to presentation orders in the error data for the 24 different orders of presentation for five-digit strings. A similar analysis accounted for 96% of the variance in the error data for four-digit strings. In fact, even the quantitative estimates of the five parameters from the two analyses were very similar. Smith and Mynatt (1977) also used the five processes to analyze study times in the self-paced procedure. They found that subjects studied pairs requiring the D2 process much longer than pairs requiring the D1 process. However, they also found that even with almost 8-sec additional study time when the D2 process was required, subjects made errors in constructing the ordering over half the time (as compared to error rates of 6% to 10% for other presentation orders). This finding suggests that the D2 process may have exceeded the subjects' storage capacity, a contingency not explicitly provided for in the model.

The effects of linguistic variables.   The model of constructive processes described above appears to be a promising account of how subjects combine the information from ordered pairs to form a single linear ordering. The specific formulation given is by no means precisely linked to the data. Instead, it should be seen as representative of a class of models that are capable of providing a quantitative account of the data from experiments on digit-string construction. However, the interest in refining such models would be considerably lessened if it should turn out that the processes under study were limited to the construction of strings from pairs. Certainly, the initial purpose of such studies was to uncover constructive processes of a general nature. The earlier results of Smith and Foos (1975), using sentences with such relations as "to the left of" and "to the right of," contained hints of these constructive processes, but the predicted differences between presentation orders were not statistically significant. There remains the possibility that different constructive processes occur with sentences.

These concerns motivated a doctoral dissertation at Bowling Green State University by Paul Foos (1975). In this study, Foos used two types of pairs—pairs of digits and pairs of words. He also presented the same relations in sentences using the phrases "to the left of" and "to the right of." His results with pairs of words and pairs of digits were highly consistent with those previously obtained with pairs of digits. Pairs of words and pairs of digits produced the same pattern of difficulty for presentation orders of both four- and five-term series that Foos et al. had reported. This result corroborates Smith and Mynatt's (1977) results, reported earlier. However, when the information was presented in sentences, the pattern of difficulty was consistently different. Sentences did yield a reliable difference between match and nonmatch orders, but the difference was significantly smaller than that found for pairs. More important, Foos found that for sentences, order 5 was more difficult than order 6 under some conditions. Remember that when pairs are presented in order 5, the model says they are reduced to the final ordering by a single rearrangement of pairs followed by a series of deletions. However, in order 6, the model specifies that two rearrangements, each followed by a deletion, are required.

Foos (1975) proposed an explanation of his results based on the assumption that sentences are inherently more internally organized and stable than pairs. He argued that the structure of a sentence can serve the same function as a marker element. Both devices segregate two elements from the other elements in memory and maintain them as two-term suborderings. Moreover, sentence organization is assumed to be more reliable and durable in memory than markers. However, when the memory load can be reduced by combining two pair-wise relations into a single three-term subordering, as in match orders, both sentence organization and markers are abandoned in favor of a single linear subordering. According to this explanation, integration reduces the memory load both by eliminating duplicate items and also by removing either markers or sentence structures. Precisely because nonmatch orders do not allow for such memory load reductions, they present greater difficulty. But the difficulty is partly a function of the dependability of the strategy used to keep pair-wise relations separated.

When a nonmatch order is presented in pairs, the subject has particular difficulty holding the pair-wise relations separately until he has information to integrate them. Nonterminal markers have a tendency to get lost or misplaced, during both storage and rearrangement of pairs. In contrast, when a nonmatch order is presented in sentences, the subject can more easily hold two (or even three) distinct relations and manipulate them in memory with relatively little chance of error. If the foregoing account is correct, then any process involving rearrangement would be expected to be less troublesome when relations are presented in sentences. Thus, with sentences, the difference in difficulty between match and nonmatch orders should be reduced, because rearrangements of the contents of memory should be easier. There should still be a difference, however, because nonmatch orders always involve an extra memory load no matter how the pair-wise relations are presented. Exactly this pattern of results was obtained by Foos (1975).

We have seen that the original memory load hypothesis was the starting place for both the general theory of linear order construction and the specific explanation offered by Foos (1975) to account for the differences between sentences and pairs. Foos argued that when the limits of storage capacity are reached, the information concerning the identity of individual pair-wise relations is the first to be abandoned. Either the markers between pairs are discarded, or the sentences are reduced to a string of elements without markers. The process is functionally equivalent to integrating pairs in match orders. It reduces memory load. There is, of course, a price to be paid for this type of reduction, because the subject can no longer be sure what the input pairs were. For example, if the pairs 30 and 71 have been presented, and the nonterminal marker is lost due to temporary memory overload, the subject is committed to the output order 3071. In the designs used in the studies reviewed in the foregoing, this hypothesis about what output order will be required was confirmed for the subject half the time, so it can be argued that abandoning a marker is more reasonable than abandoning any of the elements in the ordered string. The latter strategy leads to incorrect output sequences in almost all cases.

The central point of the extension of the memory load hypothesis by Foos (1975) was that when the total demands on memory exceeded capacity, both markers for pairs and sentence organization are abandoned, leaving an ordered string of elements in memory. In two similar experiments, he had found that digit pairs and isomorphic sentences about digit pairs describing four-digit strings produced different results in two respects. With sentences, there was no difference between orders 5 and 6, and the size of the match-nonmatch difference (orders 1, 2, 3, and 4 versus orders 5 and 6) was smaller. Foos took this result to mean that with sentences, the total demand on memory capacity was not being taxed to the point where sentence organization was abandoned, even with nonmatch orders. However, he reasoned that with longer strings of five or six digits, the total demand on capacity should be increased to the point where the results for pairs and sentences should become more alike.

Foos (1975) first tried a selected set of presentation orders for five-digit strings, comparing presentation in unadorned pairs with isomorphic sentences describing pairs. The pattern of results was similar to what he had found with four-digit strings. Even with six-digit strings in a final experiment, Foos obtained the same pattern of results as long as only one nonmatch situation occurred in the presentation order. However, Foos included in this last experiment two presentation orders for six-digit strings that had two nonmatch situations, so that the subject at one point was forced to maintain three separate pairs (or sentences) before beginning to integrate pairs and forming suborderings of three or more digits. For this special class of presentation orders, the orders that required the D2 process involving two rearrangements were more difficult than orders that required the D1 process involving a single rearrangement. That is, when the information to produce the string 123456 was presented in the order, 56, 34, 12, 45, 23, more errors were made than when presentation order was 12, 34, 56, 23, 45. This difference was obtained for both presentation of digit pairs and isomorphic presentation in the form of sentences. The difference was, however, relatively small when the information was presented in sentences. In other words, if Foos' hypothesis is correct that sentences are more stable, and the subject is more inclined to hold information in separate pairs when it is given in sentence form, then it is quite difficult to overload this sentence-memory system and force the subject into a strategy of concatenating nonmatch pairs. However, it appears that the results do agree, in outline, with Foos' hypothesis.

More recent experiments suggest an even more complicated picture of the role played by various aspects of linguistic setting in which the pair-wise relations are presented. In many of the experiments in which the elements and the relationships all appear in sentence form, the experimenter has varied the particular relation word used, sometimes saying, for example, that A is to the left of B, sometimes that B is to the right of A. In a recent experiment, Mynatt and Smith (1977) presented relational information visually in the form of sentences in a self-paced procedure and measured study time. This procedure had previously yielded data consistent with the constructive processes proposed by Foos et al. (1976) when pairs were used. The pattern of results in the new experiments depended on how the relations were presented. If every sentence was

of the form "Ann is friendlier than Bill," always using the same relation said in
the same way, then the pattern of results was very similar to that found with unadorned pairs of digits or words. But in another condition of the experiment,
Mynatt and Smith used sentences like "The red one is above the green one" or
"The brown one is below the white one." Both "above" and "below" typically
appeared within a single trial of three and sometimes four sentences. With these
sentences, seven out of eight subjects showed a pattern of results different from
the pattern found with "friendlier" and with digit pairs. In particular, order 5
consistently took more time and led to more errors than order 6.

The first conclusion to be drawn from Mynatt and Smith's (1977) study is
that the mere presence of a sentence frame is not the determining factor, because
when the information was presented in a series of sentences all using the same
adjective, like "Sue is friendlier than Bill, Tom is friendlier than Ann," etc., the
data came out very much like the results with pairs of digits in the Foos et al.
(1976) study. In this case, it was order 6 that took more time and led to more
errors than order 5. In other respects, the data also resemble the pattern of study
times obtained by Mynatt and Smith with pairs of digits and pairs of words.
These results indicate that there are experimental arrangements, using sentences
to present relations, that subjects handle like a sequence of pairs.

Mynatt and Smith's (1977) results also establish that there are situations
in which sentences produce results unlike those found with digit strings. The
contrasting results were obtained from the same subjects, so we can rule out the
possibility of a simple variation across individuals in preferred strategy for hand-
ling pair-wise relations. On the other hand, the contrasting results occurred when
the sentence frame varied; that is, when both "above" and "below" appeared in
the set of sentences. Such variation would be expected to draw the subject's
attention to linguistic aspects of the materials, thereby introducing a factor that
is not present in the digit-string experiment. It is possible that the salience of
the linguistic aspects, and the fact that the subject must use a fairly elaborate
process of interpreting the direction of the adjective when he combines "A is
above B" with "C is below B," is the cause of the change in the data configuration.

The salience of the sentence frame cannot be the full explanation of differences, however. In two experiments, Mynatt and Smith (1977) presented
relations in the form of sentences that ordered five profession names like "doctor" and "soldier" with varied combinations of both "taller" and "shorter." In
one case the results fit very well with predictions of the Foos et al. model. The
third sentence of order 6 was studied longer than the corresponding sentence of
order 5. Moreover, sentences with "shorter" were studied longer than sentences
with "taller," and this difference suggests that a conversion process was occurring when the former comparative was used. However, in another experiment
that was designed to completely replicate the one just described, neither of these
results was obtained. Furthermore, orders 5 and 6 did not differ in other conditions of the experiment in which the following pairs of relational phrases were

used: (1) to the left of—to the right of; (2) better than—worse than; and (3) is the father of—is the son of. Some of the same subjects showed the configuration expected with pairs when later tested with pairs of digits and pairs of words, again ruling out an explanation in terms of simple individual differences.

In the Mynatt and Smith (1977) study, the sentences that produced data like the digit strings not only used the same adjective all the time but also used as stimulus elements common boys' names, which would have limited powers of eliciting imagery, along with a comparative adjective, "friendlier," which also lacks any simple image. In contrast, the materials that produced data different from the digit strings used colors as elements and the adjectives "above" and "below," which at once permit spatial mappings and spatial imagery. It seems possible that colors ordered in a vertical array might easily give rise to a concrete visual image incorporating some analog information. Moreover, the spatial aspect of such an image suggests still another way in which subjects could maintain the integrity of two-term orderings in the nonmatch situation. That is, the ordering of red above green can be kept separate from the ordering of brown below white by placing the second ordering next to first so that no commitment needs to be made regarding the relation between green and white. It also seems likely that when the third sentence is presented, and integration becomes possible, the elements of such a visual image might be searched in a different manner from elements in a rehearsal buffer. Specifically, what is searched first might not necessarily be the first element in the buffer, if indeed a rehearsal buffer is maintained in parallel with the image. (Informal observations and subjects' comments suggest that both forms of storage are being used at the same time.) Minor changes in where the search begins can be shown to have major consequences for the model's predictions of the relative difficulty of the D1 and D2 processes. Thus it appears feasible to explain the reversal of orders 5 and 6 in terms of the influence that a particular mode of representation has on the order of operations in the Foos et al. model.

Unfortunately, from the data at hand, we cannot say with certainty whether it is the use of varying adjectives, with the resulting linguistic complication, or the use of materials that can be readily imagined, that produces the different data patterns. However, the results to date suggest that sentence frames interact in a complicated fashion with individual differences. Subjects appear to differ in their tendency to use imaginal representations. However, the individual predisposition is never so strong that it fully determines whether or not images are used. There appear to be some conditions in which virtually all subjects construct and use images and other conditions in which virtually all subjects depend exclusively on rehearsal. However, there is also a large set of conditions in which a confusing pattern of results emerges because they arise from a mixture of different strategies operating in different subjects. It was partly because Mynatt and Smith (1977) suspected such an interaction of conditions and materials with individual biases toward different strategies that they confounded imagery and sentence frame factors in the study reported in the preceding.

In summary, the research we have described clearly shows that a complicated process, involving short-term memory and rearrangement of relations, occurs when subjects build a linear ordering out of component relations. Deeper analysis of this process should enable us to predict experimental conditions under which people would be unable to build linear orderings and possibly may lead to discoveries of several different processes that produce orderings, possibly orderings with different psychological properties.

A Developmental Approach to the Construction of Linear Orderings (Riley)

The central focus of the work done by Kirk Smith and his colleagues has been an examination of the processes involved in constructing linear orders from a set of relations between pairs of elements. Thus, given the relations between A and B, B and C, and C and D, how is the order $ABCD$ constructed? Smith has addressed this question by presenting the relations between adjacent elements in the order to subjects and then asking the subject to recall the complete linear orderings. A major variable of interest in these studies is how the presentation order of the relations affects the subjects'subsequent success in recalling the complete ordering. Smith's results point out the importance of memory load considerations in constructive processes. In general, subjects were most successful when the second, and subsequent relations presented, contained only one new item. When two relations have a common element, e.g., $A > B$ and $B > C$, the new element in the second relation can be added to the first relation yielding the order $A > B > C$. However, if the second relation does not share an element with the first, e.g., $A > B$ and $C > D$, both relations must be held separately in memory until an additional relation(s) containing elements in common with AB and CD is presented. Thus, Smith observes, subjects are much more likely to recall the complete ordering when presented the relations in the order $A > B$, $B > C$, $C > D$ than when presented the relations in the order $A > B$, $C > D$, $B > C$.

On the surface this result appears to conflict directly with the assertion of Riley and Trabasso (1974), that linear orderings are constructed by an "ends-inward" process, first isolating the end anchors, and then inserting the remaining elements from the ends inward. Thus, in a six-term series ($ABCDEF$), the subject would first isolate the ends A and F and note that they are the anchors at the end of a scale. Then the relations $A > B$ and $E > F$ are noted, allowing the subject to insert B and E into the linear orders A, B, and E, F. Next, elements C and D are inserted: A, B, C, and D, E, F. Finally, the relation between C and D is noted, completing the ordering $ABCDEF$. This process is very similar to processes that have been proposed in the past to describe the learning of serial lists (cf. Wishner, Shipley, & Hurvich, 1957; Feigenbaum & Simon, 1962; Bower, 1971). Thus, one might expect, based on the ends-inward process, that in Smith's task, subjects would perform better when they were presented first with relations containing end terms ($A > B, C > D, B > C$) rather than the opposite finding that he obtained.

In order to evaluate whether there is, in fact, any contradiction between Smith's findings and the model for the construction of linear orderings proposed by Riley and Trabasso, it is necessary to consider the objectives of the research program of Trabasso, Riley, and their colleagues, and the task that they used. The original concern of this program was to examine the logical abilities of young children and, in particular, to examine the role of task factors such as memory and language in tasks traditionally used to assess children's logical abilities. The task examined by Trabasso and Riley was a problem known in the developmental literature as the "transitivity task." Piaget (1970; Piaget, Inhelder, & Szeminska, 1960) has asserted that children are unable to make transitive inferences, i.e., infer $A > C$ given $A > B$ and $B > C$, until they reach the stage of concrete operations (about 7 or 8 years of age). The transitivity task has been used as a diagnostic procedure for evaluating intellectual growth; that is, on the basis of a child's success or failure on such a task, one infers whether or not the child has certain logical abilities. Bryant and Trabasso (1971) argued that factors other than logical ability can affect a child's performance on reasoning tasks. Specifically, if the child does not remember the premises ($A > B, B > C$), one cannot say anything about his or her logical abilities if he or she fails to make the inference, A > C. The procedures developed by Bryant and Trabasso, and subsequently used by Riley and Trabasso (1974), Trabasso (1975), Trabasso, Riley, and Wilson (1975), and Riley (1976), make use of lengthy training procedures to ensure that the "premises" in the task are learned and make use of testing that measures both retention of the original premise relations and inference making.

These procedures have now been used with both children and adults using both five-term and six-term series; the basic paradigm is outlined in Fig. 8. In this task there are a number of sticks that differ in color and length. Stick 1 is the shortest. The subject is first trained to make relational choices (longer or shorter) on each of the premise relations involving adjacent pairs of sticks. On choice trials, pairs of sticks are presented in a box so that only the color codes can be used to predict the length relations. Feedback is given on training trials (either visual, i.e., presenting the actual sticks, or linguistic, i.e., stating the relations verbally). The pairs are presented in block randomized order, and training is continued until a stringent memory criterion is reached. Following training on adjacent pairs, the person is tested on all possible member pairs without feedback.

Bryant and Trabasso, using a five-term series, found that four- to six-year-old children performed significantly above chance levels on the critical inferential question (Stick 2 versus Stick 4) following training to ensure retention of the premise relations. Thus they concluded that previous failures on this task by young children were probably due to failures to recall the premise relations

Training	Testing	2	3	4	5	6
1<2, 2>1	1	TE	E	E	E	E
2<3, 3>2	2		T	I1	I2	E
3<4, 4>3	3			T	I1	E
4<5, 5>4	4				T	E
5<6, 6>5	5					TE

T = Training Pair

E = End-anchored Pair

Ii = Inference Pair of Step-size i, i = 1, 2

FIG. 8   Schematic outline of training and testing relations for five-term series problems. (From Trabasso & Riley, 1975.)

rather than the absence of the logical abilities necessary to make transitive inferences.

Riley and Trabasso (1974) replicated and extended the work of Bryant and Trabasso (1971). Their major purpose was to examine some linguistic factors in Bryant and Trabasso's procedures that appeared important for the success of young children in the inference task. They demonstrated that the use of both forms of the comparative, longer and shorter, is necessary for teaching young children (4-year-olds) the relations between pairs of sticks. For present purposes, however, one of the most important aspects of the Riley and Trabasso study was their focus on children's performance in the acquisition, as well as testing, phase of the task. The training data showed a striking serial-position effect. The number of errors on training pairs (premises) containing end terms was significantly less than on relations in the middle of the five-term ordering. A reexamination of Bryant and Trabasso's data indicated a serial-position effect in their training data as well. Riley and Trabasso suggested that such a serial-position effect would be obtained if children were constructing orderings from the ends inward rather than storing each "premise" relation separately in memory. This possibility, although not the only explanation for why relations containing end terms would be easier to learn than relations from the middle of the ordering, was compelling for several reasons. First, serial-position effects had been observed in numerous studies of serial-list learning and in situations in which subjects learned to map responses onto existing continua (cf. Bower, 1971). In fact, Bower had shown that a serial-position effect arises whenever elements are mapped onto a linear order and that the existence of such a serial-position effect can be taken as *prima facie* evidence for the construction of a linear order. In addition, a major problem for young children in a task such as this is the memory load. The linear-order representation eliminates the redundancy contained in encoding a set of ordered relations with common elements, thus reducing the memory load. The argument that people will construct integrated memory representations rather than simply storing copies of the inputs in memory tasks had been made by a number of researchers studying adults' memory for verbal materials (Bransford & Franks, 1971; Potts, 1972; Barclay, 1973).

Riley and Trabasso argued that the children in their task were able to isolate the end anchors from the randomly presented series of premise relations by finding those sticks that were only shorter and only longer (Sticks 1 and 5). Once the ends of the series are isolated, the child can use a linear, spatial image (like that described by DeSoto, London, & Handel, 1965) and place the shortest element on one end and the longest on the other. Construction of the linear ordering would proceed by adding elements to this spatial image from the ends in toward the middle until all of the elements presented in the random training sequence were included in the ordering. With a five-term series, however, one cannot discriminate between the construction of a linear ordering and a simpler explanation of the serial-position effect based on factors such as response competition. Because pairs (1, 2) and (4, 5) each contain a member that has only a single comparative associated with it, these pairs should be easier to learn than pairs (2, 3) and (3, 4), in which all three elements have two comparatives associated with them. Thus the serial-position effect could be observed even if the children were storing each relation separately as an ordered pair.

In order to discriminate between these two alternatives, Trabasso, Riley, and Wilson (1975) extended the foregoing work using six-term series. In the acquisition phase of the experiment, explanations of the serial-position effect based on factors such as response competition would predict that pairs (1, 2) and (5, 6) would be learned quickly and that pairs (2, 3), (3, 4) and (4, 5) would be equal in difficulty. The ends-inward model predicts that pair (3, 4) would be acquired later than (2, 3) or (4, 5). Table 2 presents the acquisition data collected by Trabasso et al.. (1975) from six-year olds, nine-year olds and college students, which clearly supports the ends-inward model. Although there was a reliable decrease in the total number of errors (and numbers of trials to criterion) made with increasing age, the patterns of errors were similar across age groups.

The pattern of errors in acquisition was the same for conditions in which the feedback in training was a presentation of the actual sticks differing in length and in which the feedback was only linguistic. These data are important for the developmental concerns of Trabasso et al. (1975), because they indicate that both children and adults learn a series of comparative relations in the same way, by constructing a single ordering of all the elements. This constructive process involves the use of inferential processes, combining premise relations via their common elements. Thus young children are not only capable of making transitive inferences, they also use these inferential processes before they are specifically required to do so by the task, i.e., before questions requiring inferences are posed in the test phase of the task.

TABLE 2

Relative Percent Trials to Criterion for Each Pair in Training
[Data from Trabasso, Riley, & Wilson (1975)]

			Pair		
Age	(1, 2)	(2, 3)	(3, 4)	(4, 5)	(5, 6)
6	11	24	28	26	11
9	18	23	28	23	12
Adult	11	18	26	24	12
Average relative difficulty	13	22	28	24	12

Riley (1976) has demonstrated that the construction of a single linear ordering from a series of pair-wise relations does not depend on the use of perceptual stimuli (colored sticks differing in length) or a spatial comparative such as length. Eight-year-old chilren were taught a six-term series using comparisons of height, weight, happiness, or niceness. The stimuli were drawings of children's faces that did not provide any clues about the actual height, etc., of the depicted children. In a condition that replicated the training procedures used by Trabasso et al. (1975), no significant differences were found in either the number of errors or pattern of errors for the four comparatives. The relative percent trials to criterion for training pairs (1, 2), (2, 3), (3, 4), (4, 5), and (5, 6) were 12, 25, 28, 23, and 12%, respectively; values that are very close to those observed by Trabasso et al. (1975) in their task using colored sticks. A second condition in Riley's experiment reveals more compelling evidence for children's ability to construct linear orderings. The children were given a set of the pictures of the faces that were used as stimuli in the experiment and were told to use these pictures to help them remember the training pairs. Of the 48 children, 41 arranged the pictures into a linear ordering, and the remaining 7 children arranged the pictures as ordered subsets (e.g., 123 456). The number of trials to criterion for this "Memory Aid" condition was reduced by 84% relative to the condition without the memory aids. In addition, in subsequent testing, with memory aids removed, the overall error rate of the Memory Aid condition was 10% compared to 18% for the No Memory Aid condition.

The remarkable facilitation in training when the children were allowed to use the memory aid (which provided only organizational information, not information about actual heights, etc.) shows the importance of memory considerations in a task of this sort. A linear ordering is a desirable representation for a series of comparative relations, because it reduces the actual amount of information that must be stored in memory, because a single ordering of six contains six elements, whereas five ordered pairs contain 10 elements. In order to construct such an ordering in the aforementioned task, a subject must store all the premise relations in memory in the order in which they are presented and then organize and integrate them into the ordering, which places a substantial memory requirement on the subject. Alternatively, without as great a demand on memory but requiring more trials to reach criterion, the subject may begin by trying to organize the input, adding to his or her representation as the randomly presented series of training trials progresses. The relations involving the end terms can be sorted out first, because they have only a single comparative associated with one element. The memory aid given to the children was so effective, because it allowed them to organize the inputs without requiring them to hold any of the premise relations in memory. Thus all the "working space" of their short-term memory could be used to organize the relations. Once the relations were organized into the complete ordering, this ordering could be easily encoded. On the average, the last error made by these children occurred in the third block of training trials (each relation presented once in a block) compared to the seventeenth block in the No Memory Aid condition.

These results and the ends-inward model can now be compared to the conclusions drawn by Smith. In Smith's studies, subjects learned 24 different linear orderings; their task was to recall the ordering after one presentation of the relations from which it could be constructed. The performance measure was a within-subject comparison of the success in recalling the complete ordering given different presentation orders. The subjects in the studies done by Trabasso, Riley, and colleagues learned only a single ordering, and they were trained until they learned all the relations from which it could be constructed. Explanations for the results of both studies rely on memory considerations. Smith's task demanded that subjects attempt to store all relations given a single-presentation; they knew that it could be structured as a linear order. Trabasso and Riley's subjects were not told that the relations presented could be organized as a single ordering. In addition, the task did not require that all the relations be stored in memory following a single presentation. One reason their task is difficult is precisely because the relations presented in training are rarely presented in what one would predict to be an optimal ordering based on Smith's data. Indeed, pilot data collected by Riley comparing acquisition of a six-term series given a random presentation of premise relations to an ordered training series [e.g., $(1, 2), (2, 3)$, $(3, 4), (4, 5), (5, 6)$ in each trial block] shows considerable facilitation of training in the latter condition for 8-year-old children. (The facilitation is not as great as that observed with the foregoing memory aid, however.) Thus these two research programs investigating processes for constructing linear orderings have not given contradictory findings. One can conclude that both children and adults can and will construct linear orderings from pair-wise comparative relations. A major value of a linear ordering is a reduced memory load, and memory factors affect its construction. Subjects are most successful when relations presented together contain a common element and can be integrated without the need to store both relations separately in memory. When subjects are presented a random sequence of relation, they begin to store the information by isolating the least confusable elements and then add elements to an ordered representation when relations that contain an element already contained in the representation are presented.

END-TERM EFFECTS

Although distance effects are very pronounced in all of the experiments described so far, there is one important case in which such effects are absent. This occurs for test pairs that include one of the end terms of the ordering. One frequently observes that reaction time to any pair containing an end-term is unusually short and that no distance effects are observed for these terms. If one of the terms is an end term, reaction time is equally short regardless of what the second term is (a notable exception to this statement is the number-comparison experiments in which no end-term effects are observed; no agreement was reached on the reason for the absence of end-term effects in this paradigm). The end-term effect is usually taken to indicate that subjects recognize the most extreme elements in the ordering and, upon detecting one of these elements in a test question, they can respond immediately without retrieving the second term.

Riley begins by describing the end-term effects obtained in her paradigm. She then presents data to suggest that a major difference between experiments using existing orderings and those using orderings constructed as part of an experiment is in the nature of the end-term effect. Potts has also obtained strong end-term effects in his paradigms, but they are of a different kind than those obtained by Riley. He presents data to suggest that the differing results are a function of the type of test employed.

End-term Effects and the Retrieval of Ordered Information (Riley)

Trabasso et al. (1975) and Riley (1976) investigated the process by which information is retrieved from a linear ordering. Response times were recorded on all test trials. Trabasso et al. (1975) and Riley used the pattern of response times as evidence for the assertion that both adults and children stored the "premise" relations in the inference problem as a single linear ordering and that during testing, questions requiring "inferences" were answered by accessing the ordering directly rather than by retrieving and coordinating "premise" relations when the inferential question was posed. The data supporting this assertion was the finding that reaction times on test trials requiring a simple retrieval of a premise relation were slower than reaction times on test trials requiring inferences. The simplest description of the data they observed is: The farther apart two elements were in the ordering, the faster they could be compared. This finding was observed for all of the ages, feedback conditions, and comparative relations discussed in the foregoing. Thus they argued that the processes used by people to answer inferential questions may not be the deductive processes of formal logic. Because any two elements could be compared directly in the ordering, all the "logical" processes occur in the construction of the ordering.

Trabasso et al. (1975) observed a reliable ordering of reaction times on the different pairs presented in the testing phase of their task. In addition to the foregoing training conditions, their study included conditions in which the subjects were shown physical displays of six colored sticks, ordered by height, and were asked to respond to test pairs by looking at the display and noting the length relation. They also showed one group of subjects a display that contained six colored sticks all the same length and asked them to imagine that the stick on the left (or right) was the longest and the one on the right the shortest. The agreement across the twelve conditions that they studied was very high; the coefficient of concordance was $w = .89, p < .01$. The ordering observed by Trabasso et al. (1975) agrees nearly perfectly with that obtained by Riley and also, in a somewhat different procedure, with that obtained by Potts (1974).

The following tabulation shows the ordering observed by Trabasso et al., (1975); lower rank represents faster reaction time. Pairs with similar reaction times are included in the same rank but are listed within the rank in order. The same ranking is obtained if pairs are ordered by error rates, with fewest errors occurring for *fastest* times.

Rank	Test
1	Both anchors: (1, 6)
2	Long anchor: (3, 6), (5, 6), (2, 6), (4, 6)
3	Short anchor: (1, 5), (1, 4), (1, 2), (1, 3)
4	Two-step inference: (2, 5)
5	One-step inference: (3, 5), (2, 4)
6	Premise or adjacent pairs: (4, 5), (2, 3), (3, 4)

The pairs in the middle of the ordering (ranks 4, 5, and 6) show the distance effects mentioned previously that are comparable to the effects discussed in earlier sections for existing orderings such as digits or animal sizes. The pairs included in the first three ranks show an "end-anchor" effect, which is generally observed in all studies that ask subjects to make comparative judgments based on orderings that are constructed during the experiment. Responses to all pairs including end anchors are faster than responses to nonanchored pairs. Responses to pairs including the long anchor (or the anchor on the linguistically unmarked end of any comparative dimension) are faster than responses to pairs including the short anchor. Generally, reaction times are approximately equal for all long-anchor and all short-anchor pairs. Once a subject has defined an element in the ordering as the "longest" or the "shortest," he or she can identify the longer or shorter member of any pair containing one of these anchors without considering the value or position of the second element. Thus decisions can be made rapidly, and distance effects would not be predicted. An additional factor is present in the end-anchor data of Trabasso et al. (1975). In half of their test trials, the subject was asked to identify the longer element in the test pair, and in the other half, the shorter element. Generally, the response times were faster when the question was "Which stick is longer?" [This is the linguistic marking effect discussed by Clark (1969)]. For the end-anchor pairs, however, a congruence or question-matching effect was observed. Subjects were faster on pairs containing the long anchor when asked to identify the longer element and faster on pairs containing the short anchor when asked to identify the shorter element. This effect was also observed by Clark (1969) in his work on three-term series problems and is similar to the congruity effect described by Banks.

The reaction-time data collected by Trabasso et al. (1975) and Riley cannot be used to clearly distinguish between the analog and discrete comparison models described earlier in this chapter. The consistency of their findings with other results discussed in this chapter contributes to establishing the importance and generality of the linear ordering in a variety of cognitive tasks. The results suggest, however, that it may not be possible to postulate a single process that can account for the results of all the experiments described here. Consideration of the end-anchor data are especially important. Although it is possible to use an analog comparison process to account for the reaction times to pairs in the middle of the orderings constructed by Trabasso et al.'s (1975) subjects, subjects appear to alter the comparison process when comparing the elements of pairs containing end anchors. In addition, linguistic factors have important effects in subjects' performance on end-anchor pairs.

Trabasso and Riley (1975) present several models developed to describe the pattern of reaction times obtained by Trabasso et al. (1975). An important consideration in these models is the nature of the representation of the linear orderings. Two types of representations were considered: a spatial image and associations of elements (colors) to ordinal locations that have associated semantic codes (long and short). They assumed in both cases that either the distance between elements in the spatial image or the strength of the associations of colors to locations would be a function of the confusability of elements in acquisition, with greatest separations or strongest associations for end anchors. The comparison process depends on locating two elements and noting their relative locations or generating length codes for the two elements and comparing their strengths using a choice axiom (Luce, 1959). Trabasso and Riley demonstrated that both these models would yield excellent fits, with rank order correlations of observed and predicted reaction times of $r = .96$. They also showed that the models, although different in their assumptions, made isomorphic predictions; both relied on the use of the "relative discriminability" of the elements (Murdock, 1960). Both use the ordinal position of elements rather than observed or generated magnitudes. Linguistic codes are important as in the discrete model described by Banks.

The generation of magnitude codes is appealing when considering detailed knowledge of the world (animal sizes) or experiments such as Moyer and Bayer (1976) in which subjects learn labels for perceptual stimuli. However, the use of such codes rather than ordinal positions and associated semantic codes seems implausible for at least some of the conditions studied by Trabasso et al. (1975) and Riley (1976), as Trabasso (1975) has noted. In their tasks, knowledge of the absolute values of elements on a comparative dimension was never required. The input was frequently verbally presented comparative relations, and the dimensions used have included abstract ones such as niceness. The establishment of ordinal positions on a continuum defined by the comparative is sufficient for success in this task.

Moyer and Bayer have argued that the range effects that they observed are powerful evidence *supporting* an analog model for comparison processes. Riley and Goodman have recently collected data designed to examine the range effect in an ordering previously studied by Moyer (1973), animal sizes. Following the logic of Moyer and Bayer, subjects compared pairs of animals from a six-term ordering with either a large range (flea to whale) or small range (cat to moose). Riley and Goodman added an additional factor, because they were interested in comparing the comparison process used for existing orderings with that used for orderings constructed for the experiments. Half of the subjects in each size-range condition were pretrained on the set of animals to be later compared. They were taught the set of animals from largest to smallest by a serial anticipation procedure to a 600% overlearning criterion. Thus subjects in the training condition could learn the ordinal positions of animals in the six-term series. Subjects in the no-training condition had repeated exposures to the six animals used, so this condition provides a weaker test of analog comparisons than found in the recent procedures used by Paivio (1975), in which no animal name was repeated. Riley and Goodman used test procedures similar to Trabasso et al. (1975), requiring subjects to identify the smaller animal on half the trials and the larger animals on the other half. The importance of end anchors in orderings constructed for an experiment is illustrated by the following findings. If pairs including end anchors are excluded from the analysis, Moyer and Bayer's findings are replicated. Reaction times are faster in the large-range condition than in the small-range. The data can be described by an inverse relation between reaction time and the log of the difference in animal sizes, as observed by Moyer

(1973). The only effect of training is an overall decrease in reaction time, which does not reach significance. The training manipulation has a considerable effect on end-anchored pairs, however. The mean difference in reaction time for all end-anchored pairs between the large- and small-range groups is 142 msec in the no-training condition, but it is only 12 msec in the training condition. In addition, training significantly decreases overall reaction times on end-anchored pairs, especially in the small-range set. Within the end-anchored pairs, the pattern of reaction time is similar to that observed by Trabasso et al. (1975). These results are consistent with the assertion that end anchors have a special role in orderings constructed for an experiment, even when the ordering constructed consists of elements for which magnitude codes appear to be available. The comparison process is simplified when these end anchors can be defined.

End-term Effects and Type of Test (Potts)

Our initial experiments using four-term orderings employed a true-false sentence verification task. Subjects were given a sentence (e.g., "the fish is friendlier than the duck") and were required to indicate whether the sentence was true or false. Reaction times were measured. A typical reaction-time profile is presented in Fig. 9. Although all nine predictions of an analog distance model were met for both true and false sentences, the data present a serious problem for such a model because of the strong interaction between truth value and specific pair. The distance between the terms of a true sentence is obviously the same as the distance between the terms of the corresponding false sentence. Hence, if distance between the terms is the only factor controlling reaction time, then the relative difficulty of the pairs should be the same regardless of whether they are part of a true or false sentence (of course, there might be a main effect of truth value).

The explanation for the obtained interaction becomes clear when one notes that for true sentences beginning with the first term (A) in the ordering (e.g., $A > B$?), reaction time is extremely short. It is much shorter than reaction time to false sentences that end with the first term in the ordering (e.g., $B > A$?). For sentences containing the last term (D) in the ordering, reaction time is shorter to false sentences that begin with this term (e.g., $D > B$?) than to true sentences that end with this term (e.g., $B > D$?). In short, reaction time is short to any test sentence that *begins* with one of the end terms of the ordering. Potts (1972, 1974) proposed that in responding to a test sentence, subjects first check to see whether the first term in the test sentence is the first term in the ordering. If it is, they respond "true" immediately. If it is not, then a certain proportion of subjects (see Potts, 1972, 1974, for details) check to see whether it is the last term in the ordering. If it is, they respond "false" immediately. Figure 10 presents the reaction time profile for a six-term ordering and reveals that a similar

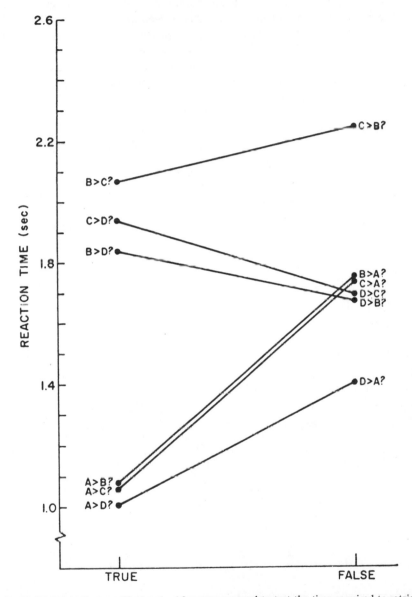

FIG. 9   Reaction-time profile for the 12 sentences used to test the time required to retrieve information about a four-term ordering. (From Potts, 1974.)

end-term processing strategy is used for this larger ordering (the solid lines represent pairs containing an end term). For pairs that do not contain an end term, however, no interaction between true and false sentences is observed. A true distance effect is observed with reaction times being a monotonic function of the distance separating the pairs.

There is a key difference between our end-term effects and those obtained by Riley. Riley reported short reaction times to all test pairs containing the end

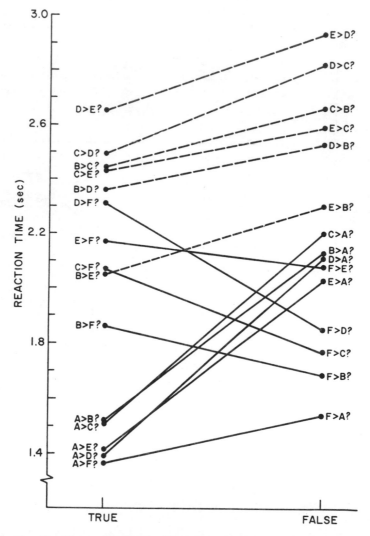

FIG. 10   Reaction-time profile for the 30 sentences used to test the time required to retrieve information about a six-term ordering. Those sentences containing an end term, *A* or *F*, are designated by solid lines; dashed lines are used to designate sentences containing only inner terms, *B-E* (From Potts, 1974.)

term congruent with the test question. It did not matter whether the end term was on the left or right of the test pair. In our experiments, on the other hand, facilitation was observed only when the end term was the first term in the test sentence.

Polich and Potts (1977) examined the possibility that different testing procedures were responsible for the differing results. Riley (as well as most other investigators) presented subjects with a pair of terms and asked them to indicate which was larger; we presented a sentence and asked subjects to indicate whether it was true or false. To test the effect of type of test, we used the same type of study materials employed by Potts (1972, 1974). During the test phase, we presented subjects with pairs of terms but varied the instructions. One group of subjects was told to press the button under the larger term in the test pair as in the experiments by Riley. The second group was told to press the button marked "true" if the test terms were in the order indicated by the paragraph and to press the button marked "false" if the terms were reversed. This condition is analogous to the true-false test used in our previous experiments. The procedure is especially interesting because not only were the test stimuli identical in the two conditions but the actual physical responses required were also identical (i.e., subjects in both conditions should respond to the pair "$A > B$" by pressing the left button and "$B > A$" by pressing the right button.)

The results are shown in Fig. 11. Clearly, the instructions had a dramatic effect on the reaction-time profile. Performance in the true-false condition was identical to performance in our previous experiments. Reaction time was short

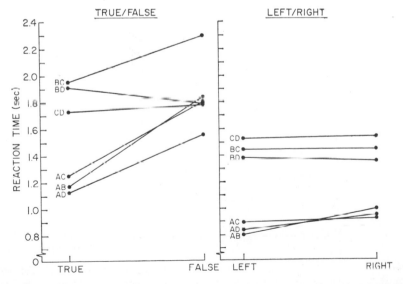

FIG. 11   Reaction-time profiles for a four-term ordering as a function of type of test. (From Polich & Potts, 1977.)

on pairs that began with one of the end terms. Performance in the paired-comparison condition, on the other hand, corresponds closely to performance in Riley's experiments. Reaction time is short on any pair containing the end term congruent with the test question regardless of whether that end term is the first or second element in the pair.

Figure 12 presents the reaction-time profile for a six-term ordering under the paired-comparison instructions. Performance again matches that reported by Riley with reaction time to any pair containing the A end term being extremely short. Further, this profile shows a strong *max* effect. Reaction time is an inverse monotonic function of the size of the largest term in a pair; pairs containing an A are fastest, followed by pairs containing a B, C, D, and E, respectively. The only violation of this pattern is found among terms containing the opposite end term, F. Reaction time to these pairs is shorter than would be predicted by the *max* effect. Examination of the data presented in Trabasso et al. (1975) reveals a similar tendency in their experiments. Polich and Potts argued that this

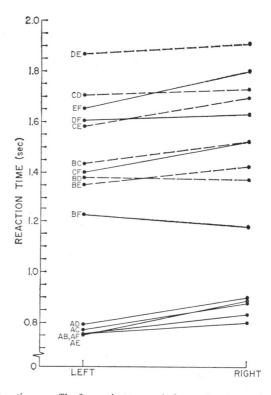

FIG. 12   Reaction-time profile for a six-term ordering under the left/right testing condition. (Those test pairs containing an end-term, A or F, are designated by solid lines; dashed lines are used to designate test pairs containing only the middle terms, $B-E$. (From Polich & Potts, 1977.)

pattern reflects the tendency for at least some subjects to adopt a strategy of checking the test pair for an A, then for a B, etc., and pressing the first one found. This corresponds closely to Parkman's (1971) analysis by synthesis model described in Bank's review of the number-comparison literature. The short reaction times to terms containing an F can again be explained by arguing that some subjects recognize that F is the smallest term and immediately press the opposite button.

These experiments reinforce Riley's suggestion that it may be impossible to postulate a single process (analog or otherwise) that can account for all the comparison judgment data. Although the distance effect is clearly a very general effect, we must remember that subjects have a variety of strategies available to them for dealing with any particular task and that even seemingly minor procedural variations can lead subjects to alter their choice of strategy.

ACKNOWLEDGMENTS

The work of G. Potts was supported in part by NSF Grant BMS 75-10424. The work of W. Banks was supported in part by NSF Grant BMS 75-20328 and the Pomona College Research Committee. The work of K. Smith was supported in part by NSF Grant BMS 75-19313 (B. Mynatt, co-principal investigator). The work of S. Kosslyn was supported by NIH Grant MH 27012-01 and NSF Grant BNS 76 16987.

REFERENCES

Atkinson, R. C., & Shiffrin, R. M. The control of short-term memory. *Scientific American,* 1971, *225*(2), 82-90.

Banks W. P , & Flora, J. Semantic and perceptual processes in symbolic comparisons. *Journal of Experimental Psychology: Human Perception and Performance,* 1977, *3*, 278-290.

Banks, W. P., Fujii, M., & Kayra-Stuart, F. Semantic congruity effects in comparative judgments of magnitudes of digits. *Journal of Experimental Psychology: Human Perception and Performance,* 1976, *2*, 435-447.

Banks, W. P., & Hill, D. K. The apparent magnitude of number scaled by random production. *Journal of Experimental Psychology,* 1974, *102*, 353-376 (Monograph).

Barclay, J. R. The role of comprehension in remembering sentences. *Cognitive Psychology,* 1973, *4*, 229-254.

Birren, J. E., & Botwinick, J. Speed of response as a function of perceptual difficulty and age. *Journal of Gerontology,* 1955, *10*, 433-436.

Bower, G. Adaptation-level coding of stimuli and serial position effects. In M. H. Appley (Ed.) *Adaptation-level theory.* New York: Academic Press, 1971.

Bransford, J. D., & Franks, J. J. The abstraction of linguistic ideas. *Cognitive Psychology,* 1971, *2*, 331-350.

Bryant, P. E., & Trabasso, T. Transitive inferences and memory in young children. *Nature,* 1971, *232*, 456-458.

Buckley, P. B., & Gillman, C. B. Comparisons of digits and dot patterns. *Journal of Experimental Psychology,* 1974, *103*, 1131-1136.

Cattell, J. McK. The time of perception as a measure of differences in intensity. *Philosophische Studien,* 1902, *19*, 63-68.

Clark, H. H. Linguistic processes in deductive reasoning. *Journal of Experimental Psychology*, 1969, *76*, 387-404.

Cooper, L. A. Mental rotation of random two-dimensional shapes. *Cognitive Psychology*, 1975, *7*, 20-43.

Crossman, E. R. F. W. The measurement of discriminability. *Quarterly Journal of Experimental Psychology*, 1955, *7*, 176-195.

Curtis, D. W., Paulos, M. A., & Rule, S. J. Relation between disjunctive reaction time and stimulus difference. *Journal of Experimental Psychology*, 1973, *99*, 167-173.

DeSoto, C. B., London, M., & Handel, S. Social reasoning and spatial paralogic. *Journal of Personality and Social Psychology*, 1965, *2*, 513-521.

Fairbank, B. A., Jr. *Experiments on the temporal aspects of number perception.* Unpublished doctoral dissertation, University of Arizona, 1969.

Fairbank, B. A., Jr., & Capehart, J. Decision speed for the choosing of the larger or the smaller of two digits. *Psychonomic Science*, 1969, *14*(4), 148.

Feigenbaum, E. A., & Simon, H. A. A theory of the serial position effect. *British Journal of Psychology*, 1962, *53*, 307-320.

Foos, P. W. *Constructive memory: Inversion effects for pairs and sentences.* Unpublished doctoral dissertation, Bowling Green State University, 1975.

Foos, P. W., Smith, K. H., Sabol, M. A., & Mynatt, B. T. Constructive processes in simple linear order problems. *Journal of Experimental Psychology: Human Learning and Memory*, 1976, *2*, 759-766.

Frase, L. T. Maintenance and control in the acquisition of knowledge from written materials. In J. B. Carroll & R. O. Freedle (Eds.), *Language comprehension and the acquisition of knowledge.* Washington, D.C.: Winston, 1972.

Friedman, A. *Comparing words: An "internal psychophysics" for a nonphysical dimension.* Paper presented at the XXIst International Congress of Psychology, Paris, July 1976. (To appear in the proceedings.)

Gillman, C. B., Buckley, P., & Theios, J. M. *Numeric comparison.* Paper presented at the Fourteenth Annual Meeting of the Psychonomic Society, St. Louis, Mo., Nov. 1973.

Goodman, N. *Languages of art: An approach to a theory of symbols.* Indianapolis, Ind.: Bobbs-Merrill, 1968.

Gravetter, F., & Lockhead, G. R. Criterial range as a frame of reference for stimulus judgment. *Psychological Review*, 1973, *80*, 203-216.

Groen, G. J., & Parkman, J. M. A chronometric analysis of simple addition. *Psychological Review*, 1972, *79*, 329-343.

Halff, H. M., Ortony, A., & Anderson, R. C. A context-sensitive representation of word meanings. *Memory & Cognition*, 1976, *4*, 378-383.

Henmon, V. A. C. The time of perception as a measure of differences in sensations. *Archives of Philosophy, Psychology, and Scientific Methods*, 1906, No. 8, 1-75.

Holyoak, K. J. The form of analog size information in memory. *Cognitive Psychology*, 1977, *9*, 31-51.

Holyoak, K. J., & Walker, H. J. Subjective magnitude information in semantic orderings. *Journal of Verbal Learning and Verbal Behavior*, 1976, *15*, 287-300.

Huttenlocher, J. Constructing spatial images: A strategy in reasoning. *Psychological Review*, 1968, *75*, 550-560.

Jamieson, D. G., & Petrusic, W. M. Relational judgments with remembered stimuli. *Perception & Psychophysics*, 1975, *18*, 373-378.

Johnson, D. M. Confidence and speed in the two-category judgment. *Archives of Psychology*, 1939, No. 241, 1-52.

Johnson-Laird, P. N. The three-term series problem. *Cognition: International Journal of Cognitive Psychology*, 1972, *1*, 57-82.

Kosslyn, S. M. Scanning visual images: Some structural implications. *Perception & Psychophysics*, 1973, *14*, 90-94.

Kosslyn, S. M. Information representation in visual images. *Cognitive Psychology*, 1975, *7*, 341-370.

Kosslyn, S. M., Murphy, G. L., Bemesderfer, M. E., & Feinstein, K. J. Category and continuum in mental comparisons. *Journal of Experimental Psychology: General*, in press.

Kosslyn, S. M., & Pomerantz, J. R. Imagery, propositions, and the form of internal representation. *Cognitive Psychology*, 1977, *9*, 52-76.

Leech, G. *Semantics*. Baltimore: Penguin, 1974.

Lemmon, V. W. The relation of reaction time to measures of intelligence, memory and learning. *Archives of Psychology*, N.Y., 1927, *15*, No. 92.

Luce, R. D. *Individual choice behavior*. New York: Wiley, 1959.

Miller, G. A. The magical number seven, plus or minus two: Some limits on our capacity for processing information. *Psychological Review*, 1956, *63*, 81-97.

Moyer, R. S. Comparing objects in memory: Evidence suggesting an internal psychophysics. *Perception & Psychophysics*, 1973, *13*, 180-184.

Moyer, R. S., & Bayer, R. H. Mental comparison and the symbolic distance effect. *Cognitive Psychology*, 1976, *8*, 228-246.

Moyer, R. S., & Landauer, T. K. The time required for judgments of numerical inequality. *Nature*, 1967, *215*, 1519-1520.

Moyer, R. S., & Landauer, T. K. Determinants of reaction time for digit inequality judgments. *Bulletin of the Psychonomic Society*, 1973, *1*(3), 167-168.

Murdock, B. B., Jr. The distinctiveness of stimuli. *Psychological Review*, 1960, *67*, 16-31.

Mynatt, B. T., & Smith, K. H. Constructive processes in linear order problems revealed by sentence study times. *Journal of Experimental Psychology: Human Learning and Memory*, 1977, *3*, 357-374.

Paivio, A. Perceptual comparisons through the mind's eye. *Memory & Cognition*, 1975, *3*, 635-647.

Parkman, J. M. Temporal aspects of digit and letter inequality judgments. *Journal of Experimental Psychology*, 1971, *91*, 191-205.

Parkman, J. M., & Groen, G. J. Temporal aspects of simple addition and comparison. *Journal of Experimental Psychology*, 1971, *89*, 335-342.

Piaget, J. *[Genetic epistemology]* (Eleanor Duckwork, trans.) New York: Columbia University Press, 1970.

Piaget, J., Inhelder, B., & Szeminska, A. *The child's conception of geometry*, London: Routledge & Kegan Paul, 1960.

Polich, J. M., & Potts, G. R. Retrieval strategies for linearly ordered information. *Journal of Experimental Psychology: Human Learning and Memory*, 1977, *3*, 10-17.

Pollack, I. The information of elementary auditory displays. I. *Journal of the Acoustical Society of America*, 1952, *24*, 745-749.

Potts, G. R. Information processing strategies used in the encoding of linear orderings. *Journal of Verbal Learning and Verbal Behavior*, 1972, *11*, 727-740.

Potts, G. R. Storing and retrieving information about ordered relationships. *Journal of Experimental Psychology*, 1974, *103*, 431-439.

Potts, G. R. *The role of inference in storing real and artificial information*. Paper presented at the American Psychological Association symposium, "Deductive Reasoning," Washington, D.C., September 1976.

Potts, G. R., & Scholz, K. W. The internal representation of a three-term series problem. *Journal of Verbal Learning and Verbal Behavior*, 1975, *14*, 439-452.

Pylyshyn, Z. W. What the mind's eye tells the mind's brain: A critique of mental imagery. *Psychological Bulletin*, 1973, *80*, 1-24.

Pylyshyn, Z. W. *Do we need images and analogues?* In the *Proceedings* of the conference on Theoretical Issues in Natural Language Processing, M.I.T., June 1975.

Restle, F. Speed of adding and comparing numbers. *Journal of Experimental Psychology,* 1970, *83,* 274-278.

Riley, C. A. The representation of comparative relations and the transitive inference task. *Journal of Experimental Child Psychology,* 1976, *22,* 1-22.

Riley, C. A., & Trabasso, T. Comparatives, logical structures and encoding in a transitive inference task. *Journal of Experimental Child Psychology,* 1974, *17,* 187-203.

Sekuler, R., Rubin, E., & Armstrong, R. Processing numerical information: A choice times analysis. *Journal of Experimental Psychology,* 1971, *89,* 75-80.

Shepard, R. N. Studies of the form, formation, and transformation of internal representations. In R. Solso (Ed.), *Information processing and cognition: The Loyola Symposium.* Hillsdale, N.J.: Lawrence Erlbaum Associates, 1975.

Shepard, R. N., Kilpatric, D. W., & Cunningham, J. P. The internal representation of numbers. *Cognitive Psychology,* 1975, *7,* 82-138.

Sloman, A. *Afterthoughts on analogical representation.* In the *Proceedings* of the conference on Theoretical Issues in Natural Language Processing, M.I.T., June 1975.

Smith, E. E. Choice reaction time: Analysis of the major theoretical positions. *Psychological Bulletin,* 1968, *69,* 77-110.

Smith, K. H., & Foos, P. W. Effect of presentation order on the construction of linear orders. *Memory & Cognition,* 1975, *3,* 614-618.

Smith, K. H., & Mynatt, B. T. On the time required to construct a simple linear order. *Bulletin of the Psychonomic Society,* 1977, *9,* 435-438.

Trabasso, T. Representation, memory and reasoning: How do we make transitive inferences? In A. D. Pick (Ed.), *Minnesota Symposia of child psychology* (Vol 9). Minneapolis: University of Minnesota Press, 1975.

Trabasso, T., & Riley, C. A. On the construction and use of representations involving linear order. In R. L. Solso (Ed.), *Information processing and cognition: The Loyola Symposium.* Hillsdale, N.J.: Lawrence Erlbaum Associates, 1975.

Trabasso, T., Riley, C. A., & Wilson, E. G. The representation of linear order and spatial strategies in reasoning: A developmental study. In R. Falmagne (Ed.), *Psychological studies of logic and its development.* Hillsdale, N.J.: Lawrence Erlbaum Associates, 1975.

Walker, J. H. Real-world variability, reasonableness judgments, and memory representation for concepts. *Journal of Verbal Learning and Verbal Behavior,* 1975, *14,* 241-252.

Welford, A. T. The measurement of sensory-motor performance: Survey and reappraisal of twelve years' progress. *Ergonomics,* 1960, *3,* 189-230.

Wishner, J., Shipley, T. E., & Hurvich, M. S. The serial-position curve as a function of organization. *American Journal of Psychology,* 1957, *70,* 285-262.

Wittgenstein, L. *Philosophical investigations.* New York: Macmillan, 1953.

Author Index

Subject Index

315

H

Hazard function, 217
Hit and false alarm probabilities, 123, 196
Holograms, 203*n*
Hybrid models, 267*ff*
    symbolic distance effect, 267

I

Ideal observer, 164
Identifiability, 195
    quasi-nonidentifiability, 179
    and reaction-time models, 178*ff*
Illusions
    Baldwin, 3
    Delboeuf concentric circles, 76
    Müller-Lyer, 86
    Size-contrast, 75
Imagery and ordering, 289
Information processing, 116
Information theory, 144
Informed Guessing Model, 143, 181
    estimation, 186
    identifiability, 195
    tachistiscopic presentation, 192–195
    test, 184*ff*
Interval scaling, 2, 33
    meaning, 43
    and ratio scaling, 37

J

Judgment
    linear judgment function, 43, 200
    processes, 69
    ratios and differences, 54
    (*See also* Choice Behavior; Relative
        Judgment Theory)

L

Lambda scale, 11
Latency, 117
    operating characteristic, 150*n*
    (*See also* Reaction time)
Letter recognition, 236
Likeableness judgments
    difference of differences model, 63

Likelihood ratio, 141, 149
    (*See also* Bayesian Statistics; Estimation
        techniques)
Linear
    additivity, 19
        of loudness, 16
    congruity, 257
    filter, 158
    judgment function, 43, 200
    orderings, 260–261
        analysis, 273–274
        construction, 271
        developmental approach, 290–296
        end-inwards model, 290
        linguistic variables, 285
        memory load hypothesis, 276
        from pairwise relations, 275
        serial position effects, 272
        theory for construction, 279
Linear system theory, 43, 200
    feature matching model, 201*ff*
Linguistic variables and ordering, 285
Logistic random variable, 101
Loudness, 95
    additivity, 2, 4
    judgment of sequential tones, 27*ff*
    scales
        and additivity, 23
        and analytic addition, 20
        of auditory intensity, 14
    scaling, 8–14, 11
    summation, 14

M

Magnitude estimation, 2, 70
    scales, 19–20
Memory load
    hypothesis, 286
    and linear orderings, 276
Memory scanning, 164
    and reaction time, 190
Mental processes and reaction time,
        194–195
Mental standard, 120
Metathetic continua, 68
Models
    additive, 53
    metric implications, 41
    multiplicative, 53